Dein Englischbuch enthält folgende Teile:

Units 1 2 3	die drei Kapitel des Buches
Getting ready for a test	Hier kannst du dich gezielt auf einen Test vorbereiten.
Extra: English for jobs	Hier kannst du typische Situationen des Berufsalltags üben.
Extra: Exam File	vielfältige Prüfungsaufgaben zur Vorbereitung auf die Abschlussprüfung
Extra: Text File	viele interessante Texte zum Lesen (passend zu den Units)
Skills File (SF)	Beschreibung wichtiger Lern- und Arbeitstechniken
Grammar File (GF)	Zusammenfassung der wichtigsten Grammatikthemen der Bände 1–6; Übersichten über die Zeitformen (*present, past, future*)
Vocabulary	Wörterverzeichnis zum Lernen der neuen Wörter jeder Unit
Dictionary	alphabetisches englisch-deutsches Wörterverzeichnis

Die Units bestehen aus diesen Teilen:

Lead-in	Einstieg in das neue Thema
Part A, B (Unit 1: Part C)	neuer Lernstoff mit vielen Aktivitäten
Practice	Übungen
How am I doing?	Hier kannst du dein Wissen und Können überprüfen.

In den Units findest du diese Überschriften und Symbole:

STUDY SKILLS	Einführung in Lern- und Arbeitstechniken
Dossier	Schöne und wichtige Arbeiten kannst du in einer Mappe sammeln.
EVERYDAY ENGLISH	Hier übst du wichtige Alltagssituationen.
MEDIATION	Hier vermittelst du zwischen zwei Sprachen.
VIEWING	Aufgaben zu Filmausschnitten
Now you	Hier sprichst und schreibst du über dich selbst.
REVISION	Übungen zur Wiederholung
WORDS	Übungen zu Wortfeldern und Wortverbindungen
	Partnerarbeit / Gruppenarbeit
	nur auf CD / auf CD und im Schülerbuch
	Filmausschnitte auf DVD
>	Textaufgaben
Extra	zusätzliche Aktivitäten und Übungen
○ ●	leichtere Übungen / schwierigere Übungen
//○ //●	parallele Übungen auf zwei Niveaus
more help	Hier findest du zusätzliche Hilfen für das Lösen einer Aufgabe.

Contents

Love life!	The world we live in	Have your say!

Love life!

The world we live in

Have your say!

an exciting drama series for young people

The characters

Toby

He's very confident, very charming and very good-looking. Lots of girls fancy him and he knows it. Some people think he's arrogant – and he is a bit. But he's a loyal friend too. Toby and his girlfriend Elly have been together for eight months.

Minty

(real name Katy Minton) Everyone respects Minty. She has lots of confidence and isn't afraid to say what she thinks. She's the class rep. She's quite serious and a bit bossy. She's attractive but she doesn't care about her appearance. She's completely different from her brother, Toby.

Ed

(real name James Ford) The first things you notice about Ed are his size (he's really tall!) and his bright red curly hair. He has a great sense of humour and is very easy-going. He hasn't got a girlfriend but would really like one. Ed and Peanut are old friends.

Bex

(also known as Becky) She's Minty's best friend. Unlike Minty she's very relaxed and laughs a lot. And you never see Bex without her make-up. Bex fancies Ed a lot, but he hasn't noticed and she hasn't told him – yet.

The episodes

Episode 1:
Just be cool

Peanut is excited. He has met a girl and she has said she'll go out with him, but now she isn't answering his calls.

[»]

Episode 2:
Top chat-up lines

Ed wants to ask a girl out. But he doesn't know how.
Peanut has some suggestions.

[»]

Peanut
(real name Philip Nutt)
A lovable geek. He's thin with big glasses. He knows everything about everything, from science to football to music. He's quite shy, but he's popular. Lots of people like him, girls and boys, because he's very cool in an uncool kind of way.

1 Who is it?

Read about the characters. Finish the sentences.

1 ... and ... are best friends.
2 ... and ... have been friends for years.
3 ... and ... are going out.
4 ... and ... are brother and sister.
5 ... has lots of friends.
6 ... fancies ...

2 Just be cool (Episode 1)

a) *Listen and answer these questions.*

1 What does Peanut want from Toby?
2 Does Toby give it to him?
3 How many times has Peanut called the girl?
4 What does Toby advise Peanut to do?

b) *Do you agree with Toby? Why (not)?*

3 Top chat-up lines (Episode 2)

a) *Listen to **part 1** and answer these questions.*

1 What is Peanut's first tip for Ed?
2 What is the second tip?
3 What does Toby think of Peanut's advice?
4 Who could Ed speak to next and why?

b) *Discuss what might happen next. Then listen to **part 2** and see if you were right.*

c) *Which statement sums up best **part 2**?*

1 Minty thinks Ed is interested in Bex so she advises Bex to ask Ed out.
2 Ed asks Bex about her favourite pizza because he wants to go out with her.
3 When Ed asks Bex about her favourite pizza, she asks him out. ► SF Listening (p. 140)

d) *Think of good ways of starting a conversation with someone you fancy. Report your best idea to the class.* more help ► D p. 103
► SF Having a conversation (p. 147)

e) ► D p. 103

4 Extra Now you

Do you like the West Street series? Why (not)? Make appointments with two partners. Say what you think about the characters and the plot.
► WB 1–2 (p. 2)

REAL-LIFE RELATIONSHIPS

1

Got a problem? Write to Jake about it.

I don't want to go to Spain

I don't know what to do. My mum died three years ago. My dad now has a new girlfriend and wants to make a new start – in Spain! He's found a job in a holiday place and he's found a school for me and my sister. My sister (she's 13, I'm 16) thinks it's a great idea. But I really don't want to go. I have a girlfriend and our relationship is really important to me. And I hate the idea of moving and making new friends. I could stay here and live with my granny or a friend, but I don't really want to do that either.
Whatever happens, I'm not going to Spain! I think my dad is so unfair. We argue all the time. What can I do? *Sam*

Jake says:

This is a hard one, Sam. If I were you, I'd try to talk to your dad in a calm way. You should listen to what he has to say. He probably thinks that he's doing the best thing for your family. You could stay with your grandmother and spend the school holidays in Spain. But perhaps it would be an idea to go to Spain for a year and see if you like it. Only you can decide what to do, but I suggest that you talk to your dad and try to understand his reasons.

Good luck!

Your comments:

☐ What about going to Spain for the school term? You could come back in the holidays – and see your friends and spend time with your girlfriend then. Could your girlfriend come and visit you in the holidays? *Ally x*

☐ I think your dad is really mean. He shouldn't put you in this situation. *Dani*

☐ I think you should go to Spain instead of staying with your granny – it might be fun! And with the internet and cheap phone calls you can keep in touch with your friends. *JC*

1 *Why doesn't Sam want to go to Spain? Give two reasons.*
2 *Imagine you are Sam's sister. Tell Sam how you feel about going to Spain and why.*
3 *What advice does Sam get from Jake, Ally, Dani and JC? Do you agree? Why (not)?*
4 *Look at the answers to Sam's problem. Write down at least four phrases you can use to make suggestions or give advice.*

▸ *SF Skimming and scanning (p. 142)*

2 More problems for Jake

✉ We have the same friends

I like this girl, but she hangs out with the same group of friends as me. Some of the people in the group have been out with each other, but usually they break up and stop speaking to each other. That makes things very difficult. Usually one of the two people stops hanging out with the group. I don't want to mess things up like that. But I do like her a lot. Should I ask her out or not? *Matty*

✉ She doesn't hang out any more

My best friend spends all her time with her new boyfriend and doesn't hang out with her old friends any more. I've talked to her about it but she says I'm just jealous. I think she's stupid. Her relationship with her boyfriend probably won't last, and then she'll need her friends. But I don't know whether I'll want to spend time with her after all this. *Nikki*

✉ My girlfriend's best friend is flirting with me

I've been with my girlfriend for 11 months and I really love her. But recently her best friend told me that if I get bored with my girlfriend, she'll always be there for me. This other girl is very attractive. She always stands really close to me and texts me all the time. I don't know what to do. Should I tell my girlfriend or not? They've been friends for 12 years. *Mel*

Send your comments to jake@r-lifemag.co.uk and we'll print them next week with Jake's comments.

Match each problem to one of these comments.

1 Why not tell her that you'd like to be more than 'just friends' and see how she feels.
2 If you want to stay with your girlfriend, you should explain this very clearly to the other girl.
3 When people start a new relationship, they often forget that it's important to find time for old friends too.

3 Now you

a) *With your partner, choose one of the problems above. Discuss possible answers.*

b) *Together write a comment for the problem. Put it up on the wall.*

c) *Walk around and read all the comments for the problem that you wrote about. Choose your favourite comment. Report to the class.*

d) **Extra** *Work on your own. Choose one of the problems and write a detailed answer.*

▸ *SF Writing course (pp. 151–152) • WB 3 (p. 3)*

4 Role play

Partner B: Go to p. 98.

a) *Partner A: Tell your partner about your problem and ask for advice.*

Your results in your last exams weren't very good and your parents want you to repeat the year. They say you spend too much time with your friends and not enough time on your school work. You don't want to change class.

b) *Listen to your partner's problem. Try and give him/her some advice.*

P1 WORDS Describing people: appearance and character

a) *Read the description of the girl below and start to collect adjectives and phrases for describing people. Use a dictionary if you need to. Organize the words in a network or a chart.*

► *SF Using a dictionary (p. 136)*

b) *Add as many words as you can to your collection (e.g. polite, reliable, ...). Try to think of words with the same meaning (easy-going = relaxed) and words with the opposite meaning (confident ◄► shy).*

c) *Write a short description of yourself. Collect all the descriptions. Someone should read them out loud. Can you guess who it is?*

more help ► *D p. 103*

d) **Extra** *Describe one of the following people:*
– your best friend
– someone from your family
– a dream/nightmare girlfriend or boyfriend.

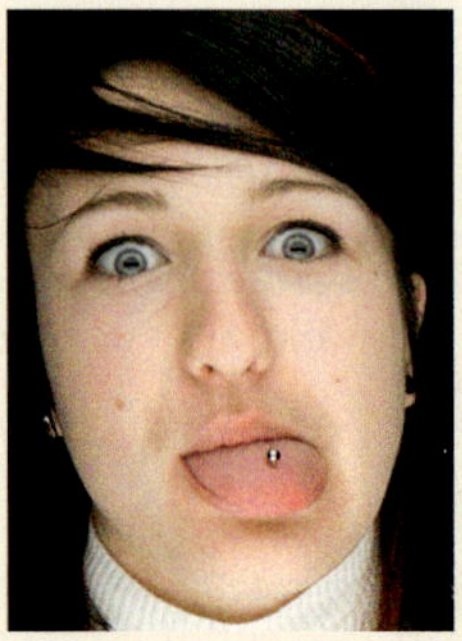

I'm short and a bit fat, with grey eyes and short, straight, black hair. I've got a piercing in my tongue. (I also want a tattoo, but I suppose I'll have to wait until I'm 18 for that.) I'm not a very serious or hard-working person – actually, I'm a bit silly and VERY lazy. (But of course I don't mention that in my CV!)

P2 //O REVISION A group of friends (Present tenses) ► *D p. 104*

a) *Complete the text with the correct forms of the verbs in brackets. Use the* ***simple present*** *or the* ***present progressive****.*

1 These people ... (be) at a summer camp in the US.
2 The sun ... (shine) and everyone ... (have) a good time.
3 The girl who ... (play) the guitar is Rose. On her right is her boyfriend Seb, the guy with the curly brown hair and the white T-shirt.
4 He ... (~~smile~~) – that's typical of Seb. He always ... (look) very serious.
5 Rose's brother Jake ... (sit) behind her.
6 Usually he ... (~~wear~~) hats. I ... (~~know~~) why he ... (wear) one in this photo.
7 The girl on Jake's left is Ruby. She ... (come) from South Africa, but she ... (spend) the summer in the US.
8 The guy with the yellow T-shirt is Josh. As you can see, he ... (kiss) his girlfriend Kate. They ... (like) each other very much.
9 And the others? The two guys on the left ... (come) from Germany, but I ... (~~remember~~) their names. And the good-looking guy with the short hair and the big smile? Well, that's me.

► *GF 3: Talking about the present (p. 162) • GF 6: The simple form and the progressive form (pp. 166–167)*

b) **Extra** ● *Find a photo of you and your friends and write about it.*

► *SF Describing pictures (pp. 133–134) • WB 4–5 (pp. 3–4)*

P3 SPEAKING Keeping a conversation going

a) *Listen to the conversation between Ed and Nadia. Ed is finding it difficult to keep the conversation going. What do you think Ed is doing wrong? What could he do better?* ► SF Having a conversation (p. 147)

b) *Look at the dialogue between Ed and another girl, Holly. What do you think he should say? Write down your ideas. If you need help, look at the box below.*

Ed Hi, I'm Ed.
Holly Hi.
Ed Er, (1) ...
Holly Oh right. I'm Holly.
Ed Hi Holly. Er, (2) ..., Holly?
Holly It's not really my kind of music.
Ed Really? (3) ...?
Holly Well, I don't know really. Not this kind. I only came because Peanut wanted to come.
Ed Oh (4) ...?
Holly Yes, he's my cousin.
Ed Oh that's a surprise, (5) ...
Holly Really? Well, he has.
Ed So (6) ...?
Holly No, I'm from Scotland.
Ed From Scotland. Wow! That's why you have that great accent. (7) ...?
Holly You wouldn't know the place.
Ed I might. I've been to Scotland a few times and (8) ...
Holly Really? Well, do you know Fort William?
Ed Of course.
Holly Well, it's not far from there.
Ed Wow, (9) ...

c) *Now listen to Ed and Holly. Compare your ideas with what Ed says. Are his conversation skills better this time?*

How to keep a conversation going

Find out his/her name, where he/she is from etc.
- Hi, I'm ... And what's your name?
- Sorry, I didn't catch your name. / Sorry, what was your name?
- So do you live around here? / Where exactly is that?

Ask lots of open questions (what, where, when, why, how, ...).
- What do you think of this music/the weather?
- Where do you go to school?
- So, who do you know here?

If one topic isn't working, change it!
- By the way, do you like ...?
- Anyway, there's something I really wanted to ask you ...

Encourage the person to talk about his/her interests.
- You know, I really like your mobile. How long have you had it?
- So you like films. What's your favourite film?
- What kind of films/music/... do you like?
- I see you're reading ... What's it like?

Show surprise or interest.
- No! I don't believe it.
- Really? That's amazing. / That's a surprise. / I didn't know ...
- That sounds great.
- I've been there too! I love it there.
- I love your jacket. Is it new?

d) *Imagine you meet someone at a party for the first time. Start a conversation and talk to each other for as long as you can.*

more help ► D p. 105 • WB 6 (p. 5)

ON-SCREEN RELATIONSHIPS

1 The best films on TV this week

What was the last film you watched on TV?
What do you look for in a film?

(500) Days of Summer ★★★★★

(Wednesday 8.00 pm, Sky 1)

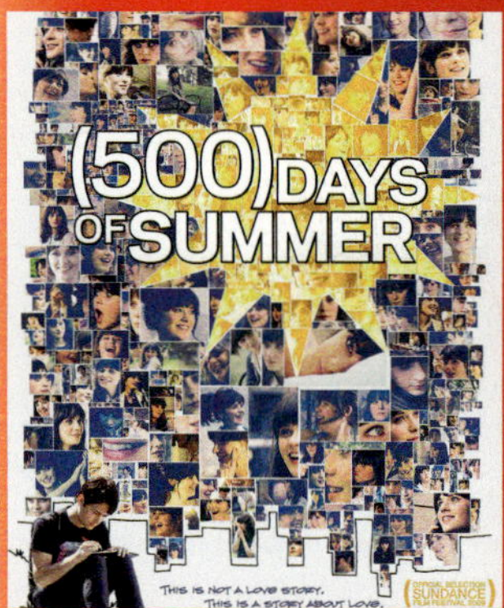

Boy meets girl. Boy falls in love. Girl doesn't. This anti-love story about a 500-day relationship between two young people, Tom and Summer, is not your typical Hollywood romantic comedy. In fact, Tom is dumped by Summer at the start, so we know the ending first. The film is set in LA and was directed by Marc Webber. It stars Joseph Gordon-Levitt as Tom and Zooey Deschanel as Summer and there is an interesting soundtrack with a good mix of old and new songs.

Bend it like Beckham ★★★★★

(Friday 9.00 pm, Virgin 1)

You've probably seen it already, but this comedy is one that everyone will enjoy watching again and again. Football-mad Jess (Parminder Nagra) is 18 and lives in London. She wants to play for a top women's football team. The problem is that her traditional Indian parents want her to find a nice Indian husband, learn how to cook and study law! Although it's a very funny film, it also looks at serious topics (like racism and parent-teenager relationships) and there is an important message: Don't be afraid to be yourself.

Twilight ★★★★★

(Friday 9.40 pm, Film 4)

Twilight is a drama, fantasy, love story and thriller based on Stephenie Meyer's bestseller. Kristen Stewart plays Bella, who has just moved to a small town in the north-west of the US. At her new school, Bella fancies Edward, played by Robert Pattinson. But there's a problem: Edward is a vampire! He's worried about what could happen if he and Bella get together. But the problem is not that she could get pregnant. There's a different danger: he might lose control and bite her! Fans of the book will love this film. But even if you don't think it's your kind of film, you should try it. The special effects are amazing.

a) *Choose the right answer.*
All the films are ... (A) romantic comedies. (B) set in America. (C) about young people.

b) *What does each film review mention? Copy the chart and make notes.*

Title	Kind of film	Plot and characters	Actors	Who will like it	Soundtrack	Special effects
(500) Days						
Bend it...						
Twilight						

► SF Skimming and scanning (p. 142) • WB 7 (p. 6)

c) *Which of the films would/wouldn't you watch? Say why.*
I like/don't like thrillers/... , so I'd watch/I wouldn't watch ...
I think ... sounds good/boring/... because the review says ...

2 VIEWING A review of *Juno*

a) *Make a chart like the one on page 12. Then watch the review. Which points about the film does the reviewer mention? Tick (✓) the right boxes.*

b) *Watch the review again. Which of these things does the reviewer say?*

1 He's a big fan of romantic films.
2 Juno is an unattractive character.
3 Juno wants to find perfect parents for her baby.
4 Juno talks to her dad about relationships.
5 Paulie Bleaker is nervous and uncool through the whole film.
6 4 out of 5 is the right score for the film.

c) *What did you find good (or bad) about the review?*

3 The perfect partner

a) *In the film Juno is trying to find out what makes a relationship successful. What would you look for in a partner? Write down five things:*
I think it's important that a partner ...

is good-looking • is fashionable • has a good sense of humour • has a lot of money • is relaxed • has the same interests as me • has the same religion • is very intelligent • is patient and kind • is confident • comes from a good family • is a happy, positive person • has/doesn't have tattoos/piercings • ...

b) *Make appointments with three partners. Tell each other about the things that are important to you in a relationship.*
– To me it's important that a partner is ...
– I agree, but I think it's more/less important that a partner ...
– I disagree. I don't think that's important because ...

c) *Report back to the class. What things do most people think are important in a relationship?*

4 Extra SONG All I want is you

a) *Read the first two verses of the song from the film* Juno. *Then listen to the song.*

If I was a flower growing wild and free,
All I'd want is you to be my sweet honey bee.
And if I was a tree growing tall and green,
All I'd want is you to shade me and be my leaves.

All I want is you, will you be my bride?
Take me by the hand and stand by my side.
All I want is you, will you stay with me?
Hold me in your arms and sway me like the sea.

by Barry Louis Polisar

b) *What do you think of the song?*
– The song makes me want to laugh/sing along/run away/...
– The music is energetic/old-fashioned/...
– The words of the song are easy to understand/funny/silly/romantic/...
– The singer's voice is beautiful/annoying/...

c) *What tells you that this is a love song? Do you like to listen to love songs? If you do, what are your favourite love songs?*

► **Text File 1** *(pp. 112–114)* • *WB 8 (p. 6)*

P1 WORDS Describing films

a) *Organize the words and phrases from the orange box into a chart or a network. You can use the headings on the right.*

b) *Add more words and phrases to your collection. Look back at the film reviews on p. 12 for ideas.*

c) *Compare your collection with a partner's.*

d) *Choose a word to complete the sentences. Put the verbs in the correct forms.*

1 The film ... Julia Roberts and George Clooney. (play/star)
2 This exciting ... is set in 18th century England. (historical drama/western)
3 It's a typical ... with a happy ending. (horror film/love story)
4 In *Twilight*, Robert Pattinson ... Edward the vampire. (direct/play)
5 The ... is played by Brad Pitt. (actor/hero)

Film people and what they do | Kind of film | +Reviewer's opinion | Plot | What's special about the film

action film • actor • boring • brilliant • cartoon • character • +costumes • (to) direct • director • exciting • famous • happy ending • hero • historical drama • horror film • music • (to) play • scene • science fiction film • +sentimental • (to) star • strange • western • (to) win an Oscar

6 My favourite ... in the film is where the hero kisses Elizabeth. (plot/scene)
7 The ... on the soundtrack go well with the story. (songs/special effects)
8 I'd recommend the film because it's really ... (boring/exciting)

e) **Extra** *Decide on a film that you and your partner have both watched. Work on your own and write at least three sentences about the film. Use words that you have collected in your chart or network. Then compare your sentences.*

P2 SPEAKING About a film

a) *Give a talk on a film you have seen. The ideas below can help you to structure your talk.*

Introduction
- title of the film
- kind of film
- names of main actors
- name of director

Plot
- where the film is set
- when it takes place
- what happens
- kind of ending

Tip
Give a short summary of the film (use the **simple present**). Don't tell the full story.

Main characters
- names
- age
- appearance
- what they're like

Special information
- soundtrack
- special effects
- costumes
- awards

Personal opinion
- reasons why you liked/didn't like the film
- favourite/least favourite scenes
- if you can recommend the film
- who you think would like it

more help ► D p. 105

► SF Giving a presentation (p. 138) • WB 9–12 (pp. 7–9)

b) **Extra** *Record your talk.*

P3 WRITING A film plot (Creative writing)

a) *Read the beginning of the film plot on the right.*

b) *In a group, brainstorm ideas on how the story could continue.*
What will happen when Hailey finds out about the bet? Will Hailey be prom queen? How will Alexis react? What kind of ending would work best (dramatic/funny/romantic/sad/...)?
Write down some of your ideas.

► *SF Brainstorming (p. 149)*

c) *Work on your own and write the rest of the plot.*

Remember

- Use adjectives (**empty**, **great**, ...) and adverbs (**nervously**, **really**, ...).
- Use time phrases and linking words (**now**, **because**, **but**, **when**, ...) and relative clauses (**who ...**, **that ...**).
- Read and correct your text.

► *SF Writing course (pp. 151–152)*

Chaz, the most popular guy in school, is dumped by his girlfriend, Alexis. He has a bet with his best friend, Tyler. Chaz says that he can change even the most boring and unattractive girl so that she can become the most popular girl in school and win the election for prom queen[1]. Tyler can choose the girl. And he chooses Hailey, a quiet, unpopular girl who is interested in art, politics and the environment ...

[1] prom queen *girl chosen by her classmates to be the queen of the formal party (prom) at American high schools*

d) *In your group read the different endings and vote for the best one.*

P4 MEDIATION Which film?

Partner B: Go to p. 98.
Partner A: Partner B visits you with a friend from England. You want to watch a film together.

a) *Read about the film* Crazy. *Explain in English what the film is about.*

Der 16-jährige Benni (Robert Stadlober) wird von seinen Eltern wegen seiner schlechten Mathenoten in ein Internat geschickt. Es ist nicht sein erster Schulwechsel, und meist war es für den halbseitig gelähmten Jungen schwer, Freunde zu finden. Diesmal geht es einfacher – zunächst. Benni teilt sich das Zimmer mit Janosch (Tom Schilling), der sich mehr für Mädchen und Spaß als für die Schule interessiert. Die Jungen freunden sich an – bis sich beide in ihre Klassenkameradin, die schöne Malen (Oona-Devi Liebich), verlieben. Dass das zu Konflikten führt, ist klar, und die Freundschaft zwischen Benni und Janosch wird auf eine echte Probe gestellt.
In diesem Film über die schwierige Zeit des Erwachsenwerdens und das Spannungsfeld zwischen Freundschaft und Liebe kommen auch Spaß und Abenteuer nicht zu kurz.

b) *Partner B will talk about a different film. Listen carefully.*

c) *The English visitor can't decide which film to watch. You and partner B have to choose. Say which film you think is better and why. Then listen to partner B's opinion and agree on a film.*

► **Text File 2** *(pp. 115–120)* • *SF Mediation (p. 157)* • *WB 13–15 (pp. 9–10)*

Extra The Absolutely True Diary of a Part-time[1] Indian

(Extracts from the novel by Sherman Alexie, adapted and abridged)

The story so far

Arnold lives and goes to school on the Spokane Indian Reservation in Wellpinit, Washington State. The Indians on the reservation are very poor and Arnold can see that most of them have no hope for the future. He makes a brave decision. He leaves the reservation school and starts at Reardan High School. Reardan High is an all-white school in a town 22 miles outside of the reservation. Arnold is the odd one out[2]: a poor Indian boy in a rich, racist town. But slowly he starts to make friends at his new school. He even starts to go out with the beautiful Penelope.

► SF Reading English texts (p. 144)

Me (drawn by me)

Penelope in her dad's old hat (drawn by me)

BIG DREAMS

Everybody is absolutely shocked that Penelope chose me to be her new friend. I am an absolute stranger at the school.

And I am an Indian. And Penelope's father, Earl, is a racist. The first time I met him, he said, "Kid, she's only dating you because she knows it will piss me off[3]. So I ain't going to get pissed. And if I ain't pissed then she'll stop dating you."

Okay, so you're probably thinking that Penelope was dating me ONLY because I was the worst possible choice[4] for her. She was probably dating me ONLY because I was an Indian boy. And, okay, so she wasn't seriously dating me. We held hands sometimes and we kissed once or twice, but that was it. I don't know how important I was to her. I think she was bored of being the prettiest, smartest and most popular girl in the world. She wanted to do something a little crazy, you know?

But, hey, I was kind of using her too. After all, I suddenly became popular. Penelope had shown that she thought that I was cute, and so all of the other girls in school decided that I was cute[5] too. I was allowed to hold hands with Penelope, and kiss her goodbye when she jumped on the school bus to go home, and so all of the other boys in school decided that I was cool. I was different.

I looked and talked and dreamed and walked differently than everybody else. I was new.

So okay, those are all the obvious[6] reasons why Penelope and I were friends. But what about the bigger and better reasons?

"Arnold," she said one day after school, "I hate this little town. It's so small, too small. Everything about it is small. The people here have small ideas. Small dreams. They all want to marry each other and live here forever."

"What do you want to do?" I asked.

"I want to leave as soon as I can. I think I was born with a suitcase."

Yeah, she talked like that. All big and dramatic. I wanted to laugh, but she was so serious.

"Where do you want to go?" I asked.

"Everywhere. I want to walk on the Great Wall of China. I want to walk to the top of pyramids in Egypt. I want to swim in every ocean. I want to climb the highest mountain. I want to go on an African safari. I want to do everything and see everything."

Her eyes had this strange, dreamy look. I laughed.

---

[1] part-time *Teilzeit-* [2] odd one out *hier: das fünfte Rad am Wagen, Außenseiter* [3] (to) piss sb. off *(infml, vulgär) jn. wütend machen, jn. ankotzen* [4] choice [tʃɔɪs] *(Aus-)Wahl* [5] cute [kjuːt] *niedlich, süß; (AE infml auch:) sexy* [6] obvious ['ɒbviəs] *offensichtlich, naheliegend*

"Don't laugh at me," she said.

"I'm not laughing at you," I said. "I'm laughing at your eyes."

"That's the problem," she said. "Nobody takes me seriously."

"Well, come on, it's kind of hard to take you seriously when you're talking about China and Egypt and stuff. Those are just big, crazy dreams. They're not real."

"They're real to me," she said.

"Why don't you tell me what you really want to do with your life," I said. "Make it simple."

"I want to be an architect."

"Wow, that's cool," I said. "But why an architect?"

"Because I want to build something beautiful. Because I want to be remembered."

And I couldn't laugh at that dream. It was my dream too. But Indian boys shouldn't dream like that. And white girls from small towns shouldn't dream big either. We should be happy with what we have. But there was no way Penelope and I were going to sit still. No, we both wanted to fly.

This bird is an Australian Arnelope. It is good at flying long distances.

PANCAKES[1] OF DOOM[2]

Arnold often hitchhikes[3] between Reardan and home. But he doesn't tell his classmates because he doesn't want them to know how poor he is. One night after a school dance, Arnold plans to wait until everybody has gone, and then hitchhike home in the dark. But Penelope's friend, Roger, has a different idea.

Roger and a few of the other popular guys decided they were going to drive into Spokane and have pancakes at a twenty-four-hour diner[4] and Roger invited us to come along.

Penelope was very excited about the idea. I was so scared that I felt sick. I had five bucks[5] in my pocket. What could I buy with that? Maybe one plate of pancakes. Maybe. What a nightmare[6].

"What do you say, Arnie?" Roger asked. "Do you want to come with us?"

"What do you want to do, Penelope?" I asked.

"Oh, I want to go, I want to go," she said. "Let me go and ask Daddy."

Oh, man, I saw my only chance to escape. I could only hope that her father wouldn't let her go. Only Earl could save me now.

I needed Earl to save me. That's how bad my life was at that moment.

"Hey, I'll go with you," Roger said. "I'll tell him you guys are going with me."

As they walked together towards the car, I saw that Roger and Penelope looked good together. They looked natural. They looked like they should be a couple.

And after everyone found out I was a poor Indian, I knew they would be a couple.

Come on, Earl! Come on, Earl! Break your daughter's heart!

But Earl loved Roger. Everybody loved Roger. He was the best football player. Of course they loved him. All real Americans love the best football player.

Me being absolutely terrified

I was angry and jealous and absolutely terrified.

"I can go! I can go!" Penelope said, as she ran back to me and hugged[7] me hard.

An hour later, about twenty of us were sitting in Denny's in Spokane.

Everybody ordered pancakes.

I ordered pancakes for Penelope and me. I ordered orange juice and coffee and toast and hot chocolate and French fries too, even though[8] I knew I wouldn't be able to pay for any of it.

---

[1] pancake ['pænkeɪk] *Pfannkuchen* [2] doom [du:m] *Verderben, Verhängnis, Untergang* [3] (to) hitchhike ['hɪtʃhaɪk] *trampen, per Anhalter fahren* [4] diner ['daɪnə] *(bes. AE) einfaches, meist preiswertes Restaurant* [5] buck [bʌk] *(bes. AE, infml) Dollar* [6] nightmare ['naɪtmeə] *Albtraum* [7] (to) hug (-gg-) [hʌg] *umarmen* [8] even though ['i:vn,ðəʊ] *selbst wenn*

I decided it was my last meal before my death, and I was going to have a feast[1].

Halfway through our meal, I went to the bathroom[2]. I thought maybe I was going to throw up. Roger came into the bathroom.

"Hey, Arnie," he said. "Are you okay?"

"Yeah," I said, "I'm just tired."

"All right, man," he said. "I'm happy you guys came tonight."

"Hey, listen," I said.

I thought about telling him the whole truth[3], but I just couldn't.

"The thing is," I said, "I, er, forgot my wallet[4]. I left my money at home, man."

"Dude[5]!" Roger said. "Man, don't worry about it. You should have said[6] something earlier."

He opened his wallet and gave me forty bucks.

I couldn't believe it.

What kind of kid can just give someone forty bucks like that?

"I'll pay you back, man," I said

"Whenever, man. Just have a good time, all right?"

We walked back to the table together, finished our food and Roger drove me back to the school. I told them my dad was going to pick me up there.

"Dude," Roger said, "It's three in the morning."

"It's okay," I said. "My dad works nights. He's coming here from work."

"Are you sure?"

"Yeah, everything is cool."

So Penelope and I got out of Roger's car to say goodbye.

"Roger told me he lent you some money," she said.

"Yeah," I said. "I forgot my wallet."

"Arnold."

"Yeah."

"Can I ask you something big?"

"Yeah. I guess[7]."

"Are you poor?"

I couldn't lie[8] to her any more.

"Yes," I said, "I'm poor."

I thought she was going to march out of my life right then. But she didn't. Instead she kissed me. On the cheek. I guess poor guys don't get kissed on the lips. At first I was annoyed[9] at her for not kissing me properly[10]. But then I understood that she was being my friend. Being a really good friend in fact.

"Roger guessed you were poor," she said

"Oh, great, now he's going to tell everybody."

"He's not going to tell anybody. Roger likes you. He's a great guy. He's like my big brother. He can be your friend too."

That sounded pretty good to me. I needed friends.

"Is your Dad really coming to pick you up?" she asked.

"Yes," I said.

"Is that true?"

"No," I said.

"How will you get home?" she asked.

"I usually walk home. I hitchhike. Somebody usually picks me up. I've only had to walk the whole way a few times."

She started to cry.

FOR ME!

I didn't know that a girl could look so sexy when she cried.

"Oh, my God, Arnold, you can't do that," she said. "I won't let you do that. Roger will drive you home. He'll be happy to drive you home."

Penelope ran over to Roger's car and told him the truth.

And Roger drove me home that night.

And he drove me home lots of other nights too.

If you let people into your life a little bit, they can be pretty damn[11] amazing.

---

1 feast [fi:st] *Festessen, Festmahl* 2 bathroom *hier (AE): Toilette* 3 truth [tru:θ] *Wahrheit* 4 wallet ['wɒlɪt] *Brieftasche* 5 dude [dju:d] *(bes. AE, infml) Mann* 6 you should have said sth. *du hättest etwas sagen sollen* 7 I guess *Ich schätze schon* 8 (to) lie [laɪ] *lügen* 9 annoyed [ə'nɔɪd] *verärgert* 10 properly ['prɒpəli] *richtig* 11 damn [dæm] *(adv, infml) verdammt*

Working with the text

1 //O Tell the story
▸ D p. 106

Match the sentence halves.

1 Arnold thinks Penelope is dating him because …	a leaving Reardan and doing something big and important.
2 Both Arnold and Penelope dream about …	b tells her the truth.
3 After the school dance, Penelope wants to …	c Roger gives him some money.
4 At the diner Arnold feels sick because …	d he hasn't got any money.
5 Arnold tells Roger that he has forgotten his wallet, so …	e Roger drives him home.
6 Later, Penelope asks Arnold if he is poor, and Arnold …	f go to a diner with Roger and some friends.
7 Penelope doesn't want Arnold to hitchhike, so …	g she is bored and wants to do something a bit crazy.

2 ● What do they mean?

Who says this and why?

1 "But, hey, I was kind of using her too." (l. 28)
2 "Nobody takes me seriously." (ll. 65–66)
3 "No, we both wanted to fly." (ll. 84–85)
4 "Break your daughter's heart!"(ll. 122–123)
5 "Man, don't worry about it." (ll. 157–158)
6 "If you let people into your life a little bit, they can be pretty damn amazing." (ll. 225–226)

3 The characters

What kind of people do you think Arnold, Penelope and Roger are? Find examples in the story to support your opinion.

I think Arnold/Penelope/Roger is …
because in line … the text/Arnold/…
says that …

ambitious • attractive • charming • cheeky • confident • crazy • dramatic • easy-going • helpful • generous • jealous • likeable • loyal • patient • popular • proud • romantic • serious • shy • successful • thoughtful • …

4 ● Penelope's diary

Imagine you are Penelope. In your diary, write about what happened at the diner.

more help ▸ D p. 106

5 A review

a) *Talk to your partner about the extract. You could use these phrases to help you:*

The extract is from the novel … by …
The story is set in … / It's about …
The main character is … He's …
The story is exciting/funny/boring/…
The ending is strange/silly/happy/sad/…
I enjoyed/didn't enjoy the story because …
After reading this extract I would/wouldn't like to read the whole book.
People who like/are interested in … should read the book.

b) ● *Write a review of a different story that you have read recently.*

more help ▸ D p. 106

▸ SF Writing course (pp. 151–152) • WB 16 (p. 11) •
Exam Check WB (pp. 12–21)

1 A holiday by the sea is more exciting (Comparison of adjectives)

What do you think? Write complete sentences. Use the words in brackets.

1 a holiday by the sea / a holiday in the mountains (exciting) *I think that … is more … than …*
2 travelling by train / travelling by car (comfortable) *In my opinion … is / isn't as comfortable as …*
3 a sports holiday / a holiday at the beach (cool)
4 beaches in Spain / beaches in Germany (crowded)
5 a camping holiday / staying at a B&B (expensive)
6 visiting a science museum / visiting a zoo (interesting)
7 going on holiday with lots of friends / going with your partner (exciting)

▸ *GF 12: Adjectives: comparison (p. 175)*

2 SPEAKING Making holiday plans

a) *Sarah and her classmate Dustin are planning a class trip. Put their phone call into the correct order.*

*Dustin*___ Hello.
*Sarah*___ Hi, Dustin! This is Sarah. I'm phoning about the class trip. Do you have any ideas?
*Dustin*___ …

A Oh, Norwich sounds OK, but do we have to sleep in tents at the camp?

B Yes, I have. What do you think about a trip to the country? There's this sports camp in the Norfolk Broads …

C Cities? Oh, I don't know, I like holidays in the country much better than holidays in the city. And you can do so many different sports in the Norfolk Broads: play football, hike, ride bikes, go canoeing, …

D A sports camp? In the country? Sounds a bit boring. I like cities better because I like more action.

E No, they offer cheap houses for school groups. Oh, and by the way, they even have an indoor swimming pool and that's free.

F Well, Norwich isn't far away – and it's a beautiful city. You can go shopping and do some sightseeing there.

G Yes, but I'm afraid some of our classmates hate sports. What else can you do there?

H Good idea. I hope everyone will like our plans. See you tomorrow.

I Now, that sounds good. Let's talk about it in class next week.

b) *Act out the conversation with a partner.*

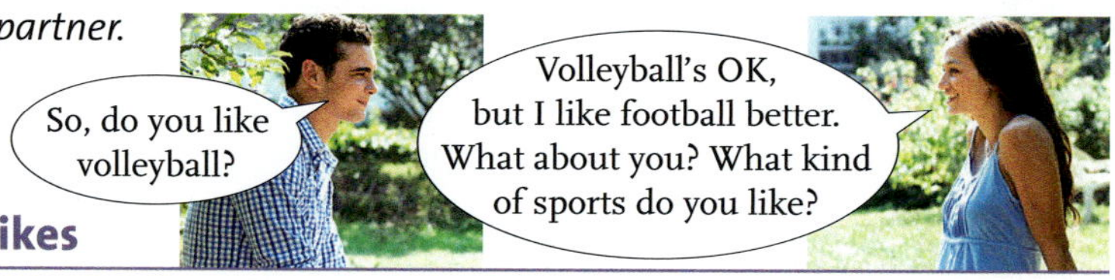

3 SPEAKING Likes and dislikes

Ask your partner about free time activities (sports, holidays, …). The phrases below will help you.

I like … 	**I love …** 	**I hate …** 	**I don't mind …** 
I quite like …	I like … a lot/very much.	I can't stand …	… is OK/all right.
I like … better than …	I like … the best/most.	I like … the least.	I don't like … very much.
… is pretty/quite good.	… is great/fantastic.	… is terrible/awful.	I'm not very interested in …
I'm looking forward to …	I can't wait to …	I'm afraid/scared/ terrified of …	I'm easy-going/relaxed about …

4 WORDS A teenage magazine

a) Zink! *is a teenage magazine with six sections:*

CINEMA & TV | SPORT | HEALTH | MUSIC | BOOKS | COMPUTER

Make a list of words under each heading. First use the words from the box. Then add more words.

Tip
Some words can go under more than one heading.

CINEMA & TV	SPORT	...
cartoon	athletics	...
...	...	

active • athletics • cartoon • cable • channel • comic • competition • concert • exercise • fruit • healthy food • (to) install • label • link • lyrics • menu • novel • pitch • playlist • plot • presenter • prime time • (to) recommend • (to) release • repeat • (to) save • scene • sound file • (to) surf the internet • (to) train • vegetables • whole-grain • writer • ...

b) *You want to tell your friend about some of the things you have read in* Zink!. *Choose the right word for each sentence.*

1 If you want to stay fit, you should eat healthy food and do daily exercise/repeat/competition.
2 Don't spend hours in front of the TV or the computer. Go outside with your friends and be more interested/relaxed/active.
3 Helsinki Motel have just installed/released/watched their new album. *Zink!* thinks it's hot.
4 *Zink!* says the new software is cheap and easy to install/join/repair.
5 Don't miss tonight's rehearsal/repeat/revision of *The English Patient* if you haven't seen it yet. *Zink!* loves it.
6 For something a bit different, *Zink!* recommends a concert/playlist/tune of religious music at Bristol Cathedral tomorrow.

▶ *You could now do tasks 1 and 2 in the Practice test on p. 24.*

5 WORDS Talking about religions

a) *For each group, find the word that doesn't fit.*
1 Jewish • English • Hindu • Muslim
2 Catholic • cathedral • Christian • Protestant
3 church • mosque • palace • synagogue
4 minister • imam • priest • technician
5 bell • funeral • wedding • service
6 believe • bell • cathedral • tower

b) *Complete the sentences with a word from each group in a).*
1 Our friend Murat is Turkish. Like most Turkish people, he's a ...
2 My wife and I are both Christians, but she's a Catholic and I'm a ...
3 Our Jewish friends go to the ... on Saturdays.
4 My uncle is a Catholic ... but we don't go to his church. It's too far from where we live.
5 You can hear the church ... a mile away.
6 Jews, Muslims and Christians all ... in one God.

6 WORDS The world of soap opera

a) *Who's who in this soap opera? Read these statements. Then complete sentences 1 to 6 with a word from the box.*

- Amy and Bill live together, but they aren't married.
- Chris fancies Amy, but he's married to Diana.
- Ella's mother is Fay. She's single.
- Gary is Ella's grandfather. His wife died.
- Hanif is Layla's brother. He has a secret relationship with Diana.
- Layla is Ella's aunt. She's divorced from Bill.

ex-husband • father • granddaughter • lover • uncle • wife

1 Gary is Fay's ...
2 Hanif is Ella's ...
3 Ella is Gary's ....
4 Diana is Chris' ...
5 Hanif is Diana's ...
6 Bill is Layla's ...

b) *Fay and Layla are at a café. Complete their conversation with words from the box.*

baby • divorced • father • love • relationship • single

Fay Hi, Layla. Guess what! I've just heard that Chris and Diana are getting (1) ...
Layla What? Is that because Chris has fallen in (2) ... with Amy?
Fay I don't know but maybe it's because he's heard about Diana's (3) ... with Hanif.
Layla Actually, I saw her today. I think she's going to have a (4) ...
Fay No! But who's the (5) ...? Her husband or her lover?
Layla Well, let's hope it's Hanif so they can get married quickly. Who wants to be a (6) ... mum? Oh – sorry, Fay!

7 Are you fit and healthy? (Simple present: questions)

a) *Write the questions in the* **simple present**. *Use the verbs in brackets.*

1 ... you ... a healthy life? (live)
Do you live a healthy life?
2 ... you ... any sports in your free time? (play)
3 How often ... you ... every week? (train)
4 ... you ... to school by bike? (go)
5 What do you think: ... the food that you eat healthy? (be)
6 How many meals ... you ... every day? (have)
7 What ... you usually ... for breakfast? (have)
8 How often ... you ... fresh fruit and vegetables? (eat)

9 ... you ... enough sleep every night? (get)
10 What else ... you ... to stay fit and healthy? (do)

b) *Answer the questions in a) for yourself.*

c) *Ask your partner the questions and take notes about your partner's answers.*

d) *Write two or three more questions to find out about somebody's lifestyle.*
Do you like fast food / soft drinks / ...?
How much water do you drink? ...

► GF 2: Making questions (p. 161) • GF 3: Talking about the present (p. 149)

▶ You could now do tasks 3 and 4 in the Practice test on p. 25.

8 Being a teenage mum is not easy

a) *Zink!* chat *is an online forum where people can write about their problems and give advice. Read about Rebecca's problem and then read Maria's advice.*

I was 16 when I got pregnant. I had been with my boyfriend for six months and he was the first boy I had sex with. I was on the pill[1] but sometimes I forgot to take it. My parents were really upset, but I wanted to keep the baby. At first my boyfriend stayed with me but then he left me because he wanted to live his own life – without a baby.

Now I live alone with my son. I love him but being a teenage mum is not easy. You have to grow up quickly. A baby isn't always sweet and it's hard when your baby is screaming at 3 am because he is hungry.

I want to go back and finish school, but I will need help from my parents. I think it will be hard to study and be a mum at the same time. But my parents are still upset and do not believe that I've grown up. What can I do?

Rebecca

Talk to your parents about your plans for the future. Explain to them what you want to do and tell them that you need their help. When they see how much you have grown up, I'm sure that they will try to help you. Good luck!

Maria

[1](to) be on the pill *die (Antibaby-)Pille nehmen*

b) *Complete the following sentences. Use information from a).*

1 Rebecca got pregnant because ...
2 When she told her parents that she was pregnant they ...
3 Rebecca lives alone with her son because ...
4 Rebecca thinks you shouldn't be a mum at 16 because ...
5 In the future, Rebecca wants to ...
6 Rebecca wants help from her parents because ...
7 Maria thinks Rebecca should ...
8 Maria thinks that Rebecca's parents will ...

9 SPEAKING Giving your opinion

a) *Read the dialogue about teenage mums. Swap the phrases in blue for phrases from the boxes and practise the dialogue with your partner.*

A: I feel that young girls shouldn't be mothers. → I think (that) ... • If you ask me ...

B: It's true that it's not an ideal situation, but it's not impossible. → You're right (that) ..., • I agree that ...

A: I believe that it isn't good for the baby, and it's hard for the mother too. → In my opinion ... • I think that ...

B: Well, I definitely think you're wrong there. It isn't too bad, especially if the mother gets enough help. → I just don't think that you're right. • I'm afraid that I disagree. • I'm sorry, but I can't agree with you there.

b) *Choose one of these topics for discussion or agree on a different one. Use phrases from a) to give your opinion.*

- Watching a film at home is better than going to the cinema.
- Fast food, soft drinks and sweets shouldn't be sold in schools.
- Violent video games should be banned.

► SF Having a discussion (p. 148)

1 LISTENING What can we do this weekend?

a) *First read the summaries below. Then listen carefully to the girls talking and decide which summary fits their phone call best.*

A Two girls are planning their weekend together. Tina has lots of interesting ideas, but Helen decides that she wants to plan a surprise for Tina.

B Tina phones Helen because the girls want to spend Saturday evening together. Helen has got some ideas, but Tina does not like them. In the end Helen is fed up with Tina and decides to stay at home alone.

C It is a phone call between two girls who want to spend Saturday evening together. Although Helen has lots of ideas, they cannot agree on how to spend the time together. Helen is fed up with Tina and decides to spend the weekend with her cousin Wendy.

D Two girls are making plans for the weekend. They want to go to their athletics training on Saturday and to visit Manchester on Sunday. After their training they are going to meet at Helen's house. They decide to watch a film on TV and listen to some music together.

b) *Listen again and take notes in a chart. What are Helen's ideas for Saturday evening? How does Tina react?*

Helen's ideas	Tina's reaction
go to the theatre	boring – sth more modern
play new computer …	

2 SPEAKING Holiday plans

a) *With a partner, use the information in the chart below to prepare a dialogue for this situation:*

You want to go on holiday with your friend after your exams[1], but you both have different ideas about what you want to do. You both talk about your ideas and try to agree on a holiday plan.

Partner A: The exams are over at last. Now we can have some fun!
Partner B: Great! Let's talk about holiday plans!
Partner A: OK. Well, what do you think about …

	Partner A	Partner B
1 Idea	a youth hostel – near the sea	camping – in the mountains
2 What does it cost?	15 euros a night	35 euros a night
3 What can you do there?	swimming, surfing, beach volleyball	hiking, mountain biking, swimming in lakes
4 Location	500 metres from railway station and beach	60 km from nearest town
5 Go just with your friend or go in a group?	Just you and me: – easier to plan holiday – fun to spend time together	Group: – more fun – could be cheaper

b) *Act out the dialogue with your partner.*

[1] exams *Prüfung, Examen*

3 LISTENING Living together

You will hear a radio phone-in programme about relationships between people of different religions. Look at the statements below for half a minute. Then listen and choose the correct answers (A, B, C or D). You will hear the phone-in twice.

1 *All about me* is about ...
- A life 50 years ago.
- B English cities.
- C married people with problems.
- D a successful mixed relationship.

2 Sharon's ...
- A parents are both Muslims.
- B mum is a Muslim.
- C dad is a Muslim.
- A parents have lots of problems.

3 Sean ...
- A has a girlfriend who is a Catholic.
- B has a girlfriend who often goes to church.
- C is a Protestant.
- D tries to go to church every week.

4 Afra ...
- A isn't with her boyfriend now.
- B is a Hindu.
- C has children.
- D says mixed relationships aren't a problem.

5 Bob ...
- A met his girlfriend in England.
- B has an Italian girlfriend.
- C is Irish.
- D is English.

6 Bob says that ...
- A he plays rugby.
- B he's a rugby fan.
- C his girlfriend is a rugby fan.
- D his team always wins.

4 LISTENING Radio adverts

Listen to three radio adverts. You will hear the recordings twice.
Are the following statements true or false?

A	1 Although the woman is on a diet[1], the man has bought her chocolates.
	2 *Her World* sells flowers[2] and special chocolates for women.
B	3 The second advert is for people who are happily married.
	4 *A lifetime's love* is the title of a book.
C	5 The third advert is for men.
	6 The main topic of the third advert is magazines.

[1] diet *Diät* [2] flower *Blume*

5 SPEAKING Too young to be a mum?

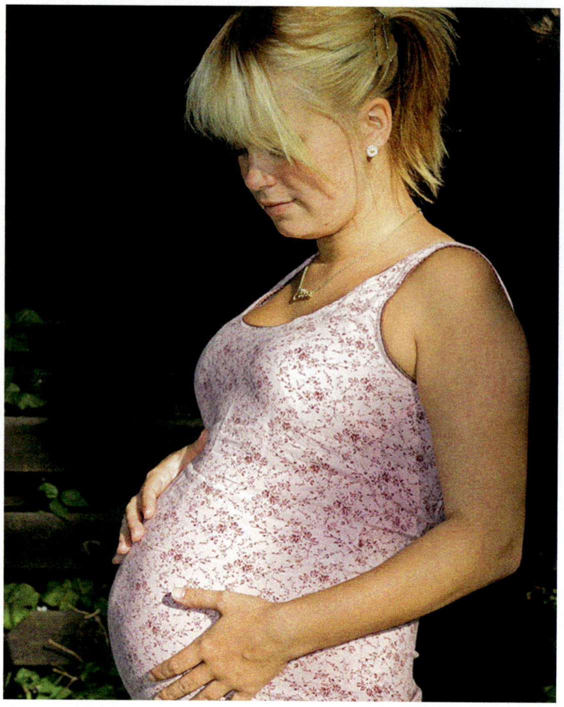

Talk about the pictures. The following questions can help you:
- What can you see in the pictures?
- What do you think the girls are thinking?
- How do you think their parents and friends reacted to the news that they were pregnant?
- How does having a baby change a teenager's life?
- What role should the baby's father play?
- What do you think is the best age to have a baby? Why?

6 PRESENTATION My lifestyle

Tell the class how careful you are (or aren't!) about looking after yourself and keeping healthy.

Talk about:
Food: likes/dislikes • healthy/unhealthy food
Exercise: keeping fit • the role of sport
Social life: friends • free-time activities

Prepare your presentation before you talk to the class. Use good, clear notes in English.

How am I doing?

In the Practice test you did some typical exam (Abschlussprüfung) tasks. If you found some tasks difficult, the questions below will help you to find out what you need to practise.

Listening (Task 1, 3, 4)

Tasks 1, 3 and 4 were listening tasks. Check your answers on p. 230 and decide how easy/hard you found them.

1 How easy or hard was each task?

	easy	OK	quite hard	very hard
Task 1				
Task 3				
Task 4				

If you found any of the tasks quite hard or very hard, look at 2 and say why.

2 What was difficult about the listening tasks?

a) I didn't understand the task.
b) People spoke too quickly.
c) I found the accents difficult.
d) There was a lot of information. I couldn't find the exact answers.
e) There were words and phrases that I just couldn't understand.
f) I didn't have time to finish all the tasks.

3 How did you do the tasks?

a) I looked quickly at the tasks first but only read them carefully while I was listening.
b) I read the tasks carefully first so I knew what I had to do.
c) I wrote as many answers as I could the first time I heard the text and checked them the second time.
d) There were lots of things that I couldn't understand and I panicked.

► *SF Listening (p. 140)*

▶ *You will find more LISTENING tasks in the Exam File, pp. 87–89.*

▶ *You will find more SPEAKING tasks in the Exam File, pp. 80–82.*

Speaking (Task 2, 5, 6)

Tasks 2, 5 and 6 were speaking tasks. Decide how easy/hard you found them.

4 How hard or easy was each task?

	easy	OK	quite hard	very hard
Task 2				
Task 5				
Task 6				

If you found any of the tasks quite hard or very hard, look at 5 and say why.

5 What was difficult about the speaking tasks?

a) I felt very nervous.
b) I didn't know what to say.
c) I didn't know enough about the topic.
d) I couldn't think of the right words.

Ask your teacher for a copy of the assessment sheet and fill it in.

Assessment sheet	☹		😐		☺	
Name ...	**1**	**2**	**3**	**4**	**5**	**Comm**
2 SPEAKING Holiday plans						
a) We listened to each other and tried to agree on a holiday plan.						
b) Our answers were long enough.						
c) We both showed interest in what our partner said.						
d) We were able to keep the conversation going.						
5 SPEAKING Too young to be a mum?						
e) I understood the message of the pictures and explained my ideas well.						
f) I used the questions to get ideas and to structure my talk.						
g) I said enough about the topic.						
h) I spoke clearly and loudly.						
6 PRESENTATION My lifestyle						
i) I spoke clearly and loudly.						
j) I talked about all the important points.						
k) I used visual materials (posters, ...) and explained them well.						
l) I looked at the audience and not at my notes most of the time.						

► *SF Speaking course (pp. 147–148)*

Unit 2 The world we live in

1 Technology in your life

a) *Look at the picture above. Try to name all the examples of technology shown.*

b) *How often do you or your family use the things in the picture? Make notes.*

I / We have (haven't) got a/an ...
I / My family never / always / often use a/an ...
I / We use a/an ... every day / week / ...

c) *Form a double circle. Use your notes. Talk to at least three partners about technology in your life. Try to find someone like you.*

Well, I'm very different from you. I never/often ...

I've got a/an ... too. / I haven't got a/an ... either.

I'm just/quite like you. I use a/an ... all the time.

d) *Read Tasha's text and write a similar text about yourself. You can put your text in your DOSSIER.*

▸ *SF Writing course (pp. 151–152)*

Tasha says:
1 July 2010 at 9.50 pm

I know that we must all try to use less energy, but it's not easy when you're a technology fan like me.

I live in a house with lots of electronic appliances: four computers, two games consoles, four TVs, two DVD players. I use an electric toothbrush and a hairdryer every day. Like most people, we have a dishwasher, a washing machine, a microwave and a fridge. Dad uses an electric razor every morning. All these appliances use a lot of energy.

We often go by car because it's so much quicker and easier than going by bus or cycling. And our family holiday this year wasn't very green either – we flew to New York. (What a great place!)

But now I've decided to try to use less energy. I cycle to school every day (it's not too far) and I usually remember to unplug my phone charger and my other appliances. When I'm cold, I put on a pullover first, before I turn up the heating. But I think I could do more for the environment.

2 What is it?

Listen to the CD. Guess what appliances the people are talking about and write them down.

▸ *SF Listening (p. 140)* • *WB 1 (p. 22)*

> Find phrases in the text that could be used as captions for the photos.

3 How big is your footprint?

We need a lot of energy to use computers, TVs, microwaves, cars, ... the list is endless. When we burn fossil fuels to produce all this energy, we send carbon dioxide (CO_2) into the atmosphere. CO_2 is one of the greenhouse gases that cause global warming. The result is climate change. Climate change has serious effects on living conditions everywhere. Some places are getting hotter and drier and in some places there is too much water. Many animals are in danger because their homes and food are disappearing.
The amount of CO_2 that you produce is called your carbon footprint. Every time you turn on the heating, play a video game or have a bath, you produce carbon emissions and your carbon footprint gets bigger.

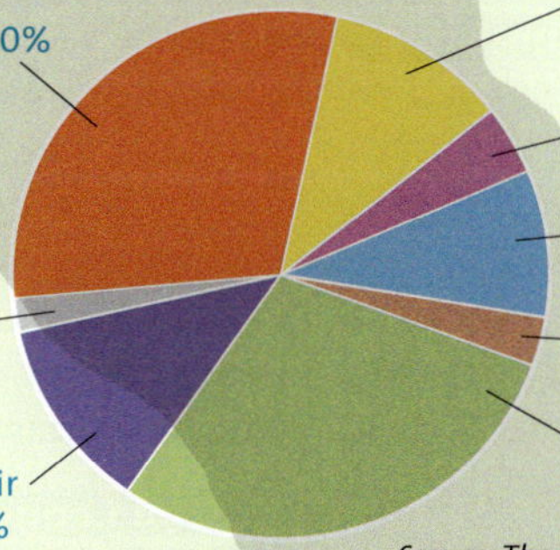

Source: The Open University

The average person in the UK has a carbon footprint of 9.8 tonnes of CO_2 per year. The pie chart shows how the average footprint in the UK is made up.

> *What does the pie chart tell us? For example: In the home, what produces the most CO_2?*

► *SF Talking about charts (p. 139)*

Average carbon footprints in tonnes of CO_2 per person per year (2009)

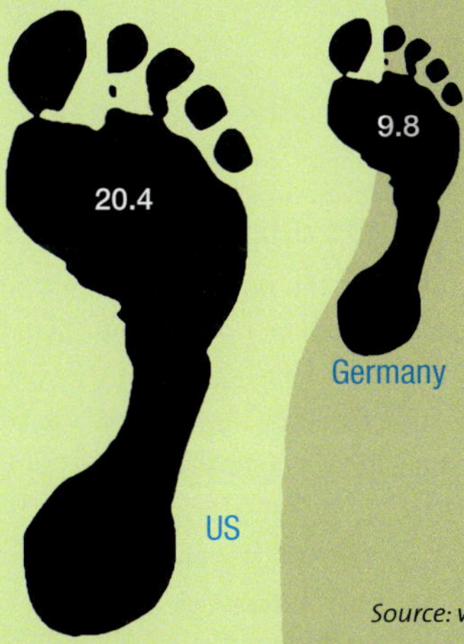

Source: www.carbonfootprint.com

2 Target for the world to stop climate change

a) *Calculate your carbon footprint. Use the carbon calculator at www.englishg.de/footprint. Are you above or below the German average? How far are you from the world target?*

b) *Why is your carbon footprint big/small? What could you do to reduce it? Think about: home, school, holidays, transport, energy, ...*

To reduce my carbon footprint I could ...
- use public transport/... more often.
- go by car/eat meat/... less often.
- turn off the TV/the lights/... when I'm not using it/them.
- ask my parents to use green energy/buy an electric car/get better insulation/turn down the heating/...

► **Text File 3** *(p. 121)* • *WB 2–4 (pp. 23–24)*

LIVING WITH TECHNOLOGY

The Daily News, 1st April 2009

Inventions that changed the world

This week British scientists named the top ten modern inventions that, they say, changed the world.

1 GPS technology

It was developed for the US army in 1978, but GPS (Global Positioning System) is now used in cars, planes, boats, and even mobile phones. Before we had GPS, people used maps or asked people for directions.

2 The Sony Walkman®

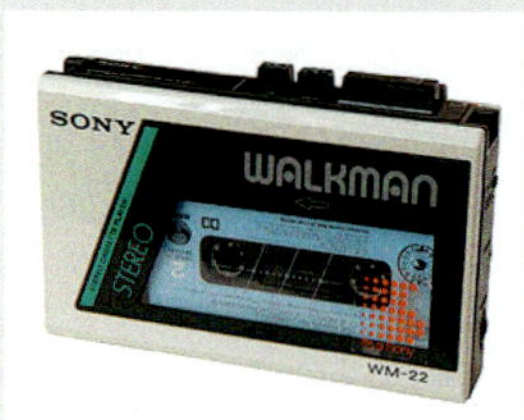

This famous personal stereo changed music forever. For the first time it was possible for people to listen to music on the way to work or during a run in the park. Then, in 2000, the Apple iPod® was invented and people could carry all their music in one pocket.

3 Trainers

They were invented in the US in 1892. At first they were worn only for sports, but they became really popular in the 1970s and since then they have changed fashion. They have also changed our feet: the army says that young people's feet are now too soft to wear traditional army boots.

4 TV dinners

'Ready' meals became popular in the 1970s because they saved a lot of time. They changed the way families ate meals. Since then it has become normal for people to sit in front of the TV to eat. Many people think that we were healthier before TV dinners because there is a lot of unhealthy fat, salt and sugar in them.

5 The PlayStation®

There were games consoles before 1994, but they were usually only found in teenagers' bedrooms. When Sony's PlayStation was introduced in 1994, games consoles arrived in living rooms, and adults became more interested in them.

6 Social networking sites

Every day people spend more than three billion minutes on Facebook. Facebook and other social networking sites like MySpace or Twitter have completely changed the way we communicate. In the past we lost contact with friends. Now we can find them again online.

7 Text messages

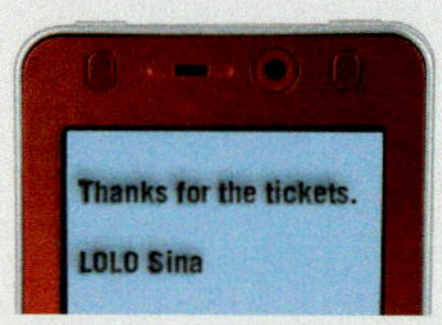

The first text message was sent in December 1992. Today the number of text messages received every day is more than the population of the planet. Text messages have created a new language. LOLO (lots of love) and IDK (I don't know) are now part of everyday English.

8 Electronic money

Credit cards made it easier for us to spend money in shops, on the internet or anywhere in the world. They also made it easy for people to spend more money than they really had.

9 Microwaves

Microwaves gave us a new, fast way to cook food, but the same technology is used for lots of other appliances. Communication equipment like mobile phones, internet and satellite TV all use microwaves to send information.

10 The Language Mediator

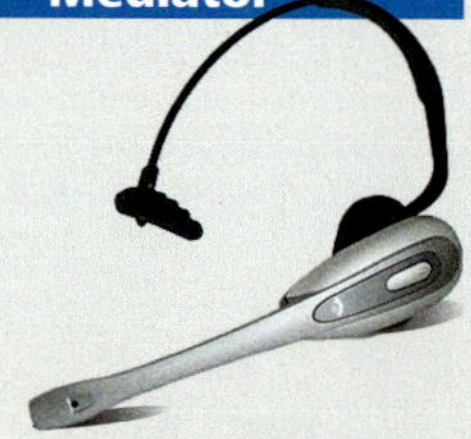

This invention allows us to communicate with people anywhere in the world. Put on the headphones and the machine translates what you hear and what you say. Now the British don't have to speak English very s-l-o-w-l-y and LOUDLY to foreign people when they are on holiday!

▶ *One of these inventions is actually a joke! Can you guess which one it is? (The answer is on p. 235.)*

1 Inventions that changed the world

a) *Complete the sentences with the inventions from p. 30.*

1 ... made it easier to stay in contact with friends.
2 ... gave people something to listen to while they were running.
3 ... are used for lots of different things, from communication to cooking.
4 ... save time but aren't good for your health.
5 ... can cause financial problems.
6 ... was only used by soldiers. Now it's used by sailors, drivers and lots of other people.
7 ... added new words to the English language.
8 ... could be bad news for language teachers.
9 ... brought fun to older generations too.
10 ... became popular more than 100 years after they were invented.

b) Think *about the inventions on p. 30. Which do you think are the most important? Make a list of your Top 3. Give reasons for your choices.*
Pair: *Talk about the advantages and disadvantages of your choices with a partner. Agree on your Top 3.*
Share: *Discuss with another pair. Agree on the Top 3 in your group.*

- For me the most important invention is ... because with (without) it/them we can (couldn't) ...
- I (don't) agree. I think ... is/are more important because ...

c) *Present your Top 3 to the class. Explain each choice in two or three sentences.*

- We think ... is the most important ... because for the first time ...
- Next we chose ... We think this is important because ... But it isn't as important as ...
- Our final choice is ...

d) **Extra** *Think of another important invention. Do some research to find out more about it (Why is it important? Who invented it? When was it invented? What's interesting about it?). Make a poster. You can put it in your DOSSIER.*

► *SF Research (p. 137)*

2 VIEWING Human Power Station

In the TV programme *Human Power Station*, the Collins family are taking part in an experiment. They are going to live in a special house for a day, but they don't know what the experiment is.

a) *Look at the photo and the title of the programme. Guess the connection between the cyclists and the special house.*

b) *Watch **scene 1** without the sound. Explain the connection between the cyclists and the man in the shower. Then watch the scene with the sound. Explain the experiment.*

c) *The Collins family have gone out for a walk and one of the presenters goes into the house. Watch **scene 2** and answer these questions:*

1 What does the presenter discover in the house?
2 How much money does this behaviour cost people in the UK every year?
3 What does the presenter want to show us when he burns the 'money'?

d) **Extra** *Does the programme make you think about what you do at home? Discuss in class.*

► **Text File 4** *(pp. 122–124)* • *WB 5–6 (p. 24)*

P1 //O REVISION Things are different today (Simple present and simple past) ► D p. 107

a) *Choose the correct tense:* ***simple present*** *or* ***simple past****.*

When I was a boy we ... (have to/had to) get up off the sofa to change channels because we ... (don't/didn't) have a remote control for the TV. We ... (watch/watched) programmes in black and white. My family ... (sits/sat) together in one room to watch TV because it ... (is/was) the only one in the house. We often ... (argue/argued) about which channel to watch. Now we ... (have/had) three TVs in our house, and we can watch programmes on the computer too, so there ... (are/were) no more arguments. This also means that today we ... (don't/didn't) sit together as a family as much and we ... (don't/didn't) talk about the programmes we watch. In my opinion that ... (is/was) a shame.

b) *Look at the chart on the right. Make sentences about what people did in the past and what they do now, for example:*

> *When people didn't have clocks, they looked at the ... to ... Today we have clocks to find out ...*

In the past, people ...
When people didn't have ..., they ...
Now we/a lot of people drive/go by/have/look at/use/write/...

► *GF 3: Talking about the present (p. 162)* • *GF 4: Talking about the past (p. 163)*

In the past ...	Now ...	to ...
sun 	clocks 	find out the time
ships 	aeroplanes	travel to Australia
horses 	cars and motorbikes	travel short distances
salt 	fridges	keep food fresh
letters 	computers 	communicate with friends

P2 WORDS Technology

a) *Collect words and phrases on the topic of TECHNOLOGY from pp. 28–31. Make a mind map. Find your own headings for the mind map.*
more help ► *D p. 107*

b) *Compare your results with a partner. Add more words and phrases if you can.*

c) *Write a short text about three inventions that you use every day and that are very important to you. Think about:*
– what you use them for
– what people did before they were invented.

> *The first invention that I use every day is my computer. I really couldn't live without it because I use it for so many things. For example, I can send e-mails to friends in seconds. I also use it to ...*
> *Before computers were invented, people ...*

d) **Extra** *Think of an invention that people use today. Describe it to your group (but don't name it). Can they guess what it is?*
It's an appliance/a machine that you use to ...
more help ► *D p. 107*

► *SF Paraphrasing (p. 149)* • *WB 7–9 (p. 25)*

P3 LISTENING A science competition

Jake and his gasifier

a) *New Zealand high school student Jake Martin won an award for a gasifier that he built for the 'Realize the dream' science competition. Look at the photo. What do you think his gasifier does? Then listen and see if you were right.*
– It looks like a machine that you can use to ...
– It might be an engine for a car/boat/...

b) *Listen again and answer these questions. Check with a partner.*
1 How much did Jake win?
2 What does he burn in his machine?
3 How long does it have to run to give a house power for a day?
4 How did he get the idea?
5 What is he going to spend his money on?
6 What is he going to do after school?

► *SF Listening (p. 140)*

P4 SPEAKING Making compliments

a) *Imagine you're talking to students at a science competition. Which phrases can you use to make compliments about their work?*
A You've done a very good/amazing/... job.
B I didn't expect such exciting/interesting/... results.
C Congratulations.
D Your results are really impressive/exciting/...
E That's cool. Where did you buy it?
F This is the most interesting project that I've seen.
G Well done!
H That ... looks great on you.

b) *Listen to two conversations. Which of the phrases do you hear?*

c) *Choose one of the examples below. Work out a dialogue where one student makes compliments about the other student's work.*
1 A project that looks at the question: Do students who eat breakfast get better marks at school?
2 A computer game to help students to learn their English vocabulary and have fun.
3 A funny video which helps new students to learn the school rules.

P5 MEDIATION A smartphone application

An American exchange student at your school asks you about the application you're using on your smartphone. Explain in English what you can do with this application.

Mit der neuen Smartphone-Anwendung **AllAroundYou** von ***MobiSoft*** bist du immer auf dem Laufenden – egal wo du gerade bist.

Du willst wissen, wo du in deiner Stadt coole Outfits kaufen kannst? Du bist in einer fremden Stadt und suchst die nächste Apotheke?

Mit **AllAroundYou** findest du alles schnell und einfach! Wähle aus den verschiedenen Kategorien die gesuchte Location aus und **AllAroundYou** zeigt dir, wo sie ist und wie weit sie von dir entfernt ist. Du kannst dir die ausgewählte Location auf einer Karte anzeigen lassen, die Route dorthin anschauen, die Infos an deine Freunde schicken und vieles mehr.

Lade dir **AllAroundYou** heute noch auf dein Smartphone!

► *SF Mediation (p. 157)* • *WB 10–11 (p. 26)*

SAVING THE PLANET

The Carbon Diaries 2015 (Abridged and adapted from the novel by Saci Lloyd)

It's 2015. The UK government is the first country to introduce carbon rationing to reduce the country's carbon footprint. From 8th January 2015 people in the UK will have a carbon allowance of 200 points a month. Everything they do – like driving the car, listening to music, having a shower – will cost them carbon points on their carbon cards. What will this mean for 16-year-old Laura Brown, her older sister Kim and their family?

▸ SF Reading course (pp. 142–143)

Sat, Jan 3rd

Dad sat down with us tonight and took us through a stupid government online form to work out what our family CO_2 allowance is. It's heavy. We've got a carbon allowance of 200 Carbon Points per month to spend on travel, heat, food. All other stuff like clothes and technology and books have already got the Carbon Points in the price, so if you want to buy a PC but it's from China and they used dirty fossil fuel to build it, then you're going to pay a lot more for it in Euros – cos you're paying for all the energy needed to make it.

The worst thing is, me and Kim have to give up lots of our points for the family carbon allowance. That leaves us almost nothing for travel, college, going out ... The car is going to be used much less, all of us can use the PC, TV, stereo for only two hours a day, heating is down to 16° C in the living room and 1 hour a day for the rest of the house, 5-minute showers, baths only at weekends. We have to choose – hairdryer, toaster, microwave, smartphone, kettle, lights, fridge or cooker and on and on. Flights are a real no-no and shopping and going out not much better. It's all kind of a *choice*.

Mon, Jan 5th

Carbon cards came today ...

They've got these little blocks down the side going from green to red and as you use your year's ration they disappear one by one till you're at your last red and then you're all alone, crying in the dark. Kim doesn't want to open her card, she says if she touches it then that's all her youth gone. I feel pretty nervous when I open mine, not that I really have a youth in my family. My sister's got it.

Thurs, Jan 8th

Back to college, and I got in late cos I had to take Mum to her bus stop. Her eyes filled with tears when we walked past the Saab. She whispered, 'It's not for ever,' and softly touched it. I pretended not to see.

We missed the first bus, so we had to wait 15 minutes in the rain till the next one. When it finally came I jumped on, swiped my carbon card and started running upstairs. Mum was searching through her purse, bag and pockets. She looked up at me.

'Laura, I can't find my card. Can you lend me some ...'

The driver shook his head. 'No carbon card, no ride, love.'

'But, please ...'

A woman out in the rain shouted: 'Get off, you stupid cow! You're holding us up.'

And then Mum started to cry. I went back down and helped her off the bus. 'We'll have to go home and get your card, Mum.'

'Found it! In my coat! Bastards!' Mum shook her green plastic card at the bus as it disappeared into the traffic. 'Oh, I shouldn't get so upset. Sweetie, let's go to Alfredo's and have a cup of tea.'

'I'm so sorry, Laura.' Mum picked up her tea cup. 'I know I should be strong, but I feel so responsible for my generation – we're the ones who've messed it all up for you.'

When I finally got to college there was a huge queue cos everyone had to swipe their CO_2 cards at the gate and the machine kept breaking down. I don't know what we were swiping for anyway – the building was freezing cold.

'Welcome to the future,' said Adisa, my best mate. 'They're ripping us off already.'

Tues, Jan 13th

My family has disappeared. Dad spends all night on his laptop, Mum is always lost on a bus somewhere and Kim just lives in her room – an evil ball of silence. I feel sick in this atmosphere. She's definitely got the TV on 24/7 in her room. I can hear it through the wall.

Weds, Jan 14th

I woke up this morning and it was freezing, freezing cold. I'm only allowed heat on in my room between 7 and 8. I went and looked at the Smart Meter in the hall. It's this thing that tells you everything that's happening with energy in the house. Even for our one hour of heat Dad keeps the bedroom temperature at 15° C. What a joke – it's not even enough to melt the ice on the windows.

Thurs, Jan 15th

There's heavy snowstorms all over the south of Europe.

Mon, Jan 19th

The snowstorms in Europe are getting worse – and moving north. Italy has just lost all its electricity. The news showed the Vatican going black, window after window.

Tues, Jan 20th

We had a power cut in the night. The house is so cold now, it feels like 200 years of cold in my bones. Cuts give me the creeps – you know, when you go to turn on the light and it's dead?

Working with the text

1 Understanding the story

a) *How does the carbon rationing system work?*

b) *Find the phrases in the text that mean the same as these sentences:*

1 We really shouldn't go by plane.
Flights are a real …
2 She started to cry.
3 You can't use buses without your CO_2 card.
4 We are the people who caused all the problems.
5 She never turns off the television.
6 Our electricity was turned off.

2 Your reaction to the story

a) *What do you think of the text? Say what you (don't) like about it. Would you like to read the whole novel? Explain why (not).*

b) ● *Is the story just science fiction? Or could this happen in the future? Explain why (not).*

3 What could you give up?

a) ○ *Look at ll. 22–31. Write down two things you could easily give up and two things you couldn't give up.*

b) *Explain your choices to a partner.*

4 ● A letter to a newspaper

Imagine you visit the UK in 2015. Write a letter to a British newspaper about carbon rationing. Say if you are for or against carbon rationing and explain why.

Dear Sir or Madam
I am a visitor from Germany and I am writing to you about …

more help ► D p. 108

► SF Writing letters (p. 154) • WB 12 (pp. 27–28)

P1 You can make a difference

a) Partner B: go to p. 99.
Partner A: You and your partner have different tips under each heading in Go Green. *Read your tips and take notes in a chart (use the text headings).*

Here it says that you should buy new, low-energy appliances.

My text says that you should turn off the lights when you leave a room.

b) Ask your partner about his/her tips to go green. Add your partner's tips to your chart.

▸ SF Taking notes (p. 141)

GO Green!

Climate change is a problem for the whole world. But don't sit around and wait for governments to act. Here are some simple things that you can do to help to stop global warming.

Reduce rubbish

About 75 % of the things we throw away could be recycled. Recycling is great because it reduces rubbish and saves energy. You can recycle paper, plastic and glass.

Use less energy

Producing electricity causes a lot of CO_2. So, to save electricity, buy low-energy appliances. If your family has an old fridge, try to get a new one. New models use much less energy. They'll reduce your family's electricity bill – and your carbon footprint!

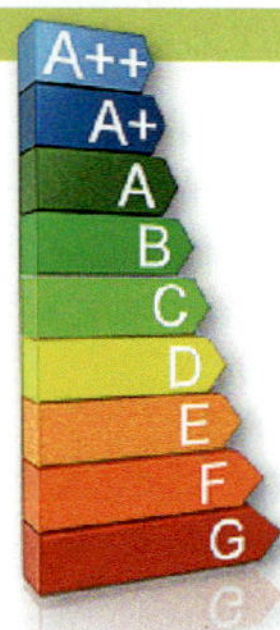

Think about your food

To help to fight against climate change, try to eat less meat. Meat has a big carbon footprint because producing it takes a lot of energy. And animals, especially cows, produce methane, which is a greenhouse gas.

Save trees

Why not plant a tree? Trees use CO_2 and they produce clean air – clean air that we need! More trees mean less CO_2 in the air.

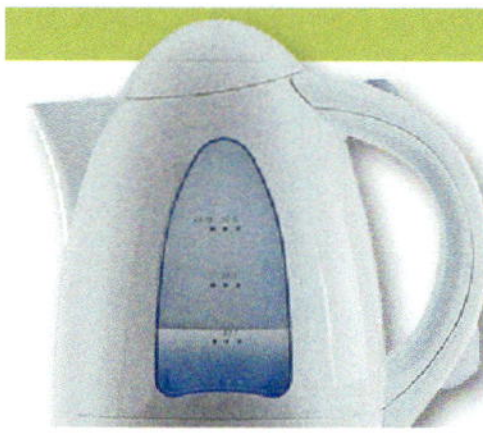

Heat less water

Heating water uses more power in houses than anything else. So when you make tea or coffee, fill the kettle only as much as you need to.

c) Which of these tips are easy to follow in your everyday life? Which are more difficult to follow? Discuss with your partner.

A: I think it's easy to turn off your computer when you're not using it. What about you?
B: …

P2 SPEAKING A cartoon (Talking about a cartoon)

a) Describe the cartoon to your partner. Then discuss what you think its message is.

b) Form a group with another pair. Compare your ideas about the cartoon. Then give your opinion of the cartoon and its message.

▸ SF Describing cartoons (p. 134) • WB 13–15 (pp. 28–29)

P3 WORDS The environment

carbon footprint • cars • emissions • fossil fuels • appliances • global • greenhouse gas • insulation • recycle rubbish • +solar energy • turn off • wind power

a) *Complete the sentences with words from the box.*

1 If there were fewer … on the roads, we could reduce carbon …
2 Good … keeps a house warm and saves energy.
3 … and … are examples of green energy.
4 We should … like glass, paper and cans.
5 Burning … is one of the main causes of … warming.
6 The average … of someone in Europe is much larger than of someone in Africa.
7 CO_2 is a …
8 To save energy we can … electric lights and electronic … when we're not using them.

b) *Find nouns that go with the following verbs.*

- **pollute** the environment, …
- **recycle** glass, …
- **save/waste** energy, …
- **destroy** forests, …

- **use** wind power, …
- **protect** …
- **clean up** beaches, …
- **burn** …

- **cause/stop** CO_2 emissions, …
- **plant/grow** …
- **reduce** …

P4 WRITING Can I save the planet? (A written discussion)

You're going to produce a written discussion of the following statement:
Carbon rationing should be introduced in Germany.

a) Collect and organize your ideas.
- *Brainstorm your ideas and make notes. (Work alone or with a partner.)*
- *Organize your ideas into arguments **for** and **against** the statement.*
- *Think of examples to support your arguments.*
- *Decide what you think about the statement.*
- *Then write an **outline** with all your arguments.*

OUTLINE
1 Introduction
2 First point of view:
Arguments and examples
3 Second point of view:
Arguments and examples
4 Conclusion

▸ SF From outline to written discussion (p. 156)

b) Write your text.
Introduction: Say what the written discussion is about and why the question is important.

I am going to discuss/write about …
Lots of people say that …
… is one of the biggest problems in the world today.
So the question is can … or not?

Points of view: Write about each point of view in separate paragraphs. List the arguments for each view and give reasons and examples.
Tip: It's often better to start with the view you disagree with.

Some people think that …
First … / Second … / Finally …
On the one hand … On the other hand …
For example, …
The reason for this is …
However, other people think that …

Conclusion: Sum up the arguments and give your own view.

In my opinion… / After looking at both sides I think …
To sum up I would say that …

c) *Read your text again and correct it. You can put your text in your DOSSIER.*

▸ SF Correcting your text (p. 152) • WB 16–18 (pp. 30–31)

1 WORDS Travel

a) *Make lists of words about travel under these headings: **air, railway, road, sea**. Use words from the box and add more if you can.*

airport • boat • cab • (to) cycle • (to) drive • ferry • flight • gate • harbour • (to) land • motorway[1] • petrol station • plane • platform • rush hour • ship • traffic jam • train • truck • the Tube • underground • ...

b) *All the verbs in sentences 1–6 are mixed up. Find the right verb for each sentence.*

1 Bob and I **drive** on a trip to Brighton last year.
Bob and I went on a trip to Brighton last year.
2 At 6 in the morning, I **went** him up at his house.
3 We had planned to **ask** on the early train.
4 But the train **travel** and the line was closed for the rest of the day.
5 So I phoned mum and she offered to **picked** us to Brighton.
6 We had to **broke down** a policeman for directions and then we were on our way. We had a great day!

2 London's underground (Simple past and present perfect)

*Complete the sentences. Use the correct tense: **simple past** or **present perfect**. Use the passive for the underlined verbs in 3 and 4.*

When London's underground – the Tube – (1) *opened* (open) in 1863, there (2) ... (be) only one line, just six km long. Since then many more lines (3) ... (add), and today's network is over 400 km. The first trains (4) ... (pull) by steam engines[2], but electric trains (5) ... (come) into use in 1890. Back in 1863, 30,000 people (6) ... (travel) on the underground on the first day. But of course the number of passengers (7) ... (rise) strongly in the last 150 years, and over three million people now use the system every day. The famous logo, which you can see in the picture, first (8) ... (appear) in 1908.

► *GF 4: Talking about the past (pp. 163–164)* • *GF 7: The passive (p. 168)*

3 Transport in London (Word order)

Read these statements about transport in London. Choose the right place for the words in brackets.

1 Julie: I love buses. I always try ... to sit ... so I can enjoy the view. (at the top)
2 Maria: I was ... in a terrible traffic jam .... (yesterday)
It took one hour ... from Piccadilly to Tower Bridge ...! (to drive)
I don't think that I'll go ... into London by car .... (again)
3 Jack: I want to reduce my carbon footprint, so I ... my car a long time ago .... (sold)
4 Mike: When I got to the stop, the last bus had ... left .... I was really angry. (early)
5 Sue: My husband and I always use ... the Tube ... when we go shopping. (on Saturdays)

▶ *You could now do task 1 in the Practice test on p. 42.*

► *GF 1: Word order (p. 160)*

[1] motorway *Autobahn, Schnellstraße* [2] steam engine *Dampflokomotive*

4 WORDS After the accident

Complete the dialogue with words from the box.

alcohol • ambulance • drunk • headache • healthy • hurts • operations • sweat • threw up • unconscious

Doctor Mike, can you hear me? You had an accident on your motorbike. Your friend Julie is still (1) *unconscious*. Both of you have broken arms and legs. You'll both have to have (2) ... But first we have to ask you some questions. Did you drink any (3) ... today?

Mike No, I didn't. Julie had one or two glasses of wine, but she wasn't (4) ...

Doctor Have you or Julie had a cold recently?

Mike No, we've been really (5) ... actually.

Doctor Good. Do you feel any pain right now?

Mike Yes, I do. My leg (6) ... terribly and I've got quite a bad (7) ... and a stomach ache too.

Doctor Well, maybe you've forgotten, but you (8) ... after the accident. You were in shock.

Mike I only remember feeling really weak. I was shaking all the time and felt cold (9) ... on my face. Doctor, who called the (10) ...?

Doctor Luckily, there was a nurse in the car behind you. He gave you first aid too.

5 Reporting what people said (Indirect speech)

Later Mike told a friend what the doctor had said. Complete Mike's sentences. Remember to change the tense of the verb.

1 *Doctor* You had an accident.
Mike He told me I had had an accident.

2 *Doctor* Julie is still unconscious.
Mike He said that Julie ...

3 *Doctor* You'll have to have operations.
Mike He added that we ...

4 *Doctor* Did you drink any alcohol?
Mike He asked if we ...

5 *Doctor* Have you or Julie had a cold recently?

6 *Doctor* Do you feel any pain?

7 *Doctor* You threw up after the accident.

▶ *You could now do task 2 in the Practice test on p. 43.*

▸ *GF 11: Indirect speech (pp. 173–174)*

6 STUDY SKILLS Writing (The 5 Ws and 'how')

a) *Use the phrases in the boxes to complete the report.*

A driving at over 80 miles per hour
B when broken glass flew into it
C in the late afternoon rush hour
D one of the worst accidents
E St Pauls and Eastville Park
F 23-year-old truck driver

Young dad loses left eye in accident

Yesterday a (1) ... was badly hurt in (2) ... in the Bristol area this year. The father of two sons had been (3) ... (where only 60 are allowed) and wasn't able to stop in time when he saw a traffic jam in front of him. Martin Smith from St Pauls in Bristol lost his left eye (4) ... Fortunately doctors were able to save the other eye. The accident happened (5) ... when thousands of people were travelling home from work. The M32 was blocked for two hours between (6) ..., and this caused traffic chaos in the centre of Bristol. Police said it was lucky that Mr Smith hadn't been killed.

b) *Match the phrases from a) to the 5 Ws and 'how'?*

▸ *SF Writing a report (p. 152)*

7 WORDS For a greener world

a) *For each group, find the word that doesn't fit.*

1 sun • plastic • paper • glass
2 oil • water • wind • sun
3 waste • recycle • reduce • save
4 help • pollute • protect • save
5 climate change • solar power • air pollution • global warming
6 trees • electricity • cars • heating

b) *Match the sentence beginnings (1–6) to the endings (a–h). There are two more endings than you need.*

1 Locally grown products ...
2 You need more energy to produce meat ...
3 You can buy cool clothes cheaply ...
4 Use a cotton shopping bag instead ...
5 Buying recycled paper can ...
6 It's much better to recycle glass ...

a than to produce vegetables.
b with public transport.
c are usually better for the environment.
d than to throw it into the dustbin.
e use green energy.
f of plastic ones.
g at second-hand shops.
h help to save trees.

8 Our green holiday (Simple past: questions)

Read the dialogue. Then use the verbs in brackets to complete the questions in the ***simple past****.*
Tip: Look at Sharon's answers first before you complete the questions.

Lucy So (1) ...? (enjoy)
So did you enjoy your holiday?
Sharon Yes, I did. I think it was the best holiday I've ever had.
Lucy Where (2) ...? (stay)
Sharon At a 'green' hotel in the south of France, near Marseille.
Lucy A 'green' hotel! That sounds interesting. How (3) ...? (find out)
Sharon Our neighbours told us about it. They were there last year.
Lucy So what (4) ...? (be)
Sharon Special? Well, the food was delicious – all locally grown.
Lucy And (5) ...? (be)
Sharon Of course it was organic food[1]. One hundred per cent! And we were allowed to help in the garden. That was great fun.
Lucy Fun? I'm not sure if I'd enjoy that. Anyway, what (6) ...? (do)
Sharon What else? Well, we went down to the beach every day.

Lucy That sounds more like a holiday. How (7) ...? (be)
Sharon It wasn't too far. Just over half a mile.
Lucy And (8) ...? (have)
Sharon Yes, we had fantastic weather. Twenty-five degrees and lots of sun every day!

► *GF 2: Making questions (p. 161)* • *GF 4: Talking about the past (p. 163)*

[1] organic food *biologisch angebaute Lebensmittel; Biokost* (organic ... *Bio-...*)

9 Ben's blog (Simple past: negative statements)

*Ben has started to 'shop green'. Read his blog. Complete the sentences with the **simple past** form of the verbs in brackets.*

Friday :-) Went shopping in town by bike today. I (1) … (~~take~~) the bus because it uses too much energy.
:-(Asked for recycled paper. Unfortunately, they (2) … (~~have~~) any.
:-) Bought some fruit. I (3) … (~~choose~~) the big red apples from Italy. Instead I chose small, locally grown ones. Cheaper too.
:-(Got some eggs for mum. Parents! I (4) … (~~be allowed to~~) buy organic eggs just because they're a bit more expensive!

Sunday :-(Went to town again. Can you believe it? I (5) … (~~can find~~) a second-hand clothes shop that was open!
:-(Bought a T-shirt made in China. I just (6) … (~~be able to~~) find one made in this country.

You could now do tasks 3 and 4 in the Practice test on pp. 43–44. ► *GF 4: Talking about the past (p. 163)*

10 WRITING A written discussion

a) Put these paragraphs in the right order (introduction, first point of view, opposite point of view, conclusion).

A On the other hand, there are arguments against buying clothes from developing countries[1], at least if the label has no reliable information about their background. First, fashion isn't everything. Second, conditions in clothes factories can be cruel. For example, one report mentions young children who work for no pay, and who are beaten if they don't produce enough.

B You often hear people say that there is a problem with clothes from developing countries. Here in Europe, these clothes can be very cheap. But the people who produce them for western markets often have to work very hard for very little. So the question is: should teenagers buy these clothes or not?

C After looking at both sides, I think it is safer not to buy clothes from developing countries if you know nothing about conditions in the factories. For me, fashion is very important, but human rights are even more important.

D On the one hand, you could say that it is not wrong to buy clothes from developing countries. First, most teenagers are interested in fashion, but they do not have much money. So it is an advantage to be able to buy clothes cheaply. Second, you cannot know the background to all the clothes you buy. And buying clothes from developing countries helps people there to make some money.

b) Write down the phrases that are used to structure the discussion in a chart with these headings: ***introduction, arguments, conclusion***

c) What other phrases can you add to the chart? ► *SF From outline to written discussion (p. 156)*

[1] developing countries *Entwicklungsländer*

1 LANGUAGE Congestion charge

Read the text. Choose A, B *or* C *from the list below to complete the text.*

They said it would never work!
It was getting worse from day to day. There were just too many cars in the centre of London. Nobody (1) ... get anywhere in time because of all the traffic. When Ken Livingstone, the Mayor of London, decided to do something about this, everybody said it would never work, but it did! In 2003, London (2) ... the first city in the world to introduce a 'congestion charge'[1]. Drivers now have to pay £8 a day to enter the centre of London. At first people said it would cause lots of problems because the technology used for paying the charge would (3) ... . It didn't! The Prime Minister[2] at that time, Tony Blair, was also very worried, but he soon discovered that he was wrong. People began to see that traffic jams weren't something that couldn't be changed.

The congestion charge has to (4) ... from Monday to Friday from 7 am to 6.30 pm. Since the introduction of the congestion charge, the number of cars per day in the centre of London (5) ... by 50,000 and traffic jams by a third. Another positive effect is that (6) ... in the congestion charge zone between Piccadilly and Tower Bridge has started to move faster. However, the managers of big (7) ... are less happy because they (8) ... fewer customers since the congestion charge was introduced. And many people said that it was unfair that only people with money could (9) ... into London, because the congestion charge AND parking are too expensive for most people.

And there are other problems too. The Mayor ordered hundreds of new (10) ... for all the extra passengers that were expected. (11) ..., however, people used the Tube instead, which was already very full. But many people think that, (12) ..., the congestion charge has been a big success. Now comes the $64,000 question: Would it work in other cities too?

1 A *can* B *could* C *couldn't*
2 A *became* B *become* C *has become*
3 A *break down* B *break up* C *cut down*
4 A *pay* B *paid* C *be paid*
5 A *goes down* B *has gone down* C *went down*
6 A *the motorway* B *the rush hour* C *traffic*
7 A *airports* B *stations* C *department stores*
8 A *had* B *have had* C *will have*
9 A *drive* B *cycle* C *walk*
10 A *buses* B *cabs* C *trucks*
11 A *Fortunately* B *Luckily* C *Unfortunately*
12 A *generally* B *although* C *always*

[1] congestion charge *City-Maut (wörtlich: Verkehrsbelastungsgebühr)* [2] Prime Minister *Premierminister/in*

2 WRITING A visit to the doctor's

a) A dialogue

You are at the doctor's. You fell off your bike yesterday evening. Your left arm hurts terribly and you have a headache and stomach ache. You threw up after the accident and felt weak. You were shaking all the time and felt cold. You want to know if your arm is broken.
In your exercise book, complete your part of the dialogue. Write about 80 words.

Doctor Good morning. And how can I help you today?
You (1) ...
Doctor Poor you! Do you feel any pain at the moment?
You (2) ...
Doctor Hmm. And do you have any pain in other parts of your body?
You (3) ...
Doctor Can you remember what happened after the accident?
You (4) ...
Doctor That can't have been very nice for you. But don't worry about it. You were probably in shock. Did you feel weak?
You (5) ...
Doctor OK. So let me have a look at your arm. Does that hurt?
You Yes, it does. (6) ...?
Doctor No, it isn't. You were lucky. Your arm will feel better in a couple of days' time. Try not to use it too much. And here, take this to the chemist's and they'll give you something for your head and stomach. You should be able to go back to school tomorrow.
You (7) ...

b) An e-mail

Write an e-mail to your best friend. In your email tell your friend about your visit to the doctor's.
You could write about:

– how long you had to wait.
– what the doctor asked you.
– what you told her.
– what the doctor advised you to do.

3 WRITING A report

Choose one of the following three topics and write a report about it. Remember to answer the 5 Ws and 'how'. Write about 100 words.

A You and your family were going on holiday, but you missed your flight because you arrived late at the airport.

B You saw an accident between a car and somebody on a bike.

C You spent a 'green' holiday in the country with your parents.

4 WRITING A shopping survey

Answer the questions below.

Shopping – for myself and my world

1 Do you help to write your family shopping list? Why (not)?
2 Do you think it's a good idea to buy organic food? Why (not)?
3 Do you agree it's better to eat less meat and more vegetables? Why (not)?
4 Do you think it's a good idea to buy recycled paper? Why (not)?
5 Do you use plastic shopping bags more than once? Why (not)?
6 Have you ever bought clothes at second-hand shops? Why (not)?

5 WRITING A letter to a newspaper

Child slaves work for western fashion companies

Two journalists have discovered a factory in Delhi where clothes for western markets were produced by children between the ages of eight and fifteen.

The reporters pretended to represent a large British fashion company and so were able to enter the factory. They described the conditions they saw inside as unbelievable. 'The children were working in dark and dirty rooms. Most of them were wearing almost nothing. They looked very tired and very hungry.'

Later the journalists returned with the police and the children were taken to the local police station, where they answered questions. They described how they worked for long hours for almost no money and said they were often beaten by the factory owners. Most of the children came from poor families who weren't able to support them.

One of the reporters, Julian Thomson, said: 'This shows that it's really important for shoppers in the West to find out where clothes were made before they buy them.'

Read the newspaper article. Then write a letter to the newspaper and say
– how you felt when you read it
– what you think about children working and why
– how you and other shoppers in your country could react.

6 WRITING Opinions

Choose one of the following statements and produce a written discussion about it. Write about 100 words.

A City centres would be nicer places if there were fewer cars there.
B The most important thing about food is that it is cheap.
C I can't worry about what workers in clothes factories earn. I don't have enough money myself.

How am I doing?

In the Practice test you did some typical exam (Abschlussprüfung) *tasks.*
If you found some tasks difficult, the questions below will help you to find out what you need to practise.

1 How easy or hard was each task?

	easy	OK	quite hard	very hard
Task 1				
Task 2a				
Task 2b				

Language (Task 1)

Check your answers on p. 232

2 Why was the language task difficult?

a) I didn't understand the task.
b) I found the multiple choice format difficult.
c) I couldn't decide which answer was correct.
d) I didn't understand all the text and panicked.

Writing (Tasks 2–6)

3 Why were the writing tasks difficult?

a) I felt nervous.
b) I didn't know what to write.
c) I couldn't find the right words.
d) I wasn't sure about the rules for writing different kinds of text (e.g. e-mail, report, etc.).
e) The texts I wrote weren't clear enough.
f) I made a lot of spelling and grammar mistakes.
g) I didn't have time to finish all the tasks.

► *SF Writing course (pp. 151–152)*

4 How did your partner do the writing tasks?

Ask your teacher for a copy of the assessment sheet on the right. Use it to assess your partner's work.

You will find more WRITING tasks in the Exam File, pp. 83–86.

Assessment sheet	☹		😐		☺	
Name ...	1	2	3	4	5	Comr
2 a) WRITING A dialogue: Did your partner ...						
a) answer all the doctor's questions?						
b) use all the ideas in the instructions and write enough?						
2 b) WRITING An e-mail: Did your partner ...						
c) use all the ideas in the instructions?						
d) use indirect speech?						
3 WRITING A report: Did your partner ...						
e) structure the report and say clearly what happened?						
f) start with the most important information and then go on to the details?						
g) answer the 5 Ws and 'how'?						
h) use the *simple past*?						
4 WRITING A shopping survey: Did your partner ...						
i) answer all the questions?						
j) give a reason for each answer?						
k) write enough?						
5 WRITING A letter to a newspaper: Did your partr						
l) write their address, the date, and the name and address of the newspaper in the right place?						
m) start and end the letter correctly?						
n) explain their opinion clearly?						
o) use long forms (of verbs)?						
6 WRITING Opinions: Did your partner ...						
p) structure their text?						
q) write enough on the topic and give examples for the arguments?						
r) use linking words to connect longer sentences?						
s) sum up the arguments for and against and express their opinion?						

Have your say!

1 What's the issue?

a) *Look at the photos. Choose one that you find interesting and describe it to your partner. Say what you think of when you look at it.*

▸ *SF Describing pictures (pp. 133–134)*

b) *What issues do these photos represent? Match the photos to the phrases in the box below.*

I think photo A/... is about ...

child poverty • discrimination • the environment • fair pay for young people • facilities for young people • the right to vote

2 What we care about

a) *Listen to eight young people. They're talking about the things they care about. Match the speakers to the photos A–F.*

Tip: For two speakers there are no photos.

b) *Listen again. In a chart, write down key words and phrases for the things the speakers care about.*

▸ *SF Taking notes (p. 141)*

Speaker	Key words and phrases
1	environment, pollution, ...

c) *Compare your charts. Can you add more key words?*

Speaker 1/... is talking about ...

I think he/she cares about ...

3 Now you

a) *Which issue do you care about most? Say why.*

b) ▸ *D p. 109*

▸ *WB 1 (p. 32)*

QUIZ

How much do you care?

If you think something is unfair, do you care enough to get up and do something about it? Take this quiz to find out.

1 You need a new T-shirt. Do you buy the one with the trendy label or the fair-trade label?

- A If the two T-shirts are the same price, I'd probably buy the fair-trade T-shirt.
- B I always choose fair-trade products because fair trade means fair pay for the people who make the products.
- C The trendy label. It's really important to look good. I don't care about fair trade.

2 There's a new student at your school. You try to talk to him, but he doesn't speak your language very well. What do you do?

- A I wait until he's learned to speak my language. It's too difficult to communicate.
- B I ask him to play football or another game where language isn't important.
- C I smile at him whenever I see him so he knows I want to be friendly.

3 Do you leave your mobile phone on charge overnight?

- A Sometimes. But I feel a bit guilty because I know it uses a lot of electricity.
- B Of course. This way my phone is always ready for me to use.
- C I would never do that! In the UK we waste £27 million a year this way!

4 Are you interested in the news?

- A No – but I sometimes look at the TV pages in the newspaper, and the sports pages too.
- B Not really, but I sometimes notice something interesting on the TV news when my parents are watching it.
- C Yes, I get information from lots of sources: news programmes, online news sites, blogs, …

5 You have three wishes. What's your first wish?

- A Good health for my family and friends.
- B World peace.
- C To be rich and good-looking.

6 Which statement do you agree with most?

- A If you don't vote, you don't have the right to complain if you don't like something.
- B Voting is a waste of time. Politicians don't listen anyway.
- C Voting is important, but you also have to get up and do something.

7 They want to close your youth club because the neighbours say there's too much noise. If they do, your band will have nowhere to practise. What do you do?

- A I email my local newspaper, start an online campaign, go on a demonstration in front of the town hall … anything I can do to save my youth club.
- B I sign a petition or join an online group.
- C Nothing – no one will listen to a group of kids.

4 How much do you care?

a) *Do the quiz. Then go to p. 236 to find your result.*

b) *Find out the results of the people in your group. Are you surprised by the results? Why (not)?*

– It says that I/you …
– I'm (not) surprised by that. I think that I/you …
– Really? I think it's true that I/you … but I don't think that I/you …

5 Extra The story behind the picture

Choose a person from one of the photos on page 46 and write 120 words about him/her. Say where the picture was taken and what the person is doing/thinking/feeling/… Where was the person earlier in the day? Where will he/she be later?

▸ SF Describing pictures (pp. 133–134) • WB 2 (p. 33)

YOUR RIGHT TO BE HEARD

1 What's the right age?

a) At what age are you allowed to do these things in Germany? Copy the chart. Discuss with your partner and try to complete the chart.

	United States	Germany
get married	14–17*	...
drive a car (on your own)	16–18*	...
vote in a national election	18	...
buy cigarettes	18	...
buy alcohol	21	...
leave home	18	...

* The rules are different in different states.

A: I think that in Germany you have to be 18/... before you can ...
B: I agree. / I disagree. I think that you have to be older / can be younger.
(Look at p. 235 to see if you were right.)

b) **Extra** *Try to find out about other countries that you know.*

c) At what age should you be allowed to do these things? Discuss with your partner.
- I think that 14/... is too young/too old/the right age to ... because ...
- I could/couldn't wait until I was 21/... to ...
- It's more/less/just as likely that young people would get divorced/have accidents/ have alcohol problems/...

▸ *SF Having a discussion (p. 148)*

2

COMMENTS E-MAIL PRINT

WE ARE PEOPLE TOO! by Oliver Munslow (16) – 23 August 2010

Look at the title of the article and the pictures. What do you think Oliver cares about? Who do you think he's talking to (adults or teenagers)?

To everybody out there that thinks young people are different, you're right! We're younger than adults. But that doesn't mean you don't need to listen to us or you don't have to respect us. We have feelings and (this might surprise some of you) we are people too.

Did you know that here in Britain every citizen under 18 has important rights? For example, we all have the right to be listened to and taken seriously, and we have the right to get together with our friends in public (as long as we respect the rights of other people and do not break the law).

But British children aren't taken seriously until they're 18. Too many adults think that our views just don't count and that we don't deserve equal rights. Here are some examples of discrimination against teenagers from my everyday life (in fact, most of these things happened to me this week).

Every day I see signs on shop doors that say '2 children at a time', 'no school bags', or even 'no children unless they are with an adult'. Children must wait outside and watch adults going in and out of the shop in front of them. Then, when they go into the shop, they must leave their bag outside. It doesn't matter if they have an expensive

laptop, tennis racket or saxophone in the bag. It has to stay outside.

If I want to meet my friends outside the shops or the burger restaurant near where I live, I can't wait for them there. Why? Because they are using that horrible 'mosquito'. Now this really makes me angry!

The mosquito is a machine that makes a terrible noise that only teenagers can hear. It hurts our ears, and shop owners use it to keep anti-social teenagers away. But it also keeps nice friendly teenagers away, people like me and my friends. In fact, teenage troublemakers make up only a very small percentage of the youth population. But did anyone think about the huge majority of young people who do not cause problems?

If I go to the cinema, I have to pay the same price as an adult because I am over 15. My sister is 19, but she pays less than me because she goes to university. So why can't you get a cheaper ticket if you're still at school? If I had a job, I would only get about £3 an hour because of my age, compared to £4.60 an hour for 18 to 21-year-olds and £5.52 for workers over 22. So, 16-year-olds earn less than adults but pay full price. That just doesn't make sense to me.

This country is a democracy. Every day, MPs and town councillors make decisions that make a big difference to our lives. But, as a 16-year-old, although I can leave home, get married, apply for a job, fight in the army, and pay taxes to the government, I don't have the right to vote. Why should political parties care about young people's wishes, when we can't vote for or against them?

We are old enough to breathe the air that has been polluted by the industries that you control. We are old enough to walk on the streets that are unsafe because of the drugs and crime problems that you haven't been able to solve. Surely we are old enough to help to improve things. Adults should start to understand that we have important things to say and that we have the right to be heard. ▲

a) // O *Match the sentence halves.* ▸ *D p. 109*

1 Oliver says teenagers are only different because ...
2 He thinks that some adults might be surprised that teenagers ...
3 The mosquito makes a noise that ...
4 Teenagers earn less than adults, so Oliver thinks it's unfair when teenagers ...
5 Young people can't vote and Oliver thinks that's why political parties ...
6 At the end of the article, Oliver says that he wants adults to ...

→

a can only be heard by teenagers.
b don't care about young people's issues.
c they are younger than adults.
d understand that young people have the right to be heard.
e are people too.
f must pay the same price for cinema tickets.

b) *Oliver thinks that teenagers are discriminated against. Find examples for his point of view in the article.*

3 Now you

a) *Discuss with a partner.*

– Are the things Oliver criticizes really discrimination against teenagers or are they sensible rules? Give reasons.
– Have you ever been in a similar situation? Talk about it. ▸ *SF Having a discussion (p. 148)*

b) ● *Write an e-mail to Oliver.*

– Say what you think of his article.
– Tell him what points you agree or disagree with. Say why.
– Say how the situation is for you in Germany.

more help ▸ *D p. 110* • *SF Writing course (pp. 151–152)* • **Text File 5** *(pp. 125–129)* • *WB 3–5 (p. 34)*

P1 WORDS Have your say

a) *Find words and phrases from pp. 46–49 for these three headings. Collect them in a mind map or word chart.*

1 **Issues:** the environment, ...
2 **Sources of information:** TV news, ...
3 **Action you can take:** buy fair-trade products, organize a march, ...

b) *Compare your words and phrases and add more words if you can.*

c) *Make appointments with three partners. Tell each partner:*

– what issues you care about most
– what sources of information you use most
– what kinds of action you take.

P2 VIEWING The mosquito: An anti-teenager device!

a) *Before you watch the news report: What is the mosquito device?*

b) *Look at the stills from the news report and try to guess the answers to these questions:*

1 Who will the reporter speak to?
2 What will they say?

c) *Watch the news report. Were you right?*

d) *Watch again and answer the questions in the box below.*

1 Where did the idea for the device come from?
 A Canada
 B Great Britain
 C the US
2 The mosquito can be heard by ...
 A little kids, teenagers and dogs.
 B teenagers and dogs.
 C teenagers.
3 Which of these comments was not made by the teenagers in the report?
 A It's disgusting.
 B It's like ringing in your ears.
 C It's really bad for our ears.
4 Why is Riverside Elementary School using the mosquito?
 A To stop teenagers bullying little kids.
 B To stop teenagers hanging around outside the school and drinking.
 C To make sure that students leave school quickly at the end of the day.
5 How does one dad use the mosquito with his daughter?
 A To call her on the phone.
 B To tell her to come inside.
 C To wake her up.

e) Extra *After watching this report, what do you think about the mosquito device?*

▸ WB 6–7 (pp. 35–36)

P3 REVISION Will the mosquito device keep troublemakers away? (*will*-future)

a) *Tom and Jill are thinking about using the mosquito outside their shop. Tom thinks it's a good idea, but Jill thinks it's a bad idea. Write down their arguments. Use* **will** *and* **won't**.

Tom (for the mosquito)

1 mosquito – keep troublemakers away
2 our customers – feel safer
3 more people – come and shop here
4 there – not be big groups of teenagers outside shop
5 we – not have to pick up their rubbish

Jill (against the mosquito)

1 mosquito – not stop troublemakers
2 they – go somewhere else and cause trouble
3 noise – annoy all young people
4 teenagers – not shop here any more
5 teenagers – not have a safe place to meet parents or friends

▸ GF 5: Talking about the future (p. 165)

b) *Act out the dialogue between Jill and Tom.*

▸ SF Having a discussion (p. 148)

c) *What do you think about using the mosquito outside your school? Write down your arguments in a list. Then discuss your opinion with two different partners.*

P4 SPEAKING Role play: A discussion about video cameras at school

There are problems with smoking, vandalism, graffiti and bullying at school. The head teacher wants to install video cameras outside the school and in the corridors and classrooms. There is a meeting to discuss this question:
Will video cameras make the school a cleaner and safer place?

a) *Decide who takes the role of moderator. The rest of the class makes five groups.*
Moderator: *Your job is to allow everyone to have their say (not to give your opinion) and to keep the discussion going.*
- *Go to p. 100.*
- *Read through your role card and practise the phrases quietly.*
- *Think of more questions you could ask to keep the discussion going.*

Other students: *Go to p. 100.*
- *Each group, choose a role card and think of arguments (and examples to support them).*
- *Make notes.*
- *Remember phrases you can use in a discussion.*

▸ SF Having a discussion (p. 148)

b) *Have the discussion. You could use the fishbowl method.*

c) *Which side had the better arguments? Vote in class.*

d) **Extra** *Write a short text: Should there be video cameras at your school? You can put your text in your DOSSIER.*

▸ SF From outline to written discussion (p. 156)

Fishbowl

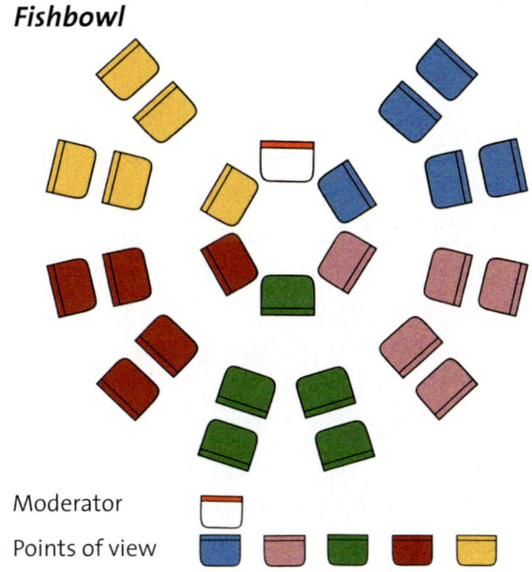

▸ WB 8–10 (pp. 36–37)

SPEAKING OUT

A class debate (Adapted from the novel *Speak* by Laurie Halse Anderson)

Speak is a novel about Melinda, who learns that it is important to speak out. In this text Melinda, the narrator of the story, describes a History class.

> *When you read the story, don't stop for every difficult word. You don't need to understand every word to understand the story. If the word is important, try to guess its meaning. If that doesn't work, use a dictionary.*

► *SF Working out the meaning of words (p. 142) • SF Reading English texts (p. 144)*

Mr Neck storms into class like a bull. We slide into our seats. I'm sure he's going to explode.

IMMIGRATION. He writes it on the board. I'm pretty sure he spelled it right.

Mr Neck: "My family has been in this country for over two hundred years. We built this place, fought in every war from the first one to the last one, paid taxes, and voted."

There's a cartoon bubble over the heads of everyone in the class. ("WILL THIS BE ON THE TEST?")

Mr Neck: "So tell me why my son can't get a job."

A few hands go up. Mr Neck ignores them. It isn't a real question, it's one he asked so he could give the answer. I relax. This is like when my father complains about his boss. The best thing to do is to stay awake and look sympathetic.

His son wanted to be a firefighter, but didn't get the job. Mr Neck is sure that this is some kind of reverse discrimination. He says we should close our borders so that real Americans can get the jobs they deserve.

I concentrate on trying to draw a pine tree.

Mr Neck writes on the board again: "DEBATE: America should have closed her borders in 1900." That gets a reaction. I can see kids counting on their fingers, trying to figure out when their grandparents or great-grandparents were born, when they came to America. When they figure out they would have been stuck in a country that hated them, or a place with no schools, or a place with no future, their hands shoot up. They do not share Mr Neck's opinion.

I don't know where my family came from. I don't know how long we've been in America. We've been in this school district since I was in first grade; that must count for something. I start drawing an apple tree.

The arguments jump across the room. A few kids quickly figure out which side Mr Neck is on, so they fight to throw out the "foreigners". Anyone whose family immigrated in the last century has a story to tell about how hard their families have worked, what they do for the country, the taxes they pay. A member of the Archery Club tries to say that we are all foreigners and we should give the country back to the Native Americans, but she's buried under disagreement. Mr Neck enjoys the noise, until one kid challenges him directly.

Brave kid: "Maybe your son didn't get that job because he's not good enough. Or he's lazy. Or the other guy was better than him, no matter what his skin color. I think the white people who have been here for two hundred years are the ones pulling down the country. They don't know how to work – they've had it too easy."

Mr Neck: "You watch your mouth, mister. You are talking about my son. I don't want to hear any more from you. That's enough debate – get your books out."

The Neck is back in control. Showtime is over. I try to draw a branch coming out of a tree for the 315th time. It looks terrible. I'm concentrating on the drawing, so I don't notice at first that David Petrakis has stood up. The class stops talking. I put my pencil down.

Mr Neck: "Mr Petrakis, take your seat."

David Petrakis is never, ever in trouble. What is he thinking? Has he finally gone crazy under the pressure of being smarter than everyone?

David: "If the class is debating, then each student has the right to say what's on his mind."

Mr Neck: "I decide who talks in here."

David: "You opened a debate. You can't close it just because it is not going your way."

Mr Neck: "Watch me. Take your seat, Mr. Petrakis."

David: "The Constitution does not recognize different classes of citizenship based on how long you've lived here. I am a citizen, with the same rights as your son, or you. As a citizen, and as a student, I am protesting the tone of this lesson as racist, intolerant, and xenophobic."

Mr Neck: "Sit your butt in that chair, Petrakis, and watch your mouth! I try to get a debate going in here and you people turn it into a race thing. Sit down or you're going to the principal."

David stares at Mr Neck, looks at the flag for a minute, then picks up his books and walks out of the room. He says a million things without saying a word. I make a note to study David Petrakis.

Working with the text

1 The story

Finish these sentences.

1 Mr Neck starts a debate about ...
2 He's upset because his son can't ...
3 Mr Neck believes that ...
4 He stops the debate when ...
5 David Petrakis says that Mr Neck can't ...
6 At the end, David ...

2 The characters

a) *Collect facts from the text about Mr Neck and David:*

Mr Neck: teacher, son wants to be a firefighter, ...
David: student, never in trouble, ...

b) *Think of adjectives, or use the ones in the box, to describe Mr Neck and David. Find quotes in the text that support your choice.*

angry • arrogant • brave • calm • clever • easy-going • confident • fair • impatient • patient • prejudiced • racist • rude • scary • strong • stupid • unfair • weak • ...

► *SF Drawing conclusions (p. 143)*

3 Now you

a) Think and make notes: *Think of a situation when someone didn't speak out, but you think he/she should have said something. Then think of a situation when someone spoke out.*
Here are some ideas:
– Someone made a racist comment.
– Someone was bullied.
– A teacher blamed the wrong student.

b) Pair: *Describe the situations to your partner. (What happened? How did others react?)*

c) Share: *Report your discussion to another pair. Then discuss this question:*
When should you speak out?

► *SF Having a discussion (p. 148)*

4 Extra VIEWING *Speak*

a) *Watch the film version of the classroom scene. Are the characters as you expected?*

b) *What's different from the book and what's the same? Think about*
– the way the characters are represented
– what people say
– what's missing in the film or book.

► **Text File 6** *(pp. 130–131)* • *WB 11 (p. 38)*

P1 WRITING Should young drivers be banned from driving at night?

a) *Some people want to ban drivers under 25 from driving after 10 pm. Would you support this idea?*

b) *Listen to a radio programme. Take notes on the arguments. You can listen twice.*

for	against
lots of accidents at night	not fair to responsible drivers
...	...

c) *Collect more arguments for and against.*

d) *Imagine German politicians want to ban drivers under 25 from driving after 10 pm. Email your English friend and say what you think about the idea and why. Write at least 120 words.*

▸ *SF From outline to written discussion (p. 156)*

P2 Mediation The rules for alcohol

Your family is visiting the US. Your parents want to know about the rules for alcohol there. Read this online article and answer your parents' questions in German.

- Gelten überall in den USA dieselben Regeln?
- Wo kann man Alkohol kaufen?
- Wie sollte man sich verhalten?

Visiting the US 1 2 **3** 4 5 ▸

Alcohol

In the US the rules for alcohol are decided by the individual states. Bars close at different times in different cities, and some parts of the US are still 'dry'. This means that you cannot buy alcohol anywhere in that area. In some states you can only buy alcohol in special shops, called ABC (Alcohol and Beverage Control) stores.

You cannot drink alcohol in public. Taking a beer out of a bar onto the sidewalk is illegal in most states. Walking down the street with a beer will certainly get you into trouble with the police. Since 1984, it has been illegal in all states in the US for people under 21 to buy alcohol or to drink alcohol in public. Even if you are a grey-haired old lady, you often have to show an official document (for example, a driving licence or a passport) that shows your picture and your birth date if you want to buy alcohol.

Many people in the US think the alcohol rules are unfair because young people are seen as adults in most other areas of life. 18- to 20-year-olds can get married, have children, buy cars, homes and guns, but they can't drink a glass of wine in a restaurant, or even a glass of champagne at their own wedding.

▸ *SF Mediation (p. 157) • WB 12–15 (pp. 39–41)*

P3 SPEAKING Solving conflicts

EVERYDAY ENGLISH

a) *Choose boxes with phrases to ...*

1 start a conversation
2 name a problem
3 disagree that there is a problem
4 say that you're sorry
5 end a conflict.

A
– What annoys me is ...
– I don't like the way you ...
– The problem is ...

B
– I don't see what's wrong with ...
– Where's the problem?

C
– Don't worry about it.
– OK. No worries.

D
– Can I have a word with you?
– Excuse me, but ...

E
– I'm sorry, I didn't mean to ...
– I'm sorry, I didn't know ...

b) *Look at these two dialogues between people at a youth hostel. Complete them with phrases from a).*

Fin Mia, (1) ...?
Mia Yes, of course.
Fin Er ... Your perfume – it's very strong!
Mia Great, isn't it? It was from my boyfriend.
Fin Well, (2) ... that it isn't great for me. Can you stop using it please?
Mia Sorry, but (3) ... it. Are you crazy?
Fin I just have problems with perfume. It hurts my eyes and my skin goes red. And we share a room, so I can't sleep.
Mia Oh dear. Of course I'll stop using it. (4) ... it had that effect on you.
Fin (5) ... And thanks.

Ali (1) ... did you use my shampoo?
PJ Oh yeah. I forgot mine, so I used yours.
Ali OK, but (2) ... that you've used it all.
PJ There's still some in the bottle, so (3) ...?
Ali Yeah, there's a bit in the bottle, but not much. And (4) ... you didn't ask me first.
PJ But you weren't there. Anyway, (5) ... use so much. It was an accident.
Ali (6) ... it does come out of the bottle very quickly.
PJ Yes, it does. But I'll buy you some more later, OK?

c) *Listen and check your answers in b).*

d) *You're sharing a room. One of you has annoyed the other. Discuss the problem. Choose one of these situations or use your own ideas. Make a dialogue.*

– You don't like your partner's music.
– The battery of your MP3 player is dead. You think that your partner forgot to turn it off.
– Your partner is always on the phone and speaks quite loudly.
– It's too cold for you with the window open.
– Your partner's trainers smell really bad.
– Your partner practises the trumpet in the room and you're really annoyed.

▸ WB 16 (p. 41)

1 WORDS Getting involved

Choose the right word to complete each sentence.

1 We have decided to practise/protect/protest against plans to close our youth club.
2 At a meeting last week, the club leader got up and made a chat/speech/talk about what we should do.
3 Then we all had a chance to give/have/speak our say.
4 Lots of people took part/place/turns in the discussion.
5 Some people thought we should advise/start/play a petition.
6 Others wanted to rise/raise/grow money for the club.
7 I complained/signed/volunteered to organize a jumble sale.
8 We have decided to go on a protest journey/march/ride through the town centre.
9 I'm sure the politicians will listen to us because we'll soon be old enough to present/spend/vote in elections!

2 READING Which event? (Drawing conclusions)

a) *Read the information about Lily. Then read about the two events. Which event is more suitable for Lily? Give reasons.*

About Lily
Lily, 17, wants to get involved in helping animals. As a student she has very little money and spends most of it on her dog.

RSPCA[1] Christmas Event
Are you a dog owner who would like to help animals in need? Here's one way to give money to the RSPCA at Christmas time. Buy a decoration[2] for our Christmas tree. We will put your dog's picture in the decoration and hang it from our tree in December. The decorations aren't cheap, but your money will help to pay for vets to look after homeless and sick animals.

RSPCA Volunteer Information Day
Volunteering with the RSPCA is a great way to meet people who share your love of animals. As a volunteer you'll be able to look after animals in need and make a real difference.
Come to Volunteer Information Day and hear other volunteers talk about their experience of helping animals. Anyone between the ages of 16 and 70 can volunteer.

b) *Read the information about Ella and Adam. Then read about the three events. Which event is most suitable for Ella and which is most suitable for Adam? Give reasons.*

About Ella
Ella works in a supermarket, but would love to be a gardener. Hobbies: action films, hiking

About Adam
Adam is a biology student. He's very interested in global warming. Hobbies: singing, acting

EVENT 1 Film and discussion
Earth 2100 is a documentary that explores how our world might look at the start of the next century if we do not take action immediately on climate change. The film, based on the latest research, also shows ways of creating a different future.

EVENT 2 Queen's Park project week
Act now to create a greener and more beautiful public space. The Friends of Queen's Park's spring project needs volunteers with green fingers who can help to clean up after the long winter. A chance to practise your garden skills and maybe get a few tips from the experts.

EVENT 3 Westport Lake clean-up
On World Environment Day this year we are going to walk around Westport Lake and collect all the rubbish that we can find. Come and help us … and bring your kids too. Remember: If children never experience nature, they'll never learn to love and protect it.

▶ *You could now do tasks 1 and 2 in the Practice test on pp. 59–60.* ▸ *SF Drawing conclusions (p. 143)*

[1] RSPCA (Royal Society for the Prevention of Cruelty to Animals) *britischer Tierschutzverein* [2] Christmas tree decoration *Christbaumschmuck*

3 Are you going to work in the holidays? *(going to-future)*

a) *Complete the dialogue. Use the* going to-*future.*

Ava (1) ... (you – work) in the holidays?

Are you going to work in the holidays?

Jon Yes. At least (2) ... (I – look for) a job. What about you?

Ava Well, (3) ... (Sam and I – work) in Mum's shop.

Jon That sounds really boring.

Ava Yeah, but (4) ... (we – not – do) it for the whole holidays. Just for a few weeks. And after that (5) ... (we – spend) a week with Dad in London.

Jon And (6) ... (he – show) you the sights?

Ava Well, maybe a few sights. But (7) ... (he – not – spend) too much time with us – I hope! We want to do some things on our own. Anyway, what about you? (8) What kind of job ... (you – look for)?

Jon Well, I'd like a job in a park or a garden. Or something similar. But one thing is sure. (9) ... (I – not – work) in a shop or anywhere inside. Not if I can be in the open air.

b) *Prepare a dialogue about your future plans (for next weekend, the holidays, ...). Act it out.*

► *GF 5: Talking about the future (p. 165)*

4 WORDS Paraphrasing

If you can't think of an English word, you can paraphrase it. Match the sentence halves to paraphrase the words in the box.

Abgeordnete(r) • (TV-)Gastgeber(in) • Partei • Untertitel • Wirtschaft • Ziel

1 It's an organization that ...
2 They're words at the bottom of a screen ...
3 It's a person who represents ...
4 It's somebody who interviews guests ...
5 It's something that you ...
6 It's our system for ...

► *SF Paraphrasing (p. 149)*

a	... producing and selling things.
b	... you in parliament.
c	... really want to be able to do in your life.
d	... in a discussion (on TV, etc.).
e	... people can vote for in elections.
f	... that help you to understand a film in a foreign language.

5 EVERYDAY ENGLISH Making suggestions

a) *You have a guest from abroad*[1]*. You're busy today, so make suggestions about what your guest could do. Choose the correct phrase to complete each suggestion:* **A** *or* **B**

	A	B	
1	I suggest	You could	... spend the morning in the technology museum.
2	Why don't	Why not	... you check the opening hours on the internet?
3	If I were you,	I suggest	... I'd take the underground into town.
4	Why don't	Why not	... ask at the station how much an all-day ticket costs?
5	If I were you,	I suggest	... that you have lunch in town.
6	You could	I'd recommend	... the Italian restaurant near the market.

b) *Use phrases from a) to make suggestions about what your guest could do after lunch. The ideas in the box can help you.*

watch a film • phone cinema for film times • walk to cinema • meet in café after film • ...

[1] from abroad *aus dem Ausland*

6 WORDS Politics

Find a similar way of expressing the ideas in each of the sentences below. Replace the underlined words with words/phrases from the box.

citizen • criticize • discriminates against • elect • illegal • responsibility • the majority

1 In the UK we vote for a new government every five years.
2 Every man and woman in this country has the right to say what they think.
3 It's the government's job to look after the economy[1], the health system and the schools.
4 This law isn't fair to young people.
5 More than half of the people want a change in the law.
6 Discrimination against minorities is against the law.
7 We all have the right to say what we don't like about the system.

7 READING What does it mean? (Working out the meaning of words)

a) *How can you work out the meaning of the **green** words in the box? Make a copy of the chart and write down the **green** words under the right headings. Sometimes there is more than one way to work out what a word means.*

1 The German word is similar	2 I know part of the word	3 The context helps
opposition, ...	...	...

b) *Compare your results with a partner.*

Opposition is the same in German.

The context helps too. The sentence is about what the government party did after they lost the election.

c) *There are nine words in the article below that you haven't learned in this book. But you can probably understand most of them. Read the text. Then say which **red** words you understood, and why.*

1 At 16 you can work and pay taxes but you are not **permitted** to vote.
2 If politicians want to improve their **popularity**, maybe they should try to be more interesting.
3 The government party lost the election and went into **opposition**.
4 The **maximum** age for members of the UK Youth Parliament is 18.
5 Parliament doesn't **sit** during the summer.
6 The South-East is the richest **region** in the UK.
7 The Youth Parliament **conference** in Dublin brought together 230 **representatives** from 32 European countries.

Ticket prices cause angry protests

Passengers are angry about plans for a 10% **increase** in bus ticket prices.
The cost of a **monthly** ticket will rise from £60 to £66. A **spokesperson** from the bus company, Jean Simons, said: 'It's a **moderate** increase and we hope it won't cause too much **hardship**. We're sorry, of course, but rising costs and **inflation** mean that we have to ask passengers to pay a bit more.'

Sanjay Patel, who represents local students, doesn't agree. 'This isn't **acceptable**. It will make things **extremely** difficult for a lot of people. We need lower ticket prices, not an increase.
There'll be a demonstration at the town hall this weekend. We **call on** everyone who is against the increase to support us.'

► SF Working out the meaning of words (p. 142)

[1] economy *Wirtschaft*

1 READING Events

Five teenagers are looking at a youth club notice board for events that would be suitable for them. Read the teenagers' statements and the descriptions of the events (A–E). Then decide which event would be best for each person.
Copy the names and write the correct letter next to each name.

Jill: I live 15 miles from the next town and I'm too young to drive. I can now get home by bus on Saturday nights – thanks to our protests. But the bus is still too expensive.

Megan: I have lots of different rights. But I'm still 'too young' to choose the person who represents me in Parliament. Something has to be done to improve this situation.

Sally: For adults it's clear enough what the law allows. And it's the same for young kids. But if you're a teenager, it's almost impossible to know what is allowed and what isn't.

Ben: I can't imagine living anywhere else. I love the fresh salt air and the little harbours with their colourful boats. Unfortunately lots of day tourists from big cities come here. And many of them make quite a mess because they don't tidy up after their picnics.

Ethan: I'm really interested in politics but most of my friends aren't. And most young people don't show enough interest in what happens across the Channel[1]. We need to be more open to ideas from our partner countries on the Continent.

A
Political Friday
This week's debate is about changing the law on the voting age. Fran Lloyd, Mayor of Norton, thinks that young people learn a lot between the ages of 16 and 18 and that 16 is too early to vote. Diana Gee, from Radio Kent, says that 16-year-olds already know enough to vote. Expect an exciting discussion.

B
Beach clean-up weekend
Once again local clubs are being asked to come to the beach (meet at North Bay) on Saturday or Sunday to help to tidy it up after the summer. Please take part. Wear gloves[2], bring plastic bags and give a couple of hours of your time for our most popular place.

C
Bus trip to Europe's capital
Join us on a trip to Brussels to visit the European Parliament. We will have space for 50 people on the bus. The trip is supported by the EU and will cost only £15. We leave Dover on 7th July at 4 am (sorry!) and get back late the same day (about midnight). Passport needed!
More info at www.kentineurope.org.uk

D
Teen rights, OK?
Local citizens' advice bureau[3] worker Diane Fry explains what young people can and can't do. Find out about your rights and responsibilities[4] in many areas: voting, working, cheaper travel tickets, drinking, smoking, driving, passports, boy-friends, girlfriends, etc., etc.
Sunday 10 am

E
March to Town Hall
Young people over 14 pay as much as adults on our local buses – a problem if you need the bus to get out at weekends. It's a £6 bus ride to and from the cinemas and clubs in and around Canterbury. Join our protest march to the town hall.
Saturday, 2 pm

[1] the Channel *der Ärmelkanal* [2] gloves *Handschuhe* [3] citizens' advice bureau *Bürgerberatungsstelle* [4] responsibility *Verantwortung, Pflicht*

2 MEDIATION An advertisement

Du willst im Sommer in Großbritannien arbeiten und hast die folgende Anzeige online gefunden. Um deine Eltern von deinem Plan zu überzeugen, mach dir Notizen auf Deutsch zu den folgenden Punkten:

1 wo du wohnen und arbeiten wirst
2 was deine Hauptaufgabe sein wird
3 welche Voraussetzungen du unbedingt mitbringen solltest
4 was du verdienen wirst
5 welche Vergünstigungen geboten werden.

Torbay International Youth Camp is looking for …

➢ ***Service team volunteers***

Your main job will be to
- organize daytime activities and evening entertainment for young people from all over the world

You will also be responsible for
- helping in the dining room during meals

You must be
- between 17 and 20 years old
- able to communicate with 11- to 15-year-olds
- organized and energetic
- a team player

It will be an advantage if you
- have experience of working with young people
- can speak at least one foreign language
- have a driving licence

We offer you
- free travel to Torbay (second class only)
- a free room in our international village
- breakfast and two hot meals a day
- £25 pocket money per week
- a chance to meet and speak with people from different backgrounds

Interested? Apply online

3 MEDIATION Helping a visitor to Germany

Your Scottish friend, Maggie, is staying with you and would like to find out about politics in Germany. You find two interesting events in the newspaper. Maggie is out and you have to leave before she returns. Write a message for her. Describe each event in English. Do not translate word for word – just give the main information.

Mit Cartoons in die Politik einsteigen

Wir werden eine DVD zeigen, die die Programme der im Deutschen Bundestag vertretenen politischen Parteien erklärt. Die unterschiedlichen Bereiche der Politik wie zum Beispiel Außenpolitik, Innenpolitik, Gesundheit und Wirtschaft werden mit Comicfiguren und lustigen Zeichnungen illustriert.
Der Film dauert ca. 45 Minuten und hat englische Untertitel.

Was noch?
Anschließend werden wir diskutieren. Danach gibt's Livemusik von Poll Position.

Wann und wo?
Freitag, 19.30, Jugendzentrum, Böllstraße 22

Live-Polit-Talk mit Studiogästen

Thema:	Wohin, Europa?
Gastgeber:	Tom Meyer
Gäste:	EU-Abgeordnete aus Deutschland, Großbritannien und Spanien
Wann:	Freitag 18.30–20.00
Wo:	Fernsehzentrum Köln

Meyer wird jungen Europa-Abgeordneten Fragen zur Zukunft Europas stellen. Insbesondere geht es um die Einbeziehung junger Wählerinnen und Wähler in politische Planungen.

Die Diskussion wird simultan ins Englische übersetzt.

Hi Maggie,
I've found two events that you might be interested in. You could go to the youth club in Böllstraße, where they're going to …

4 READING Notices, short ads and signs

Read each short text. Then decide if the statements below are true or false.

Need a weekend job?
We're looking for a reliable and friendly student to help out with selling snacks in our sandwich bar on Saturdays and/or Sundays. You must be 16 or older and have a clean and tidy appearance. You will earn £8 an hour.
For more information, come in and talk to the manager.

BRIDGETON TENNIS CLUB

Rules for Members

1 Tennis shoes must be worn on court.
2 Sports clothes must be worn during play.
3 A maximum of four people are allowed on each court.
4 Nets must be taken down at the end of play.
5 All rubbish must be taken away.
6 Under-18s are not allowed to buy alcohol at the club bar.

They're watching you
There are over 4 million video cameras (CCTV) in Britain. They're watching you in the street, in shops, at railway stations, everywhere. Find out more on Panorama next Monday at 8.30 pm on BBC 1.

How well can you drive?
The RoSPA[1] Young Driver Assessment will tell you how good a driver you are. The assessment is for drivers aged between 17 and 24, and can be taken from six months after passing the driving test.

Trip to the Houses of Parliament
Newton Youth Forum is organizing a special day trip to London, where our local MP Mike Worth will take us on a two-hour tour of the Houses of Parliament.
Tour starts: May 5th, 8.45 am
Departure from: Newton Station
Cost: £5 per person (Forum members pay only £3)
Return to Newton: 6.30 pm
More information and booking:
www.newtonyouthforum.org.uk

1 At the tennis club, members can wear whatever they like.
2 The sandwich bar needs someone to tidy up.
3 If you're interested in the job in the sandwich bar, you should go and see the manager.
4 The Newton Youth Forum trip to London starts at the Houses of Parliament.
5 The BBC TV programme is about CCTV cameras in public places in Britain.
6 RoSPA helps young people to pass the driving test.
7 You must not leave any rubbish at the tennis court.
8 If you go on the trip to London, you will return to Newton the same day.
9 Only good drivers can do the RoSPA Young Driver Assessment.
10 The BBC programme about CCTV cameras is on in the morning.
11 Members of Newton Youth Forum have to pay £3 for the trip to London.
12 They don't sell alcohol at the tennis club bar.

[1] RoSPA (Royal Society for the Prevention of Accidents) *britische Gesellschaft zur Förderung der Straßensicherheit*

5 READING A news report

Read the text and do the tasks below.

Sunderland votes in UKYP election

Over 16,000 young people will be able to vote in the Sunderland region in this year's election to the UK Youth Parliament (UKYP). Voting at 55 schools will take place over 7 days from 26th February. On 5th March, the names of the four winners will be announced.

> UKYP is an organization that allows young people between the ages of 11 and 18 to have their say. There are no parties and no government or opposition. The 600 Members of Youth Parliament (MYPs) come together to debate and to organize campaigns for change. An MYP can sit in the UK Youth Parliament and in local youth parliaments.

This year, 22 candidates are standing for election in the Sunderland region, more than ever before. We spoke with a few of those candidates.

The youngest, 11-year-old Will Black from West Windon Primary School, wants free recycling at all schools. 'At the moment, schools have to pay for the collection of all rubbish. We should have free collections for anything that can be recycled. Then schools would have a reason to recycle as much as possible.'

Barbara McKenzie, 16, from St Ambrose School for Girls, believes public transport for students should be cheaper. 'Young people need to be mobile, but they can't pay the full ticket price for buses and trains while they're at school. We should only have to pay half of what adults pay.'

The oldest candidate in this year's election, 17-year-old Jack Smith, says that there aren't enough places for young people. 'There isn't a suitable place for music concerts in the area. The places we can use are too small, or they aren't free when we need them.'

Jack, from Rosebrook Technology College, said: 'There's so much negative stuff about young people in the media, but many of us are working hard to change the situation.'

> The UK Youth Parliament sits at different places each year. This year's main sitting, in July, will be held at the University of Ulster in Northern Ireland, where there will be three days to debate issues and plan campaigns. And during the year, there will probably be a sitting in the House of Commons[2].

1 True, false or not in the text?
A The article is about the results of the Youth Parliament elections.
B Adults vote in Youth Parliament elections.
C Members of Youth Parliament are called MYPs.
D Sunderland is the biggest region in the UK.

2 How many people from Sunderland will be elected to the UK Youth parliament?
A 4 B 22 C 55

3 MYPs can sit
A only in the UK Youth Parliament.
B in the UKYP and local youth parliaments.
C only in a local youth parliament.

4 Complete the sentences.
A For Will Black, ... is very important, so ...
B Barbara McKenzie cares about ... and wants young people to ...
C Jack Smith would like more ...

5 The UKYP always meets in the House of Commons. This statement is true/false because the text says ...

[2] House of Commons *Britisches Unterhaus*

How am I doing?

In the Practice test you did some typical exam (Abschlussprüfung) tasks. Check your answers on pp. 234. If you found some tasks difficult, the questions below will help you to find out what you need to practise.

1 How easy or hard was each task?

	easy	OK	quite hard	very hard
Task 1				
Task 2				
Task 3				
Task 4				
Task 5				

Reading

Tasks 1, 4 and 5 were reading tasks. The following questions will help you to think about how you did.

1 What was difficult about the reading tasks in general?

a) Some of the texts were quite long and/or complicated.
b) There were words and phrases that I just couldn't understand.
c) There was a lot of information in the texts. I sometimes couldn't find the exact answers.
d) The tasks weren't like the tasks that we usually do in class.

2 Problems with specific tasks:

Task 1
- I understood most of the texts but it was still hard to find the information that I needed to match people and events.

Task 4
- The mixture of text types (e.g. notices, ads, signs) made it hard to concentrate on the content.
- I wasn't always sure which text contained the information I needed to do the task.

Task 5
- The newspaper article was hard to read.
- The mixture of task types (e.g. true/false/not in the text, multiple choice, etc.) made it more difficult to find answers.

3 How did you do the tasks?

a) I read each task carefully so that I knew what to look for in the texts.
b) I tried to understand the main ideas of each text first. That helped me to guess words and phrases that I wasn't sure about.
c) I scanned the texts when I was looking for a special piece of information.
e) If there was a task that I wasn't sure about, I left it out and came back to it later.
f) I checked my answers at the end and corrected any mistakes that I found.

▸ *SF Reading course (pp. 142–143)*

Mediation

Tasks 2 and 3 were mediation tasks. The following questions will help you to assess how you did. Ask your teacher for a copy of the assessment sheet and fill it in.

	Assessment sheet	☹		😐		☺	
	Name ...	**1**	**2**	**3**	**4**	**5**	**Comments**
2	a) It was easy for me to take notes on the English text in German.						
	b) In my notes, I concentrated on the most important information and didn't translate word for word.						
	c) I found information on all the important points (a–e).						
3	d) I found it easy to use German texts to write a message in English.						
	e) In my message, I only gave the most important information about the events (when, where, what). I didn't translate word for word.						
	f) I used short and simple sentences.						
	g) If I didn't know an important word in English, I tried to paraphrase it or to use a similar word or phrase.						

▶ *You will find more READING and MEDIATION tasks in the Exam File, pp. 90–97.*

English for jobs

Das Kapitel **English for jobs** bereitet dich auf Situationen in deinem zukünftigen Berufsalltag vor, in denen du Englisch brauchst.

Du verfolgst den beruflichen Werdegang von zwei englischen Jugendlichen von der Bewerbung über den damit verbundenen Schriftverkehr und das Vorstellungsgespräch bis hin zu verschiedenen Situationen am Arbeitsplatz.

Anhand realistischer Situationen, wie z. B. dienstliche Telefonate, Kundengespräche oder Präsentationen von Produkten, kannst du auf den folgenden Seiten wichtige Wörter und Wendungen für den englischsprachigen Arbeitsalltag auffrischen, ergänzen und anwenden.

EFJ 1 1 Two personal statements

Sarah Dee and Nat Wilde are finishing school this year.

Which of these plus points do Nat and Sarah say they have? Listen and write them down in a copy of the chart.

▸ SF Taking notes (p. 141)

- can explain technology
- communicates well
- enjoys travelling
- speaks foreign languages
- has internet skills
- is a team worker
- is sporty
- likes music
- is organized
- is reliable
- likes helping others

Nat	Sarah
enjoys travelling	…

2 Company websites

a) *Read some job information that Sarah and Nat have found on the internet. Check the chart you made in 1 and decide which company they should apply to.*

GHC career possibilities

GHC is a private health care service[1] with 97 hospitals in the UK. We are always looking for nurses who are able to travel around the country and help out when a colleague[2] is ill or on holiday. A perfect job for those who like to help others. Send in your CV with a letter of motivation.[3]

WOW ELECTRONICS

Imagine working for an exciting company with first-class training programmes to support you. The UK's number one electronics store is looking for new sales assistants[4]. You work well in a team? You like good service and contact with customers? You can explain how a camera or an MP3 player works? You're looking for a career where you can rise to the top? Then send in your CV.

SAYGO CAREERS

Welcome to Saygo's careers website. With 15,000 employees[5] in the UK and abroad[6], we're Britain's big player in the holiday industry. We offer career possibilities in our UK offices and at our holiday destinations[7] abroad. At Saygo we work to make our customers' dreams come true. If you'd like to join us, why not send in your CV? It could be the best career decision you make.

b) *Explain your decision to your partner.*

3 A letter of motivation

a) *Read about letters of motivation in the Skills File.* ▸ SF Writing letters (pp. 154–155)

b) *Choose three key points from the list for a letter of motivation. Decide the best order.*

– information on my qualifications and skills
– my reason for writing
– information on the history of the company
– thanks for reading the letter

c) *You want to apply to a company from 2. Complete this letter of motivation.*

…
I am writing to you about the career possibilities that you mention on your company website. I would be very interested in working as … / in …
I am 17 years old and will finish school in …

[1] health care service *Gesundheitspflegedienst* [2] colleague *Kollege/Kollegin* [3] letter of motivation *Begleitbrief* [4] sales assistent *Fachverkäufer/in* [5] employee *Angestellte/r* [6] abroad *das/im Ausland* [7] holiday destination *Urlaubsziel*

EFJ 2

1 Accepting an invitation

Sarah has been invited to an interview.

WOW ELECTRONI

Ms Sarah Dee
12 Hallow Road
Redhill RH1 6DF

Dear Ms Dee

Thank you for your letter of motivation. We would like to invite you to an interview at our office in Brighton in the week 14th–18th June. Please let us know which date works best for you.

Train and bus connections to Brighton are excellent. If you like, we can help you to plan your trip.

We plan to interview ten candidates each day, and there will be a chance for group discussions during lunch in our canteen.

We look forward to hearing from you, if possible by e-mail to the address below.

Yours sincerely

Petra Pym
pym@wow.co.uk

a) *Sarah would like to travel to the interview by car. She's also a vegetarian. Read the letter from WOW Electronics. Which of the points below will she need to ask about?*

place of interview • interview dates • interview times • public transport • car parking facilities • whether there will be a meal • the kind of food the canteen offers

b) *Put the sentences from Sarah's e-mail to Petra Pym in a suitable order.*

It will be interesting to meet other candidates during lunch.

Dear Ms Pym

I would like to travel to Brighton by car.

Yours sincerely Sarah Dee

Can you tell me if your canteen offers vegetarian food?

Please let me know when I should arrive at your office.

Thank you for your letter of 25th May.

Is there a car park near your office?

I would like to come for an interview on Wednesday 16th June.

I look forward to meeting you.

c) *Compare your e-mail with a partner.*

2 Agreeing on details

27th May

Dear Ms Dee

Thank you for your e-mail of 26th May. I saw that you can come for an interview on Wed.16th June. Would you like an interview at 9.30 am or 2.30 pm? If you choose the afternoon interview, please arrive in time for lunch at 12.15 pm.

I am afraid we do not have car parking facilities for candidates. It would probably be easier to come to Brighton by train or bus. If you decide to do this we can book your tickets for you.
I am happy to say that our canteen offers vegetarian dishes too.

I look forward to meeting you.

Yours sincerely
Petra Pym

Read Petra Pym's e-mail. Then complete Sarah's answer.

… Ms Pym

Thank you …
… at 2.30 pm and will make sure that I arrive …
I have decided to … to Brighton by … I would be very happy if you could … as you offered in your mail.
I am very glad … vegetarian … Many thanks.
I … meeting you and the other candidates.

Yours …

► SF Writing letters (p. 154)

[1] (to) make arrangements *Verabredungen treffen*

EFJ 3

1 Giving good answers

a) *How should Nat answer Ms Wood's questions? Choose A or B.*

Nat has been invited to an interview too. It takes place today ...

Ms Wood Hello, nice to meet you, Nat. My name is Polly Wood.
Nat A Hello Ms Wood. Nice to meet you. B Hi, Polly!
Ms Wood Well, Nat. Thank you for your interest in Saygo. Maybe you can tell me why you'd like to work for us.
Nat A Because travelling is really cool. B Well, I really enjoy travelling and being in other countries.
Ms Wood Maybe you can say something about your strengths. What are you good at?
Nat A Well, I'm really brilliant at languages. And I'm just so organized and reliable. B Well, I speak two foreign languages quite well. And I'm very organized and reliable.
Ms Wood If you worked for Saygo abroad, you would have to spend a lot of time looking after tourists with questions or problems.
Nat A I hope they won't have too many problems! B Problems are there to be solved. I think I can do that.
Ms Wood Of course, there would also be quite a lot of desk work to do.
Nat A I can imagine that. I'm very happy to do office work. B No worries, Ms Wood!

b) *Compare your answers with a partner. Say why you chose one answer and not the other. Was it because of the content[1], the kind of language used, or both?*

c) *Read the rest of the interview. Say why Nat's answers aren't very good. Think of better answers.*

Ms Wood Are you confident with using a computer?
Nat Sure, I spend lots of time surfing the internet.
Ms Wood OK, imagine everybody wants something from you at the same time. What do you do?
Nat I tell them to be patient. I'm not a machine.
Ms Wood How soon would you be able to start if we offered you a job?
Nat I don't know. Maybe next month.
Ms Wood Why should we choose you?
Nat Why not?
Ms Wood Well, that's it. Thank you for coming. We'll contact you soon. Goodbye.
Nat See you.

▸ *SF Taking part in a job interview (p. 147)*

2 Now you: Role play

Think of a job and the strengths that you need for it.

Partner A
- Start the interview.
- Find out about the candidate's strengths.
- Suggest a problem that might happen.
- Ask if B could start in May.
- Ask if B has any questions.
- Finish the interview.

Partner B
- React to the opening question.
- Say what your strengths are.
- Say how you would solve the problem.
- If you got the job, you could start in June.
- Ask a good question.
- Say goodbye.

[1] content *Inhalt*

EFJ 4

1 Leaving a message

Sarah has started at WOW Electronics. Right now, she's making a phone call ...

a) *Put Sarah's telephone conversation in the right order and write it down.*

Thank you, Tim. Bye.

01705 – 4912214

OK. That's great. Thanks.

Can I leave a message?

Hello, Tim. This is Sarah from WOW Electronics. Can you put me through[2] to Jane Parks, please?

Sure, I'll get a pen ... OK, your message?

Yes, hold on[1], please. ... I'm sorry, Sarah, but Jane isn't answering her phone.

Yes, of course. Can you give me your last name, Sarah?

CX Computers. Tim speaking.

And your phone number?

Could you ask her to phone me when she has a moment?

Dee. I'll spell it. D double E.

b) *Listen and check. Then practise the conversation. Use different names and phone numbers.*

2 More telephone phrases

a) *You will hear six short phone conversations. In which conversation do you hear the English phrases for these German ones?*

A Am Apparat.

B Kann ich etwas ausrichten?

C Sie müssen sich verwählt haben.

D Bleiben Sie am Apparat.

E Ich gebe Ihre Nachricht weiter.

F Ich verbinde.

b) *Listen again. Write down the phrases from a) in English. Compare with a partner.*

c) *Practise the phrases in short dialogues, like this:*

Can you tell Mrs Parks that I'll call back later?

Of course. I'll give her your message as soon as[3] I see her.

3 Now you: Guided dialogue[4]

Prepare a dialogue and act it out.

Partner A: You get a call from a customer.

Partner B: You want to order something.

A: Grüße und nenne den Namen deiner Firma.

B: Stelle dich vor. Sage, mit wem du sprechen möchtest.

A: Sage, dass du am Apparat bist. Frage, wie du helfen kannst.

B: Sage, was du bestellen willst.

A: Sage, dass Tim dafür zuständig ist. Biete an, B mit ihm zu verbinden.

B: Sage, dass du am Apparat bleibst.

A: Entschuldige dich: Tim antwortet nicht.

B: Frage, ob Tim dich zurückrufen kann. Nenne deine Telefonnummer.

A: Wiederhole die Telefonnummer. Bitte B, ihren/seinen Nachnamen zu buchstabieren.

B: Reagiere.

► WB 1–3 (pp. 42–44)

[1] (to) hold on *am Apparat bleiben* [2] (to) put sb. through *jn. durchstellen/verbinden* [3] as soon as *sobald* [4] guided dialogue *gelenkter Dialog*

EFJ 5 1 Speaking to a visitor

Nat is working at Saygo's office in Malaga. Last week he had a meeting there with Karin Lang, from Saygo's German office.

Thanks for a successful meeting.
The weather here has been like this for weeks.
Bye, Karin.
This is delicious!
Where would you like to go for lunch?
How was your trip?
Was the flight OK?
It was nice to meet you.
What about somewhere with Spanish food?
Can I call you a taxi?
This is a nice building.
Have you heard that joke about ... ?

a) *Look at the sentences above. When are they used during the meeting? Complete a copy of the chart.*

Start of the meeting	Break for a meal	End of the meeting
Was the flight OK?	Where ...	...

b) *Listen and check. Then compare your chart with a partner.*

c) *How can you react when somebody*
– thanks you?
– apologizes to you?
– says something you agree with?
Find phrases in the box for each situation.

Don't mention it. • Don't worry about it. • No problem. • Not at all.[1] • That's fine with me.[2] • That's OK. • That's true. • You're quite right. • You're welcome.

d) *Listen again and check. Then compare your answers with a partner.*

2 Now you: Guided dialogue

Prepare a dialogue and act it out.

Partner A: You work for a German company.	Partner B: You're a guest from abroad.
Begrüße B. Frage, wie die Reise war.	Beschreibe deine Reise. Entschuldige dich, dass du zu spät kommst. Erkläre den Grund.
Reagiere auf die Entschuldigung.	Sage, dass das Wetter sehr angenehm ist.
Stimme zu. Sage, wie lange es schon gutes Wetter gibt.	Sage etwas Nettes über das Büro von A.
Erkläre, dass das Gebäude ganz neu ist. Sage, wann die Firma eingezogen ist.	Frage, was das für ein Gebäude links ist.
Antworte. Biete B etwas zu trinken an.	Bedanke dich.
Reagiere. Frage, wann B essen möchte.	Frage, ob 12.30 in Ordnung wäre.
Reagiere. Schlage vor, dass ihr mit der Arbeit beginnt.	Stimme zu.

► WB 4–6 (pp. 44–46)

[1] Not at all! *Bitte schön!* [2] That's fine with me. *Von mir aus gerne.*

EFJ 6

1 Reacting to problems

a) *Read the dialogue. What's wrong with the way Sarah speaks to the customer?*

Today Sarah is working in one of WOW's big stores. She has a customer with a problem. Unfortunately, she didn't sleep very well last night …

Sarah	What do you want?
Customer	I bought this mobile last week and it doesn't work very well.
Sarah	'Doesn't work very well.' What does that mean? Listen, mate. Just say exactly what's wrong with it.
Customer	Well, the keys[1] are hard to press and it doesn't take good photos.
Sarah	What do you expect if you buy a cheap phone?
Customer	Maybe you're right. Anyway, I'd like to change it. I don't mind paying more for a better phone.
Sarah	Wait there! I'll ask the manager.
Customer	Thank you. Could I ask you to be quick? I'm a bit late for a doctor's appointment.
Sarah	Well, why didn't you come here earlier? Honestly! Customers!

b) *Find better phrases for Sarah below. Then act out a dialogue that sounds more polite.*

Starting a conversation
- Good morning / … How can I help you?
- Can I do anything for you, sir/madam?

Sounding friendly
- I see.
- Of course, sir/madam.
- That's no problem. I'll …
- Could I ask you to …

Reacting to problems
- What seems to be the problem?
- Could you be a bit more specific?
- I'll see what I can do.
- Of course, there are sometimes problems with less expensive models/older models/…
- I'm sorry, but …

► *SF Having a conversation (p. 147)*

2 Now you: Role play

Partner B: Go to p. 101.
Partner A: Read the background information on the left. Then follow the instructions on the right. Be as polite and friendly as you can.

You're a sales assistant in an electronics store. The latest model of a popular TV has just arrived. Last week the older model was sold at a reduced price in a sale. Your company policy[2] is not to change products that were sold in a sale. However, you know that your manager sometimes makes exceptions[3], especially if this helps to keep good customers. The manager is at a meeting today, so you can't speak to him till tomorrow. A cuatomer comes up to you.

- Start the conversation.
- Ask about the reason.
- Ask if the customer still has a receipt.
- React. Explain your company policy.
- Explain why you can't give an answer today.
- React.

► *WB 7–9 (pp. 46–47)*

[1] keys *(pl) Tasten* [2] company policy *Unternehmenspolitik* [3] exception *Ausnahme*

EFJ 7 1 Deciding what to say

a) *Look at Sarah's list below. Then listen to Sarah's conversation with her colleague. Which points does she decide to drop from her list? Why? Do you agree with her?*

Sarah has to present a new mobile to WOW sales assistants. She's discussing her list of points with a colleague[1]. Is it too long?

SAMTO: New mobile
1 How mobile phone technology works
2 Earlier SAMTO models and history of product
3 Country of production
4 What the new SAMTO can do
5 How to use the new SAMTO
6 SAMTO uses 35 per cent less energy.
7 Super ringtones!
8 Price
9 Details about guarantee[2]
10 Dangers of using mobile while driving a car

b) *Read Nat's list and agree on five points to drop from it. Then listen to his presentation. Did he drop the same points as you?*

Nat has to present a hotel to his colleagues. He wants to reduce the number of points in his list from 10 to 5.

Beach City Hotel, Malaga
1 Location: central, but busy street
2 Extra: tennis club near hotel
3 Rooms – clean, comfortable
4 Hotel bar – happy hour until 7 pm
5 Restaurant – good breakfast, lunch/evening meal also offered
6 Staff[3]
7 New air conditioning[4] next year
8 Shuttle service[5] to airport
9 Prices
10 Other hotels in Malaga

2 Structuring a presentation

a) *Make a chart with headings for the different parts of a presentation:* **Introduction**, **Main part**, **End**. *Match the points on the right to the correct heading.*

b) *Go to p. 148. Find phrases that you can use for each point in a). Add them to your chart.*

c) *Listen to Nat's presentation again. Which phrases from your chart does he use?*

- Go into detail about your main points.
- List the points you plan to make.
- Sum up your main ideas and say what your conclusion is.
- Thank your audience and offer to answer questions.
- Tell your audience what your main topic is.
- Use pictures to illustrate[6] your main points.

3 Now you: Presentation

Prepare a short presentation. You could talk about a hotel, a mobile phone or some other appliance or product.

► *SF Giving a presentation (pp. 138, 148)*

[1] colleague *Kollege/Kollegin* [2] guarantee *Garantie* [3] staff *Personal* [4] air-conditioning *Klimaanlage* [5] shuttle service *Zubringer(bus)*
[6] (to) illustrate *bildlich darstellen*

EFJ 8 1 Giving the figures

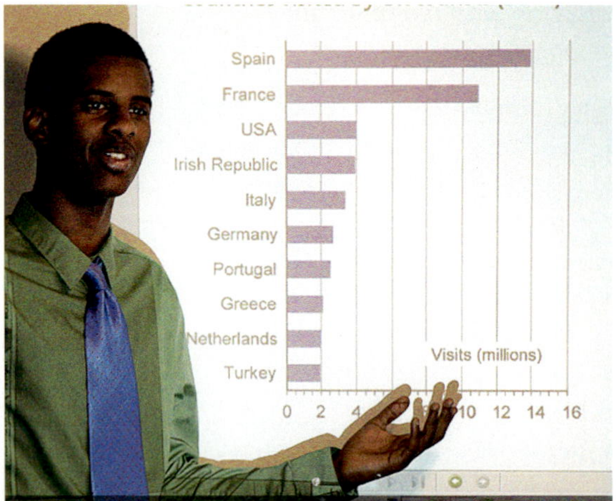

Nat has to present some statistics[1] about holidays abroad[2] by UK citizens. He's already prepared some charts and graphs[3]...

Remember

When you talk about statistics you usually ...

describe The chart here shows ...

explain As you can see, there are ...

evaluate[4] It's very clear that ...

Sometimes you'll also want to ...

draw conclusions This means ...

▸ *SF Talking about charts (p. 139)*

a) *Look at the two charts below and complete Nat's presentation text. What else could Nat say in his evaluation[5] and conclusion? Write down some ideas. Then listen and compare.*

Countries visited by UK tourists (2008)

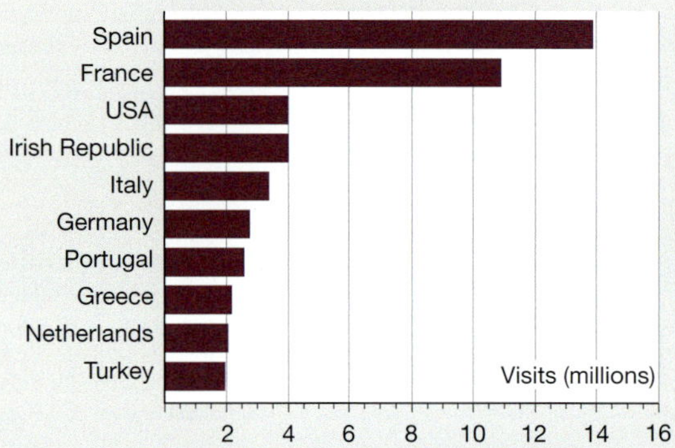

The chart here shows which countries people from the UK visited in 2008.
As you can see, there were just under 14 million visits to Spain and about 11 million visits to ... 4 million people went to ... Over 2 million travelled to Germany, ... And almost exactly 2 million went to ...
It's very clear that ... and ... are the most popular destinations[6] ...
This means we'll need to offer quite a lot of holidays in ...

How UK citizens travelled abroad (2008)
Number of travellers: 68.9 million

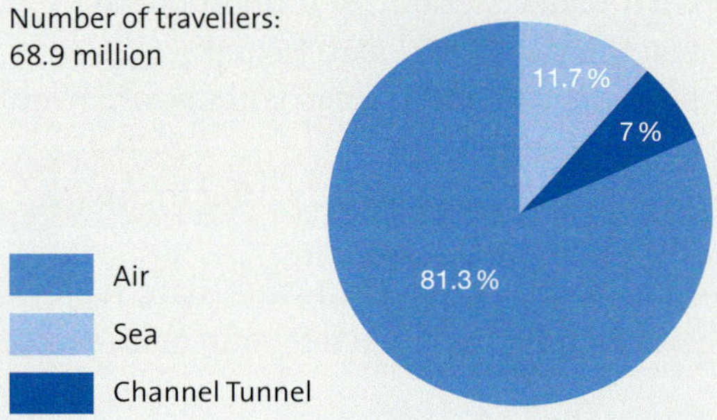

In the second chart we can see how ...
81 per cent of travellers went by ...
Almost 12 per cent ... And 7 per cent used the ...
The most popular kind of transport is ...
This means ...

Source statistics: Office for National Statistics

b) *Look again at what Nat says in a). Write down the words he uses with numbers, e.g.* ***just under 14 million****. With a partner try and think of similar words and add them to your list.*

[1] statistics *(pl) Statistiken* [2] abroad *ins/im Ausland* [3] graph *(Kurven-) Diagramm* [4] (to) evaluate *bewerten* [5] evaluation *Bewertung* [6] destination *Reiseziel*

2 Talking about trends[1]

Look at the graphs and add the missing figures to Nat's presentation text.
What could Nat say in his conclusion? Write down some ideas. Then listen and compare.

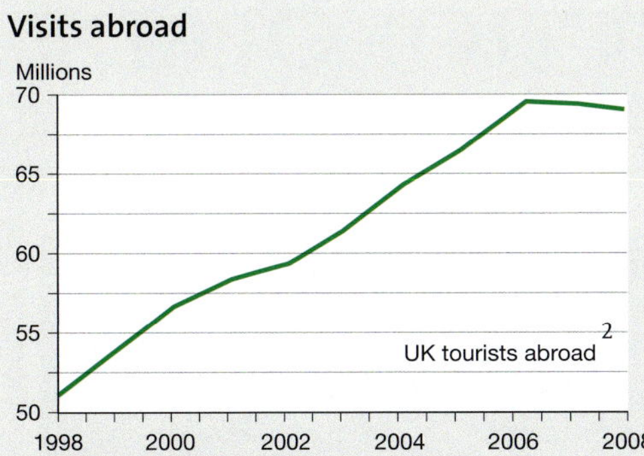

The first graph shows how many people travelled abroad from the UK between 1998 and 2008.
As you can see, the numbers rose from about 50 million in ... to just under ... million in 2006, but fell again in ... and ...

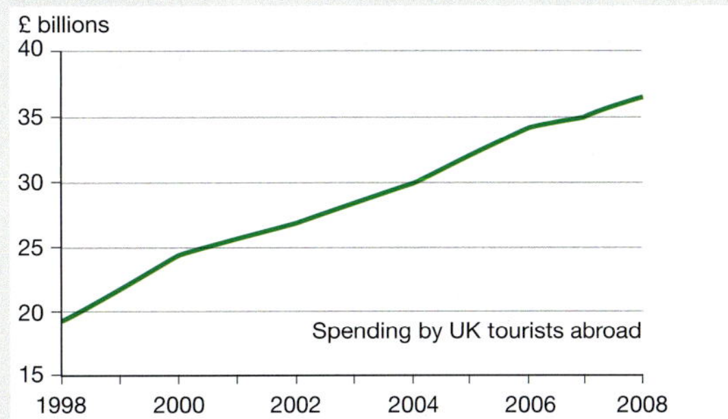

The second graph shows how much money people from the UK spent abroad.
The most interesting thing is that spending rose from under £35 billion[3] in 2006 to almost £37 billion in ...
So it's clear that spending rose although the number of travellers fell. It means that ...

Source statistics: Office for National Statistics

► *SF Talking about charts (p. 139)*

3 Now you: Presentation

Prepare a presentation of the statistics in these graphs and charts. Join up with another pair. Give your presentations. Discuss how they could be improved.

► *SF Using visual materials with a presentation (p. 138)*

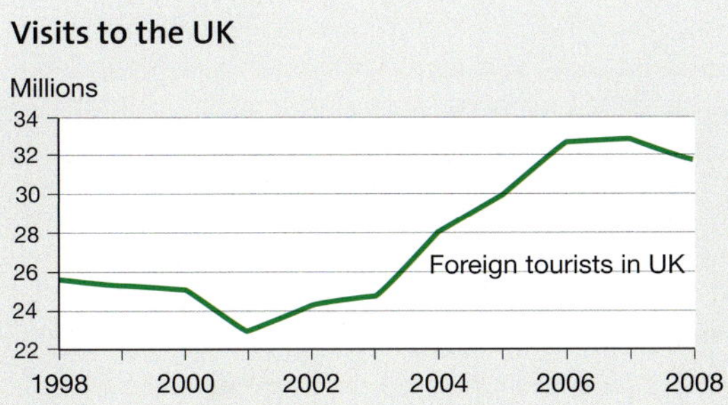

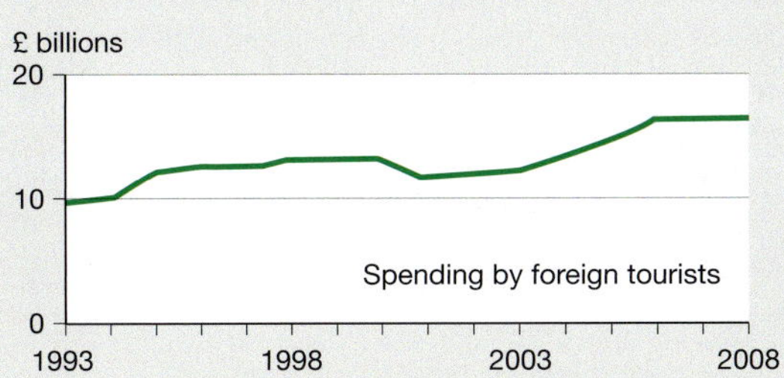

Source statistics: Office for National Statistics

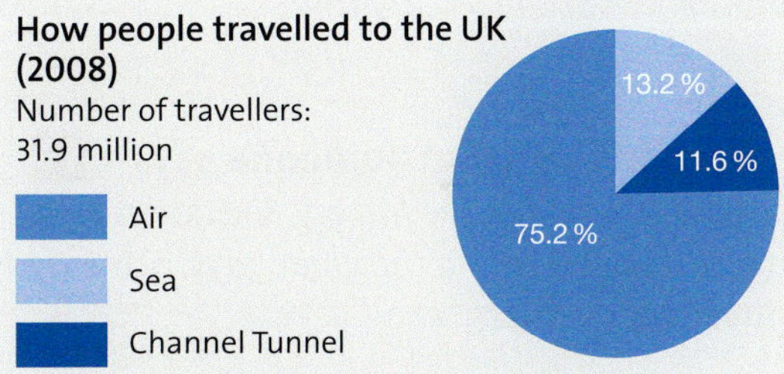

[1] trend *Trend, Entwicklung* [2] abroad *im Ausland* [3] billion *Milliarde*

EFJ 9

1 Explaining a brochure

Sarah's on holiday. She's visiting you! You know she loves chocolate and cocoa[1], so you've decided to visit a famous chocolate factory with her …

a) *Read the brochure on the right. Make notes in English. Your notes should include[2] four things that visitors to Schmidt-Schokolade can do, the opening hours and the cost of admission.*

b) ***Partner A:*** *Use your notes from a) to talk about the factory tour.*
Partner B: *Listen to your partner. Ask at least one question about the factory tour.*

SCHMIDT-SCHOKOLADE

Erleben Sie die Welt der Schokolade in unserer spannenden Ausstellung!

Öffnungszeiten: Mo–Fr 8.00 bis 18.30 Uhr, Sa 9.00 bis 18.00 Uhr.

Der Eintritt ist frei.

Woher kommt eigentlich der Kakao? Wie sieht ein Kakaobaum überhaupt aus? Wie gelangt die frische Joghurt-Füllung in die Tafel? Die unterhaltsame Ausstellung beantwortet viele Fragen rund um Schokolade und ist dabei eine Entdeckungsreise mit allen Sinnen: Sehend, hörend, riechend, schmeckend und fühlend erfahren neugierige Schokoladen-Liebhaber alles rund um die „Speise der Götter", den Kakao. Interaktiv und Schritt für Schritt wird der gesamte Prozess von der Kakaobohne bis hin zur fertigen Schokolade erklärt. Ein spannendes Quiz bietet Kindern und auch Erwachsenen viel Spaß – so lässt sich spielerisch die Welt der Schokolade entdecken!

Genießen Sie die ganze Vielfalt der Schokolade in unserem Schoko-Geschäft neben der Ausstellung. Probieren Sie unsere leckeren Schokoladen, bevor Sie sie kaufen, entdecken Sie neue Sorten und versorgen Sie sich mit leckerem Proviant für unterwegs. Außerdem gibt es in unserem Fabrikverkauf immer wieder günstige Angebote und ein umfangreiches, wechselndes Sortiment. Lassen Sie sich überraschen!

Nach Voranmeldung bieten wir auch Rundgänge durch unsere Fabrik an.

2 Explaining what someone says

You're with Sarah in the factory. She doesn't understand everything the guide says. Listen and answer her questions.

What was that about?

He's going to tell us …

▸ *SF Mediation (p. 157)*

3 Passing on questions[3]

Sarah wants you to ask the guide some questions. What do you say to him in German?

1. Can you buy Schmidt chocolate in England?
2. How many kilograms of chocolate are produced every day?
3. What percentage of production is for Christmas?
4. Which sort of chocolate is the most popular?
5. Who invents the new sorts of chocolate?
6. Does the company make organic[4] chocolate too?

[1] cocoa (bean) *Kakao(bohne)* [2] include *beinhalten/einschließen* [3] (to) pass on questions *Fragen weitergeben* [4] organic *Bio-*

Inhalt

Im **Exam File** findest du ein breites Angebot an Prüfungsaufgaben. Damit kannst du
- das Trainingsangebot der *Getting ready for a test*-Seiten abrunden
- dich gezielt in verschiedenen Kompetenzen und wichtigen Aufgabenformaten testen
- dich selbstständig oder gemeinsam in der Klasse auf die Prüfung vorbereiten
- den „Ernstfall" der Abschlussprüfung üben.

Natürlich können hier nicht alle denkbaren Aufgabentypen geübt werden, aber du kannst davon ausgehen, dass dir die verschiedenen Übungen wichtige Hilfen für eine gelungene Prüfungsvorbereitung sind.

Weitere Hilfe bei der Prüfungsvorbereitung bieten die Tipps auf Seite 76 sowie der Prüfungswegweiser auf den Seiten 77–79.

► Wenn du eine *Listening*-Aufgabe zu Hause machen willst, geh zu www.englishg.de.
Wähle die B-Ausgabe und gibt dort den Web-Code ein, der bei deiner *Listening*-Aufgabe steht.
Die Lösungen zu allen **Exam File**-Aufgaben findest du unter www.englishg.de/examfile.

Dein Weg zum Prüfungserfolg

Eine Prüfung ist eine Gelegenheit zu zeigen, was du gelernt hast. Du brauchst keine Angst davor zu haben, denn alles, was in der Prüfung drankommt, kennst du schon aus dem Unterricht.

Während des Schuljahres

1 Bereite dich langfristig vor, nicht erst am Abend vor der Prüfung.
2 Überlege, welche Bereiche du wiederholen solltest. Besprich das auch mit deinem Lehrer/deiner Lehrerin. Mach dir einen Plan, wie du deine Vorbereitung am besten einteilst.
3 Denk daran: Dein *Skills File* enthält viele nützliche Tipps und Hilfen.
4 Mach dich mit verschiedenen Prüfungsformaten vertraut. Hierzu gibt es im **Prüfungswegweiser** auf den Seiten 77 bis 79 hilfreiche Hinweise.

Im **Prüfungswegweiser** findest du
- eine Beschreibung typischer Prüfungsformate
- Verweise auf Beispiele für die verschiedenen Formate
- eine Übersicht typischer Arbeitsanweisungen
- Tipps und Verweise auf das. *Skills File.*

Am Abend vor der Prüfung

1 Entspanne dich. Du kannst lesen, dich in die Badewanne legen, Musik hören, fernsehen, ...
2 Geh zur gewohnten Zeit ins Bett.

Am Tag der Prüfung

1 Stehe rechtzeitig auf, damit du nicht hetzen musst.
2 Nimm dir Zeit für ein entspanntes Frühstück.
3 Lies etwas „zum Aufwärmen“, aber schau nicht mehr in dein Schülerbuch.
4 Denk daran, du hast dich gut vorbereitet. Es gibt keinen Grund, nervös zu sein.

Während der Prüfung

1 Konzentriere dich auf den Test, lass dich nicht ablenken.
2 Lies dir die Aufgaben genau durch.

Bevor du die Aufgaben bearbeitest, überlege genau, was du tun sollst. Lies die Aufgabenstellung langsam und gründlich durch. Sollst du z. B. ganze Sätze schreiben oder dir nur Notizen machen? Du kannst besonders wichtige Dinge in der Aufgabenstellung unterstreichen und die Aufgabe, wenn nötig, für dich in einzelne Schritte unterteilen.

3 Löse zuerst die Aufgaben, die dir einfach scheinen. Wende dich erst danach den schwereren Aufgaben zu.
4 Aufgaben, die du bearbeitet hast, hakst du ab. So siehst du, wie du vorankommst, und behältst den Überblick.
5 Schau ab und zu auf die Uhr. Du solltest dir für den Schluss noch Zeit einplanen, um deine Antworten noch einmal durchzulesen und zu korrigieren.

Good luck!

VIEWING ***Mr Bean – The Exam***

Watch the video. What tipps would you give Mr Bean?

Prüfungswegweiser

Typische Aufgaben ▸ *Beispiele im* Exam File	**Typische Arbeitsanweisungen** ▸ Skills File
SPEAKING	
Talking about photos, cartoons, etc. ▸ *S. 80, Aufgaben 1, 2, 3* Über Fotos, Cartoons usw. sprechen (allein oder in Partnerarbeit)	• *Talk about the photo/cartoon (to a partner).* • *Look at the photo/cartoon and describe what's happening /...* • *What is the message of the photo/cartoon?* • *Show your photo/cartoon to your partner and describe ...* • *Discuss ...* ▸ *SF Describing pictures (p. 133–134)* ▸ *SF Describing cartoons (p. 134)*
Simulated situations ▸ *S. 81, Aufgaben 4, 5* Simulierte Situationen im Dialog bewältigen (z. B. Vorhaben, Auswahl, ... diskutieren oder erklären)	• *Choose ... and make a list. Then talk to your partner. Explain your choice. Finally, try to agree on ...* • *Look at the list/chart and think about/talk about ... Decide together on ...* ▸ *SF Having a discussion (p. 148)*
Guided dialogue ▸ *S. 82, Aufgabe 6* Einen gelenkten Dialog führen	• *Prepare a dialogue (with your partner). Act it out.* • *Act out the conversation in English.* ▸ *SF Having a conversation (p. 147)*
Role play ▸ *S. 82, Aufgabe 7* Rollenspiel zu einer Situation, die auf einer Rollenkarte beschrieben wird	• *Look at the role card and act out the conversation (with your partner).* • *Look at the picture/role card. Discuss the situation with your partner.* ▸ *SF Having a conversation (p. 147)* ▸ *SF Having a discussion (p. 148)*

In der mündlichen Prüfung kann es sein, dass zwei oder mehr Kandidat(inn)en gleichzeitig getestet werden. In diesem Fall können folgende Redemittel nützlich sein:

Einen Einstieg finden

- Would you like to begin?
- I'll start if you like.
- You first, please.
- Is it my turn or yours?

An den Partner/die Partnerin übergeben

- That's your special field.
- Maybe you can answer that question.
- Have you got any views on this?

Deinem Partner/deiner Partnerin zustimmen/widersprechen

- I agree. / I think so too.
- You're quite right.
- I don't agree. / I don't think so.
- I don't think you're right there.

Wenn du deinen Partner nicht verstehst

- Could you say that again, please?
- Could you repeat that, please?
- I'm not sure if I understand what you mean.
- Can you explain what you mean, please?

Typische Aufgaben ► *Beispiele im* Exam File	Typische Arbeitsanweisungen Tipps ► Skills File

WRITING

Questionnaire/Form ► *S. 83, Aufgabe 1* Fragebogen/Formulare ausfüllen	• *Fill in the questionnaire/form.* • *Complete the survey.* • *Answer the questions …* **Tipp** Oft musst du keine ganzen Sätze schreiben. Achte genau auf die Arbeitsanweisung.
Story ► *S. 83, Aufgabe 2; S. 84, Aufgabe 3* Geschichten zu Bild- oder Textimpulsen schreiben	• *Look at the pictures. Then write a story (of about … words).* • *Tell the story behind the picture. Use your imagination.* ► *SF Writing course (pp. 151–152)*
Email/Letter/Postcard/Letter of application ► *S. 84, Aufgabe 4; S. 85, Aufgabe 5c* E-Mails, Briefe, Bewerbungsschreiben usw. verfassen	• *Write an e-mail/a letter/a postcard/a letter of application to …* • *Answer (Jack's) email/letter.* • *Write for more information.* ► *SF Writing letters (p. 154)*
Working with texts ► *S. 85, Aufgabe 5; S. 86, Aufgabe 6* Schreibaufgaben, die sich auf einen längeren Sach- oder Literaturtext beziehen.	• *First read the text. Then do the tasks below.* **Tipp** Hier helfen auch die Lesetechniken, die du gelernt hast. ► *SF Reading course (pp. 142–143)* ► *SF Writing course (pp. 151–152)*
Summary ► *S. 85, Aufgabe 5a; S. 86, Aufgabe 6b.1* Texte (Literatur, Sachtext, …) oder einzelne Fakten zu einem Thema zusammenfassen	• *Sum up the story/article/main points …* • *Give a short summary of …* • *Write a summary of (100) words.* • *Say what happened (in the story/…)* ► *SF Summarizing texts (p. 150)*
Description/Creative writing ► *S. 85, Aufgabe 5b; S. 86, Aufgabe 6b.4* Beschreibung, Charakterisierung, kreatives Schreiben	• *What does the text say about …?* • *Describe …* • *Continue the story.* • *What happens next/when …?* **Tipp** Wenn du nach Ideen suchst, helfen dir die Brainstorming-Techniken, die du gelernt hast. ► *SF Brainstorming (p. 149)*
Article/Report ► *S. 85, Aufgabe 5d* Artikel/Bericht für ein Print- oder Onlinemagazin verfassen	• *Write an article for your school mag/ …* • *Write a report on/about …* ► *SF Writing a report (p. 152)*
Giving your opinion ► *S. 86, Aufgaben 6b.2; 3* Die eigene Meinung zu einem Thema formulieren	• *What do you think about …? Give reasons for your opinion.* • *Write/give your opinion.* • *What would you do or say if …?* • *Should/Would …?* ► *SF From outline to written discussion (p. 156)*

Typische Aufgaben ► *Beispiele im* **Exam File**	Typische Arbeitsanweisungen	Tipps ► **Skills File**
LISTENING		
True/False ► *S. 87, Aufgabe 1* Entscheiden, ob Aussagen zum Hörtext richtig oder falsch sind	• *Decide if the statements are true or false (right or wrong).* • *Tick the correct answer.*	1 Du wirst **verschiedene Textsorten** (Dialoge, Bekanntmachungen ...) und **verschiedene Akzente** hören. Manchmal sollst du zeigen, dass du Details verstanden hast, z. B. einen Preis, Abfahrtszeiten o. Ä. Bei anderen Aufgaben geht es um die **Kernaussage**, z. B. ob jemand mit seinen Eltern klar kommt oder sich optimistisch oder pessimistisch gibt. ► *SF Listening (p. 140)*
Multiple choice ► *S. 87, Aufgabe 2* Aus mehreren Antworten die richtige auswählen	• *Choose/Write down the correct answer for each task.* • *Tick the right statement.*	
Missing information ► *S. 88, Aufgaben 3, 4; S. 89, Aufgabe 6* Lücken in Sätzen/Tabellen ergänzen	• *Complete the missing information.* • *Fill in the missing information.*	
Matching ► *S. 89, Aufgabe 5* Zuordnungsaufgaben	• *Choose the right statement.* • *Match the sentence parts.*	
READING		
Matching ► *S. 90, Aufgabe 1* Einen Text einem Bild oder einem anderen Text zuordnen	• *Match the tips to the photos.* • *Which statement/... goes with which picture/description/...*	1 In der Prüfung kann es **verschiedene Textsorten** geben: Listen, Poster, Blogs, Sachtexte, Kurzgeschichten ... 2 Manchmal geht es um die **Hauptaussage** des Textes, manchmal um **Details**, und manchmal sollst du **Schlussfolgerungen** ziehen. 3 Bei der Bewältigung unterschiedlicher Aufgaben helfen dir die verschiedenen **Lesetechniken**, die du gelernt hast. ► *SF Reading course (pp. 142–143)*
Completing a chart ► *S. 91, Aufgabe 2 b* Textinhalte tabellarisch wiedergeben	• *Complete the chart/table/grid ...* • *Fill in the chart/timeline/...*	
True/false ► *S. 93, Aufgabe 3 b* Entscheiden, ob Aussagen zu einem Text richtig oder falsch sind	• *Are these statements true or false (or not in the text)?* • *Correct the wrong statements.*	
Multiple choice ► *S. 93, Aufgabe 3 c; S. 94, Aufgabe 4 b* Die richtige Antwort auswählen	• *Decide which answer is correct.* • *Tick the right/correct/best answer.* • *Mark the correct statement.*	
Finish sentences ► *S. 93, Aufgaben 3 d* Sätze über den Text vervollständigen	• *Complete/Finish these sentences (using information from the text).*	
Questions on the text ► *S. 93, Aufgabe 3 e; S. 94, Aufgabe 4 c* Fragen zum Textinhalt beantworten	• *Answer these questions.* • *Answer the questions in complete sentences.*	
MEDIATION		
English ► German ► *S. 95, Aufgaben 1, 2; S. 96, Aufgabe 4, S. 97, Aufgabe 5* Sprachmittlung Englisch ► Deutsch	*Typische Arbeitsanweisungen* • *beschreiben die Situation (**Du bist mit deiner Familie in Urlaub in England** o. Ä.).* • *nennen häufig die Punkte, die du in der Zielsprache wiedergeben sollst.*	1 Hier kommen **mehrere Sprachkompetenzen** zum Einsatz – z. B. liest du einen Text, um dann Fakten mündlich oder schriftlich weiterzugeben. 2 Nennt die Arbeitsanweisung nicht die Punkte, die du vermitteln sollst, gib nur die **Kerninformationen** weiter. ► *SF Mediation (p. 157)*
German ► English ► *S. 96, Aufgabe 3* Sprachmittlung Deutsch ► Englisch		
German ► English ► German ► *S. 97, Aufgabe 6* Sprachmittlung zwischen 2 Personen		

SPEAKING

1 Talking about a photo

Talk about the photo. The questions below can help you:
- Why do you think the girl is standing at the side of the road?
- Where do you think she wants to go?
- What could she have in her bag and suitcase?
- If you could travel somewhere now, where would you go?
- What would you take with you?

2 Talking about a cartoon

Talk about the cartoon. The questions below can help you:
- What's happening?
- Why is the boss unhappy with the apprentice?
- What does the cartoon tell us about modern life?
- Do you agree with the message of this cartoon? Give reasons.

build a house • communicate • communication • hammer • nail[1] • send a message on twitter

3 Discussing photos

Work with a partner. Partner B: Go to p. 102

a) *Partner A: Show Partner B your photo and describe what you can see in it. Then Partner B will talk about his/her photo.*
Discuss the different things that dogs can do for people. Say how you feel about dogs and why.

b) *Partner A: Show Partner B your photo and describe what you can see in it. Then Partner B will talk about his/her photo.*
Discuss different ways that people can spend their holidays. Say what kind of holiday you like best and why.

[1] nail *Nagel*

4 Choosing presents for an English family

You and your partner are going to stay with the Smith family in London for two weeks and you want to choose five typical German presents to take with you. You need presents for Mr and Mrs Smith and for each of their three children, Daniel (16), Laura (13) and Tim (7). Choose five of the things below and make a list. Then talk to your partner. Explain your choices. Finally, try to agree on one list. Our Choices: 1. ___, 2.

5 Deciding on a day trip to a theme park

You and your friend are in Ontario, Canada. You want to go on a day trip together to visit a Canadian theme park. Here is a programme with all the trips you can do today.

a) *Look at the list and think about these questions:*

– Which trip sounds really interesting to you? Why?
– Is there a trip you wouldn't like to go on? Why not?

b) *Work with a partner. Talk about the different trips and theme parks. Decide together on the best day trip.*

Trip	Theme park	What does the theme park offer?	What is included?	Price / person
1	Marineland (Niagara Falls)	Lots of sea animals. Exciting water shows with dolphins and sharks[1]. Also many rides[2] and roller coasters[3].	Bus ride, admission.	$ 89.00
2	Storyland (near Ottawa)	Fairy-tale trail[4]. Mini-golf course. Small water park. Different playgrounds[5]. Paddle boats. Daily shows.	Bus ride, admission, lunch in café.	$ 39.95
3	African Lion Safari (near Hamilton)	More than 1,000 animals from all over the world in a wildlife park. 'Jungle[6] Playground'.	Bus ride, admission. Guided bus tour through park plus choice of guided boat tour or elephant ride in the park.	$ 65.99
4	Canada's Wonderland (near Toronto)	Over 200 attractions. 15 roller coasters! Big water park. Live shows.	Bus ride, admission, lunch.	$ 55.00

[1] shark *Hai* [2] ride *Fahrgeschäft* [3] roller coaster *Achterbahn* [4] fairy-tale trail *Märchenpfad* [5] playground *Spielplatz* [6] jungle *Dschungel*

6 Talking about holiday jobs

Two friends, Joe and Lucy, meet in the street. They're talking about holiday jobs. Prepare a dialogue with your partner. Act it out.

Partner A (Joe)

Begrüße Lucy und frage sie, wie es ihr geht.

Partner B (Lucy)

Grüße zurück und sage, dass es dir gut geht, und dass du gerade einen Ferienjob angefangen hast.

A: Frage Lucy, was für einen Job sie macht.

B: Erzähle, dass du Zeitungen austrägst.

A: Frage, ob das Zeitungsaustragen ein guter Ferienjob ist.

B: Antworte, dass es bei gutem Wetter richtig Spaß macht, und frage Joe, ob er einen Ferienjob hat.

A: Antworte, dass du in einer Fabrik arbeitest.

B: Frage, um was für eine Fabrik es sich handelt.

A: Antworte, dass in der Fabrik Maschinen hergestellt werden, du aber nur am Computer sitzt.

B: Frage, ob Joe diese Arbeit gefällt.

A: Antworte ja, aber es fällt dir schwer, immer so früh aufzustehen.

B: Sage, du wettest, Joe steht nicht so früh auf wie du.

7 Role plays: Solving problems abroad[1]

Partner B: Go to page 102.

a) *Partner A: Look at the role card and act out the conversation with your partner.*

You're in an internet café in a town abroad. You need a cheap hotel. You find one on the internet, but you aren't sure how far away it is or what kind of area it is in. You speak to the person at the next PC.

- Ask if he/she lives in this town.
- Give the name of the hotel you've found. Ask if your partner knows it.
- Give the address of the hotel. Ask how far it is from the café.
- Ask what kind of area it is in.
- Ask if your partner could suggest something else.
- React positively to this information. Ask for directions.
- React.

b) *Partner A: Look at the role card and act out the conversation with your partner.*

Your holiday in Spain is over. All European airports have been closed for a week for safety reasons. You can't fly back home. You are at a travel agent's. You want to find an alternative to flying.

- Explain why you can't fly.
- Say where you want to go and ask if you can buy a train ticket.
- You have to be home sooner. Ask about buses to Germany.
- Ask about your arrival time.
- Ask about the price.
- React and say if you want to buy the ticket.

[1] abroad *im Ausland*

WRITING

1 Guided writing: A questionnaire

A class from a school in the UK wants information about life in Germany. Answer the questions below. You must fill in each item. You may use your imagination. You needn't write complete sentences.*

Hi from St Mary's school! We would like your help with our European project. We're sorry we don't know much German, so we hope you can understand English.
What is life like in Germany?
Please fill in the questionnaire and give it back to your teacher.

Country:	Town/City:	Age: ....
Questions:		**Answers:**
1. What do you have for breakfast?		
2. What time do you have to be at school?		
3. How long is a typical school day?		
4. What do you have for lunch?		
5. What after-school activities do you do?		
6. How much homework do you get and when do you do it?		
7. What do you have for your evening meal?		
8. What do you do in the evening on school days?		
9. Do you have to wear a school uniform?		
10. Would you like to visit the UK? Why (not)?		

* Write in your exercise book or ask your teacher for a copy of the form.

2 Picture story: A parcel for Darkwood

Look at the pictures. Then write a story (about 100 words). You can use the key words in your sentences. Use your imagination to explain what happened after Joe pressed the bell. What made him run away?

A Joe Lee – Whizz Parcel Service

B parcel for Dr Bones, The Old House, Darkwood

C long drive – big, old house – tall trees

D big door – bell

E hear noise – terrified

F end of day – back at Whizz – explain what happened

3 The story behind the picture

Tell the story behind the picture. Use your imagination. The questions below can help you:
- Who is the man?
- Who or what is he looking at?
- How does he feel?
- What is his life like?
- What will he do next?

4 A summer job

a) *Read the job advertisement.*

b) *You're interested in the job. Write an e-mail to ask for more information. Use the ideas below. Before you write, decide the best order for the different points:*
- where the school is
- how you can get there
- exact dates
- why you want to be in the soap
- where you can sleep
- three important facts about yourself
- how much you'll earn.

c) *Imagine you got a part in the TV soap. What happened on the first day of filming? Write a report.*

TV Europe: Summer jobs for students

We are filming an episode for a new European TV soap. This summer we are filming in a German school while the students are on holiday. We are looking for reliable young people (14–19) with a good level of English. Would you like to be one of the students in the film (non-speaking role)?

Write an e-mail today to:
j.gubbins@tv-europe.de

5 Text-based writing: A teen mag article

First read the text. Then do the tasks below.

SURVIVAL TRIP

Last summer four teachers and a national park ranger took a group of 20 students from Riverside High School in Launceston, the second largest city on the island of Tasmania, Australia, to Mt Cameron National Park.

They were away from 'civilization' (houses, shops, restaurants, roads, cinemas, etc.) for three days. The trip was to teach the students to look after themselves in a difficult situation. Each student was only allowed to take one bag with them for their sleeping bag, clothes and washing gear – but they had to make the bags themselves! Joseph Shrimpton, 17, told us he had made his bag from an old potato sack. The most difficult part was the strap[1], which he made by putting pieces of material together. It wasn't a very good bag and he was worried that the strap would break. Later, in the middle of the bush, the strap broke ... Walking with the bag wasn't so easy after that!

On the first part of their journey from Launceston, the students went by normal coach.[2] However, on the second part, they travelled in special minibuses for the bush. They had to wear blindfolds[3] so that they couldn't see where they were going. When they were far enough into the national park, the buses stopped, the blindfolds were taken off, and the students were on their own!

They had to find out where they were and then, using their map-reading skills and finding the answers to questions the teachers had given them, they had to hike to where the park ranger had left basic equipment so that they could make 'tents' for the night. They hiked for three days, 20 kilometres per day, with two nights in the bush. They also had to discover where food had been hidden. There was food powder[4] (not very nice!) and a few cans of chilli con carne, which were for the student who had answered the most questions correctly during the hike each day. He or she was allowed to put the chilli con carne on the camp fire and eat it out of the can. Each of the others had to take turns at heating up their food powder with some water in the empty chilli con carne can, because they had no cooking things or plates with them. One evening the park ranger brought some insects[5] which he cooked on the camp fire. Some students were brave (or hungry!) enough to eat them.

After three long days in the bush the buses were waiting to take the students back to Launceston. The teens were tired and dirty but most of them, at least, were very happy. They had survived! Carla McBeath said, 'Although it was hard, I learned to look after myself. But the insects were really awful!' ■

a) *Sum up the article. Say what happened before and during the trip.*

b) *What does the text say about food? Describe what the students ate and how they felt about it.*

c) *Choose task 1 or 2. Write about 120 words.*

1 Write a letter to a friend about a hike you did.

2 Tasmania National Parks are looking for young people to help with survival camps in the summer. Write a letter of application to Phil Wilson, GPO Box 1751, HOBART, TAS 7001.

d) *Write an article for your school mag. Write about 120 words. Choose topic 1 or 2.*

1 My most exciting holiday

2 My best class trip

[1] strap *Tragegurt* [2] coach *Reisebus* [3] blindfold *Augenbinde* [4] food powder *Lebensmittelpulver* [5] insect *Insekt*

6 Text-based writing: A short story

a) *First read the text.*

Back home

Jody Miller from Chicago sat on the train, looking out of the window at the fine old trees whose leaves were just beginning to change colour as autumn got nearer. She was getting nearer by the minute to high school and the last year there before college. Her year in Germany was over. She was back home, in the Midwest. The college football season was starting – Jody wondered if her cheerleader's costume would still fit her after all that German food – and it would soon be time for the baseball World Series. And then there was football's Super Bowl in the winter. But right now she couldn't stop thinking about her time as an exchange student for a year at a *Realschule* in Freiburg, a beautiful, warm, busy town in the south-west of Germany, full of students, sun, restaurants and cafés. As her train arrived at the station and she realized it was time to get off, she thought about the wonderful trips she had made from Freiburg, up into the Black Forest for picnics, hiking and, in the long winter, cross-country skiing.

She got off the train and walked the last few minutes to her high school. She couldn't see any of her friends. She felt lonely. Where were they all? 'Come on,' she said to herself. 'The place isn't that bad. And you couldn't have stayed in Germany. Well, maybe for one more year. But this is your home. This is where you'll get a job one day.'

She couldn't stop thinking about Benny, a student at her school in Freiburg. He had helped her with homework, explained all those difficult German words to her and been her partner at the end-of-year school dance. She couldn't forget him, his blue eyes, his long blond hair, the way he spoke English, the way he looked at her. He would have been a reason for staying in Germany forever. But what had he said to her at that dance, holding her in his arms? 'I'm sorry, Jody. I already have a girlfriend. She's in California as an exchange student at the moment.' He already had a girlfriend! Why did she think he was only interested in her? Why hadn't she asked? Why hadn't he told her earlier? Why? And what if she had stayed, would he have changed his mind? What if ...? Stop it!

She opened the door of the classroom and twenty happy faces were looking at her – her best friends Mel and Davina, Rosie, Helen and, in the corner, Dave. He had changed a lot in the time she had been away. Wow! There was a banner across the classroom. 'Welcome back, Jody!' it said. Everybody was clapping. And then the teacher came in. She came over to Jody and hugged[1] her. Then the clapping stopped and they all turned to the flag in the corner of the room, as the well-known tune of the National Anthem[2] sounded from the loudspeaker of this classroom in downtown Chicago. Jody smiled. She was back home, and it felt good!

b) *Now do these tasks.*

1. Sum up what we learn about Jody from the text. Give at least five facts. (Write about 50 words)
2. Should Jody have stayed another year in Germany? Give reasons for your opinion based on the information in the text.
3. What do you think about exchange visits? Support your opinion with examples from the text. (Write about 120 words)
4. Continue the story: imagine Jody goes back to Freiburg in her next holiday. What happens? (Write about 150 words)

[1] (to) hug *umarmen* [2] National Anthem *Nationalhymne*

LISTENING

1 Report: Belinda's Britain

Web-Code: EG21-D6-EA-087-1

a) First read the statements (1–8).

1 Belinda reports from the UK for viewers in the United States.
2 The topic of last week's report was transport.
3 The British use public transport more than cars.
4 Travelling by train is more expensive than travelling by bus.
5 A lot of travelling within Britain is by air.
6 People in Britain often walk when they don't have far to go.
7 Belinda likes driving in London better than driving in San Francisco.
8 If you park your car where it is not allowed, your car will be taken away.

b) Now listen to the report and decide if the statements (1–8) are true or false. Write your answers down.

c) Listen again and check your answers.

2 Announcements

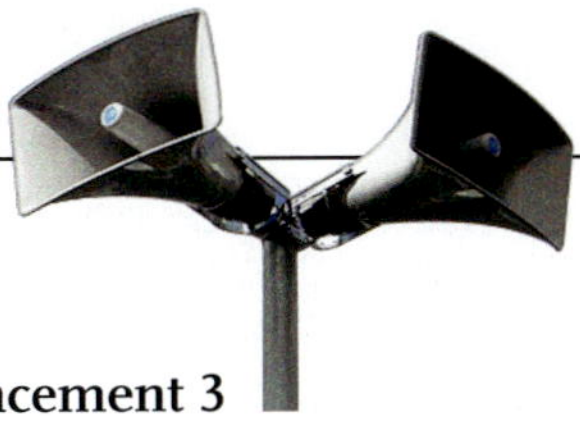

Web-Code: EG21-D6-EA-087-2

You are going to hear four announcements.

a) First read the tasks (1–10).

Announcement 1

1 The non-stop train to York will leave today from platform
A 3. B 4. C 5.

2 The non-stop train to York will be ...
A 5 minutes late.
B 10 minutes late.
C 30 minutes late.

3 The train that stops in Peterborough will leave at ...
A 5.53. B 6.03. C 6.30.

Announcement 2

4 You can buy a pair of Janglers jeans for
A £10. B £49. C £59.

5 The café is on the
A first floor.
B second floor.
C fifth floor.

Announcement 3

6 There are refreshment stations[1]
A every 2 kilometres.
B every 5 kilometres.
C every 42 kilometres.

7 The disco starts at
A 5 pm. B 8 pm.
C 10 pm.

8 The marathon finishes at
A Milson's Point.
B Harbour Bridge.
C Sydney Opera House.

Announcement 4

9 At 10.30 BBC 1 will show ...
A Jim in Germany.
B Red Roses.
C EastEnders.

10 You can watch the news on BBC 1 at
A 9.30 pm. B 10 pm. C 10.30 pm.

b) Now listen to the announcements. Write down the correct letter (a, b or c) for each task (1–10) while you are listening. Choose only one letter for each task.

c) Listen to the announcements again and check your answers.

[1] refreshment (station) *Erfrischung(sstation)*

3 Dialogue: Shopping

Web-Code: EG21-D6-EA-088-3

a) First read the statements (1–10).

1 Diana ordered ... tops from an online shop.
2 Only ... of the tops have arrived.
3 Diana has paid ... for the tops.
4 The online shop's service number is ...
5 Prices at *Just Jeans* are reduced by ...
6 *HK Fashion* is ... *Just Jeans*.
7 Pete asks Diana to go ... with him.
8 Diana says the shops will be closed in ...
9 Pete wants to look at the ... in the *VG Comp* store.
10 Diana suggests that Pete tries the *VG Comp* ...

b) Now listen to the dialogue. Write down the missing words to complete the statements (1–10) while you are listening.

c) Listen to the dialogue again and check your answers.

4 Dialogue: Practising for an interview

Web-Code: EG21-D6-EA-088-4

Dayamayee has a job interview at a call centre in Delhi tomorrow. In the dialogue she is practising with her friend Harita, who plays the interviewer.

Name	Dayamayee
Personal qualities	good at ... enjoys ...
Computer skills	can use ...
Attitude to modern technology	has got ...
Level of English	always got good ... speaks ... listens ...
Knowledge of Britain	has visited her ... reads ...
Work experience	part-time: ... weekend job: ...
Weaknesses	forgets ...

a) Listen to the dialogue and complete the candidate profile for Dayamayee.

b) Listen to the dialogue again. Add any missing information.

Web-Code: EG21-D6-EA-089-5

5 Personal statements: My future

a) *First read statements A–F below.*

b) *Next listen to the speakers. Choose the right statement for each speaker.*
*While you listen, write the correct letter (A–F) next to the speaker's name.**
Be careful. There is one more statement than you need.

c) *Listen again and check.*

Statements

A I don't want my parents to plan my future for me.
B I don't know yet which career is right for me.
C I want to get advice from my parents before I decide what to do.
D My parents don't really understand how much I need a break.
E I plan to combine[1] travelling with getting work experience.
F I don't think it'll be easy to find a good job in my country.

Speaker	Statement
1 Pia	
2 Mikael	
3 Frans	
4 Marietta	
5 Sally	

* *Copy the chart into your exercise book.*

Web-Code: EG21-D6-EA-089-6

6 Radio advertisement

a) *Listen to the advertisement.*
Complete the missing information.

1 The boy in the advertisement phones his ... because ...
2 BBB offers ... for ...
3 To book a room ...
4 In the second message, the boy ...
5 The advertisement speaks to ... and promises ...

b) *Listen again and check your answers.*

[1] (to) combine *kombinieren, verbinden*

READING

1 A list of tips: What to do when you're down

a) First read the text.

Ten top tips when you're down

TIP 1 Talk to a friend. Good friends will want to help. So why not call one of your mates and tell them about your problem?

TIP 2 Talk to your parents. Listen to their advice. Try to understand them. Remember: they were young once too and had similar problems.

TIP 3 Sometimes it can help if you express[1] your feelings in a creative way. Write a story or poem, draw or paint something or maybe write some music.

TIP 4 Physical activity can make you feel happier. Go swimming or running, or do some other sport. Be active.

TIP 5 Light makes us feel better. On a grey winter's day, try using a sun lamp. But nothing can beat real sunlight. So go out in the sunshine if you can.

TIP 6 The beauty of nature can make us feel more relaxed. Go for a walk outdoors and breathe in the fresh air.

TIP 7 Be kind to your body. Fill a bath and lie back in the hot, soapy water. Maybe try a massage or do yoga.

TIP 8 A great therapy if you're feeling down is simply to laugh or smile. You could try watching a comedy on TV or reading a funny book.

TIP 9 Helping others can make you feel better about yourself. Why not volunteer to work with children or to help people who can't look after themselves?

TIP 10 Do something nice for yourself. Buy something that you really want – maybe the latest computer game or some trendy clothes.

b) *Now match each tip (1–10) to one of the pictures below (A–L). There are two more pictures than you need.*

c) *Read the tips again. Choose three tips that you find helpful. Give reasons.*

---

[1] (to) express *ausdrücken, äußern*

2 A short biography: Jérôme Boateng, footballer

a) Read the text first. Then do the tasks below.

Jérôme Boateng (born 3 September, 1988 in Berlin; height: 1.92 metres) is a German footballer who plays for the English Premier League team, Manchester City. Boateng is a defender[1].

Boateng has both German and Ghanaian nationality. His mother is German, his father Ghanaian. His two half-brothers, Kevin-Prince and George, are also footballers. Kevin-Prince plays for Ghana's national team. Football is a bit of a tradition in the Boateng family. Jérôme's uncle also played for Ghana.

Boateng is a strongly built sportsman who can play any full-back position[2]. His career began in 1994 with the youth team of Tennis Borussia Berlin. Then in July 2002, when he was 13 years old, he joined Hertha BSC Berlin. In January 2007, at only 18, he became a Hertha first team member. He played his first match against Hannover 96 in the 2006–07 Bundesliga season.

Boateng was offered a five-year contract[3] with Hertha, but decided against staying on with the Berlin team. Instead, he moved to Hamburger SV in August 2007 for a fee of € 1.1 million. There, he continued to develop his game and became one of the key players in Hamburg's defence. Other clubs were soon interested in him, including VfL Wolfsburg, Arsenal and Manchester City. In June 2010, it was announced that Boateng was moving to Manchester – this time for a fee of over £ 10 million. The move was a big step in his career and he felt very excited about it. 'I'm looking forward to the challenge[4],' he said. Boateng's contract with City runs for five years.

Boateng also has an impressive international career. He played for the German U-16, U-17 and U-19 teams several times. He is also a former[5] German U-21 international player and won the 2009 UEFA European Under-21 Football Championship with the German team.

In October 2009, Boateng played his first match with the (adult) German national team against Russia, but was sent off in the second half after receiving two yellow cards. This was not typical of Boateng. People who have seen him play describe him as calm and disciplined. Because he had always played with a minimum of fouls, he himself was annoyed by his behaviour on the field. But German national coach, Joachim Löw, was sure that Boateng would learn the right lessons from his mistake.

In the summer of 2010, Boateng was a member of the German team in the FIFA World Cup in South Africa. In Germany's match against Ghana, he played against his own half-brother. This was the first time that brothers played against each other in the World Cup. Germany beat Ghana 1–0.

b) *Copy and complete the chart with the information from the text.*

Name	*Jérôme ...*
Place/Date of birth	
Nationality	
Family (one detail about each member)	
Clubs (dates)	*Tennis Borussia (1994 – ...)*
International experience	

c) *What does the text tell us about Boateng's character?*

d) *What was special about the 2010 World Cup?*

[1] defender *Abwehrspieler/in* [2] full-back position *Abwehrposition* [3] contract *Vertrag* [4] challenge *Herausforderung* [5] former *ehemalige/r*

3 A short story: Money isn't everything

a) *First read the text.*

Tim and Lisa had been going out together for six weeks now and it was time for Lisa to meet Tim's parents. She had been invited for tea at Tim's house on Sunday.

Lisa was very nervous. She had met Tim at the local youth club, but he lived on the other side of town. He only went to the same youth club because his grandma lived near there and he liked to visit her once a week between leaving school and going to the youth club.

Tim's parents had a lot of money, not like Lisa's parents. Her mum was a single parent and worked at a supermarket. Her dad had disappeared, to New Zealand her mum thought, when Lisa was only two. But Lisa wasn't unhappy. She had great fun with her mum and her younger brother. Money wasn't everything. And her home? Well, Lisa really didn't mind living in a caravan. Although, when Tim asked her where she lived, she just said the name of the village outside the town where the youth club was.

'OK, this is our house,' said Tim, as they walked up to the front door.
'House?' said Lisa. 'It's a palace! I knew your parents were rich, but I never expected a huge place like this. Bye, Tim. I'm going home.'
'Lisa, please,' said Tim. 'Don't be so nervous. They're only my parents.'
He squeezed her hand.
Lisa smiled. 'OK, I'll stay. But I'm not looking forward to this.'

They walked into the big, square hall.
'I'll introduce you to my parents,' Tim said.
'Mum! Dad!' he called. But nobody came.
'That's funny,' said Tim. 'I told Mum we were coming, so why aren't they here?'
'Are you sure they want to meet me?' Lisa asked.
Tim took Lisa's hand again. 'Of course they want to meet you! They can't wait. Come on. Let's go into the living room. I'm sure they'll be here in a few moments.'

Lisa followed Tim across the hall into the living room. She looked around and saw beautiful furniture[1], expensive lamps, a plasma TV and a Danish stereo system. Modern paintings hung on the walls.
Lisa wanted to be polite. 'It's a very nice room,' she said to Tim.
'Do you really like it?' asked Tim.
Lisa didn't. 'It doesn't feel as if people live here,' she thought. 'It's so cold and impersonal.'

They waited for a few minutes, but there was still no sign of Tim's parents.
'Maybe they're in the garden,' Tim said. 'I'll go and look.'
He went outside while Lisa stayed in the living room. After some minutes she heard the sound of voices, loud and angry.
'Somebody's having an argument,' she thought. 'Maybe Tim and his parents are arguing about me.'
She walked out to the hall to be able to listen better.

Standing in the hall, Lisa could hear that the voices were coming from upstairs. There were two people, a man and a woman.
'I don't understand you,' the man said. 'We've got everything money can buy, but still you aren't happy.'
Then the woman: 'Money isn't everything. You're my husband, but you're never at home. We have a beautiful house, but you spend all your time at the office. What kind of life is this?'

[1] furniture *Möbel*

Lisa shivered[1]. 'Tim's parents can't be very happy,' she thought.

'What do you mean?' the man asked. 'I'm at home today. I'm not at the office. It's Sunday.'

'Yes,' the woman answered. 'Sunday. A day for the family, but we can't enjoy our house together. No, we have to go downstairs and talk to that girl Tim met at that awful youth club.'

'Why don't you want to meet our son's girlfriend?' the man asked. 'I don't see a problem.'

'You don't see a problem?' the woman shouted. 'That girl comes from the worst part of town. Why your mother still lives there I don't know. But I do know that I'd like someone better for my son. ... No! Don't say anything! Let's just go downstairs and be nice to her, if we have to.'

At that moment Tim came into the hall. 'What's the matter, Lisa?' he asked.

b) *Decide if these statements (1–5) are true, false or not in the text. Write your answers down.*

1 Lisa has often been invited to Tim's house.
2 Lisa and Tim have different family backgrounds.
3 Lisa's father works at a supermarket in New Zealand.
4 Lisa thinks you can be happy without a lot of money.
5 When Lisa met Tim, she told him that she lived in a caravan.

c) *Read the tasks (1–3) and decide which answer (A – D) is correct. Choose only one letter for each task.*

1 When Lisa sees Tim's house, she
- A is surprised at how small it is.
- B turns around and goes home.
- C feels more relaxed about meeting his parents.
- D feels more nervous about meeting his parents.

2 When Tim and Lisa enter the house,
- A Tim is surprised that his parents aren't there.
- B Tim's parents are there to welcome them.
- C only Tim's mum is there to welcome them.
- D Tim's parents are waiting in the living room.

3 When Lisa sees the living room in Tim's house, she
- A immediately likes it.
- B makes a polite comment about it.
- C tells Tim what she thinks about it.
- D wonders why nobody is there.

d) *Complete these sentences (1–4).*

1 Tim went into the garden because ...
2 Lisa went into the hall because ...
3 Lisa thinks Tim's parents can't be happy because ...
4 Tim's mother doesn't want to meet Lisa because ...

e) *Answer these questions (1–3). Use examples from the text to support your answers.*

1 Why do you think Lisa feels uncomfortable about meeting Tim's parents?
2 How does Tim try to make Lisa feel more relaxed?
3 Describe the relationship between Tim's parents.

f) *How do you think the story ends? Write 60–80 words.*

[1] (to) shiver *erschauern, zittern*

4 A holiday blog: One island, two countries

a) *First read the text.*

Hi. This is Wendy. Tim and I are just back from Ireland. Here are a few notes.

▪ **Thursday 25th August:** Drove to Stranraer in Scotland and took the ferry. Flying is cheaper, but we wanted to use our car for the trip. Less than two hours at sea (ferry was really fast) and we were in Belfast, still in the UK. Northern Ireland is the part of Ireland that is still British.

▪ **Friday 26th August:** The conflict between Catholics and Protestants in Northern Ireland killed so many people. But now – thankfully – it's over, and tourists go there to shop and enjoy the nightlife. Other attractions in Belfast (the capital): the shipyards[1] where the *Titanic* was built (great!) and the wall paintings done by Protestants and Catholics in their areas of the city.

▪ **Sunday 28th August:** Crossed the border into the Irish Republic today. We didn't need passports and, like in the UK, you drive on the left. But distances[2] are in kilometres, not miles. And we had to change money – they use euros, not pounds. Dublin, the Republic's capital, is full of history – and full of people, with so many shops, cafés and pubs. Once, the Republic was quite poor. But joining the EU was good for Ireland. The economy[3] improved and the Republic became the 'Celtic Tiger'. OK, so Ireland has had some economic problems recently. But I'm still writing on a laptop that was 'Made in Ireland' and there's a one in four chance that your computer was made there too.

▪ **Tuesday 30th August:** But enough about industry. South-west of Dublin there's an absolute 'must' for tourists – the Rock of Cashel, a great collection of medieval architecture[4] and Celtic art. We loved walking around the historical buildings.

▪ **Wednesday 31st August**: Another highlight was the Ring of Kerry, a 170 km narrow road around the Iveragh Peninsula. As we drove along, we stopped again and again to look at the mountains and the amazing views out to sea. At times we wished[5] there were fewer other tourists. Later, there was a big Irish welcome at a great little bed and breakfast. We were sorry we couldn't stay longer.

b) *Now read the tasks (1–3) and decide which answer is correct: A, B or C.*

1 Wendy and Tim went to Northern Ireland by ferry because they
- A wanted to save time.
- B wanted to save money.
- C wanted to take their car with them.

2 Wendy says tourists in Northern Ireland
- A can get killed in the religious conflict.
- B can enjoy the shopping and nightlife.
- C can paint walls in Belfast.

3 In the Irish Republic Wendy noticed that
- A cars drove on the right.
- B distances were in miles.
- C distances were in kilometres.

c) *Answer these questions (1–4).*

1 What does Wendy say about the Irish economy? (at least two things)

2 Which sight does Wendy describe as a 'must' for tourists? Why?

3 What is the Ring of Kerry? What did Wendy and Tim do there?

4 Name at least four things that Wendy liked about her holiday in Ireland.

[1] shipyards *Werft* [2] distance *Entfernung* [3] economy *Wirtschaft* [4] medieval architecture *mittelalterliche Architektur*
[5] (to) wish *(sich) wünschen*

MEDIATION

1 Signs

Du machst mit deiner Familie Urlaub in England. Deine Eltern verstehen nicht viel Englisch und wollen wissen, was diese Schilder bedeuten. Erkläre es ihnen kurz auf Deutsch.

2 A poster

Du bist mit deiner Familie im Urlaub in Nova Scotia in Kanada. Dein kleiner Bruder fragt, was die auf dem Poster beschriebene Tour bietet. Erkläre ihm kurz auf Deutsch

- was man auf der Tour alles sehen kann.
- wie man sich mit dem Kapitän verständigen kann.
- wie lange die Tour dauert.
- wie man sich an Bord verpflegt.

3 What's on TV this evening?

Your American guest has asked you to suggest some German TV programmes that she could watch this evening. Read this page from a TV magazine. Write her a message in English with the main information (one or two sentences for each programme). Do not translate word for word.

FERNSEHEN Tagestipps ab 17 Uhr

19:40 | RTL | SOAP

Gute Zeiten schlechte Zeiten:

Will Pia keine lockere Beziehung?
Pia tut zwar furchtbar cool, wenn es um John geht, doch als dieser mit einem anderen Mädchen flirtet, wird sie eifersüchtig. John entgeht ihr Gefühlschaos nicht. Er stellt sie zur Rede.

20:15 | ARD | KRIMI

Tatort: „Tempelräuber"

Im heutigen Fall aus Münster muss Kommissar Thiel den Mord an einem Priester aufklären. Sein Partner Professor Boerne befindet sich diesmal in der ungewohnten Rolle des Zeugen.

20:15 | Pro 7 | SHOW

Schlag den Raab

Wer tritt heute im Wettkampf gegen Moderator Stefan Raab an? Den Kandidaten erwarten Spiele zu den Bereichen Sport, Quiz, Geschicklichkeit und noch vielen anderen. Dem Sieger winkt ein Gewinn von 1 Million Euro.

21:15 | RTL | DOKUSOAP

Bauer sucht Frau

Bauer Heinrich gibt die Hoffnung nicht auf und sucht noch immer nach einer liebevollen Partnerin. Heute startet er einen neuen Versuch.

4 A school brochure

You would like to spend a school year in England. You have found this information on the internet.

★★★ THE ROYAL BLUE COATS SCHOOL ★★★

The Royal Blue Coats School, founded by Charles II in 1666, is a day school for boys and girls aged 12 to 18. It is situated in Hexham in the northeast of England in a quiet corner of the old town.

We offer 26 subjects including music, drama, art and design. Students can also choose between many different extra-curricular activities and clubs.

- ✶ Sports: There are the traditional sports – rugby, cricket and hockey – and many other choices, for example basketball, tennis and swimming (in our own swimming pool).
- ✶ Fees: £3,502 per term. This includes tuition[1] and books. (The school year, starting in September, has 3 terms.)
- ✶ Scholarships[2]: There are free places for a small number of students. For information, contact the school office.
- ✶ School lunches: The cost is £167 per term in Years 7 to 9 and £180 per term in Years 10 to 13. We also offer breakfast and snacks during mid-morning break.

[1] tuition *Unterricht* [2] scholarship *Stipendium*

Berichte deinen Eltern in Stichworten auf Deutsch:

1 was es für eine Schule ist.
2 wo sich die Schule befindet.
3 was zum regulären Unterricht und zu weiteren Angeboten gesagt wird.
4 welche Sportarten angeboten werden.
5 wie hoch das Schulgeld ist.
6 wie die Kosten reduziert werden können.
7 was über Verpflegung gesagt wird.

5 A flyer

Du hast mit deiner Familie eine Reise nach Arizona gewonnen. Deine Eltern verstehen diesen Flyer nicht. Erkläre auf Deutsch, was man bei einem Ausflug in den Canyon beachten sollte. Nenne drei Punkte.

Beautiful, but ...

Every year thousands of visitors go to the Grand Canyon and look down to the Colorado River one mile below. The view is absolutely fantastic, and some people decide to hike down to the river. This can be quite difficult, because the paths into the canyon are steep[1] – and then, when the visitors get to the bottom, they have to climb back up the path again. That's even harder! It can take a very long time, especially in the summer when it can get really hot (40 degrees Celsius). The National Parks Service does NOT recommend doing the hike there and back in one day. Instead you can get a backcountry permit[2] and spend the night on a campsite. Or there is a small number of beds at the Phantom Ranch in the canyon.

The Grand Canyon is a beautiful place, but it can be dangerous too. Plan your trip well and be careful. Many people have gone down into the canyon and not come out again – at least, not alive ...

6 Passing on[3] questions and answers

During your stay in Arizona, you and your family talk to Susan Diefenbacker, a ranger at the Grand Canyon National Park. Your parents' English is not very good, so you must help them.

Mutter Frag mal bitte, ob man heute in den Canyon hinabwandern kann.
You ...
Susan I wouldn't recommend it in this heat. And it's really too late in the day now.
You ...
Vater Schade. Ich würde gerne zum Fluss hinunter. Frag, wie es morgen wäre.
You ...
Susan If you leave very early in the morning, it should be OK.
You ...
Vater Toll! Gibt es sonst etwas, das wir beachten müssen?
You ...
Susan Make sure you have suitable footwear – a good pair of strong shoes. It's a long and difficult walk.
You ...
Mutter Und wie ist es, wenn wir auf dem Campingplatz im Canyon übernachten wollen? Muss man reservieren?
You ...
Susan Yes, but there are always a few backcountry permits available on the same day. Just come to the Visitors Center when we open in the morning.
You ...
Mutter Frag bitte, wann das Center öffnet.
You ...
Susan At 8 o'clock in the morning.
You ...
Vater Gibt es etwas Besonderes, was wir auf die Wanderung mitnehmen sollten?
You ...
Susan Lots of water! Four liters per person per day. Food and snacks – and lots of of time! Good luck to you all! Be safe and enjoy your visit!
You ...
Mutter Bedanke dich bitte und sage ihr, dass wir hoffen, dass wir die Genehmigungen bekommen.
You ...

---

[1] steep *steil* [2] backcountry permit *Erlaubnis(schein) für Übernachtung in der Wildnis* [3] (to) pass on *weitergeben, übermitteln*

Unit 1 Part A

4 Role play ▸ Unit 1, Part A (p. 9)

a) *Partner B: Listen to your partner's problem. Try to give him/her some advice.*

b) *Now tell your partner about your problem and ask for advice.*

You're worried about a friend. She misses a lot of school and is getting bad marks. She doesn't hang out with you and her other friends any more. You think that the kids that she hangs out with aren't good for her. You think she's unhappy. You want to help her, but you don't know what to do.

Unit 1 Part B

P4 MEDIATION Which film? ▸ Unit 1, Part B (p. 15)

Partner B: You visit partner A with your friend from England. You want to watch a film together.

a) *Read about the film* Die fetten Jahre sind vorbei.

b) *Partner A will talk about a different film. Listen carefully. Then explain in English what your film is about.*

Die Freunde Jan (Daniel Brühl) und Peter (Stipe Erceg) sind Mitte 20, leben zusammen in Berlin und finden, dass die Welt sehr ungerecht ist. Und wie protestieren sie dagegen? Sie brechen nachts in die Villen reicher Leute ein. Dort stehlen sie nichts, sondern stellen die Möbel auf den Kopf, hängen die Bilder um und hinterlassen Botschaften wie „Die fetten Jahre sind vorbei". Die Probleme beginnen, als Jan und Peters Freundin Jule (Julia Jentsch) in die Villa eines wohlhabenden Managers (Burghart Klaußner) einbrechen. Jan und Jule, zwischen denen sich eine Liebesbeziehung entwickelt, werden auf frischer Tat ertappt. In ihrer Panik kidnappen sie den Manager. Gemeinsam mit Peter, der nichts von der Beziehung zwischen Jan und Jule weiß, halten sie ihre Geisel auf einer kleinen Berghütte gefangen – und aus Spaß wird krimineller Ernst.

c) *Your English friend can't decide which film to watch. You and partner A have to choose. Listen to partner A's opinion. Then say which film* you *think is better and why. Agree on a film.*

▸ SF Mediation (p. 157)

Unit 2 **Part B**

P1 You can make a difference ▸ *Unit 2, Part B, p. 36*

a) *Partner B: You and your partner have different tips under each heading in* Go Green. *Read your tips and take notes in a chart (use the text headings).*

My text says that you should turn off the lights when you leave a room.

Here it says that you should buy new, low-energy appliances.

b) *Ask your partner about his/her tips to go green. Add your partner's tips to your chart.*

▸ *SF Talking notes (p. 141)*

GO Green!

Climate change is a problem for the whole world. But don't sit around and wait for governments to act. Here are some simple things that you can do to help to stop global warming.

Use less energy

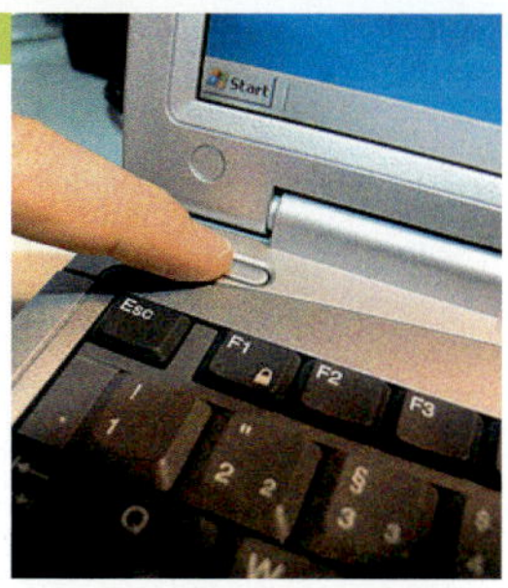

Producing electricity causes a lot of CO_2. So, to save energy, always turn off the lights when you leave a room. And when you're not using your computer, TV or stereo, turn them off completely.

Save trees

Every day forests are cut down to make new paper. But we need trees to reduce CO_2 in the air. Think about the paper that you use. Is your printer paper 100% recycled? And what about your toilet paper?

Reduce rubbish

Everyone loves new stuff, but when we throw away our old stuff we produce a lot of rubbish and collecting rubbish costs energy. So why not buy second-hand stuff: clothes, books, mobile phones – anything. Buying second hand will also save you a lot of money!

Think about your food

To help to fight against climate change, try to eat more local food. Local food has a small carbon footprint because it doesn't have to travel a long way to your local shop.

Heat less water

Showers cause over 65 per cent of home water-heating costs. Try taking shorter showers to save energy.

Unit 3 Part A

P 4 SPEAKING Role play: A discussion about video cameras at school

Role cards

▸ Unit 3, Part A (p. 51)

Moderator

You can use these phrases to ...

▸ ***start the discussion***
- Hello everyone. Thanks for coming to the meeting today.
- Our question/topic is ...
- So, who would like to start the discussion?

▸ ***ask questions***
- What's your opinion?
- Do you agree with that point?
- Can you explain that? / What do you mean?
- How? / Why?

▸ ***end the discussion***
- Time is up*, I'm afraid.
- Thank you all for taking part in the discussion.
- Let's vote now: Who is for/against ...?
- The result is that most people in this class ...

* time is up *die Zeit ist zu Ende*

Teacher AGAINST video cameras
- You think it's <u>your</u> job to make sure that students behave.
- You don't want to be watched by cameras.
- The school should use the money for other things (computers, books, ...).
- You think that students will be afraid to speak openly.
- ...

Student 1 FOR video cameras
- With cameras, you would feel safer.
- Your cousin's school uses cameras and now there's less bullying.
- Nice students don't need to worry about the cameras, only the troublemakers.
- Cameras should also be in toilets because there's a lot of bullying and vandalism there too.
- ...

Head teacher FOR video cameras
- You watched a news report on TV about a school in London with cameras: the school is cleaner, safer and students' grades are better.
- There were a lot of problems at your school last year: computers were stolen, students were bullied, graffiti was written on the walls.
- It's expensive to buy new computers, to clean the graffiti, and to repair things in the school.
- ...

Parent FOR video cameras
- Troublemakers will be caught more easily.
- If the school doesn't have to spend so much money on repairing things, there will be more money for school trips, ...
- If teachers don't have to look after troublemakers all the time, they'll have more time for teaching.
- The school will be a nicer, cleaner place for everyone.
- ...

Student 2 AGAINST video cameras
- Bullying won't stop, it will take place outside school.
- Troublemakers shouldn't be watched by cameras, they should be watched by real people.
- There are cameras at your friend's school. Your friend says that it feels like a prison.
- You can't talk openly when you know that there are cameras and microphones.
- ...

▸ SF Having a discussion (p. 148)

English for jobs

2 Now you: Role play ▸ *English for jobs (p. 70)*

Partner B: Read the background information on the left. Then follow the instructions on the right. Be as polite and friendly as you can.

Last week you bought a new TV at a reduced price in a sale. When you unpacked[1] the TV at home, however, you saw that the screen was much too big for your living room.
Now you're going back to the store to ask if you can change your new TV for a smaller one. You know that some stores don't change sale goods[2]. However, you're a good customer there and you don't mind paying more if a smaller TV is more expensive.

- Your partner will start the conversation.
- Say you would like to change your TV.
- Give the reason.
- Explain about the sale.
- Ask if A can make an exception[3]. Give a reason.
- Ask when you can expect an answer.
- Thank A and say when you'll return.

[1] (to) unpack *auspacken* [2] sale goods *Ausverkaufsware* [3] exception *Ausnahme*

Exam File

3 Discussing photos ▸ p. 80

a) *Partner B: Listen to Partner A talking about his/her photo. Then show Partner A your photo and describe what you can see in it.*
Discuss the different things that dogs can do for people. Say how you feel about dogs and why.

b) *Partner B: Listen to Partner A talking about his/her photo. Then show Partner A your photo and describe what you can see in it.*
Discuss different ways that people can spend their holidays. Say what kind of holiday you like best and why.

Exam File

7 Role plays: Solving problems abroad ▸ p. 82

a) *Partner B: Look at the role card and act out the conversation with your partner.*

You're in an internet café in your town. The person at the PC next to you asks you some questions.
- Say how long you've lived in the town.
- You don't know the hotel your partner asks about. Ask the name of the street.
- Say how far it is.
- Say that you don't like the area and explain why.
- Say that you can recommend a good, cheap hostel close to the internet café. Describe what it's like.
- Offer to show Partner A the way to the hostel.

b) *Partner B: Look at the role card and act out the conversation with your partner.*

You work at a travel agent's in Spain. All European airports have been closed for a week for safety reasons. You have a lot of customers looking for an alternative way home. Many of them are very stressed. Your next customer comes to your desk and describes his/her situation.
- You know all about the situation. Describe the reactions of some of your customers.
- All trains are booked out for the next days. Say the earliest date your customer could travel.
- You can offer a bus seat for tomorrow. Give the departure time.
- Journeys to German cities take between 25 and 30 hours. Say when the bus will arrive.
- Say a ticket costs €190.
- React.

Unit 1 Lead-in

3 Top chat-up lines (Episode 2)

d) more help ▸ *Unit 1, Lead-in (p. 7)*

Think of good ways of starting a conversation with someone you fancy.
– Look at the phrases below and choose the five best chat-up lines.
– Then compare with a partner. Together try to agree on your top five chat-up lines.

Say hello
Hello. My name's ...
Hi. How are you?
Hi. It's hot/cold today, isn't it?

Ask a question
What's your name?
What did you think of the football/film/... last night?
Did you see the programme on TV about ... last night?
Are you enjoying yourself?
How was your day?
What did you do last weekend?
What are your plans for this weekend?
I don't think I know you. Are you from here?
Excuse me. Do you know how this phone/laptop/... works?
Could you tell me the way to the park/the post office/...?

Say something nice
I really like your shirt/...
That's a really cool mobile phone/...

Try to say something funny
Hi, I'm Mr/Miss Perfect. You were looking for me.
There's something wrong with my phone: it hasn't got your number in it.
I've lost my phone number. Can I have yours?
Excuse me. My friend wants to know if you like me.
Well done. / You're very lucky. You've just won the competition for the most attractive person in the room. And the prize is an evening out with me.

▸ *SF Having a conversation (p. 147)*

Unit 1 Lead-in

3 Top chat-up lines (Episode 2) ▸ *Unit 1, Lead-in (p. 7)*

e) ● *Write a dialogue between two people in which one person asks another person out.*

Unit 1 Part A

P1 WORDS Describing people: appearance and character ▸ *Unit 1, Part A (p. 10)*

c) more help *You have to write a short description of yourself. Here are some ideas. Don't forget to use the phrases that you collected in 1a) and b).*

I'm (quite/really) tall/short/thin/...
My eyes are ...
I've got long blond/straight brown/curly black/... hair.
I've got a piercing/tattoo on/above/... my ...

People say I'm easy-going/friendly/...
My friends say I'm ...
I think I'm (a bit) bossy/shy/...
I like/don't like/love ...
... is/isn't important to me.

Unit 1 **Part A**

P2 //● REVISION A group of friends (Present tenses) ▸ Unit 1, Part A (p. 10)

a) *Complete the text about the photo with the correct form of the verbs in the box. Use the* ***simple present*** *or the* ***present progressive****. (Use the words in the box on the left for sentences* ***1*** *to* ***6****, and the words in the box on the right for sentences* ***7*** *to* ***9****.).*

be • have • not know • look • play • shine • sit • not smile • wear • not wear

1 These people ... at a summer camp in the US.
2 The sun ... and everyone ... a good time.
3 The girl who ... the guitar is Rose. On her right is her boyfriend Seb, the guy with the curly brown hair and the white T-shirt.
4 He ... – that's typical of Seb. He always ... very serious.
5 Rose's brother Jake ... behind her.
6 Usually he ... hats. I ... why he ... one in this photo.

come (2x) • kiss • like • not remember • spend

7 The girl on Jake's left is Ruby. She ... from South Africa, but she ... the summer in the US.
8 The guy with the yellow T-shirt is Josh. As you can see, he ... his girlfriend Kate. They ... each other very much.
9 And the others? The two guys on the left ... from Germany, but I ... their names. And the good-looking guy with the short hair and the big smile? Well, that's me.

▸ *GF 3: Talking about the present (p. 162) • GF 6: The simple form and the progressive form (pp.166–167)*

Unit 1 **Part A**

P3 SPEAKING Keeping a conversation going

▸ Unit 1, Part A (p. 11)

d) ● more help 👥 *You meet someone at a party for the first time and you have to talk to him/her for as long as you can. You'll be more successful if you prepare well. Here are some ideas:*

*Write down some useful phrases that you can **start the conversation** with.* →	Hi, I'm ... What's your name? / How are you? / How're you doing? / ...
*Prepare **some topics** before you start. Make notes for useful questions you can ask.* →	**Possible topics** **Music:** What kind of music? My favourite group is ... Do you like them too? **TV programmes:** What kind of ...? **Sport:** I like ... What about you? Do you play ...?
*Think of a few **extra questions** if you want to change the topic or to keep the conversation going! Look back at the ideas you had for 3 a) and b).* →	What's your favourite pizza? • What do you think about ...? • By the way, do you like ...?
*Think about how to **finish the conversation**. Don't just stop talking!* →	I have to go now. • It was really nice talking to you. • Talk to you later. • See you later. • Can I have your phone number? • ...

▸ SF Having a conversation (p. 147)

Unit 1 **Part B**

P2 SPEAKING About a film

▸ Unit 1, Part B (p. 14)

a) more help *Prepare a talk about a film that you have seen. Here are some useful phrases.*

Introduction title of the film • kind of film • names of main actors • name of director →	Today I'm going to talk about the film ... It's a ... (horror film/comedy/science fiction film/love story/cartoon/...) It stars ... It was directed by ...
Plot Give a short summary of the film. →	The film is set in ... • The story takes place in ... • It's about ... / It tells the story of ... • At the beginning .../Later/During the film ...
Main characters Name one or two main characters and describe them. →	The main/My favourite character is ... He's/She's .... (What do they look like? How old are they? What are they like?)
What's special about the film? Talk about things that are special about the film. →	So what's special about this film? Well, ... It has a good soundtrack/brilliant special effects/amazing costumes/... It won an Oscar.
Personal opinion Say what you liked about the film. • Would you recommend the film to other people? →	To sum up, I love this film because ... My favourite part/scene in the film is when ... Everybody/People who like ... will like this film. I'd give it ... stars out of five./You must see it!

Unit 1 Part C

1 // ● Tell the story
▸ Unit 1, Part C (p. 19)

Finish these sentences.

1 Arnold thinks Penelope is dating him because ...
2 Both Arnold and Penelope dream about ...
3 After the school dance, Penelope wants to ...
4 At the diner Arnold feels sick because ...
5 Arnold tells Roger that he has forgotten his wallet, so ...
6 Later, Penelope asks Arnold if he is poor, and Arnold ...
7 Penelope doesn't want him to hitchhike, so ...

Unit 1 Part C

4 ● more help Penelope's diary
▸ Unit 1, Part C (p. 19)

Step 1: *Imagine which details could be important to Penelope. Make notes.*

I wanted to go to the diner. / I felt excited. / Arnold looked a bit scared. I didn't know why ...

Step 2: *Try to make your text more interesting by using linking words (after that, a few minutes later, then, next, but, so ... that, and, because, ...).*

I wanted to go to the diner, but Arnold looked a bit scared. Arnold ordered our food, then he looked a bit sick. A few minutes later he got up ...

Step 3: *End your diary text by giving a personal view:*

I don't care what Daddy says, I think ...
I want Arnold to know that he doesn't have to lie to me / he's got friends / ...

▸ Writing course (pp. 151–152)

Unit 1 Part C

5 A review
▸ Unit 1, Part C (p. 19)

b) ● more help *Use these questions to make notes about a story that you've read. The words in the boxes might help you.*

- What's the title?
- Who wrote it?
- What kind of story is it?
- What's the story about?
- When and where does it take place?
- Who are the main characters?
- What's good/bad/interesting about it?
- What's the ending like?
- Would you recommend it to other people?/ Who should read it?

▸ Writing course (pp. 151–152)

Kinds of stories
a short story • a novel • a love story • a science fiction story • a comedy • a drama • an adventure story • a historical story • an action story • a crime story • a detective story • a horror story • a mystery story • ...

Words to describe a story
amazing • awful • boring • brilliant • clever • exciting • fantastic • horrible • perfect • realistic • sad • scary • silly • strange • stupid • surprising • terrible • violent • ...

Unit 2 **Part A**

P1 // ● REVISION Things are different today (Simple present and simple past)

▸ *Unit 2, Part A, p. 32*

a) *Complete the text with the correct form of the verbs in brackets (**simple present** or **simple past**).*

When I was a boy we ... (have to) get up off the sofa to change channels because we ... (~~have~~) a remote control for the TV. We ... (watch) programmes in black and white. My family ... (sit) together in one room to watch TV because there ... (be) only one in the house. We often ... (argue) about which channel to watch.
Now we ... (have) three TVs in our house, and we can watch programmes on the computer too, so there ... (be) no more arguments. This also means that today we ... (~~sit~~) together as a family as much and we ... (~~talk~~) about the programmes we watch. In my opinion that ... (be) a shame.

b) *Look at the chart on the right. Make sentences about what people did in the past and what they do now, for example:*

When people didn't have clocks, they looked at the ... to ... Today we have clocks to find out ...

▸ *GF 3: Talking about the present (p. 162)* • *GF 4: Talking about the past (p. 163)*

In the past ...	Now ...	to ...
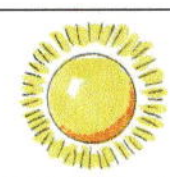		find out the time
		travel to Australia
		travel short distances
		keep food fresh
		communicate with friends

Unit 2 **Part A**

P2 WORDS Technology

▸ *Unit 2, Part A, p. 32*

a) more help *Collect words and phrases on the topic of TECHNOLOGY from pp. 28–31. Make a mind map. Use the headings on the right or find other headings. Then add the words and phrases that you collected.*

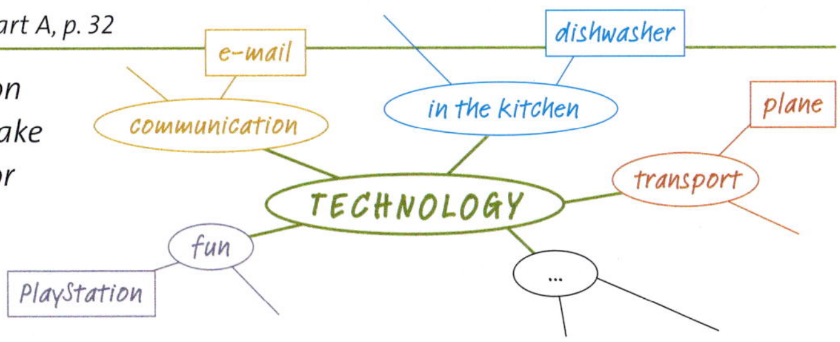

d) **Extra** more help
Think of an appliance or a machine that people use today. Look at your mind map from 2a) again for ideas. Then describe the appliance or machine to your group (but don't name it).
Here are some useful phrases:

It's an appliance/machine that you use to ... • You use it when you want to ... • Most/some people use it every day. • I've got one in my bedroom/kitchen/living room/bathroom/... • I have/haven't got one. • I want/don't want one. • If you like/don't like ..., then you should get one of these.

▸ *SF Paraphrasing (p. 149)*

Unit 2 Part B

4 ● more help A letter to a newspaper

▸ Unit 2, Part B, p. 35

Write a letter to a British newspaper about carbon rationing. In your letter say if you are for or against carbon rationing. Give reasons for your opinion.

1. Collect your ideas. ▸ SF Brainstorming (p. 149)
2. Write the letter. ▸ SF Writing letters (p. 154)
3. Correct your letter. ▸ SF Correcting your text (p. 152)

Start the letter. → Dear Sir or Madam

Say why you are writing. → I am a visitor from Germany and I am writing to you about ...

Say what you think. → In my opinion ...

Give reasons why you think carbon rationing is good/bad. → First ... / Second ... / Another reason is ... / Finally ... / So ...

End the letter. → Yours faithfully
Lena Schneider

These comments on an internet forum might give you some ideas for your letter:

Bob says:
I hate carbon rationing and I want it to stop. Life is so horrible now and everyone is unhappy. It's dark and cold and there is nothing good to look forward to.

jj says:
I agree with Bob. It's so unfair because this is the only country in Europe with carbon rationing. So people in France and Germany can turn up their heating, listen to music, watch TV and drive their cars. That's not fair!

Maggie says:
I think the government should stop carbon rationing and give money to scientists so that they can find better ways to fight global warming. There must be a better way.

C E Jones says:
People have known about global warming for a long time, but most of them didn't do anything to stop it. They kept driving their big cars and wasting energy in their houses, so the problem got worse. That's why I think carbon rationing is a good idea. The problem won't go away and so we must do something now to stop it.

TonyH says:
I think carbon rationing is hard, but it's necessary. We always expect others to do something against global warming: the government, big companies, other countries. But we must all get involved.

Unit 3 Lead-in

3 Now you

► Unit 3, Lead-in (p. 46)

b) ● *Write a short text and explain what you care about. Example:*

I care about child poverty. Some kids have nothing and ...

► SF Writing course (pp. 151–152)

Try to find a photo that goes with your text. Put up your text and the photo on the classroom wall. Go round and read the texts. Guess who wrote which text.

Unit 3 Part A

2 We are people too!

► Unit 3, Part A (p. 49)

a) //● *Finish these sentences:*

1. Oliver says teenagers are only different because ...
2. He thinks that some adults might be surprised that teenagers ...
3. The mosquito makes a noise that ...
4. Teenagers earn less than adults, so Oliver thinks it's unfair when teenagers ...
5. Young people can't vote and Oliver thinks that's why political parties ...
6. At the end of the article, Oliver says that he wants adults to ...

Unit 3 Part B

3 Now you ▸ *Unit 3, Part A (p. 49)*

b) more help *Write an e-mail to Oliver about his article.*

Say what you think of his article.
- I think your article is ... interesting/silly/unrealistic/...
- I agree with you completely.
- I'm sorry, but I don't agree with you at all. / I'm not sure if I agree with all of your points.

Tell him what points you agree or disagree with and give reasons.
- You say that ...
- I think/In my opinion you're right to say that ...
- You could be right, but what about ...?
- I agree/disagree with this point because ...
- It's true that a lot of young people ...

Say what the situation is like for you in Germany. Describe a situation that happened to you or someone you know.
- In Germany the situation is similar/quite different. For example ...
- It annoys me when ...
- Recently I/a friend was ...
- I/my friend wasn't doing anything wrong, but ...

Dear/Hi Oliver

My name is … and I live in Germany.
I think your article is …

You say that …
In my opinion …

In Germany the situation is …

Best wishes
(your name)

Useful words and phrases
bus driver • cause trouble • complain about sth./sb. • feel scared • hang out with friends • make too much noise • policeman/-woman • be polite to sb. • respect sb. • be scared of sth./sb. • be rude/unfriendly to sb. • serve sb. first/last • shop assistant • shoplift • shout at sb. • take sb. seriously • threaten sb. • ...

▸ *SF Writing course (pp. 151–152)*

TF 1–6

TF 1 My love is like ...

1 Love songs and poems

a) *Have you noticed that most songs and poems seem to be about love? What's your favourite love song or poem at the moment? What do its lyrics say about love?*

b) *Read the songs and poems. Which aspects of love from the list below are they about?*

- losing your lover
- having a laugh about love
- asking someone to be your lover
- saying how wonderful your lover is
- talking about someone else's love affair

A

Bye bye love

Chorus
Bye bye love
Bye bye happiness
Hello loneliness
I think I'm gonna cry
Bye bye love
Bye bye sweet caress[1]
Hello emptiness
I feel like I could die
Bye bye my love, goodbye

There goes my baby
With someone new
She sure looks happy
I sure am blue[2]
She was my baby
Till he stepped in[3]
Goodbye to romance
That might have been[4]
Chorus
I'm through with romance
I'm through with love
I'm through with counting
The stars above
And here's the reason
That I'm so free
My loving baby
Is through with me
Chorus

Felice Bryant (1925–2003) Boudleaux Bryant (1920–1987)

B

Love is all around

I feel it in my fingers, I feel it in my toes.
Well love is all around me, and so the feeling grows.
It's written on the wind, it's everywhere I go.
So if you really love me, come on and let it show.
You know I love you, I always will.
My mind's made up[5] by the way that I feel.
There's no beginning, there'll be no end
'Cause on my love you can depend[6].
I see your face before me as I lay on my bed.
I kinda get to thinking of all the things you said.
You gave your promise to me and I gave mine to you.
I need someone beside[7] me in everything I do.

Reg Presley (born 1943)

C

Celia Celia

When I am sad and weary[8]
When I think all hope has gone
When I walk along High Holborn[9]
I think of you with nothing on

Adrian Mitchell (1932–2008)

D

One parting[10]

Why did he write to her
'I can't live without you'?
And why did she write to him
'I can't live without you'?
For[11] he went west, she went east
And they both lived.

Carl Sandburg (1878–1967)

E

Goodbye

He breathed in air, he breathed out light.
Charlie Parker[12] was my delight[13].

Adrian Mitchell (1932–2008)

---

[1] caress [kə'res] *Zärtlichkeit, Liebkosung* [2] blue *(infml) deprimiert, down* [3] (to) step in *ins Spiel kommen* [4] ... that might have been *die hätte sein können* [5] my mind's made up *ich habe mich entschieden* [6] (to) depend on sth. [dɪ'pend] *sich auf etwas verlassen* [7] beside [bɪ'saɪd] *neben* [8] weary ['wɪəri] *erschöpft* [9] High Holborn [ˌhaɪ 'həʊbən] *(Straße in London)* [10] parting *Abschied* [11] for *denn* [12] Charlie Parker *amerik. Jazzmusiker (Altsaxophon) und Komponist (1920–1955)* [13] delight [dɪ'laɪt] *Entzücken*

2 Taking a closer look

In their poems and songs, writers use special techniques to express feelings. Read the study skills box and then answer the questions below.

a) *Write down the rhyme schemes of the two songs **A** and **B**. What effect do the rhymes have?*

b) *Listen to* Bye bye love *and describe its rhythm (fast, slow, peaceful, jumpy, ...). How does it make the listener feel?*

c) *Read the poems **C–E** again and find repetitions. What effect do the repetitions have?*

3 What do you think?

Which is the best love song/poem – the one you chose in 1a or one of the songs or poems on page 112? Give reasons. (music, rhythm, words, message, ...)

– I think ... is the best because ...
– It makes me feel happy/sad/calm/...
– want to dance/laugh/sing along/...
– The music/words/rhythm ... is/are beautiful/sad/thoughtful/...
– The message is interesting/good/... because ...

STUDY SKILLS Poem and song techniques (1)

Rhyme[1]: Rhymes create a pattern[2] you can hear. When this pattern continues through a poem or song, it gives it a rhyme scheme[3], which you can write down like this: AABBCC – ABAB – ...
Rhymes are a good way to structure a poem or song and to make it sound good.

Rhythm[4]: The variation[5] of stress on the words and syllables gives a song or poem its rhythm. The rhythm of a poem/song creates a feeling or mood[6]. For example, a slow rhythm can create a thoughtful or relaxed feeling. A fast rhythm can make it sound exciting or happy.
Repetition[7]: If a sound, a word or a phrase is repeated, this shows us that the idea is important. It can also hold the poem together.

▸ *SF Reading literature (pp. 145–146)*

[1] rhyme [raɪm] *Reim* [2] pattern ['pætn] *Muster* [3] rhyme scheme [ski:m] *Reimschema* [4] rhythm ['rɪðəm] *Rhythmus, Takt* [5] variation [ˌveəri'eɪʃn] *Veränderung, Variation* [6] mood [mu:d] *Stimmung* [7] repetition [ˌrepə'tɪʃn] *Wiederholung*

4 Pictures in the mind

a) *Read or listen to the poem on the right and draw or describe in writing the picture that it creates in your mind.*

b) *Explain your picture to your partner.*

A red, red rose

'O, my Love's like a red, red rose,
That's newly sprung[5] in June.
O, my Love's like the melody
That's sweetly played in tune[6].
As fair[7] art[8] thou[9], my bonnie lass[10],
So deep in love am I;
And I will love thee[11] still, my dear,
Till a' the seas go dry.
Till a' the seas go dry, my dear,
And rocks melt[12] wi' the sun:
I will love thee still, my dear,
While the sands o' life shall[13] run:
And fare thee well[14], my only love!
And fare thee well, a while!
And I will come again, my love,
Tho' it were ten thousand mile!'

Robert Burns (1759–1796)

STUDY SKILLS **Poem and song techniques (2)**

Images:[1]
Poets[2] paint pictures with words and show us a new way of seeing things. Sometimes these images are immediately clear, sometimes it takes time to understand them.
In a **metaphor**[3] a poet talks about something as if it is something else, e. g. The garden was a sea of flowers, or as if it can do something it cannot, e. g. *Time flies.*
In a **simile**[4], a poet creates an image by comparing one thing to another, e. g. *a face as white as snow*, or *She fights like a tiger.*

► *SF Reading literature (pp. 145–146)*

c) *Look at the following images from the poem 'A red, red rose'. Decide whether they are metaphors or similes.*
– my Love's like a red, red rose ...
– my Love's like the melody ...
– While the sands o' life shall run
– And rocks melt wi' the sun

d) *Choose one image from the poem and explain what it means and how it works. The language below might help.*

My Love's like a red, red rose ...
- is a metaphor/simile.
- It compares ... to ...
- It says that ... is like ...
- It says that ... but you can't really ...
- It means that ...
- It gives you the picture of ...

5 Now you

Choose a) or b) or c).

a) *Find your favourite word, image, rhyme or idea from the poems. Use them to write your own poem. (It doesn't have to rhyme!)*

b) *Write your own four line poem. Start each line like the Robert Burns poem on this page:*
My love is like ...

c) *Learn your favourite English poem or song and recite it to the class.*

---

[1] image ['ɪmɪdʒ] *Bild* [2] poet ['pəʊɪt] *Poet, Dichter* [3] metaphor ['metəfə] *Metapher* [4] simile ['sɪməli] *Vergleich, Simile* [5] sprung [sprʌŋ] *hier: aufgeblüht* [6] in tune [tjuːn] *gestimmt* [7] fair [feə] *(old) schön* [8] art [ɑːt] *(old) are* [9] thou [ðaʊ] *(old) you* [10] bonnie lass [ˌbɒni 'læs] *Scot: schönes Mädchen* [11] thee [ðiː] *(old) dich* [12] (to) melt [melt] *schmelzen* [13] shall [ʃəl] *hier: werden* [14] fare thee well *(old) lebe wohl*

TF 2 Making friends

start profile friends

ABOUT ME Jay

Basic Info

Sex: male[1]
Age: 16
Looking for: friends, networking
Current[2] city: Wellington, New Zealand
Hometown: London, UK
School/Job: school/yes
Status: in a relationship

Likes and Interests

Interests: evolutionary biology, space travel[3], football, cricket
Music: classical, jazz
Books: everything except novels or poetry
Movies: SF[4], documentaries on science
Television: football, SF series

1 2 3 4 5

start profile friends

ABOUT ME Dizzy

Basic Info

Sex: female[5]
Age: not telling
Looking for: LOVE & adventure
Current City: somewhere in Europe
Hometown: ditto[6]
School/Job: I work in fashion.
Status: single

Likes and Interests

Interests: celebs[7], music, clubbing
Music: hip hop, what else?
Books: love stories
Movies: Anything romantic. NO violence.
Television: Just the soaps, oh, and Next Top Model.

1 2 3 4 5

start profile friends

ABOUT ME Cate

Basic Info

Sex: female
Age: look it up
Looking for: friends
Current city: Sydney, NSW
Hometown: Melbourne, Victoria
School/Job: actor (Oscar, Elf Queen)
Status: married

Likes and Interests

Interests: Film, theatre, solar energy

start profile friends

ABOUT ME Finn

Basic Info

Sex: male
Age: 15
Looking For: cool girls and guys
Current city: Hamburg, Germany
Hometown: Hamburg, Germany
School/Job: I go to school in Hamburg.
Status: it's complicated

Likes and Interests

Interests: sports (mainly[8] sailing), parties
Music: new German bands
Books: not really
Movies: action, action, action
Television: sport

1 Confirm[9] or ignore?[10]

a) *If the people above asked to be your friend on a social networking site, which of them would you confirm as a friend? Which of them would you ignore? Why?*

b) *Discuss your reasons for confirming or ignoring with a partner.*

c) *What information do the authors of these profiles not give about themselves? What you would say in your profile. What information would you leave out?*
Share your group's ideas with the class.

---

1 male [meɪl] *männlich* 2 current ['kʌrənt] *gegenwärtige(r, s), derzeitige(r, s)* 3 space travel *Raumfahrt* 4 SF = science fiction [ˌsaɪəns 'fɪkʃn]
5 female ['fiːmeɪl] *weiblich* 6 ditto ['dɪtəʊ] *dito, ebenso* 7 celebs *(kurz für* celebrities) [sə'lebz] *Promis, Prominente*
8 mainly *hauptsächlich, vorwiegend* 9 (to) confirm [kən'fɜːm] *bestätigen* 10 (to) ignore [ɪg'nɔː] *ignorieren*

2 Cate Blanchett wants to be my friend on Facebook (a short play by Alex Broun)

Characters

Barry — worker on a building site[1]
Morris — Barry's boss
Sarah — office worker on building site
Cate Blanchett — film star

Time Morning. Working day.
Setting[2] Building site office.

Barry sits at a desk working on a computer. Morris enters.

Morris — Morning Barry.
Barry — Morris.
Morris — Are you going to start pouring that cement[3] this morning?
Barry — First thing. I'm just checking my Facebook.
Morris — Don't be too long.
Barry — I won't.

Morris looks through some folders[4].

Morris — Have you seen that bill from the cement company ?
Barry — In the folder.

Morris continues to look.

Barry — Do you know someone called *(reading)* Cate ... Blatchett?
Morris — Who?
Barry — Cate Blatchett?
Morris — Don't think so. Why?
Barry — She wants to be my friend on Facebook.

Morris stops looking in folder. Thinks. Beat[5].

Morris — How do you spell the last name?
Barry — B – l – a – n – c – h – e – t – t.

Morris thinks. Beat.

Morris — I think you'll find that's Blanchett.
Barry — Yeah.
Morris — (coming over to screen) B – l – a – n – c – h – e – t – t. Blanchett.
Barry — Right. Do you know her then?

Beat.

Morris — No, I don't think so. *(He goes back to folder.)* Are you sure that bill is in here?
Barry — Yeah. It says here she won an Oscar.
Morris — What for?
Barry — *The Aviator.* Best Supporting Actress.
Morris — Well that's clearly bullshit[6].
Barry — You think so?
Morris — Of course. If you've won an Oscar, you don't talk about it on Facebook, do you? You let people work it out for themselves.
Barry — True.
Morris — It's probably someone who just wants to be famous. Just ignore her.
Barry — But then she'll know, won't she?
Morris — No mate. That's the good thing about Facebook. People don't know when you ignore them.
Barry — But she'll see I'm not in her friend list.
Morris — It'll be some time before she works that out. How many friends has she got?
Barry — Three.
Morris — Maybe it won't be so long then. Are you sure that bill is in here?
Barry — Unless[7] Sarah has paid it already.
Morris — Is she here yet?
Barry — She's getting coffee.
Morris — Come and get me when she gets back. *(leaving)* And Baz, I really need you to start pouring that cement.
Barry — I'm on my way.

---

[1] building site *Baustelle* [2] setting ['setɪŋ] *Schauplatz, Handlungsrahmen* [3] (to) pour cement [ˌpɔː sɪ'ment] *Zement gießen*
[4] folder ['fəʊldə] *Mappe, Ordner* [5] beat *kurze Pause* [6] bullshit ['bʊlʃɪt] *(infml, vulgär) Bockmist, Schwachsinn* [7] unless [ən'les] *es sei denn*

Morris exits[1].

Barry — Confirm – ignore – confirm – ignore.

Sarah enters with coffees.

Sarah — *(passing one to Barry)* Here you go.

Barry — Thanks.

Sarah — There's a woman at the front gate for you.

Barry — Who?

Sarah — She says her name's Kate Blatchett.

Barry — Cate Blanchett?

Sarah — I'm pretty sure it was Blatchett.

Barry — What did she look like?

Sarah — Plain[2]. With a big hat. I'm not sure why. There's no sun out there.

Barry — Could she be 'beautiful in certain[3] lighting conditions[4]'?

Sarah — Maybe. Why?

Barry — *(pointing to computer)* That's what it says here, under 'About Me.' 'Beautiful in certain lighting conditions.'

Sarah — Is that her? Good picture.

Barry — She doesn't look like that?

Sarah — No way!

Barry — She wants to be my friend on Facebook.

Sarah — Yeah? What did you say?

Barry — I haven't decided yet.

Sarah — What's she doing here?

Barry — I don't know.

Sarah — Maybe she's stalking[5] you.

Barry — Yeah, right. Morris wants to know where that bill is for the cement.

Sarah — Under the folder.

Barry — Under? I said in.

Sarah — The paid ones are in. The unpaid ones are under. I told him that years ago.

Barry — Sorry. I didn't know. Hey, what do I do about Cate Blatchett?

Sarah — Wasn't it Blanchett?

Sarah exits. Barry looks at the screen again.

Barry — Confirm – ignore – confirm – ignore? *(Beat)* Ignore.

Cate Blanchett enters, wearing dark glasses and a large hat.

Cate B. — Hi, I'm Cate Blanchett.

Barry — Not Blatchett?

Cate B. — No, Blanchett.

Barry — Nice to meet you. What are you doing here?

Cate B. — I needed to speak to you.

Barry — Right. Any particular reason?

Cate B. — Many reasons.

Barry — Right. How did you find me?

Cate B. — I have people.

Barry — People?

Cate B. — Who do things for me.

Barry — What things?

Cate B. — Many and varied[6].

Barry — Great, but you're not actually allowed on the site.

Cate B. — Of course. I'll be on my way soon. But first, I'm wondering why you haven't answered my friend request?

Barry — I have answered.

Cate B. — Confirm or ignore?

Barry — *(Beat)* Confirm.

Cate B. — Let me check.

Barry — *(blocking computer)* You can't.

Cate B. — Why not?

Barry — It's a work computer. No personal surfing allowed.

Cate B. — *(looking at computer)* But I can see your Facebook profile.

Barry — I was just checking it quickly before the boss came in. But he's here now.

Cate B. — Is he?

Barry — Yes, he'll be back in a minute.

Beat.

Cate B. — So you definitely added me as a friend?

Barry — Yep.

Beat.

Cate B. — *(suddenly)* You're lying[7]!

Barry — No I'm not.

Cate B. — Yes. You are!

Barry — All right. I am. I ignored your request.

Cate B. — But why?

Barry — Does it matter now[8]?

Cate B. — Yes, it does.

Barry — I don't want to make it worse for you.

---

[1] (to) exit ['eksɪt] *abgehen, hinausgehen* [2] plain [pleɪn] *unscheinbar* [3] certain ['sɜːtn] *gewisse(r, s), bestimmte(r, s)* [4] lighting conditions ['laɪtɪŋ kən,dɪʃnz] *Lichtverhältnisse* [5] (to) stalk sb. [stɔːk] *jm. (belästigend) nachstellen* [6] varied ['veərid] *verschiedenartige(r, s)* [7] (to) lie [laɪ] *(-ing form:* lying*) lügen* [8] Does it matter? *Spielt das eine Rolle?*

Cate B. Please, Barry. If I understand why you ignored me it will help me with the pain. And help me get more 'confirms' in the future.

Beat.

Barry All right. *(Beat)* Are you sure you want to hear this?

Cate B. Go on, Barry. I can take it.

Barry Well ...

Cate B. Say it, Barry. Say it.

Barry You're an actor.

Cate B. So?

Barry Well, it's not really a very honourable profession[1].

Cate B. Isn't it?

Barry No.

Beat.

Cate B. I see. Why isn't acting an honourable profession?

Barry Well, you're kind of famous.

Cate B. Kind of? I'm ...

Barry But you don't really do anything. You're like one of those people.

Cate B. Which people?

Barry You know like Paris what's-her-name? Famous for being famous.

Cate B. That's not true.

Beat.

Barry Well actually it is.

Cate B. But I won an Oscar.

Barry Actually there's a few questions about that.

Cate B. A Golden Globe.

Barry Who hasn't?

Cate B. I won the Volpi Cup at the Venice[2] Film Festival.

Barry See, now you're just making that up[3].

Cate B. I played Galadriel in *Lord of the Rings* 1, 2 and 3.

Barry You shouldn't be telling people that.

Cate B. *Return of the King* and *Two Towers* are two of the Top Ten moneymaking movies of all time.

Barry That doesn't make them good.

Cate B. Many people have congratulated me on my role as the Elf Queen.

Barry Were any of them not members of your family?

Cate B. You didn't like it?

Barry You got the character wrong – really wrong.

Barry shakes his head sadly.

Cate B. And your profession is honourable?

Barry Now you're just being nasty[4]. And you know it.

Cate B. Sorry.

Barry That was cheap, Cate. We build. Houses for people to live in, places of work, schools, hospitals. We make things that exist in the real world. While you create –

Cate B. Fantasy?

Barry nods again sadly.

Cate B. I entertain[5]. I give those little people, out there in the dark, an escape. From their hard daily lives.

Barry At best, it gives them a few moments of pleasure[6]. At worse, it reminds them of their hard lives.

Beat.

Cate B. I'm a mother. I've raised[7] three children.

Barry There's something to be proud of.

Cate B. Then will you accept my friend request?

Barry I would if you'd put that in Facebook.

Cate B. What does it say?

Barry 'Actor. Oscar, Elf Queen.'

Cate B. I just forgot to put mother in.

Barry You forgot being a mother? I'm not sure I really want to be friends with someone who puts being an 'actor' over being a 'mother'.

Cate B. But I don't.

Barry Cate ...

Barry shakes his head again, sadly.

Cate B. But I didn't write it. One of my people did.

Barry Do you know what they say about bad builders?

Cate B. No. What do they say?

Barry Bad builders blame their tools.

Beat.

---

[1] an honourable profession [ˌɒnərəbl prəˈfeʃən] *ein ehrenwerter Beruf* [2] Venice [ˈvenɪs] *Venedig* [3] (to) make sth. up *sich etwas ausdenken* [4] nasty [ˈnɑːsti] *gemein* [5] (to) entertain [ˌentəˈteɪn] *unterhalten, zerstreuen* [6] pleasure [ˈpleʒə] *Vergnügen, Freude* [7] (to) raise children [reɪz] *Kinder großziehen, aufziehen*

Cate B. — You're not going to confirm me as a friend, are you?

Barry shakes his head.

Cate B. — Maybe if you got to know me a bit better.

Barry — I'm careful about who I accept as a friend.

Cate B. — You could come over for dinner? Andrew will cook.

Barry — I don't think it will work now.

Cate B. — Have you seen *Notes on a Scandal*? I can be pretty hot stuff.

Barry — You see, now that's just sad.

Beat.

Cate B. — *(dropping to her knees, begging*[1]*)* Barry, please!

Morris — *(entering)* I still can't find ... *(He sees Cate Blanchett kneeling in front of Barry.)*

Morris — Everything all right?

Barry — Good thanks, Morris.

Beat.

Morris — Are you getting on to that cement?

Barry — I'm just on my way.

Sarah — *(entering)*Morris, the bill is under, not ... *(She also sees Cate Blanchett kneeling in front of Barry.)*

Beat.

Sarah — In.

Beat. Cate Blanchett stands.

Barry — Morris. Sarah. This is Cate Blatchett.

Cate B. — Blanchett.

Morris — Nice to meet you.

Sarah gives a little wave.

Cate B. — Morris. Such a nice name. Strong. And Sarah. So ... pretty.

Morris — As Barry knows, we have a rule about visitors on site.

Barry — I didn't invite her. *(Beat, looking at Cate Blanchett)* Well, I didn't. *(to Morris)* She wants to know why I ignored her friend request on Facebook.

Morris — *(to Cate Blanchett)* Whatever the reason we've got a busy morning. So if you wouldn't mind ...

Morris points at the door.

Cate B. — Of course. Well Barry, see you around. Online.

Barry — No you won't. Remember – 'ignore.'

Cate B. — Maybe you'll change your mind[2]. In a month or two?

Barry — Not likely.

Cate B. — A year? Five years?

Morris — *(moving Cate Blanchett towards the door)* We're really busy this morning.

Cate B. — *(to Morris)* Would you like to be my friend?

Morris — Sorry. I've got too many already.

Cate B. — *(to Sarah)* Sarah?

Sarah — *(shaking head)* Sorry.

Barry — *(to Cate Blanchett)* You're acting desperate[3] now.

Cate B. — Is that a big turn-off[4]?

Sarah, Barry and Morris nod their heads.

Cate B. — Right, well ...

Morris — Straight down the path and back through the gate.

Cate B. — Morris, Sarah, Bazza.

Barry — It's Barry.

Cate B. — Of course. Good bye.

Cate Blanchett exits.

Barry — I thought she'd never leave.

Sarah — Sad.

Barry — Very.

Morris looks at Barry.

Barry — What? I didn't invite her.

Morris moves to the folder.

Morris — Have a word to Neil at the gate. No visitors. And cement pouring – now.

Barry — I'm on it.

Morris — That'd be good.

Barry exits.

Morris — Facebook. More trouble than it's worth. *(to Sarah)* Now, where's that bill?

End play.

---

[1] (to) beg (-gg-) *bitten, betteln* [2] (to) change one's mind [maɪnd] *seine Meinung ändern* [3] desperate ['despərət] *verzweifelt*
[4] (to) be a turn-off ['tɜːn_ɒf] *(infml) abstoßend wirken, abtörnend sein*

3 The plot

a) *Read the questions on lines 1–157 of the play. Choose a, b or c. Give reasons for your choice.*

1. At the start of the play Barry
   - A is checking his emails.
   - B is surfing the internet.
   - C is checking his Facebook.
2. Morris wants Barry
   - A to start pouring cement.
   - B to look for a bill.
   - C to look for information about Cate Blanchett.
3. Morris advises Barry
   - A to confirm Cate Blanchett as a friend.
   - B to find out more about her first.
   - C to ignore her.
4. Barry tells Morris that Cate Blanchett
   - A already knows him.
   - B hasn't got many people on her friend list.
   - C has got lots of people on her friend list.
5. Just before Cate arrives, Barry decides to
   - A confirm her friend request.
   - B ignore her friend request.
   - C think a little longer about what to do.
6. When Cate asks Barry if he has confirmed or ignored her, Barry
   - A tells the truth immediately.
   - B first tells a lie, then tells the truth.
   - C first tells the truth, then tells a lie.

b) *Look at lines 158–214. What is the main question that Cate and Barry are discussing? Who uses the following arguments?*
- Honourable people don't become actors.
- Cate is very famous.
- Cate has won important awards.
- Cate has played in films that have made lots of money.
- Cate wasn't very good in the role of Elf Queen.

What can you say now about Barry's attitude to Cate?

c) *Look at the rest of the discussion between Cate and Barry in lines 215–274. Answer the following questions.*
1. Why do Cate and Barry think that their jobs are useful?
2. How does Barry react when Cate says that she's a mother?
3. Why do you think Barry says 'You see, now that's just sad.' (l. 268)

d) *Look at lines 279–341. Why does Barry say to Cate: 'You're acting desperate now?' What do Sarah and Morris think of Cate?*

e) *Write a short magazine advertisement for the play. Explain enough about the plot to get people interested, but don't give away too much.*

4 Friends online and friends for real

a) *Is Barry's attitude to Cate fair? Is the plot realistic? Why (not)? Discuss in small groups.*
- I think Barry is friendly/unfriendly/cruel ...
- He was right/wrong to ignore her because ...
- I found the whole play realistic/unrealistic because ...
- ...

b) *Imagine a famous star sent you a friend request. What reasons might you have for confirming or ignoring it? Make notes and compare your ideas with a partner.*

c) *How many of your online friends are friends in real life too? Is there a difference when you only know someone online? Discuss.*
- None[1]/some/most of my online friends are friends in real life too.
- The difference between my real and online friends is ...
- It makes/doesn't make a difference if you've met someone in real life.
- You behave the same/differently to someone you haven't met in real life.
- ...

[1] none [nʌn] *keine(r, s)*

TF 3 The Meatrix

1 The Matrix

Read the summary of the plot of The Matrix. *Make notes under the headings in the box.*

Characters • Pills • Dream world • Real world

Neo has a feeling that somehow something isn't right in the world. Morpheus offers Neo two pills. With the red pill he will find out the truth[1]. With the blue pill his life will continue as before. Neo takes the red pill and he realizes[2] that he is living in a dream world called the Matrix. The Matrix was created by intelligent machines to control humans because they need them to provide[3] energy. The humans think that their lives are continuing as normal, but this is an illusion. In the real world they are just batteries for the machines.

2 The Meatrix

a) *Compare the* Meatrix *poster with the* Matrix *poster. What might* The Meatrix *be about?*

b) *Partner A: Watch the cartoon, but cover[4] your ears so that you can't hear the sound. Partner B: Listen, but don't look at the screen. When the cartoon ends, discuss these questions: Who are the two main characters? Where is the story set at first? Where is it set later?*

c) *Which of these statements are wrong? Correct them.*

1. At first Leo, the pig, thinks he is living on a family farm.
2. Leo tells Moopheus about the Meatrix.
3. Leo doesn't want to find out the truth about the Meatrix.
4. Leo realizes he's living on a factory farm.
5. Moopheus describes what is bad about factory farming.
6. Leo doesn't want to help stop the Meatrix.

d) *Watch the film again (with pictures and sound) and check your answers. What is the Meatrix?*

3 The message

a) *What is the main message of the cartoon?*

b) *How does* The Meatrix *use* The Matrix *to get this message across[5]? (Think about the titles, the plots and the characters of both films.)*

c) *What do you think of the cartoon?*

[1] truth [truːθ] *Wahrheit* [2] (to) realize [ˈriːəlaɪz] *erkennen* [3] (to) provide [prəˈvaɪd] *liefern* [4] (to) cover one's ears *sich die Ohren zuhalten*
[5] (to) get a message across *eine Botschaft rüberbringen*

TF 4 Uniting Europe

1 AIRBUS – a European dream?

Over the last 40 years, Airbus, a truly[1] European company, has become one of the world's two largest aircraft[2] producers.

It all started with a group of European aircraft companies in 1969. These companies – from France, Germany, Spain and the United Kingdom – had enough good ideas, but still did not build many planes. On their own, they were too small to compete with a huge American producer like Boeing. So they came together and founded Airbus.

Would it be possible for companies from four different countries to work together successfully? Roger Béteille, one of Airbus's founding fathers, was worried that national interests would make it difficult. But in the end all the partners agreed, firstly, to produce different parts at sites[3] in each country and, secondly, to use just one assembly line[4] and test flight centre in Toulouse, France.
This meant that Airbus had to develop[5] a transport system to move large aircraft parts from all over Europe to Toulouse, by road and sea and also with huge cargo planes[6] called Belugas. Today, 15 sites in France, Germany, Spain and the UK produce parts which are then transported to the Airbus assembly lines – there are three today – in Toulouse and Hamburg also and in Tianjin, Northern China.

Starting with the A300 in the 1970s, Airbus has always produced aircraft that use little fuel and are quiet and cheap to run[7]. Today the company produces a range[8] of eco-efficient planes with seats[9] for between 107 and 525 passengers.

The A380 can carry up to 525 passengers.

The A380 transport system

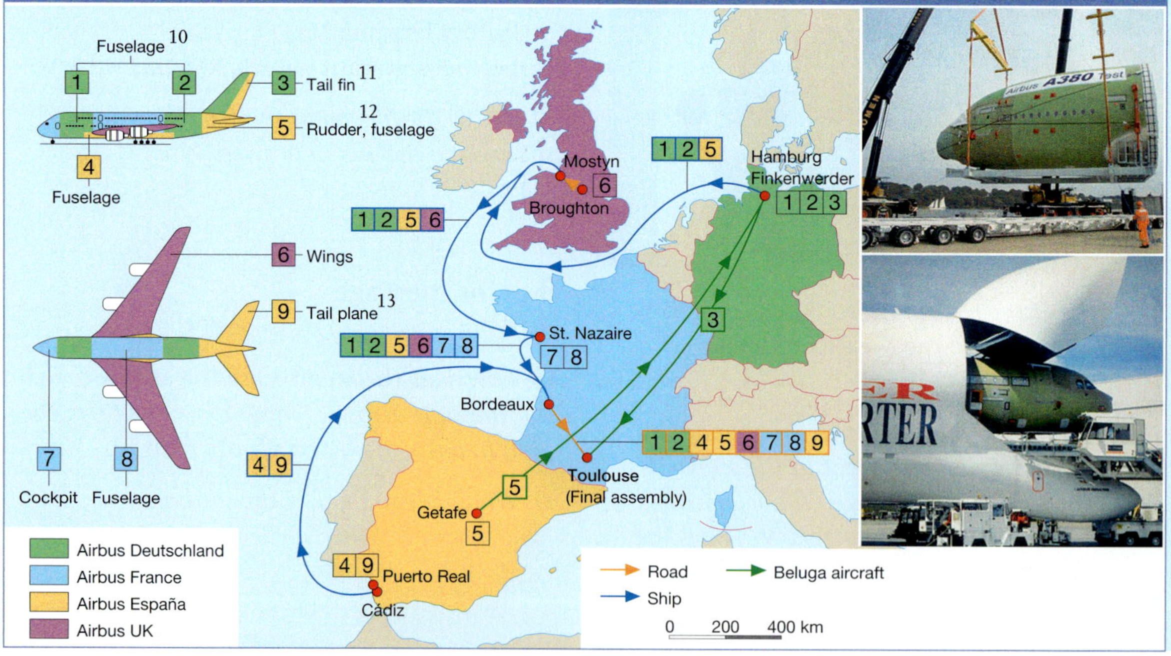

[1] truly ['tru:li] *wahrhaft* [2] aircraft ['eəkrɑ:ft] *Flugzeug* [3] site *Standort* [4] assembly line [ə'sembli laɪn] *Montagestraße* [5] (to) develop [dɪ'veləp] *entwickeln; aufbauen* [6] cargo plane ['kɑ:gəʊ pleɪn] *Frachtflugzeug* [7] (to) run *betreiben* [8] range [reɪndʒ] *Sortiment, Reihe* [9] seat [si:t] *Sitz(platz)* [10] fuselage ['fju:zəlɑ:ʒ] *Flugzeugrumpf* [11] tail fin ['teɪlfɪn] *Heckruder* [12] rudder ['rʌdə] *Seitenruder* [13] tail plane ['teɪlpleɪn] *Leitwerk*

So is Airbus a perfect model of European cooperation? When things are going well, it seems so. But there are problems too. For example, the fact that production sites in different countries used different computer software was one reason behind big delays[1] in delivering[2] the A380 to the company's customers. These delays have caused a fall in profits[3], so that since 2007 production sites have been sold off and thousands of jobs lost. When Airbus has to decide where to cut jobs, it is then that national governments disagree, and national interests begin to play at least as big a role as the idea of European cooperation.

Sam – Apprentice

'I joined Airbus as an apprentice after secondary school. I took part in an intercultural awareness[4] programme, working with British, French and German apprentices. It was a most enjoyable experience, from which I learned a lot and made a number of great friends from all three countries. I feel very lucky to have this apprenticeship. I would like to continue along the Airbus career path as far as I can, and later look for a chance to work in another country.'

a) *Read about Airbus and then try to answer these questions.*

1 What are the advantages for European countries of building planes together?

2 When does European cooperation become difficult for Airbus?

3 Why does Sam enjoy being an apprentice at Airbus?

b) *Look at the map on p. 122. With the help of the skills and language boxes say*

– what kind of map it is
– what is produced in each country and how it gets to Toulouse.

c) *Do you agree or disagree with the following?*

It would be a better idea if Airbus planes were all made in one place.

Make notes on your reasons and use them to discuss the question in class. You could think about:

European cooperation • transport problems • the environment • jobs in your country • competition with American companies • ...

► *SF Having a discussion (p. 148)*

GEOGRAPHY SKILLS **Talking about maps**

When you talk about maps,
– look at the title and the key[5] and make sure you understand what the map is about.
– start with a general statement about the map, then talk about the details.

Activate your English

– This is a physical[6]/political/thematic map.
– The map shows ...
– (Broughton) is situated[7] in/near/ ...
– ... is about ... km away from ...
– ... is between ... and ...
– The wings/... are produced/made/... in ...
– They are transported/flown from ... to ...
– They are transported by road/ship/air/cargo plane/...
– The aircraft parts are put together in ...

[1] delay [dɪ'leɪ] *Verzögerung; Verzug* [2] (to) deliver [dɪ'lɪvə] *liefern, ausliefern* [3] fall in profits ['prɒfɪts] *Rückgang der Gewinne* [4] intercultural awareness [ˌɪntəkʌltʃərəl_ə'weənəs] *interkulturelles Bewusstsein* [5] key *Legende* [6] physical ['fɪzɪkl] *physisch* [7] (to) be situated ['sɪtʃueɪtɪd] *liegen, gelegen sein*

2 Young people and the European Union

On p. 123, Sam talks about how cooperation across borders in the European Union (EU) was an advantage for him.

a) *What does the EU mean to you personally? Think about the question for a minute and write down your answers. Then collect all the answers in class.*

b) *Read the skills box on the right. Then describe the chart below. Say*
- what kind of chart it is
- what the chart is about
- what the source and date are
- what you have learned from the chart.

GEOGRAPHY SKILLS **Interpreting charts**

- Charts and graphs[1] contain statistics[2] on a specific topic. The topic and the source and date of the statistics are usually given at the top or bottom.
- The statistics can refer to a situation at a specific time or to changes over a longer period[3].
- The statistics can be presented in different forms: bar chart, pie chart or line graph.
- Be sure you know what the numbers in a chart are: ordinary[4] numbers, percentages, etc.

▸ *SF Talking about charts (p. 139)*

YOUNG PEOPLE AND EUROPE
What the European Union means for Europeans aged 15–30

I can travel, study and work anywhere[5].	90%
My rights are protected.	72%
It's good for the economy[6].	71%
It's good that there's a European government.	56%
Too many complicated rules. / It's a waste of time and money.	40%
Cultures mix too much.	35%

Source: The Gallup Organization / The European Commission (February 2007)

c) *Make a survey for your class:*
- *Copy the statements from the chart.*
- *Decide which statements express how you feel about Europe. Put a tick (✓) beside them.*
- *Collect all results and make a class bar chart.*
- *Compare your class results with the chart above.*

Activate your English
- This group's results are similar to/different from ...
- The most important issue for us/them is ...
- I find their results very interesting/strange/hard to believe/...

[1] graph [græf], [grɑːf] *Diagramm, Graph* [2] statistics [stəˈtɪstɪks] *(pl) Statistik(en)* [3] period [ˈpɪəriəd] *Zeitspanne, Zeitraum* [4] ordinary [ˈɔːdnri] *normal, gewöhnlich* [5] anywhere *hier: überall* [6] economy [ɪˈkɒnəmi] *Wirtschaft*

TF 5 If only Papa hadn't danced (by Patricia McCormick)

> *Look at the picture. Think about where the people are, who they could be, what their relationship is and what will happen next. Make some notes. Then discuss your ideas in a group.*

But who could blame him? When the results of the presidential election were tacked up on the polling station[1] doors, a lot of people danced and sang in the streets – none[2] of them more joyfully than Papa. Finally the Old Man had lost. The Old Man, who'd ruled[3] the country since Papa was a baby, had been beaten fair and square. The man who robbed[4] from the poor to make himself rich was finished.

But not everyone in the village danced that night. The rich men, the ones made fat by the Old Man, stood in the shadows and watched.

The next day, when Papa and his friends gathered around the radio, they heard that the election results had been a mistake. There would have to be a recount[5]. Papa spat in the dust and said it was a lie. A week passed, then another – while the Old Man stayed in his grand house in the capital. While his men were supposedly[6] counting the ballots[7] again. Papa and his friends grumbled among themselves, but not loud enough for anyone else to hear.

Then one night we awoke to the hot breath[8] of fire. The corn patch[9] just outside our hut was ablaze[10]. We jumped from our beds and ran to the field to beat down the flames with branches[11]. But it was no good. Our entire crop[12] was gone.

At dawn Papa sought out[13] the police. They came to our home, looked at our field with eyes of stone and told us to empty the house of all we owned.

'Take what you can,' one of the policemen said. 'They will be back tonight. This time they will torch[14] your house.'

'They?' I asked Papa when the policemen had left. 'Who are they?' Papa sighed and shook his head. 'Our neighbours and tribesmen,' he said. 'People we have known our whole lives. People whose bellies[15] have been filled by the Old Man.'

Mama clucked her tongue at Papa. 'Everyone saw you celebrating,' she said. 'They know you voted against the Old Man and now we will pay for it.' She looked out and saw the smouldering[16] remains[17] of our neighbours' fields.

The crops of those who'd danced with Papa were in ashes. The others were as lush and green as they'd been the day before.

And so we packed our things – the few we had, the fewer we could carry – into a few

---

[1] polling station ['pəʊlɪŋ steɪʃn] *Wahllokal* [2] none [nʌn] *keine(r, s)* [3] (to) rule *beherrschen; herrschen* [4] (to) rob (-bb-) [rɒb] *rauben* [5] recount ['ri:kaʊnt] *Nachzählung* [6] supposedly [sə'pəʊzɪdli] *angeblich* [7] ballot ['bælət] *Stimme, Stimmzettel* [8] breath [breθ] *Atem* [9] patch [pætʃ] *(kleines) Feld, Beet* [10] ablaze [ə'bleɪz] *in Flammen* [11] branch [brɑ:ntʃ] *Zweig* [12] crop [krɒp] *Ernte* [13] (to) seek sb. out, sought, sought [si:k, sɔ:t] *an jn. herantreten* [14] (to) torch [tɔ:tʃ] *anzünden* [15] belly *Bauch* [16] smouldering ['sməʊldərɪŋ] *schwelend* [17] remains [rɪ'meɪnz] *Überreste*

bundles and an old cardboard suitcase. I put my bundle on my head, took one last look at our home, then turned to face our future.

'Where will we go?' I asked Papa.

'We will walk until we find a friendly place where we can stay,' he said. 'When it is safe, when the recount is finished, when the rightful president takes office[1], then we will return home.'

As we came to the centre of the village, we met up with other families like ours. The fathers hung their heads, the mothers looked only at the dirt beneath their feet and the children tugged[2] listlessly at their parents' hands. 'Why?' they asked. 'Why must we leave home?' The parents did not dare[3] to answer – in case[4] 'they' were listening.

The world beyond the village was new and strange – a vast plain[5] of parched[6] grass and shimmering heat. We walked by night, through bushes alive with the sounds of frenzied insects, and slept by day under the scanty shade of the acacia tree. We walked and walked and walked.

At last we came upon a settlement. From a distance it bloomed up from the earth like a flower. We saw, shimmering on the horizon, what we thought was our safe place, the place where we would rest[7] until we could go home. But as we drew[8] near, we saw that the village looked just like ours. One house was nothing but a smouldering heap[9], the one next door untouched.

And so we walked on and on, each village the same.

We gathered news as we walked. 'The Old Man is still in power,' said people who joined our dusty procession. 'He won't give up without a fight,' they added.

I asked Papa about the man who had won the election. 'He won't give up without a fight either,' Papa told me. The next day on the radio we heard that he had fled the country.

That night, there was just one tiny strip[10] of dried meat left[11]. Mama cut it three ways and handed each of us a piece. Papa shook his head.

'Give mine to the child,' he said. 'I'm a tough old bird. I can make do.'

The next morning, when we awoke, we found corn to eat. Corn and biscuits and a bit of fruit. But Papa wouldn't touch a thing. He turned away and whispered to Mama, 'I was a fool to hope for change. And now I am a thief. Now I'm no better than the Old Man.'

In the afternoon we came upon a great river. Wide and sluggish[12], it looked as hot and steamy as we were. I knew from my studies that we had come to the edge[13] of our country. On the other side of the river was a free country, a land of cities and farms, a nation where the people had voted for a president who had spent years in jail fighting for justice.

Mama knelt[14] in the shallows and splashed water on her face. But as I knelt down next to her, I saw that she was trying to cover her tears.

'This is our homeland,' she said. 'No one wants us over there.' She gestured to the tawny hills across the river.

It was then that I saw the long metal fence which uncoiled, like a snake, all along the riverbank[15] on the other side. The fence was tall and crowned with rings of wire[16]: wire with teeth that could slice[17] the clothes from your back, the skin from your bones. In the distance I saw a man in an orange jumpsuit patching[18] a hole at the bottom of the fence – a spot where some lucky person must have slipped through the night before. His tools were at his feet, a pistol in his belt[19].

Papa came over and said I was needed. There was a sign, he said, that he needed me to read. He brought me to a spot where someone had hand-painted a warning: *Beware[20] of crocodiles.*

That night, we hid in the bushes until the sky was black. We would wade across at midnight, when the man in the orange jumpsuit had gone home and when the

---

[1] (to) take office *sein Amt antreten* [2] (to) tug (-gg-) [tʌg] *ziehen* [3] (to) dare *(es) wagen, sich trauen* [4] in case *für den Fall, dass*
[5] plain [pleɪn] *Ebene* [6] parched [pɑːtʃt] *ausgetrocknet, verdorrt* [7] (to) rest *ausruhen* [8] (to) draw near, drew, drawn *näherkommen*
[9] heap [hiːp] *Haufen* [10] a tiny strip ['taɪni] *ein winziger Streifen* [11] (to) be left *übrig sein* [12] sluggish ['slʌgɪʃ] *träge* [13] edge [edʒ] *Rand, Kante*
[14] (to) kneel, knelt, knelt [niːl, nelt] *(sich hin)knien* [15] riverbank *Flussufer* [16] wire ['waɪə] *Draht* [17] (to) slice [slaɪs] *schneiden*
[18] (to) patch [pætʃ] *flicken* [19] belt [belt] *Gürtel* [20] beware of ... [bɪ'weə] *Vorsicht vor ...*

crocodiles, we hoped, would be sound asleep.

When it was time to go, I walked straight towards the river, knowing my nerve would fail if I faltered[1] for even a moment. But Papa stopped me at the water's edge.

'Wait here,' he said. And then he scooped Mama up into his arms and waded silently into the darkness.

It seemed a lifetime until he returned. He didn't say a word, just lifted me up onto his shoulders and strode into the water. Every stick[2] I saw was a crocodile. Under every rock, every ripple[3] in the water, was a pair of ferocious jaws[4]. When we reached the other side, I leapt from his shoulders and kissed the sand.

Once more Papa stepped into the river – this time to fetch our suitcase. Surely our luck wouldn't hold again ... I watched his back disappear into the dark and thought how much I loved that broad back; how it shouldered all our woes[5], and now all our hopes. Finally Papa emerged[6] from the darkness with all our worldly possessions[7] balanced on his head.

Then we got down on our hands and knees and crawled along the base of the fence, like scorpions looking for a place to dig[8]. But the sand was unyielding and the fence invincible[9]. Everywhere our fingers scrabbled for[10] a weakness, someone – the man in the orange jumpsuit most likely – had mended[11] it with links of chain[12] held tight with wire.

The sky overhead had begun to brighten and the horizon was edged with pink. Soon it would be light[13] and we'd be trapped between the waking crocodiles and the man with the gun in his belt.

We came to a spot in the fence where a thorn bush grew on the other side. Papa said we would have to dig here: no time to keep looking. Perhaps the roots[14] of the bush had loosened the sand, he said. If not, at least we could hide behind the bush, if only for a while.

And so all three of us dug – Mama in the middle and Papa and I on either side – our hands clawing furiously at the earth. I'd only made a few inches of progress[15] when the sky turned red. It would be dawn in less than an hour. I redoubled my effort[16], working the outer edge of the bush where the soil[17] was a bit looser. Soon I'd dug a hole barely big enough for a man's foot. I lifted my head to call out to Papa to come and see my work – and saw the man in the orange jumpsuit striding towards us.

Mama wailed[18] piteously, then plucked at her hem where she'd hidden the tiny bit of money we had. She knelt in the sand, her arms outstretched, our few coins in her upturned palms[19].

But the man shook his head. He placed his hand on the belt that held his gun.

'Take me,' Papa begged him. 'Spare[20] the woman and the girl.'

Again the man shook his head. Then he reached into his pocket and took out a giant cutting tool. With one mighty snap he severed[21] the links where the fence had been patched. He yanked[22] on the fence so hard it cried out in protest, and peeled it back as if it were made of cloth.

'Hurry,' he said. 'Once the light comes, I will have to go back to patrolling.'

We didn't fully comprehend[23] what he was saying, but we didn't wait.

'You go first,' Papa said to me. 'I want you to be the first in our family to taste[24] freedom.'

I scrambled through the fence, stood next to the man in the orange jumpsuit and looked back at our homeland as the sun began to turn its fields to gold.

'You will miss it for a long time,' the man said to me. 'I still do.'

I stared up at him.

'Yes,' he said. 'I outran[25] the Old Man long ago.'

Mama crawled through and kissed the man's

---

[1] (to) falter ['fɔːltə] *zögern, zaudern* [2] stick *Stock* [3] ripple ['rɪpl] *Kräuseln, kleine Welle* [4] ferocious jaws [fəˌrəʊʃəs 'dʒɔːz] *furchteinflößende Kiefer* [5] woes [wəʊz] *(pl) Sorgen* [6] (to) emerge from [i'mɜːdʒ] *auftauchen aus, hervortreten aus* [7] possessions [pə'zeʃnz] *(pl) Besitz(tümer), Habe* [8] (to) dig, dug, dug [dɪg, dʌg] *graben* [9] invincible [ɪn'vɪnsəbl] *unbesiegbar* [10] Everywhere our fingers scrabbled for ... *Überall, wo unsere Finger nach ... suchten/wühlten* [11] (to) mend *reparieren* [12] chain [tʃeɪn] *Kette* [13] light *hell* [14] root [ruːt] *Wurzel* [15] progress ['prəʊgres] *Fortschritt(e)* [16] effort ['efət] *Bemühungen* [17] soil [sɔɪl] *Erde* [18] (to) wail [weɪl] *jammern, heulen* [19] palm [pɑːm] *Handfläche* [20] (to) spare [speə] *verschonen* [21] (to) sever ['sevə] *durchtrennen* [22] (to) yank [jæŋk] *reißen, ziehen* [23] (to) comprehend [ˌkɒmprɪ'hend] *verstehen* [24] (to) taste [teɪst] *schmecken, kosten* [25] (to) outrun sb. *jm. davonlaufen*

boots. He simply helped her to her feet.

'Quickly now,' he said, once Papa had made it through. 'Walk, as fast as you can, until you see a house with white flowers out front. Go round to the back and tell them Robert sent you. They will feed you and hide you until night. Then they will send you to the next safe house, which will send you to the next, and the next – until finally you are in the city and can be swallowed up[1] by all the people there.'

'How do we know we can trust these people?' Mama asked.

'They are our countrymen,' he said. 'You will find many of us here. Now go!'

We did as he instructed, and found the house with the white flowers just as the morning sun broke through the clouds. A woman there brought us inside, gave us water and meat and led us to mats where we could rest. It had been so long since I'd slept on anything other than bare, open ground that I fell asleep at once.

I awoke sometime later and saw that Papa's mat was empty. I stood and wandered outside. The sun was setting, so all I could see was his silhouette against the deepening sky. He raised his arms to the heavens and started to hum[2]. And then I saw Papa dance.

Working with the text

1 Your impressions[3]

Think back to your discussion on the picture on page 125. How close were your ideas to what happened in the story?

2 The plot[4]

Use the key words in the boxes to write down the plot of the short story If only Papa hadn't danced.

The narrator's[5] father dances when he hears that the Old Man has lost the election. ...

narrator's father • dance • Old Man • lose election ▶	Old Man • rule country • long time ▶	next day • recount • one night • family's fields • burn ▶	police • tell family • house will burn • next night
same thing • happen • everyone • vote against Old Man ▶	so • family • pack up their things • leave home ▶	family • walk across country • night • sleep • day ▶	one afternoon • come to • wide river • edge of their country
other side • a free country • but also • metal fence ▶	crocodiles • in river • but family decide • cross river at night ▶	father • carry wife/daughter/ possessions across ▶	then • family try to • dig hole under fence • before light
but • man in orange jumpsuit • repair fence • pistol ▶	family think • man • arrest[6] them • but • man • cut fence ▶	he • also from their country • send them • safe house ▶	that evening • narrator • see father • dance again

STUDY SKILLS Reading fiction[7] (1)

Setting[8] and plot

The **setting** of a story is the place and time it happens: the Australian outback in the 1950s, Africa today, a fantasy world in the future ...

The **plot** is the action and events that take place in a story. These events often happen because one event causes another. Stories also often use flashbacks[9] in their plots.'

▸ *SF Reading literature (pp. 145–146)*

[1] (to) be swallowed up [ˌswɒləʊd‿'ʌp] *verschluckt werden* [2] (to) hum (-mm-) [hʌm] *summen* [3] impression [ɪm'preʃn] *Eindruck*
[4] plot *Handlung* [5] narrator [nə'reɪtə] *Erzähler/in* [6] (to) arrest [ə'rest] *verhaften* [7] fiction ['fɪkʃn] *Erzählliteratur, Belletristik*
[8] setting ['setɪŋ] *Schauplatz, Handlungsrahmen* [9] flashback ['flæʃbæk] *Rückblende*

3 The characters

a) *Make a network with the characters' names:* **Old Man, narrator, Papa, Mama, man in jumpsuit.** *Add notes to show the links between them (e.g., father of, same homeland as, ...).*

b) *Choose a character from your network. Find parts of the text that tell you what kind of person he/she is. Collect information like this:*

Name	Characterization	Source
Papa	Papa spat in the dust and said it was a lie. ...	lines 17–18

c) *What conclusions can you draw from your chart? Say how you see the character you chose.*

d) *Use your chart to write a characterization.*

4 The atmosphere

a) *Without checking the text, finish this sentence:* The atmosphere in the story is ...

b) *Read the box on the right. Then find examples of how the writer creates atmosphere. Collect them in a chart like this:*

How	Example	Source
image	the hot breath of fire	lines 25–26
adjective	smouldering ...	...

c) *Compare and explain your charts.*
– 'Hot breath' makes you feel the fire is alive.
– 'Smouldering remains' gives you the feeling the family has lost everything.
– ...
Would you change your sentence from a)? Why (not)?

5 What do you think?

boring • depressing • exciting • interesting • moving[6] • sentimental • unbelievable • ...

a) *Which adjective(s) best describe the story?*

b) *Why did the narrator's father decide to leave the country with his family? Why do people leave their home country?*

STUDY SKILLS Reading fiction (2)

Characterization[1]

Writers can use words like *cruel*, *honest*, *prejudiced*, *sentimental*, etc. to tell us about the characters in a story.
Writers can also say indirectly what kind of person a character is, e. g. when they tell us what the character does, thinks or feels.
For example:

The purse was full of money. Enough to pay her bills. She picked it up and walked on.
'But it belongs to someone else,' a voice inside her whispered.
She stopped and turned slowly towards the police station. She knew she had to hand[2] it in.

In these lines, the writer tries to show us that the character is an honest person.

▸ SF Reading literature (pp. 145–146)

STUDY SKILLS Reading fiction (3)

Atmosphere

The **atmosphere** is the feeling that a writer creates in a story. It can be exciting, scary, romantic, sad etc.
To create atmosphere, a writer can work with

– images[3] (e. g. metaphors[4] or similes[5])
– adjectives (e. g. smouldering **remains**, parched **grass**)
– details of the plot (e. g.: 'The parents did not dare to answer – in case 'they' were listening.'

▸ SF Reading literature (pp. 145–146)

6 Different points of view

Write either lines 140–169 through the eyes of the father of the family or lines 197–231 through the eyes of the man in the orange jumpsuit.

▸ SF Reading literature (pp. 145–146)

You can put your text in your DOSSIER.

▸ SF Writing course (pp. 151–152)

[1] characterization [ˌkærəktəraɪ'zeɪʃn] *Charakterisierung* [2] (to) hand sth. in *etwas abgeben, einreichen* [3] image ['ɪmɪdʒ] *Bild*
[4] metaphor ['metəfə] *Metapher* [5] simile ['sɪməli] *Vergleich* [6] moving *bewegend*

TF 6 Two presidents

1 The US president

a) *Name the current president of the USA. Is there a picture of this president on the right?*

b) *Write down the names of the presidents on the right and of other US presidents you know. What else do you know about them?*

c) *What do you know about the job of the US president? Make notes and share your information in class.*

2 A social studies class

a) *Listen. Where is the class taking place? What is it about?*

b) *Copy the chart on the right. Then listen again and fill as many examples in the chart as you can.*

c) *Compare your chart with a partner and make corrections. Do the same in a group.*

What does the US president do?

Head of the government	Head of state
– The president runs ...	...

3 The president's busy life

Read the president's schedule. Find more examples of his roles as head of the government and head of state and add them to your chart.

THE WHITE HOUSE Office of the Press Secretary[1]

The President's Schedule for next week

- On Monday, the President will celebrate Father's Day. At an event in Washington, he will discuss the important role of fathers in building healthy families.
- On Tuesday, the President will discuss the political situation in the Middle East with the National Security Advisor and military advisors. Later the President will have lunch with the King of Norway. In the evening, the President will receive the women's national soccer team.
- On Wednesday, the President will meet senators[2] from both parties to discuss new laws on energy and climate. In the afternoon the President will travel to Michigan, where he will present the awards to the winners of this year's Young Scientist competition.
- On Thursday, the President will meet the Cabinet to discuss education reform. In the evening, the president will speak to the nation on television to announce new plans for dealing with[3] the economic crisis.
- On Friday, the President will travel to Banff, Canada, where he will take part in the G8 Summit[4]. In the afternoon, the President will meet the British Prime Minister to discuss political and economic cooperation between the United States and the United Kingdom. In the evening, the President will have a working dinner with G8 leaders.

[1] press secretary ['pres ˌsekrətri] *Pressesprecher/in* [2] senator ['senətə] *Senator/in* [3] (to) deal with, dealt, dealt [diːl, delt] *fertigwerden mit, umgehen mit* [4] summit ['sʌmɪt] *Gipfel, Gipfeltreffen*

4 The president of the Federal Republic of Germany

a) *Name the current German president. Collect other facts you know about him.*
Is there a photo of the current president below? Can you name any of the other presidents in the photos?

b) *Think about the statements below. Decide if they are true or false. Correct the wrong statements.*
Discuss your answers with a partner and change them if necessary.
Compare your answers in a group and share what you think with the whole class.

1 The German president is the head of state.
2 He/She is the head of the government.
3 He/She signs legislation[1] before it can become law.
4 He/She often vetoes legislation.
5 He/She chooses ministers for the cabinet.
6 He/She gives speeches on important days in the life of the country, like the Day of German Unity.
7 He/She lives in a palace in Berlin.
8 He/She represents Germany at political summits like the G8.
9 He/She makes Germany's foreign policy[2].
10 He/She is elected by the people.

c) *Explain how the role of the German president is similar to or different from the role of the US president. Which other important person in German politics plays a similar role to the US president?*

5 Talking about German politics

a) *Find more information about the role of the German president or about another role in German political life, e.g. the chancellor[3], the premiers[4] of the German states (Bavaria, Hamburg, etc.), the speaker of the German parliament, a member of parliament, the leader of a political party, etc.* ▸ *SF Research (p. 137)*

b) *Prepare a short talk to explain the political role you chose to an American student.*
The language on the right might be helpful.
Give your talk in a small group.

Activate your English

The German president/chancellor/...
– has a(n) executive[5]/political/representational[6] role.
– is elected by parliament/the people/...
– is the head of state/head of the government.
– signs legislation into law.
– chooses ministers for the cabinet.
– is in charge of[7] foreign/economic/ ... policy.
– runs the debates in parliament.
– makes speeches on ...
– meets foreign heads of government/state.

[1] legislation [ˌledʒɪs'leɪʃn] *Gesetze; Gesetzgebung* [2] foreign policy ['pɒləsi] *Außenpolitik* [3] chancellor ['tʃɑːnsələ] *Bundeskanzler/in*
[4] premier ['premiə] *Ministerpräsident/in* [5] executive [ɪg'zekjətɪv] *Exekutiv-, ausführende/r* [6] representational [ˌreprɪzen'teɪʃnl] *repräsentativ*
[8] (to) be in charge of sth. *für etwas zuständig sein, für etwas die Verantwortung tragen*

Skills File – Inhalt

Das **Skills File** dieses Bandes fasst alle Arbeits- und Lerntechniken zusammen, die du in den Bänden 1 bis 6 kennengelernt hast.

Die Themen, die in Band 6 neu sind, sind mit **NEW** gekennzeichnet:
– **NEW Describing cartoons**, Seite 134
– **NEW Reading literature**, Seite 145.

Die Hinweise im **Skills File** helfen dir bei der Arbeit mit Hör- und Lesetexten, beim Sprechen, beim Schreiben von eigenen Texten, bei der Sprachmittlung und beim Lernen von Methoden.

STUDY AND LANGUAGE SKILLS

SF Learning words

Worauf solltest du beim Lernen und Wiederholen von Vokabeln achten?

- Lerne immer 7–10 Vokabeln auf einmal.
- Lerne neue und wiederhole alte Vokabeln regelmäßig – am besten jeden Tag 5–10 Minuten.
- Lerne mit jemandem zusammen. Fragt euch gegenseitig ab.
- Schreib die neuen Wörter immer auch auf und überprüfe die Schreibweise mithilfe des *Dictionary* oder *Vocabulary*.

Wie kannst du Wörter besser behalten?

Wörter kannst du besser behalten, wenn du sie in Wortgruppen sammelst und ordnest:

- **Gegensatzpaare** sammeln, z. B. **(to) allow** ◂▸ **(to) ban**, **divorced** ◂▸ **married**, **single room** ◂▸ **double room**
- Wörter mit **gleicher oder ähnlicher Bedeutung** sammeln, z. B. **big** – **huge** – **large**; **(to) scream** – **(to) shout**
- Wörter in **Wortfamilien** sammeln, z. B. **(to) produce**, **producer**, **product**, **production**, ...; **(to) drive**, **driver**, **driving licence**, **driving instructor**, ...
- Wörter in **Wortnetzen** *(networks)* sammeln und ordnen.

SF Describing pictures

Wie kann ich Bilder beschreiben?

- Um zu sagen, wo genau etwas abgebildet ist, benutze: **at the top/bottom** • **in the foreground/background** • **in the middle** • **on the left/right**
- Diese Präpositionen sind auch hilfreich: **behind** • **between** • **in front of** • **next to** • **under**
- Um zu beschreiben, was die Personen auf dem Bild tun, benutze das **present progressive**. **Someone is riding a horse.**

Wie kann ich beschreiben, was die Personen fühlen?

Oft sollst du dich in eine Person auf einem Foto hineinversetzen und beschreiben, was sie fühlt oder denkt. Schau dir das Foto genau an und nimm dir Zeit, dir die Situation vorzustellen. Beim Formulieren helfen dir *phrases* wie:
Maybe the woman/man in the photo feels ... /is thinking about ... •
I think he/she feels/wants to/...

►►►

Manchmal sollst du dir vorstellen, was die Person getan hat, bevor das Foto gemacht wurde. Achte auf Details im Foto (Hat die Person einen Gegenstand in der Hand? Wie sieht sie aus? Was tut sie?) und überlege dir, wie es zu der im Foto gezeigten Situation gekommen sein könnte (Warum ist die Person traurig, fröhlich etc.?). Verwende die **past tenses**:
Maybe he found out that ... • Perhaps he was looking for a place to relax/...

Wenn du beschreiben sollst, was wohl als Nächstes geschehen wird bzw. was die Person danach tun wird, verwendest du die **future tenses**:
He looks as if he's going to cry/... • Maybe he'll decide to ...

SF NEW Describing cartoons ▸ *Unit 2, Part B (p. 36)*

Cartoons sind humorvolle Zeichnungen, die häufig ein aktuelles Thema aufgreifen.

Wie beschreibe ich einen Cartoon?

Bei der Beschreibung eines Cartoons gehst du zunächst vor wie bei der Beschreibung von Fotos oder anderen Zeichnungen.

1. Beschreibe die Personen oder Dinge: Was tun sie gerade? Wo befinden sie sich? usw.
   The cartoon shows ... • In the foreground/background/... there is/are ...

2. Achte darauf, ob der Cartoon eine Bildunterschrift (*caption*), Sprechblasen oder Gedankenblasen (*speech bubbles, thought bubbles*) hat.
   In the caption it says that ...

GLOBAL WARNING

Wie analysiere ich die Aussage eines Cartoons?

1. Sag, worum es in dem Cartoon geht, welches Thema er behandelt:
   The cartoon is about ...

2. Wenn du analysierst, welche Botschaft (*message*) der Cartoon-Zeichner vermitteln möchte, solltest du alle Elemente des Cartoons noch einmal zusammen betrachten: die Zeichnung sowie die Bildunterschrift und Sprech- oder Gedankenblasen. Achte darauf, ob die Personen oder Dinge positiv oder negativ dargestellt werden. Bedenke, dass ein Cartoon auch ernste Themen humorvoll darstellt und oft stark übertreibt!
   I think the cartoon shows us that ... • The artist wants to say that ...

3. Manchmal sollst du Stellung zur Botschaft des Cartoons nehmen und deine eigene Meinung sagen:
   I like/don't like the cartoon because ... • I think the artist is right/wrong because ...

SF Check yourself

How am I doing?

Damit du weißt, wie gut du die Kompetenzbereiche (**Listening**, **Speaking**, **Reading**, **Writing**, **Mediation**) beherrschst und wo du noch Schwächen hast, solltest du dich immer wieder selbst überprüfen. Das kannst du auf unterschiedlichen Wegen tun. Eine Reihe von Tipps kennst du vermutlich schon. Du kannst dich auch nach jedem *Getting ready for a test* mithilfe der *How am I doing*-Seiten selbst überprüfen. Dabei gehst du wie folgt vor:

1. Du bearbeitest die Aufgaben und überprüfst deine Ergebnisse.

2. Dann schaust du dir die Bereiche, in denen du Fehler gemacht hast, noch einmal an. Die Verweise zeigen dir, auf welchen Seiten im Schülerbuch du Tipps oder Übungen zu diesen Bereichen findest.

3. Nun solltest du gezielt diese Bereiche üben. Dies kannst du z.B. mithilfe des *Exam File* oder des *Workbook* tun. Frag auch deinen Lehrer oder deine Lehrerin, wo du noch weitere Übungen finden kannst.

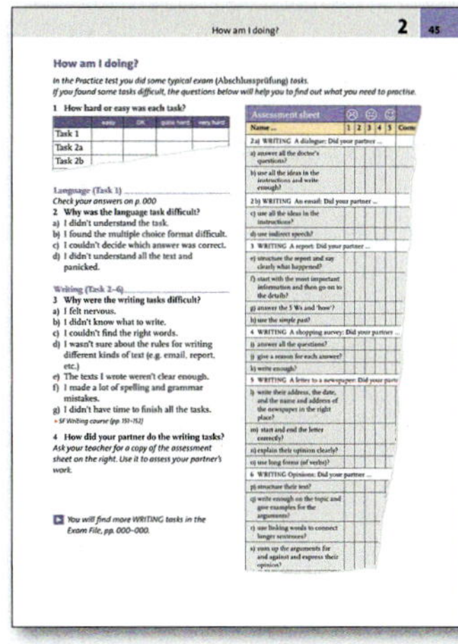
How am I doing? 2 45

How am I doing?

Die Arbeit mit einer persönlichen Fehlerliste

Führe eine Liste der Fehler, die du oft machst, und nutze sie beim Schreiben von Texten als persönliche Checkliste. Hefte diese Listen in deinem Englischordner ab oder lege dir dafür ein extra Heft an (z.B. in DIN-A5).
Das Heft kannst du z.B. nach folgenden Schwerpunkten unterteilen:

1. Drittel: *Words* 2. Drittel: *Grammar* 3. Drittel: *Spelling*

Dann untersuchst du deine Klassenarbeiten und andere schriftliche Arbeiten auf deine Fehlerquellen hin. Dein/e Englischlehrer/in zeigt durch Abkürzungen am Rand, was für eine Art Fehler du gemacht hast.

WORDS

Wrong	Correct	REMEMBER
He goes to school ~~with the~~ bus.	He goes to school by bus.	mit dem Bus fahren – go by bus
We've got a ~~strong~~ teacher.	We've got a strict teacher.	Nicht verwechseln! streng – strict / strong – stark
I climbed ~~on~~ a tree.	I climbed a tree.	auf einen Baum klettern – climb a tree

Tipp

- Ergänze das Heft jedes Mal, wenn du eine Klassenarbeit oder einen Text von deinem Lehrer/deiner Lehrerin zurückbekommen hast.
- Überprüfe, ob du bestimmte Fehler immer wieder machst. Wenn ja, such dafür Übungen in deinem Englischbuch, deinem *Workbook*, deinem *e-Workbook* oder frag deinen Lehrer/deine Lehrerin nach Übungen.
- Schau dir vor jeder Klassenarbeit die Fehler an, die du oft machst.
- Mach dir mithilfe des Grammatikteils die Regeln, die dir besonders schwerfallen, noch einmal bewusst.

SF Using a dictionary

Wie benutze ich ein zweisprachiges Wörterbuch?

Du verstehst einen Text nicht, weil er zu viele Wörter enthält, die dir unbekannt sind, und die Worterschließungstechniken (▸ *SF Working out the meaning of words, p. 142*) helfen dir nicht weiter? Du sollst einen Text auf Englisch schreiben und dir fehlt das eine oder andere Wort, um deine Ideen auszudrücken? Du willst z. B. sagen, die Handlung in *Twilight* dreht sich um die schwierige Beziehung zwischen Bella und Edward, aber du kennst das englische Wort für „drehen" nicht? In jedem Fall hilft dir ein zweisprachiges Wörterbuch.

- Die **Leitwörter** oben auf der Seite helfen dir, schneller zu finden, was du suchst. Auf der linken Seite steht das erste Stichwort, auf der rechten Seite das letzte Stichwort der Doppelseite.
- „drehen" ist das **Stichwort**. Alle Stichwörter sind alphabetisch geordnet: d vor e, da vor de und dre vor dri usw.
- Die **kursiv gedruckten** Hinweise helfen dir, die für deinen Text passende Bedeutung zu finden.
- Die **Ziffern** 1, 2 usw. zeigen, dass ein Stichwort mehrere ganz verschiedene Bedeutungen hat.
- **Beispielsätze** und **Redewendungen** sind dem Stichwort zugeordnet. In den Beispielsätzen und Redewendungen ersetzt eine **Tilde** (~) das Stichwort.
- Im englisch-deutschen Teil der meisten Wörterbücher findest du außerdem Hinweise auf **unregelmäßige Verbformen**, auf die **Steigerungsformen der Adjektive** und Ähnliches.
- Die **Lautschrift** gibt Auskunft darüber, wie das Wort ausgesprochen und betont wird.

Dr.

Dr. (*Abk. für* **Doktor**) Dr., Doctor
Drache dragon
Drachen *Papierdrachen* kite; *Fluggerät* hang glider

Drehbuch screenplay, script
drehen 1 *Verb mit Obj* turn; *Film* shoot*; *Zigarette* roll **2**: ***sich ~*** turn; *schnell* spin*; ***sich ~ um*** *übertragen* be* about
Drehkreuz turnstile; **Drehorgel** barrel organ ['ɔːgən]; **Drehort** location; **Drehstuhl** swivel chair; **Drehtür** revolving door
Drehung turn; *um eine Achse* rotation
Drehzahl (number of) revolutions *Pl od.* revs *Pl*
Drehzahlmesser rev counter
drei three
Drei three; *Note etwa* C; ***ich habe eine ~ geschrieben*** I got a C
dreidimensional 1 *Adj* three-dimensional **2** *Adv*: ***etwas ~ darstellen*** depict sth. three-dimensionally; **Dreieck** triangle ['traɪæŋgl]; **dreieckig** triangular [traɪ'æŋgjʊlə]

Tipp

Nimm nicht einfach die erste Übersetzung, die dir angeboten wird! Lies den Wörterbucheintrag, bis du die richtige Übersetzung gefunden hast.

Wie benutze ich ein einsprachiges Wörterbuch?

Wenn du englische Texte liest oder selbst einen englischen Text schreibst, kannst du auch ein einsprachiges englisches Wörterbuch zu Hilfe nehmen. Hier findest du mehr über ein englisches Wort heraus als in einem zweisprachigen Wörterbuch:

- Das einsprachige Wörterbuch erklärt die **Bedeutung** eines englischen Wortes **auf Englisch**. Manche Wörter haben mehrere Bedeutungen. Lies alle Einträge und Beispielsätze genau und vergleiche sie mit deinem englischen Text, um die richtige Bedeutung herauszufinden.
- Das Wörterbuch hilft dir auch, die passende **Verbindung mit anderen Wörtern** zu finden, z. B. mit Verben, Präpositionen oder in bestimmten Wendungen. Das ist besonders nützlich, wenn du selbst einen englischen Text schreiben willst und nach den richtigen Wörtern und Formulierungen suchst.

deadly ['dedli] *adj*
1 *able or likely to kill people* {= lethal}: This is no longer a deadly disease.
deadly to The HSN virus is deadly to chickens.
a deadly weapon The new generation of biological weapons is more deadly than ever.
2 (*only before noun*) {= complete}:
deadly silence There was deadly silence after his speech.
a deadly secret Don't tell anyone – this is a deadly secret.
in deadly earnest *completely serious:* Don't you laugh – I am in deadly earnest!
3 (*informal*) *very boring*: Many TV programmes are pretty deadly!
4 *always able to achieve something*: The new Chelsea striker is said to be a deadly

SF Research

Wo kann ich Informationen finden?

Wenn du nach Informationen suchst, solltest du immer **mehrere Quellen** verwenden. Du kannst im Internet, in einem Lexikon, Atlas, Wörterbuch, Schulbuch oder in anderen Quellen suchen. Auch CDs und DVDs sind mögliche Quellen. Benutze auch einige englische Quellen, das kann dir beim Ausformulieren deines englischen Textes helfen.

- Internet/Lexikon: alle Wissensgebiete, wichtige Personen und Ereignisse
- Atlas: geografische und politische Übersichten, Städte, Flüsse
- Wörterbücher: Rechtschreibung und Bedeutung von Wörtern
- Schulbücher: verschiedene Wissensgebiete
- Zeitungen/Zeitschriften: aktuelle Informationen zu allen Themenbereichen

Wie kann ich das Internet zur Recherche nutzen?

Eine wichtige Informationsquelle ist das Internet. Aber manchmal findest du dort so viele Informationen, dass du schnell den Überblick verlierst. Diese Tipps sollen dir helfen, damit du nicht im *world wide web* verloren gehst.

- Fertige eine Liste mit Schlüsselwörtern (**key words**) zu deinem Thema an, z. B. **carbon calculator, carbon footprint, ...**
- Probiere, mit welchem Schlüsselwort oder welcher Kombination von Schlüsselwörtern du die besten Ergebnisse erzielst: **„carbon calculator", ...**
- Wenn du dir zunächst einen Überblick verschaffen willst, kannst du auch ein Nachschlagewerk im Internet anklicken wie z. B.: www.infoplease.com www.en.wikipedia.org
  Manchmal gibt es dort auch Links, die dir weiterhelfen können.
- Suchmaschinen (wie z. B. *Google*, *Altavista* oder *Yahoo*) helfen dir, Websites zu deinem Thema zu finden. Verwende eine Suchmaschine und gib deine Schlüsselwörter in das Suchfenster ein.
- Wenn die angezeigten Websites dir nicht helfen oder du zu viele Websites angezeigt bekommst, versuch es noch einmal, indem du deine Schlüsselwörter präzisierst.

mit **allen** Wörtern	carbon calculator footprint	10 Ergebnisse
mit der **genauen Wortgruppe**	carbon calculator	
mit **irgendeinem** der Wörter		
ohne die Wörter		

Tipp

- Verwende immer mehrere Internet-Quellen, um sicherzugehen, dass die Informationen stimmen.
- Suche Antworten auf die **5 Ws** (**who**, **what**, **where**, **when**, **why**).
- Bei englischen Quellen brauchst du nicht alles zu verstehen. Konzentriere dich auf das Wesentliche.
- Schreib die Quellen nicht wortwörtlich ab, sondern mach dir Notizen in deinen eigenen Worten. ▸ *Taking notes (p. 141)* • *Reading course (pp. 142–143)*

SF Giving a presentation

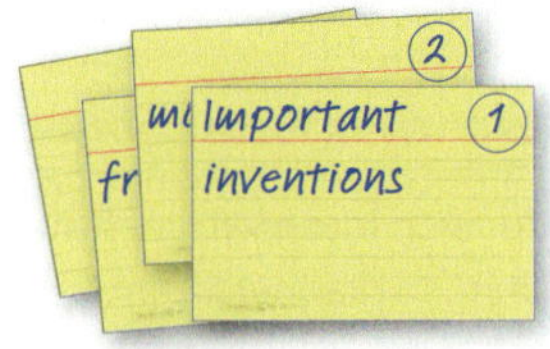

Wie mache ich eine gute Präsentation?

Vorbereitung
- Schreib die wichtigsten Gedanken in Stichworten auf, z. B. auf nummerierte Karteikarten oder in einer Mindmap.
- Übe deine Präsentation zu Hause vor einem Spiegel. Sprich laut, deutlich und langsam und mach Pausen an geeigneten Stellen.

Folien oder Poster
- Folien (für Overhead-Projektoren oder Computerpräsentationen) oder Poster sind gut, um
  - zu zeigen, wie dein Vortrag aufgebaut ist
  - Tabellen, Diagramme usw. für alle lesbar zu präsentieren
  - die wichtigsten Punkte zusammenzufassen.
- Schreib groß und für alle gut lesbar.

Durchführung
- Bevor du beginnst, sortiere deine Vortragskarten.
- Häng das Poster auf oder leg deine Folie auf den ausgeschalteten Projektor bzw. bereite den Beamer vor.
- Warte, bis es ruhig ist. Schau die Zuhörenden an.
- Erkläre zu Anfang, worüber du sprechen wirst.
- Lies nicht von deinen Karten ab, sondern sprich frei.

This picture/photo/ … shows …

My presentation is about … First, I'd like to talk about … Second, …

Schluss
- Beende deine Präsentation mit einem abschließenden Satz.
- Frag die Zuhörenden, ob sie Fragen haben. Bedanke dich fürs Zuhören.

That's the end of my presentation. Have you got any questions?

Ausführlichere sprachliche Hilfen für Präsentationen findest du unter:
► *SF Giving a presentation – useful phrases (p. 148)*

SF Using visual materials with a presentation

Wofür sind visuelle Materialien gut?

Deine Zuhörer/innen werden deinem Vortrag mit mehr Aufmerksamkeit folgen. Sie können sich viel mehr merken, wenn du nicht nur sprichst, sondern ihnen auch etwas zum Anschauen bietest (Visualisierungen). Das können z. B. Fotos, Cartoons, Landkarten, Zeitleisten, Diagramme, Poster oder Filmausschnitte sein.

Was muss ich bei visuellen Materialien beachten?

Vorbereitung
- Das Gerüst deines Vortrags sollte stehen, bevor du anfängst, dir darüber Gedanken zu machen, welche Visualisierungen gut passen könnten.
- Diagramme und Tabellen sind gut, um Zahlen zu verdeutlichen; Zeitleisten sind gut, um eine Entwicklung zu zeigen; mit Fotos und Cartoons kann man seinen Vortrag auflockern.

Durchführung
- Bezieh deine visuellen Materialien in deinen Vortrag ein, um etwas zu veranschaulichen, aber lies nicht einfach von der Folie etc. ab.

Tipp
Denke daran, dass Schriften und Bilder so groß sein sollten, dass alle im Klassenraum sie gut lesen und sehen können.

SF Talking about charts

Welche Informationen kann ich Diagrammen (charts) entnehmen?

Diagramme stellen statistische Vergleiche zwischen mindestens zwei Dingen dar. Es werden entweder absolute Zahlen oder Prozentsätze miteinander verglichen.

Welche unterschiedlichen Formen von Diagrammen gibt es?

- **Bar charts (Säulendiagramme)** beschreiben häufig die Anzahl oder Größe von zwei oder mehr Dingen.
- **Pie charts (Kreis-/Tortendiagramme)** geben einen schnellen Überblick über die prozentuale Verteilung.
- **Charts (Tabellen)** ermöglichen den Vergleich unterschiedlicher Daten anhand von Zahlen und Prozentsätzen.
- **Line graphs (Kurvendiagramme)** stellen den Zusammenhang zwischen zwei zu vergleichenden Größen dar.

Countries visited by UK tourists (2008)

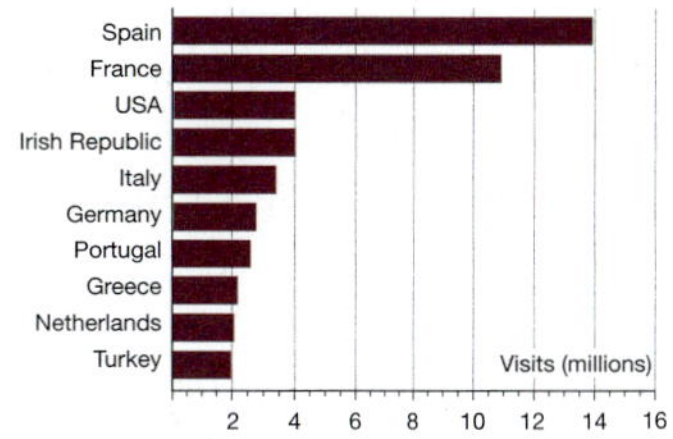

How UK citizens travelled abroad (2008)
Number of travellers:
68.9 million

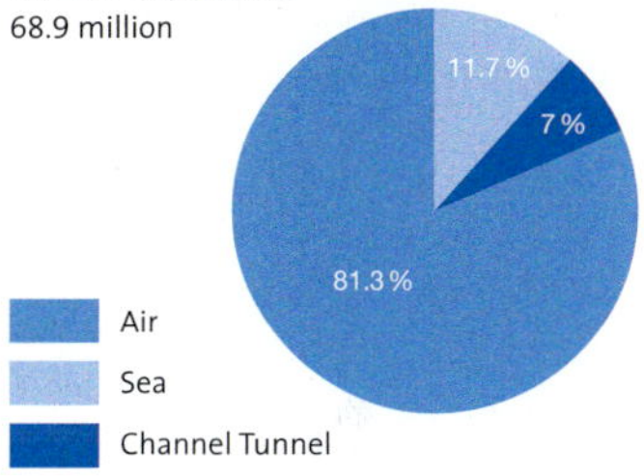

Wie kann ich beschreiben, was die Diagramme darstellen?

Um ein Diagramm zu beschreiben, solltest du folgende Fragen beantworten:

- **What is the chart/table/graph about?**
  The bar/pie chart is about ... • The line graph deals with ... •
  It is taken from ...
- **What does the chart/table/graph compare or show?**
  The chart/table/graph compares the size/number of ... •
  It shows the different ... • The pie chart is divided into ... slices that show ...
- **What does the chart tell you? What information does it give you?**
  ... has the largest/second largest • ... is twice/three times/... as big as ... •
  There are more than/nearly twice as many ... as there are ... •
  A huge majority/small minority/ ... • ... per cent of ...

Wenn vorhanden, solltest du Aussagen über den Zeitraum der Statistik ergänzen:
The chart is about the years ... • The chart shows the number of UK tourists in ...

Spending by UK tourists abroad

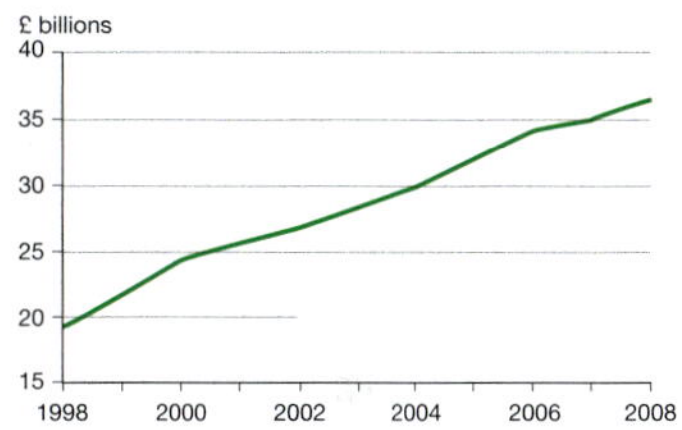

Tipp

Benutze das **simple past**, wenn du dich auf einen Zeitpunkt in der Vergangenheit beziehst: Almost 14 million tourists from the UK visited Spain in 2008.

Benutze das **simple present**, wenn du deine Schlussfolgerungen wiedergibst:
Spain is one of the most popular countries with tourists from the UK.

Benutze das **present perfect**, wenn du dich auf einen Zeitraum beziehst, der von der Vergangenheit bis heute reicht:
How many people have visited Spain since 2008?

LISTENING AND READING SKILLS

SF Listening

Was muss ich beim *listening* beachten?

Vor dem Hören:
- Überlege, worum es in dem Hörtext gehen wird. Frag dich, was du schon über das Thema weißt.
- Lies die Aufgaben gut durch, damit du weißt, worauf du achten sollst:
  - auf die **Hauptgedanken** oder die **Kernaussage** des Textes, z. B. wenn du sagen sollst, um welches Thema es geht, oder welche Meinung der Sprecher zu dem Thema hat.
  - auf bestimmte **Details**, z. B. wenn du Namen, Uhrzeiten, Jahreszahlen heraushören sollst.
- Bereite dich darauf vor, Notizen zu machen. Leg z. B. eine Tabelle oder Liste an.

Beim Hören:

- Keine Panik! Du musst nicht alles verstehen. Konzentriere dich auf das Wesentliche. Oft werden wichtige Informationen wiederholt.
- Achte auf Geräusche und unterschiedliche Stimmen. Was ein Sprecher/ eine Sprecherin besonders betont, das ist wichtig!
- Wenn du gezielt nach Informationen suchst, denk an die Aufgabe und lass dich von anderen Einzelheiten nicht ablenken. Aufgepasst: die Informationen, die du suchst, kommen vielleicht in einer anderen Reihenfolge vor, als du sie erwartest.
- Manche Signalwörter machen es dir leichter, den Hörtext zu verstehen:
  - Aufzählung: **and**, **another**, **too**
  - Gegensatz: **although**, **but**
  - Grund, Folge: **because, so**, **so that**
  - Vergleich: **larger/older/... than**, **more**, **most**
  - Reihenfolge: **before**, **after**, **then**, **next**, **later**, **when**, **at last**, **at the same time**
- Mache kurze Notizen, z. B. Anfangsbuchstaben, Symbole oder Stichworte.

Nach dem Hören:
- Vervollständige deine Notizen sofort.
- Konzentriere dich beim zweiten Hören auf das, was du beim ersten Mal nicht gut verstanden hast.

Worauf sollte ich bei automatischen Telefonansagen achten?

Wenn du eine telefonische Auskunft einholen willst, hörst du manchmal eine automatische Telefonansage.
- Keine Panik! Du kannst eine automatische Telefonansage mehrmals hören.
- Achte besonders auf Zahlen! Meist wirst du aufgefordert, bestimmte Tasten auf deinem Telefon zu drücken, um die gewünschte Information zu erhalten. Oft werden diese Zahlen wiederholt.
- Überlege dir vorher, welche Informationen du suchst und auf welche Schlüsselwörter du dafür achten solltest. Schreib sie auf.
- Höre besonders genau zu, wenn deine Schlüsselwörter genannt werden, und mach dir Notizen zu ihnen.

SF Taking notes

Worum geht es beim Notizenmachen?

Wenn du beim Lesen oder Zuhören Notizen machst, kannst du dich später besser an das Gehörte oder Gelesene erinnern. Das ist nützlich, wenn du etwas vortragen, nacherzählen oder einen Bericht schreiben sollst.

Wie mache ich Notizen?

In Texten oder Gesprächen gibt es immer wichtige und unwichtige Wörter. Die wichtigen Wörter werden Schlüsselwörter (**key words**) genannt und nur diese solltest du notieren. Meist sind das Substantive und Verben, manchmal auch Adjektive oder Zahlen.

Tipp

- Verwende Ziffern (z. B. „7" statt „seven").
- Verwende Symbole und Abkürzungen, z. B. ✔ (für „ja") und + (für „und") oder US für United States, E. für Edward.
  Du kannst auch eigene Symbole erfinden.
- Verwende not oder ✕ statt „doesn't" oder „don't".

SF Marking up a text

Wann sollte ich einen Text markieren?

Du hast einen Text mit vielen Fakten vor dir liegen und sollst später über bestimmte Dinge berichten. Dann wird es dir helfen, die für die Aufgabenstellung wichtigen Informationen im Text zu markieren.

Wie gehe ich am besten vor?

Lies den Text und markiere nur die für dein Thema wichtigen Informationen. Nicht jeder Satz enthält für deine Aufgabe wichtige Wörter, und oft reicht es aus, nur ein oder zwei Wörter in einem Satz zu markieren.

- Behalte beim Lesen die Aufgabenstellung im Hinterkopf. Wenn du die gesuchten Informationen im Text gefunden hast, markiere sie. Du kannst die wichtigen Stellen einkreisen, unterstreichen oder mit einem Texmarker hervorheben.
- Manchmal ist es hilfreich, wenn du zusätzlich wichtige Stichwörter an den Rand schreibst. Wenn du später die Informationen noch einmal benötigst, brauchst du nur die markierten Stellen und die Notizen auf dem Rand zu lesen.

ABER:
Markiere nur auf Fotokopien von Texten oder in Büchern, die dir gehören, oder verwende eine Folie und einen wasserlöslichen Folienstift.

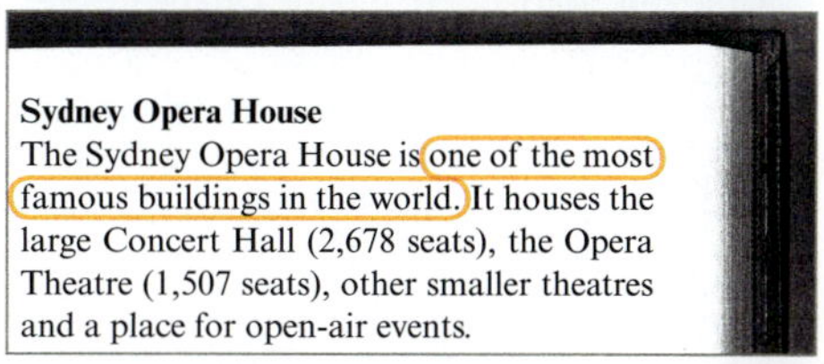

Sydney Opera House
The Sydney Opera House is one of the most famous buildings in the world. It houses the large Concert Hall (2,678 seats), the Opera Theatre (1,507 seats), other smaller theatres and a place for open-air events.

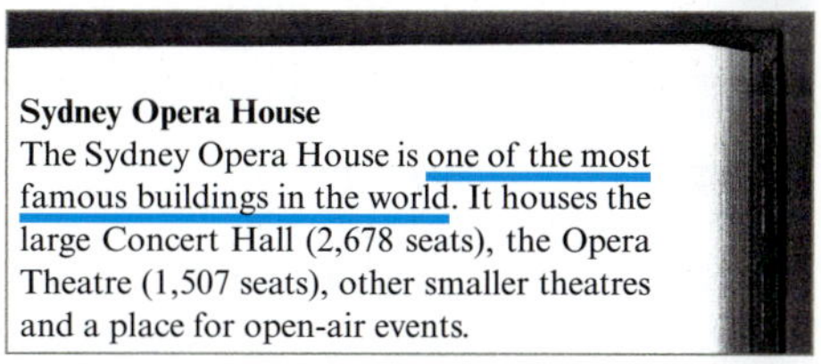

Sydney Opera House
The Sydney Opera House is one of the most famous buildings in the world. It houses the large Concert Hall (2,678 seats), the Opera Theatre (1,507 seats), other smaller theatres and a place for open-air events.

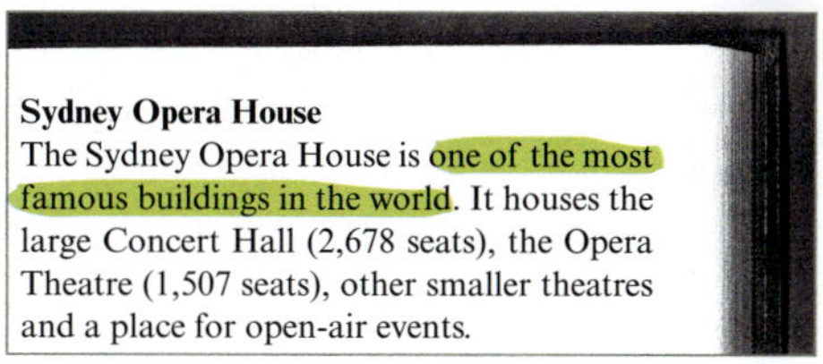

Sydney Opera House
The Sydney Opera House is one of the most famous buildings in the world. It houses the large Concert Hall (2,678 seats), the Opera Theatre (1,507 seats), other smaller theatres and a place for open-air events.

READING COURSE

Working out the meaning of words

Das Nachschlagen unbekannter Wörter im Wörterbuch kostet Zeit und nimmt auf Dauer den Spaß am Lesen. Oft geht es auch ohne Wörterbuch!

Was hilft dir, unbekannte Wörter zu verstehen?

1. **Bilder** zeigen oft die Dinge, die du im Text nicht verstehst. Wenn es Bilder zum Text gibt, dann schau sie dir vor dem Lesen genau an.
2. Oft hilft dir der **Textzusammenhang** *(context)*, z.B. *When we **reached** the station, Judy went to the ticket machine to buy our tickets.*
3. Manche englischen Wörter werden **ähnlich wie im Deutschen** geschrieben oder ausgesprochen, z.B. **excellent**, **millionaire**, **nation**, **reality**.
4. Manchmal stecken in unbekannten Wörtern **bekannte Teile**, z.B. **friendliness**, **helpless**, **understandable**, **gardener**, **tea bag**, **waiting room**.

Skimming and scanning

Skimming: Lesen, um sich einen Überblick zu verschaffen

Beim **Skimming** überfliegst du einen Text schnell, um dir einen ersten **Überblick** zu verschaffen, worum es geht. Du willst z.B. herausfinden, ob ein Text im Internet oder in einem Buch überhaupt nützliche Informationen zu deinem Thema (z.B. für ein Referat) enthält. Achte beim Skimming auf:
- die **Überschrift**
- die **Zwischenüberschriften** und **hervorgehobene** Wörter oder Sätze
- die **Bilder** und **Bildunterschriften**
- den **ersten** und **letzten Satz** jedes Absatzes
- **Grafiken**, **Statistiken** und die **Quelle** des Textes.

Scanning: Lesen, um nach bestimmten Informationen zu suchen

Beim **Scanning** suchst du in einem Text nach **bestimmten Informationen**, die z.B. für ein Referat wichtig sind. Dazu brauchst du nicht den gesamten Text zu lesen, sondern du suchst nach Schlüsselwörtern (**key words**) und liest nur dort genauer, wo du sie findest. Geh dabei so vor:

Schritt 1: Denk an das Schlüsselwort, nach dem du suchst, oder schreib es auf.

Schritt 2: Geh mit den Augen und dem Finger schnell durch den Text, in breiten Schlingen wie bei einem „S" oder „Z" oder von oben nach unten wie bei einem „U". Dabei hast du das Schriftbild oder das Bild des Wortes, nach dem du suchst, vor Augen. Das gesuchte Wort wird dir sofort „ins Auge springen". Lies nur dort weiter, um Näheres zu erfahren.

Schritt 3: Wenn das Schlüsselwort, nach dem du suchst, im Text nicht vorkommt, überleg dir, welche anderen Wörter mit den benötigten Informationen zu tun haben, und such nach diesen.

Finding the main ideas of a text

Wenn du Texte wie Zeitungsartikel, Berichte oder Kommentare richtig verstehen willst, ist es gut, wenn du ihre Hauptaussagen erkennst und nachvollziehst, wie sie zusammenhängen. Dabei hilft dir ein Blick auf die Struktur dieser Texte.

Wie finde ich die Hauptaussagen eines Textes?

① Jeder Text dreht sich um ein Thema oder hat eine Hauptaussage. Diese findest du oft im ersten Absatz. Lies ihn deshalb besonders gründlich durch.
② Die Hauptaussage wird in der Regel durch weitere Aussagen bzw. Gedanken unterstützt. Du findest sie oft im ersten oder letzten Satz der nachfolgenden Absätze.
③ Diese weiteren Aussagen bzw. Gedanken werden meist durch Beispiele und Begründungen ergänzt.

We are people too!

By Oliver Munslow (16) – 23 August 2010

① To everybody out there that thinks young people are different, you're right! We're younger than adults. But that doesn't mean you don't need to listen to us or you don't have to respect us. We have feelings and (this might surprise some of you) we are people too.

Did you know that here in Britain every citizen under 18 has important rights? For example, we all have the right to be listened to and taken seriously, and we have the right to get together with our friends in public (as long as we respect the rights of other people and do not break the law.

② But British children aren't taken seriously until they're 18. Too many adults think that our views just don't count and that we don't deserve equal rights. Here are some examples of discrimination against teenagers from my everyday life (in fact, most of these things happened to me this week).

③ Every day I see signs on shop doors that say '2 children at a time', or 'no school bags', or even 'no children unless they are with an adult'. [...]

Tipp

Die folgenden Wörter oder Wendungen werden oft im Zusammenhang mit Begründungen oder Beispielen verwendet:
and so • because • e.g. / for example • etc. • for lots of reasons • this shows that • that's why • ...

Drawing conclusions

Wenn du Fragen zu einem Text beantworten sollst oder bei einer Recherche Informationen zu einer bestimmten Frage suchst, kann es sein, dass du an mehreren Stellen schauen musst oder dass die Antwort nicht 1:1 im Text steht.

Wie funktioniert schlussfolgerndes Lesen?

1. Die einfachste Form des schlussfolgernden Lesens besteht darin, die Informationen aus verschiedenen Textstellen zusammenzuführen. Bei dem Text *The Carbon Diaries 2015* (S. 35) sollst du erklären, wie *carbon rationing* funktioniert. Dazu musst du dir mehrere Stellen ansehen.

2. Manchmal steht die Antwort auf eine Frage nicht direkt im Text. Dann musst du sie dir erschließen. Du fragst dich z. B., ob Laura Brown und ihre Familie durch die Ausnahmesituation mehr gemeinsam unternehmen. Dafür musst du Aussagen im Text finden, die etwas mit der Frage zu tun haben:

Lines 84–89: *Dad spends all night on his laptop, Mum is always lost on a bus somewhere and Kim just lives in her room – an evil ball of silence. (...)*

Conclusion: *The family don't spend more time together because of carbon rationing. In fact, they spend less time together.*

SF Reading English texts

Was unterscheidet Sachtexte und literarische Texte?

Wenn du einen Text liest, solltest du dir klar machen, ob er sich mit der Wirklichkeit auseinandersetzt, also ein Sachtext (*non-fictional text*) ist, oder ob er von einer erdachten Welt handelt, also ein literarischer Text (*fictional text*) ist.

Sachtexte (oder nicht-fiktionale Texte) sind z. B. Berichte in Zeitungen, wissenschaftliche Artikel, Kommentare, sowie Gebrauchsanleitungen und Broschürentexte. Hier informiert der Autor oder die Autorin über ein Thema der realen Welt oder nimmt Stellung dazu.

Literarische (oder fiktionale) Texte sind z. B. Kurzgeschichten und Romane. Der Autor oder die Autorin wählt Figuren (*characters*) aus und erzählt von ihren Gefühlen und Handlungen, von deren Motiven und Hintergründen. Oft verwenden Autoren für ihre Geschichten eine anschauliche Sprache (z. B. ausschmückende Adjektive, Vergleiche).

Was ist das Besondere beim Lesen von längeren literarischen Texten auf Englisch?

Geschichten lesen macht Spaß! Wenn du eine Geschichte (*story*) oder einen Roman (*novel*) liest, tauchst du in eine andere Welt ein. Dabei ist es nicht so wichtig, dass du beim Lesen jedes Wort verstehst. Lass dich einfach von der Handlung durch die Geschichte tragen.

Hier sind ein paar Tipps, die es dir erleichtern, längere literarische Texte auf Englisch zu lesen.

Vor dem Lesen:

1. Lies die **Einführung** und die **Überschrift(en)** und sieh dir die **Bilder** zum Text an. Sie geben dir erste Informationen über das, was dich erwartet. Stell dir vor, worum es in der Geschichte gehen könnte.
2. Bei Lektüren oder Romanen gibt es hinten auf dem Buchumschlag meist einen kurzen **Klappentext** mit einer Zusammenfassung der Handlung – natürlich ohne, dass das Ende verraten wird.

Während des Lesens:

1. Tauche in die Geschichte ein. Lies zügig! Kümmere dich nicht um einzelne Wörter, die du nicht verstehst. Lies einfach weiter. Das Wichtigste ist, dass du im Großen und Ganzen die Handlung verstehst.
   Wenn du merkst, dass du der Handlung nicht mehr folgen kannst, weil du zu viele Wörter nicht verstehst, dann nutze alle dir bekannten Techniken, um die Bedeutung zu erschließen:
   – Sieh dir noch einmal die Bilder an.
   – Beachte den Textzusammenhang *(context)*.
   – Kennst du ähnliche englische oder deutsche Wörter?
   – Vielleicht kennst du Teile der unbekannten Wörter?
   ► *SF Working out the meaning of words (p. 142)*
2. Wenn das alles nicht hilft, dann schlage das unbekannte Wort im Wörterbuch nach. ► *SF Using a dictionary (p. 136)*

Tipp

Beim Lesen von englischen Lektüren oder Büchern kann dir eine Lesetagebuch (**reading log**), wie du es sicher aus dem Deutschunterricht kennst, das Verstehen und Behalten erleichtern.

►►►

3. Um der Handlung besser folgen zu können, kann es helfen, wenn du nicht die ganze Geschichte hintereinander liest. Hör ab und zu auf zu lesen und denk darüber nach, was du bis dahin gelesen hast. Erzähl jemandem, was bisher geschah und was du noch nicht verstanden hast. Oft klären sich manche Fragen im Gespräch. Dann lies weiter.

SF NEW Reading literature ▸ *TF 1, TF 5 (pp. 112–114, pp. 125–129)*

Was ist das Besondere an literarischen Texten?

Literarische Texte sind oft in einer besonderen Form oder Sprache verfasst. Sie zeigen eine Welt oder Umgebung, die der Autor oder die Autorin erdacht hat. Im Englischen nennt man diese Texte auch *fiction*, weil sie von einer erfundenen (englisch: *fictional*) Welt handeln – im Gegensatz zu *non-fiction*, die sich mit der wirklichen Welt auseinandersetzt.

Alles, was du bereits über das Lesen von Texten im Allgemeinen gelernt hast (▸ *Reading course, pp. 142–143; SF Reading English texts, pp. 144–145*), wird dir auch beim Lesen von Literatur helfen.

Literarische Gattungen und ihre Merkmale

Grundsätzlich unterscheidet man drei Arten von literarischen Texten: Gedichte (*poetry*), Erzähltexte (*fiction: stories, novels, etc.*) und Dramen (*plays*).

Du kannst Literatur natürlich einfach zum Vergnügen lesen, zum Beispiel, weil dir die Geschichte, ein bestimmtes Thema oder die dargestellten Personen interessant erscheinen. Zum besseren Verständnis ist es aber hilfreich, wenn du etwas über formale, stilistische oder technische Besonderheiten des Textes weißt. Überlege dir, warum der Autor oder die Autorin gerade diese Mittel einsetzt und welche Gefühle bei dir dadurch während des Lesens entstehen.

Das sind die Besonderheiten der drei Arten von literarischen Texten:

Erzähltexte (z. B. Kurzgeschichten, Romane) bestehen aus einem fortlaufenden Text, der manchmal durch Kapitel untergliedert ist. Um die Figuren (*characters*) der Geschichte herum wird eine Handlung (*plot*) entwickelt, die in einen bestimmten Handlungsrahmen eingebettet ist: ein bestimmter Ort, eine Zeitspanne und ein näher beschriebener Schauplatz (*setting*).

Die Charakterisierung der Figuren kann direkt erfolgen, indem sie mit bestimmten Adjektiven (*cruel, sentimental, ...*) beschrieben werden (*direct characterization*). Bei der indirekten Charakterisierung (*indirect characterization*) wird beschrieben, was die Figuren sagen, tun oder fühlen.

Durch besondere sprachliche Mittel (s. Gedichte, p. 146) schafft der Autor eine bestimmte Atmosphäre (*atmosphere*). Diese kann z. B. bedrohlich oder humorvoll sein. Die Ereignisse werden von dem Erzähler (*narrator*) der Geschichte aus einer bestimmten Erzählperspektive (*point of view*) beschrieben: der Ich-Erzähler (first-person narrator) ist Teil des Geschehens und erzählt aus der Ich-Perspektive, was ihm (und anderen) widerfährt, während der Er-Erzähler (*third-person narrator*) außerhalb des Geschehens steht.

Mr. Neck storms into class like a bull. We slide into our seats. I'm sure he's going to explode. IMMIGRATION. He writes it on the board. I'm pretty sure he spelled it right.
[...]

(aus dem Roman *Speak*, S. 52)

Ich-Erzähler
(*first-person narrator*)

Jody Miller from Chicago sat on the train, looking out of the window at the fine old trees whose leaves were just beginning to change colour as fall approached. She was back home, in the Midwest.
[...]

(aus der Kurzgeschichte *Back home*, S. 86)

Er-Erzähler
(*third-person narrator*)

▸▸▸

Gedichte bestehen meist aus gebundener Sprache, d.h. aus Verszeilen (*verses*) und Strophen (*stanzas*). Die Sprache von Gedichten unterscheidet sich von der Alltagssprache oft durch die Verwendung von Reimen (*rhyme*), Rhythmus (*rhythm*) und Wiederholungen (*repetition*) sowie einer bildhaften Sprache (Bilder: *images*), z.B. Vergleiche (*similes*) und Metaphern (*metaphors*).

Dramen bestehen in der Regel aus Monologen und Dialogen in direkter Rede. Meist geben Bühnenanweisungen (*stage directions*) Handlungsanweisungen für die Darsteller, sie sind aber auch ein wichtiger Hinweis für den Leser, um sich den Schauplatz (*setting*) vorstellen oder die Aussagen der Figuren besser interpretieren zu können.

A red, red rose
O, my Love's like a red, red rose,
That's newly sprung in June.
O, my Love's like the melody
That's sweetly played in tune.
[...]

(aus dem Gedicht *A red, red rose*, S. 113)

Über literarische Texte sprechen und schreiben

Wenn du über literarische Texte sprechen oder schreiben sollst, sind folgende Formulierungen hilfreich:

Setting and plot
The story/novel/play is about ...
The story/novel/play is set in ...
The text tells the story of ...
The action takes place during/in ...

Point of view
The story is told from the main character's/... point of view.
... is the narrator of the story.

Characters and characterization
The main character(s) is/are ...
He/she seems to be a strong/weak/brave/... person.

Poems
The poem describes/imagines ...
The lines of the poem (don't) rhyme.
The poem has a slow/lively/... rhythm.
In line(s) ... you can find a simile/metaphor/...

Language
The language in the text creates an exciting/thrilling/... atmosphere.
I think ... is a metaphor/an image for ...
The word/phrase ... is repeated in line ...

Your reaction
The text made me feel happy/sad/angry/...
I liked it/didn't like it when ...
I found the ending/story/characters interesting/funny/...

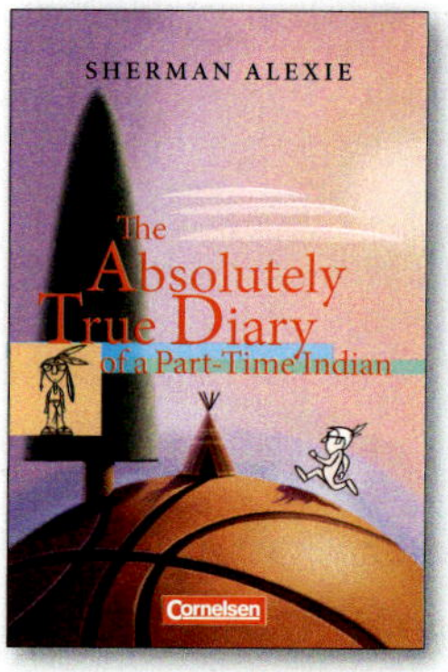

SPEAKING AND WRITING SKILLS

SPEAKING COURSE

Having a conversation

Ein Gespräch beginnen

Es gibt immer mehrere Möglichkeiten:
- **wenn du etwas erfragen willst** (z. B. den Weg oder die Uhrzeit)
  Excuse me, do you know ... • Excuse me, can you tell me ...
- **wenn du jemanden begrüßen möchtest oder kennenlernst**
  Hi. • Hello. • Good morning/evening.
  Oft kann man das Gespräch dann mit einer allgemeinen Bemerkung weiterführen: **Great day today! • That's a great ...**
- **wenn du jemanden wiedertriffst**
  Hi, how are you doing? • Hi, ..., how are things? • Hi, ... Good to see/meet you.

Ein Gespräch führen

Für den weiteren Verlauf des Gesprächs sind diese Wendungen nützlich:
- **sich vorstellen:** **By the way, my name's ... • I'm ... • Nice to meet you.**
- **Smalltalk machen:** **Have you ... before? • Have you ever ...? • Where are you from? • Do you like ...? • I like ... What about you?**
- **um Hilfe bitten und anderen helfen:** **Do you know where ...? • Can you tell me ...? • Sure, no problem • Why don't you ...?**
- **sich verabschieden:** **See you tomorrow/next week. • Bye!**

Und wenn du etwas nicht verstanden hast, kannst du immer nachfragen:
Sorry, I didn't get that. • Sorry, could you say that again, please?

Tipp

Oft hört man zur Begrüßung auch **How are you?** Es wird nicht erwartet, dass du darauf eine ausführliche Antwort gibst. Am besten sagst du einfach **Fine, thanks. How about you?**

Taking part in a job interview

Sich vorbereiten

Auf ein Vorstellungsgespräch musst du dich unbedingt vorbereiten. Du solltest Fragen zu den folgenden Bereichen beantworten können:
- deine Eigenschaften (**personal qualities**), Stärken (**strengths**) und Schwächen (**weaknesses**)
- deine Interessen (**interests**) und Arbeitserfahrungen (**work experience**)
- was dich an dem Jobangebot reizt (**why you're interested in the job**).

Überleg dir eigene Fragen, z. B. zu deinem Tätigkeitsbereich (**What kind of work would I have to do?**) oder zum Tätigkeitsbeginn (**When would I have to begin?**).

Im Vorstellungsgespräch

Im Vorstellungsgespräch ist es wichtig, dass du freundlich bist und dich als positiver und interessierter Mensch präsentierst.
- **bei der Begrüßung:** **Hello, nice to meet you. • Good morning.**
- **warum du dich bewirbst:** **I'm really interested in ... • I'm good at ..., so I think ...**
- **wenn es um deine Joberfahrungen geht:** **I really enjoyed working with ...**
- **bei der Verabschiedung:** **Goodbye and thank you very much.**

Tipp

- Hör gut zu, wenn du etwas gefragt wirst.
- Sprich nicht zu viel, aber auch nicht zu wenig.
- Sprich nicht zu schnell.

Having a discussion

Seine Meinung zum Ausdruck bringen und erklären

1. **Expressing an opinion:** In einer Diskussion ist es gut, wenn du möglichst klar und deutlich sagst, was du zu einer bestimmten Frage denkst:
   I think ... • In my opinion ...
2. **Giving reasons and examples:** Genauso wichtig ist es, dass du Beispiele und Argumente nennst, die deine Meinung unterstützen – schließlich willst du deine Gesprächspartner von deinem Standpunkt überzeugen!
   because ... • First ... / Second ... / And finally ... • For example ... • Let me explain ... • That's why ...

Auf andere in einer Diskussion reagieren

1. **Asking for clarification:** Manchmal ist es notwendig nachzuhaken, weil man ein Argument nicht verstanden hat:
   Could you say that again? • Sorry, but I don't understand what you mean.
2. **Agreeing with someone:** Wenn du die Meinung eines anderen unterstützen willst, kannst du das so zum Ausdruck bringen:
   I agree (with you/...). • That's a good point. • You're right.
3. **Disagreeing with someone:** Oft widerspricht man nicht direkt, sondern leitet seine Reaktion mit **Sorry, ...** oder **I don't think ...** ein. Zeig immer Respekt für die Meinung des oder der anderen.
   I don't think you can say ... • I see what you mean, but ... • Sorry, but that's not right. • Sorry, I don't agree with you • Yes, but ...

Giving a presentation – useful phrases

Einleitung

Nenne zu Beginn deines Vortrags dein Thema und gib einen kurzen Überblick darüber, worum es in deinem Vortrag geht:
The topic of my talk today is ... • I'm going to divide this talk into four sections. • First, I'll give you some general facts about ... • Next I'll look at ... • Finally, I'll ...

Während der Präsentation

Mach deutlich, wenn du einen neuen Abschnitt in deinem Vortrag beginnst:
Now please have a look at ... • On the next slide ... • Now I'd like to draw your attention to ... • As you can see in ...

Schluss

Fasse am Ende deines Vortrags die wichtigsten Punkte zusammen. Frag deine Zuhörer, ob sie etwas nachfragen oder kommentieren möchten.
To sum up my talk I ... • Please feel free to ask questions or comment on anything I've said.
Ausführlichere Hinweise zur Vorbereitung und Durchführung einer Präsentation findest du unter: ▸ *SF Giving a presentation (p. 138)*

SF Paraphrasing

Worum geht es beim *paraphrasing*?

Paraphrasing bedeutet, etwas mit anderen Worten zu erklären. Das ist hilfreich, wenn dir ein bestimmtes Wort nicht einfällt oder wenn dein Gegenüber dich nicht verstanden hat (siehe auch ► *SF Mediation, p. 157*).

Wie gehe ich beim *paraphrasing* vor?

- Man kann mit einem Wort umschreiben, das dieselbe Bedeutung hat:
  to train is the same as to practise
  Oder man sagt das Gegenteil: **alive is the opposite of dead**
- Manchmal braucht man mehrere Wörter, z. B. wenn man etwas beschreibt oder erklärt. Dabei benutzt man ein allgemeines Wort (**general word**) und nennt weitere Eigenschaften:
  A racing car is a very fast car.
- Oder du umschreibst das Wort mit **... is/are like ...**:
  A chef is like a cook, he or she is the main cook in a restaurant.
- Du kannst auch einen Relativsatz (**relative clause**) verwenden:
  A garage is a place where cars are checked and repaired.
  A nurse is a person who looks after people who are ill, usually in a hospital.

SF Brainstorming

Wofür ist Brainstorming gut?

Bei vielen Aufgaben ist es nützlich, wenn du im ersten Schritt möglichst viele Ideen zum Thema sammelst. Dabei hilft dir das Brainstorming.

Wie gehe ich beim Brainstorming vor?

Schritt 1:
Schreib alle Ideen so auf, wie sie dir einfallen. Es ist zunächst völlig egal, ob sie gut sind oder nicht. Du kannst die Ideen durcheinander auf einen Zettel schreiben oder schon etwas geordnet, z. B. für jede eine neue Zeile.

Schritt 2:
Lies alle deine Ideen durch und wähle die besten aus. Dann sortiere sie und fasse sie sinnvoll zusammen. Dabei kannst du folgende **Techniken** anwenden:

1. Leg eine **Mindmap** an. Schreib das Thema in die Mitte eines Blattes Papier. Überlege, welche Oberbegriffe zu deiner Sammlung von Ideen passen. Verwende unterschiedliche Farben. Ergänze jede Idee, die zu einem Oberbegriff passt, auf einem Nebenast. Nimm dafür nur wichtige Schlüsselwörter. Du kannst statt Wörtern auch Symbole verwenden und Bilder ergänzen.
2. **The 5 Ws**: Schreib die **5 W-Fragen** **Who? What? Where? When? Why?** in eine Tabelle. Die Ideen, die dir zu jeder Frage kommen, schreibst du darunter.

SF Summarizing texts

Wenn du einen Text zusammenfasst, gibst du die wichtigten Informationen oder Ereignisse in kürzerer Form wieder. Eine schriftliche Zusammenfassung nennt man im Englischen *summary*.

Wie gehe ich beim *summarizing* vor?

1. Lies den Text mindestens einmal genau durch, damit du verstehst, worum es geht. Mach dir noch keine Notizen.

2. Lies den Text erneut, Satz für Satz, durch. Am besten arbeitest du mit einer Kopie, damit du Passagen im Text markieren kannst. Markiere die Textstellen, die dir Antworten auf die 5 Ws geben.
   Wenn du keine Kopie hast, mache dir in Stichpunkten Notizen zu den **5 Ws**:
   Who? Who is the text about?
   What? What happens? / What does he/she do?
   Where? Where does it happen?
   When? When does it happen?
   Why? Why does it happen? / Why does he/she do this?

3. Schreibe eine Zusammenfassung des Texts in deinen eigenen Worten. Verwende das **simple present** (auch wenn du eine Geschichte zusammenfasst, die in der Vergangenheit spielt).
   In der **Einleitung** erklärst du in ein oder zwei Sätzen, worum es in dem Text geht:
   The story is about ... • The text describes ... • The article shows ... • In the story we get to know ...
   Im **Hauptteil** gibst du die wichtigsten Ereignisse (z. B. einer Geschichte) oder die Hauptpunkte eines Textes (z. B. eines Zeitungsartikels) wieder. Bringe die Informationen in eine logische Reihenfolge. Verwende dafür deine Notizen zu den **5 Ws**. Schreibe den Text nicht einfach ab, sondern benutze deine eigenen Worte.

4. Überprüfe deinen Entwurf. Enthält dein Text wirklich die wichtigsten Gedanken oder Ereignisse aus dem Original? Achte auch auf sprachliche Fehler und darauf, dass deine Sätze durch *linking words* verbunden sind, wie z. B.
   and • that's why • but • because • ...

5. Bei einer schriftlichen Zusammenfassung (*summary*) musst du den korrigierten Entwurf zum Schluss in eine Reinschrift bringen.

WRITING COURSE

The steps of writing

1. Brainstorming – Ideen sammeln, dann sortieren ► *SF Brainstorming*
2. Schreiben. Dabei achte darauf,
   - deine Sätze zu verbinden und auszubauen ► *Writing better sentences*
   - deinen Text gut zu strukturieren ► *Using paragraphs*
   - bei einem Bericht die 5 Ws abzudecken ► *Writing a report*
3. Deinen Text inhaltlich und sprachlich überprüfen ► *Correcting your text*

Writing better sentences

Linking words

Eine Geschichte klingt interessanter, wenn du die Sätze mit **linking words** miteinander verbindest. Dabei gibt es mehrere Möglichkeiten:
- **Time phrases** wie **at 7 o'clock**, **every morning**, **a few minutes later**, **then**, **next**
- **Konjunktionen** wie **although**, **because**, **but**, **so ... that**, **that**, **when**, **while**
- **Relativpronomen** wie **that** und **who**

Adjektive und Adverbien

- Mit Adjektiven kannst du Personen, Orte oder Erlebnisse genauer und interessanter beschreiben. Vergleiche: **The man looked into the room.**
  ► **The young man looked into the empty room.**
- Mit Adverbien kannst du beschreiben, **wie** jemand etwas macht:
  The young man looked nervously into the empty room.

Using paragraphs

Structuring a text

Bei guten Texten lassen sich drei Hauptabschnitte erkennen:
- eine **Einleitung**, die in das Thema einführt
- ein **Hauptteil**, der meist aus mehreren Absätzen besteht
- ein **Schluss**, der den Text mit einer Zusammenfassung oder etwas Persönlichem zu einem interessanten Ende bringt.

Topic sentences

Am Anfang eines Absatzes sind kurze, einleitende Sätze (**topic sentences**) gut, weil sie den Lesern sofort sagen, worum es geht, z. B.
1. Orte: **My trip to ... was fantastic.** • **... is famous for ...** • **... is a great place.**
2. Personen: **... is great/funny/interesting/clever ...**
3. Aktivitäten: **... is great fun.** • **Lots of people ... every day.**

Wie kann ich meine Absätze interessant gestalten?

- Beginne mit einem interessanten Einstiegssatz:
  You'll never guess what happened to me today! • **Did I tell you that ...?**
- Fange für jeden neuen Aspekt einen neuen Absatz an.
- Beende deinen Text mit einer Zusammenfassung oder etwas Persönlichem.

Writing a report – collecting and organizing ideas

Worauf kommt es bei einem Bericht an?

- Gib dem Leser **eine schnelle Orientierung**, was passiert ist.
- Beginne mit **wichtigen Informationen** und gib erst dann Detailinformationen.
- Ein Bericht gibt immer Antworten auf die **5 Ws**:
  Who? What? When? Where? Why? und manchmal auch auf **How?**
- Verwende das **simple past**.

Correcting your text

Ein Text ist noch nicht „fertig", wenn du ihn zu Ende geschrieben hast. Du solltest ihn immer mehr als einmal durchlesen:
- einmal, um zu sehen, ob er vollständig und gut verständlich ist
- noch einmal, um ihn auf Fehler zu überprüfen, z. B. **Rechtschreibfehler** ***(spelling mistakes)*** oder **Grammatikfehler** ***(grammar mistakes)***.

tomato [tə'mɑːtəʊ], *pl* **tomatoes** Tomate

wife [waɪf], *pl* **wives** [waɪvz] Ehefrau

drop (-**pp**-) [drɒp] fallen lassen

forget (-**tt**-) [fə'get] vergessen

Spelling mistakes

Lies deinen Text langsam, Wort für Wort, Buchstabe für Buchstabe. Wenn du unsicher bist, hilft dir ein Wörterbuch. Beachte folgende Regeln:

Tipp

- Manche Wörter haben Buchstaben, die man nicht spricht, aber schreibt, z. B. **knife**, **climb**.
- Manchmal ändert sich die Schreibweise, wenn ein Wort eine Endung erhält,
  z. B. **take** → **taking**, **terrible** → **terribly**, **lucky** → **luckily**,
  try → **tries** (**aber stay** → **stays**), **run** → **running**, **drop** → **dropped**.
- Beim Plural tritt manchmal noch ein **-e** zum **-s**, z. B. **church** → **churches**.

Grammar mistakes

Diese Tipps helfen dir, typische Fehler zu vermeiden:

Tipp

- Im **simple present** wird in der 3. Person Singular **-s** angehängt: **she knows**
- **Unregelmäßige Verben:** Manche Verben bilden die Formen des *simple past* und des Partizip Perfekt *(past participle)* unregelmäßig. Die unregelmäßigen Formen musst du lernen. Die Liste steht auf S. 239–240.
  go – went – gone; buy – bought – bought
- **Verneinung bei Vollverben:** Im *simple present* mit ***don't/doesn't***, im *simple past* mit **didn't**, z. B. **He doesn't speak French, he didn't learn it at school.**
- **Satzstellung**: Im Englischen gilt immer (auch im Nebensatz):
  a) subject – verb – object (S-V-O) **... when I saw my brother.**
  ... als ich meinen Bruder sah.
  b) Orts- vor Zeitangabe **I bought a nice book in town yesterday.**
  Ich habe gestern in der Stadt ein schönes Buch gekauft.

SF Writing a CV

Was ist ein CV?

CV bedeutet „Lebenslauf". Ein Lebenslauf ist eine Zusammenfassung deiner bisherigen Ausbildung, deiner Fähigkeiten und deiner Interessen. Du brauchst einen Lebenslauf, wenn du dich um eine berufliche Anstellung bewirbst. Amerikaner benutzen statt *CV* das Wort *resumé*.

CURRICULUM VITAE
Oliver Schäfer

Tulpenweg 34 32051 Herford, Germany
Telephone: 00 49 5221 978036
Email: oliver.schaefer@email-hf.de

Education
2004-2010 Gutenberg-Gesamtschule (secondary school), Herford, Germany
2000-2004 Regenbogen Grundschule (primary school), Herford, Germany

Qualifications
Studying for *Fachoberschulreife* (equivalent of GCSEs)
Languages: English (6 years), French (4 years)
Driving licence

Work experience
Work experience at a garage (3 weeks)

Hobbies and interests
My hobbies are cycling, doing workouts, repairing all kinds of machines. I am very interested in technical things and computers.

References
Available on request

Geburtsdatum und -ort werden in einem CV/resumé **meist nicht** genannt. In der Regel fügst du auch **kein Foto** von dir bei.

Gib deine Telefonnummer mit der **internationalen Vorwahl** an.

Fettgedruckte Überschriften und eine **klare Gliederung** erleichtern das Lesen.

GCSEs gibt es nur in Großbritannien, in den USA entspricht das dem **US high school diploma**.

An dieser Stelle kann auch eine **konkrete Person** als **Referenz** genannt werden. Selbstverständlich musst du ihn oder sie vorher fragen!

Du kannst auch den Abschnitt **Personal statement** hinzufügen, in dem du deine persönlichen Stärken hervorhebst, z.B. *I am a hard-working, reliable student and I like working in a team. I am looking forward to getting more experience in the work place.*

Tipp

Bevor du deinen Lebenslauf losschickst, geh folgende Checkliste durch:
- Habe ich weißes A4-Papier benutzt? Ist das Blatt sauber und ordentlich?
- Habe ich den Lebenslauf mit einem Computer geschrieben?
- Ist die Seite klar gegliedert und gut lesbar?
- Habe ich alle zentralen Bereiche abgedeckt: meine Erfahrungen, meine Interessen, meine Fähigeiten und persönlichen Eigenschaften?
- Habe ich auch wirklich keine sprachlichen Fehler in meinem Schreiben?

SF Writing letters

Beim Schreiben von Briefen und E-Mails musst du unterschiedliche Regeln beachten, je nachdem, ob du einen förmlichen Brief (*formal letter*) an unbekannte Personen, Behörden, Zeitschriften usw. schreibst oder einen persönlichen, informellen Brief (*informal letter*) an Freunde oder Verwandte.

Worauf kommt es bei förmlichen Briefen an? (formal letters)

(1) Schreibe deine Adresse (ohne Namen) und das Datum in die rechte obere Ecke. Verwende keine typisch deutschen Buchstaben wie z. B. ß, ä, ö, oder ü.
(2) Die Anschrift steht links.
(3) Die Anrede lautet *Dear Sir or Madam*. Wenn du den Namen des Adressaten kennst, beginne deinen Brief mit *Dear Mr/ Mrs/Ms ...*
(4) Verwende Langformen. (*I am, I would like* statt *I'm, I'd like* etc.)
(5) Nenne zu Beginn den Grund deines Briefes.
(6) Bedanke dich bei Bitten und Anfragen im Voraus. (*I look forward to hearing from you. Thank you.*)
(7) Beende den Brief mit *Yours faithfully*, wenn du den Adressaten nicht kennst. Hast du den Adressaten am Anfang des Briefes mit Namen angeredet, dann schreibe *Yours sincerely*.
(8) Unterschreibe den Brief und tippe zusätzlich deinen Namen.

Tipp

Beachte, was du zum Schreiben von Texten gelernt hast:
- Vor dem Schreiben: Ideen sammeln, dann sortieren.
- Während des Schreibens: Sätze verbinden und ausbauen; strukturieren.
- Nach dem Schreiben: Überprüfe deinen Brief inhaltlich und sprachlich. ▸ *SF Writing course (pp. 151–152)*

Example for a letter of application

(1) Schillerstr. 17
37067 Goettingen
Germany

(2) Jane Hall
Meadows Home Farm Shop
Harston
Cambridge CB22 4BE
Great Britain

4 May 2010

(3) Dear Ms Hall

(5) (4) I am writing to you about the advertisement in the Cambridge Weekly News of April 21st. I would love (4) to work for you at Meadows Home Farm this summer.

I am 16 years old and I have a good level of English but would like to improve my speaking skills. I am hard-working, friendly and a fast learner. At home I look after two horses so farm work is not new to me. I have also worked in a sports shop so I have experience in serving people and working in a team. My hobbies are horse riding, playing volleyball and hiking. Please find my CV enclosed with this letter.

Thank you for your time. I look forward to hearing (6) from you.

(7) Yours sincerely

(8) *Tamara Wille*
Tamara Wille

Was muss ich bei einem Bewerbungsschreiben beachten?

Eine schriftliche Bewerbung besteht aus einem Lebenslauf (▸ *SF Writing a CV, p. 153*) und einem Anschreiben. Bei einem Bewerbungsschreiben musst du alle Regeln für das Schreiben von förmlichen Briefen beachten.
Wenn du dich auf eine ausgeschriebene Stelle bewirbst, solltest du dich in deinem Anschreiben auf die Stellenanzeige beziehen (*letter of application*). Wenn du bei einer Firma anfragst, ob sie eine Praktikums- oder Arbeitsstelle haben, begründest du in deinem Anschreiben, warum du dich für diese Firma interessierst (*letter of motivation*).
In beiden Fällen solltest du hervorheben, warum gerade du für ein Praktikum oder die ausgeschriebene Stelle geeignet bist.

▸▸▸

Letter of application

- Sage, auf welche Stellenanzeige du dich beziehst.
  I am writing about your advertisement in ...
- Nenne deine Stärken. Gehe dabei besonders auf die Qualifikationen und Interessen ein, die in der Stellenanzeige genannt werden. Zeige auch, dass du dich über das Unternehmen informiert hast.
  I have studied English for six years and my level is quite high.
  I am a friendly, ... person and I enjoy working in a team/serving customers ...
  As you can see on my CV, I have done work experience in ...
- Danke dem Adressaten für seine Aufmerksamkeit und sage, dass du dich auf eine Antwort freust.
  Thank you very much for your time. I look forward to hearing from you.

Letter of motivation

- Sage, woher du das Unternehmen kennst und warum du dich an es wendest. Nenne den Zeitpunkt, ab dem du eine Stelle oder ein Praktikum antreten könntest.
  I learned about your company through internet research/at our school's career information day/...
  I am writing to apply for a summer job/a part-time job/...
  I am 16 years old and I will finish school in ...
- Nenne deine Stärken, Interessen und Qualifikationen, die für das Unternehmen interessant sein könnten. Zeige, dass du dich über das Unternehmen informiert hast.
  I have good computer skills/... • I am good at ...
  I am very interested in ... • I like working in a team/serving customers/...
  On your website I learned that your company ...
- Danke dem Adressaten für seine Aufmerksamkeit und kündige an, dass du dich wieder melden wirst.
  Thank you very much for your time. I will contact you in two weeks to see if you need more information.

Was ist wichtig bei einem Leserbrief an eine Zeitung oder Zeitschrift?

- Wenn du auf einen Zeitschriftenartikel reagieren und einen Leserbrief (*letter to a newspaper/magazine* oder *letter to the editor*) schreiben sollst, beginne deinen Brief mit
  Dear Sir or Madam / Dear Editor (oder mit dem Namen des Autors des Artikels)

Was ist bei persönlichen Briefen anders? (informal letters)

Hier sind die Regeln nicht ganz so streng. Aber beachte Folgendes:

- Schreibe deine Adresse (ohne Namen) und das Datum in die rechte obere Ecke.
- Verwende keine typisch deutschen Buchstaben wie z. B. ß, ä, ö, oder ü.
- Du benötigst keine Anschrift.
- Du kannst deinen Brief mit *Dear/Hello/Hi* ... beginnen.
- Nenne zu Beginn den Grund deines Briefes, stelle auch Fragen.
- Beende den Brief mit einem freundlichen Gruß/Ausblick/Erwartungen/...
- Schließe deinen Brief mit *Yours/Best wishes/Love/*... ab.

Tipp

- Dein Anschreiben sollte nicht länger als eine DIN- A4-Seite sein. Beschränke dich auf das Wichtigste.
- Gib keine Informationen zu deiner Familie.
- Frage beim ersten Kontakt nicht gleich nach der Bezahlung.
- Beschreibe deine Stärken in sachlicher Form, ohne dabei angeberisch zu wirken, z. B.: *My level in English is quite high.* (nicht: *My English is brilliant.*)
- Auch bei einer Bewerbung per E-Mail musst du alle Regeln eines förmlichen Schreibens beachten. Verwende keine unseriös klingende E-Mail-Adresse wie z. B. sexgod88@mail.de!

SF From outline to written discussion

Worum geht es bei einer *outline*?

Oft sollst du zu strittigen Fragen wie z.B. **Carbon rationing should be introduced in Germany.** schriftlich Stellung nehmen und deine Position überzeugend darlegen. Dabei sollst du zeigen, dass du dich intensiv mit dem Thema auseinandergesetzt und Pro und Kontra abgewogen hast. Dafür ist es hilfreich, wenn du erst Argumente sammelst und sie dann **vor** dem Schreiben des Textes gliederst. Diese Gliederung nennt man *outline*. Sie erleichtert dir das anschließende Schreiben.

Wie gehe ich bei einer *outline* vor?

1. Collecting ideas
Beim Sammeln von Ideen kannst du unterschiedliche Techniken nutzen. Dabei ist es sinnvoll, wenn du neben den Argumenten auch konkrete Beispiele notierst, die deine Aussage verdeutlichen.

▸ *SF Brainstorming (p. 149)*

2. Outlining
Mit Hilfe der *outline* strukturierst du die Ideen, die du zuvor gesammelt hast. Überleg dir, welche Meinung du zu der gestellten Frage hast. Führe in der *outline* erst die Argumente auf, die gegen deine Meinung sprechen. Stell erst danach die Argumente und Beispiele vor, die deine Meinung stützen.
Eine Erörterung besteht aus vier Teilen. Ordne deine Ideen stichwortartig nach dem Schema rechts.

1 Introduction
2 First point of view: Arguments and examples
3 Second point of view: Arguments and examples
4 Conclusion

Wie mache ich aus der *outline* eine Erörterung?

1. Introduction
In der Einleitung stellst du das Thema vor und beschreibst, worum es geht. Dabei kannst du von einer persönlichen Erfahrung oder einem allgemein bekannten Problem ausgehen.
Lots of people think ... • It is generally believed that ... • I once ... • You often hear people say that • ..., so the question is: should ... or not?

2. Present the first point of view
Zunächst führst du die Argumente an, die gegen deine Überzeugung sprechen.
First ...; second ... • Another argument for/against ... is ... • For example, ... • It might also be argued that ... • Finally ... • So ... • That is why ...

3. Present the second point of view
Präsentiere dann die Argumente, die deine Meinung stützen. Wichtig ist, dass du eine Überleitung schreibst und deine Argumente mit Beispielen (z.B. aus deiner eigenen Erfahrung) anreicherst.
However, lots of people feel ... • Other people disagree. They think that ... • It is also important to remember ... • It is only partly true that ...

4. Conclusion
Am Schluss wägst du das Für und Wider noch einmal ab und sagst deine Meinung. Nenn keine neuen Argumente mehr.
To sum up, I would say that ... • After looking at both sides I think ...

MEDIATION SKILLS

SF Mediation

Wann muss ich zwischen zwei Sprachen vermitteln?

Manchmal musst du zwischen zwei Sprachen vermitteln. Das nennt man *mediation*.

1. Du gibst englische Informationen auf Deutsch weiter:
Du fährst z. B. mit deiner Familie in die USA und deine Eltern oder Geschwister wollen wissen, was jemand in einem Café gesagt hat oder was an einer Informationstafel steht.

2. Du gibst deutsche Informationen auf Englisch weiter:
Vielleicht ist bei dir zu Hause eine Austauschschülerin aus den USA oder Dänemark zu Gast, die kein Deutsch spricht und Hilfe braucht.

3. In schriftlichen Prüfungen musst du manchmal in einem englischen Text gezielt nach Informationen suchen und diese auf Deutsch wiedergeben. Oder du sollst Informationen aus einem deutschen Text auf Englisch wiedergeben.

Worauf muss ich bei *mediation* achten?

- Übersetze nicht alles wörtlich.
- Gib nur das Wesentliche weiter. Oft gibt dir die Fragestellung Hinweise, worauf es ankommt.
- Verwende kurze und einfache Sätze.
- Wenn du ein Wort nicht kennst, umschreibe es oder ersetze es durch ein anderes Wort.

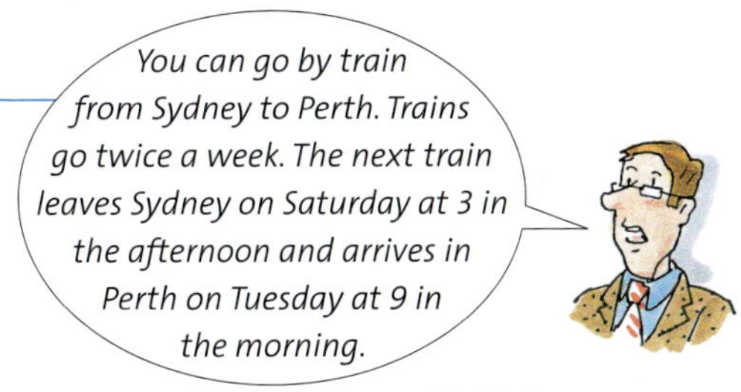

Was kann ich tun, wenn ich ein wichtiges Wort nicht kenne?

Vielleicht findest du es manchmal schwer, mündliche Aussagen oder schriftliche Textvorlagen in die andere Sprache zu übertragen, z. B. weil
- dein Wortschatz nicht ausreicht
- dir bekannte Wörter im Augenblick nicht einfallen
- spezielle Fachbegriffe auftauchen.

Manche Wörter kannst du umschreiben, z. B. mithilfe von Relativsätzen wie:
It's somebody/a person who ...
It's something that you use to ...
It's an animal that ...
It's a place where ...

► *SF Paraphrasing (p. 149)*

Grammar File – Inhalt

Im **Grammar File** (S. 158–177) werden wesentliche grammatische Themen aus den Klassen 5 bis 9 noch einmal zusammengefasst.

In der linken Spalte stehen Beispielsätze und Übersichten.

In der rechten Spalte stehen Erklärungen und Hinweise.

Indirect speech (reporting verb: simple past)

Kate said that she loved basketball. She told me she was training hard for their next match.

◄ Steht das **einleitende Verb im *simple past*** (*she said, told me, answered* usw.), werden die Zeitformen der direkten Rede meist um eine Zeitstufe in die Vergangenheit „zurückverschoben" *(backshift of tenses)*.

He said his name was Alex.
Er sagte, dass er Alex heißt.

! Im Englischen steht vor der indirekten Rede **kein Komma** und das Wort *that* wird oft weggelassen.

Veränderungen der Zeitformen bei einleitendem Verb im *simple past*

	Direct speech	Indirect speech
present ► **past**	'I don't like football.' 'I'm training hard.'	She **said** she didn't like football. She **added** that she was training hard.
past ► **past perfect**	'We played very well last week.'	She **said** they had played very well last week.
can ► ***could***	'I can get you a ticket for our next match.'	She **told** me she could get me a ticket for their next match.

Additional information

The present perfect progressive

I've **been writing** e-mails all day.
Ich **schreibe** (schon) den ganzen Tag E-Mails.

„Additional information"-Abschnitte enthalten Grammatik, die du nicht selbst zu verwenden brauchst. Du solltest aber verstehen, was dort erklärt wird, damit du keine Schwierigkeiten mit Texten hast, in denen diese Grammatik vorkommt.

GF 1 Word order Wortstellung

1.1 S – V – O

S – V – O

Subject – Verb – Object

		Subject	Verb	Object	
1		Rob	likes	ice cream.	
		The Clarks	have bought	a house	in Bath.
2		Ella	didn't like	the film.	
		Ava	can't speak	German	very well.
3	Can	Jamie	speak	German?	
	Did	you	like	the film?	

Die wichtigste Wortstellungsregel ist **Subject – Verb – Object** (Subjekt – Prädikat – Objekt). Sie gilt in bejahten und verneinten Aussagesätzen (1, 2) und in Fragen (3).

► *Fragebildung: 2 (p. 161)*

! Beachte die Unterschiede zum Deutschen:

1 We're going to have **a big party**.
Wir werden **eine große Party** veranstalten.

1 Die Teile des Prädikats (*are going to have*) dürfen nicht durch das Objekt (*a big party*) getrennt werden.

2 We **often** have fish **on Fridays**.
Wir essen **freitags oft** Fisch.

2 Prädikat und Objekt (*have fish*) dürfen nicht durch Adverbien (*often*) oder Zeitangaben (*on Fridays*) getrennt werden.

3 Yesterday **we** celebrated Grandpa's birthday.
Gestern feierten **wir** Opas Geburtstag.
When I arrived, **the film** had already begun.
Als ich ankam, hatte **der Film** schon begonnen.

3 Die Wortstellung ist auch dann S – V – ..., wenn der Satz mit einer Zeitangabe (*yesterday*) oder einem Nebensatz (*When I arrived*) beginnt.

4 He'll go out with you if you ask **him**.
..., wenn du **ihn** fragst.
Elisabeth told me that she loves **Jeremy**.
..., dass sie **Jeremy** liebt.

4 Die Wortstellung S – V – O gilt auch in Nebensätzen (*if you ask him; that she loves Jeremy*).

1.2 Adverbs and phrases of place and time

Adverbien und Orts- und Zeitangaben

1 Luckily she was able to stop the car.
At first we couldn't see anything.

1 **Satzadverbien** wie *perhaps, maybe, suddenly, luckily, finally, of course, at first* beziehen sich auf den ganzen Satz. Sie stehen in der Regel am Satzanfang.

2 We don't often get up before 10 on Sundays.
I usually make breakfast for everybody.
We had never been to Spain before.

2 **Adverbien der unbestimmten Zeit oder Häufigkeit** wie *already, always, ever, just, never, often, sometimes, usually* stehen gewöhnlich vor dem Vollverb.

3 Try to speak clearly, then you'll do well.
The guide answered the questions politely.
They went outside and played in the garden.
We're flying to Spain tomorrow.

3 Nach dem Vollverb (+ Objekt) stehen gewöhnlich
- **Adverbien der Art und Weise** (*clearly, politely, well*)
- **Ortsangaben** (*outside, in Bristol, on the roof*)
- **Zeitangaben** (*tomorrow, a year ago, in 2008*).

We were in Italy last summer.
Wir waren letzten Sommer in Italien.

! Wenn ein Satz mit einer Orts- und einer Zeitangabe endet, dann gilt die Regel **Ort vor Zeit** – wie im Alphabet: **O vor Z**.

Every Friday evening we do the shopping.
Sometimes you can see foxes from my window.
In Britain, school usually starts at 8.45 or 9.00.

◄ Manchmal stehen Adverbien, Ortsangaben und Zeitangaben auch an anderen Stellen im Satz.

GF 2 Making questions Fragebildung

Word order in questions (except in subject questions)

1 Are you from Scotland?
Do you like pizza?
Have you got a pet?
2 Where are you from?
What is your favourite food?
Why did they move to Wales?

Wortstellung in Fragen (außer in Fragen nach dem Subjekt)

1 **Entscheidungsfragen *(Yes/No questions)*** können nur mit „Ja" oder „Nein" beantwortet werden.

2 **Fragen mit Fragewörtern *(Questions with questions words)*** erfragen weitere Informationen („Wer?" „Was?" „Wann?" „Wo?" „Warum?" „Wie?").

Auxiliary	Subject	Main verb	
Can	you	**drive** a moped?	
Is	Jake	**washing** the dishes?	
Have	you	**seen** 'Twilight' yet?	
Will	they	**arrive** on time?	
Do	you	**like** pizza?	Magst du ...?
Does	she	**live** in Bristol?	Wohnt sie ...?
Did	they	**move** to Wales?	
Don't	they	**live** here any more?	

◄ **Entscheidungsfragen** beginnen immer mit einem **Hilfsverb *(auxiliary verb)***:
Can ...? Is ...? Have ...? Will ...? ...

Die Wortstellung ist also:
Auxiliary – S – V – ...

In *simple present*- und *simple past*-Fragen braucht man eine Form des Hilfsverbs ***do***:
Do ...? Does ...? Did ...?
Die deutschen Entsprechungen haben meist kein Hilfsverb.

Question word	Auxiliary	Subject	Main verb
When	can	you	**come** to Bath?
What	have	they	**bought**?
Where	will	you	**stay**?
How	do	you	**know**?
Why	does	Ella	**want** to move?
Who	did	you	**meet** in London?

◄ Auch in **Fragen**, die mit einem **Fragewort** beginnen, steht ein **Hilfsverb** vor dem Subjekt:
When can ...? What have ...? Where will ...? ...

Die Wortstellung ist also:
Question word – Auxiliary – S – V – ...

Wie die Entscheidungsfragen erfordern auch Fragewort-Fragen im *simple present* und im *simple past* eine Form des Hilfsverbs ***do***:
How do ...? Why does ...? Who did ...?

2.2 Word order in subject questions

Wortstellung in Fragen nach dem Subjekt

Question word (= Subject)	Verb	
Who	can drive	a moped?
Who	likes	ice cream?
What	makes	you laugh?
Whose sister	moved	to Bristol?
Which bus	goes	to Bath?

◄ Fragen nach dem Subjekt sind **„Wer oder was?"**-Fragen. In solchen Fragen tritt das Fragewort an die Stelle des Subjekts. Vergleiche:

***Jenny** likes ice cream.*	*Jenny mag Eis.*
***Who** likes ice cream?*	*Wer mag Eis?*

Statement	Subject question	Object question
Liz likes Jake. Liz mag Jake.	**Who** likes Jake? **Wer** mag Jake?	**Who** does Liz like? **Wen** mag Liz?
Noise causes headaches.	**What** causes headaches?	**What** does noise cause?

! Mit *who, what, whose ...* und *which ...* kann man nach dem Subjekt oder nach dem Objekt fragen. Fragen nach dem Subjekt werden **ohne *do/does/did*** gebildet.

GF 3 Talking about the present Über die Gegenwart sprechen

Du möchtest ausdrücken,

– dass etwas **regelmäßig** geschieht ▸ *The simple present: GF 3.1*	→	Hanna **gets up** at 7 o'clock every morning. Hanna steht jeden Morgen um 7 Uhr auf.
– dass etwas **gerade jetzt** geschieht ▸ *The present progressive: GF 3.2*	→	It's 7 o'clock. Hanna **is getting up**. Es ist 7 Uhr. Hanna steht (gerade) auf.

3.1 The simple present

Das ***simple present*** wird verwendet,

Dave Wilson **usually** gets the bus to school.
On Mondays his mother takes him in the car.
He **never** cycles to school because it's too far.

◂ um über Handlungen und Ereignisse zu sprechen, die **wiederholt, regelmäßig, immer** oder **nie** geschehen (oft mit Zeitangaben wie *always, never, usually, sometimes, often, every week, on Mondays* usw.).

Dave and his family live in Manchester.
He plays hockey and collects models of old cars.
His dad works for a building company.

◂ um über **Dauerzustände**, **Hobbys** und **Berufe** zu sprechen.

! *He, she, it* – das „s" muss mit.

Verneinte Sätze	I don't cycle to school.	Dave doesn't walk to school.
Fragen	Do you go to school by bus? **Where** do the Wilsons live?	Does your mother take you in the car? **When** does Dave's mother take him in the car?

3.2 The present progressive

Das ***present progressive*** wird verwendet,

What's Dave doing? – **Just now** he's cleaning his bike.

◂ um über Handlungen und Ereignisse zu sprechen, die **jetzt gerade im Gange** sind (oft mit Angaben wie *at the moment, now, just*).

Dave (on the phone) I can't talk right now, Jack. I'm cleaning my bike.

! Die Handlung, um die es geht, kann für einen Augenblick unterbrochen sein, z. B. durch ein Telefonat. Wichtig ist, dass sie noch nicht abgeschlossen ist.

This week Dave's grandma is staying at the Wilsons' because Dave's mum is ill.

◂ um über **vorübergehende Zustände** zu sprechen (begrenzter Zeitraum: *this week*).

Verneinte Sätze	The Wilsons aren't working.	Dave isn't watching TV.
Fragen	Are you watching TV? **What** are you doing?	Is Dave cleaning his bike? **Who** is Dave talking to?

Dave's dad works for a building company.
Look, he's working at his desk at the moment.

GF 4 Talking about the past Über die Vergangenheit sprechen

Du möchtest ausdrücken,

– dass etwas in der Vergangenheit **geschah**; das Geschehen ist **abgeschlossen** und **vorbei** ▸ *The simple past: GF 4.1*	→ Emma **left** school in 2007. Emma ging im Jahr 2007 von der Schule ab.
– dass etwas in der Vergangenheit **gerade im Gange (noch nicht abgeschlossen) war** ▸ *The past progressive: GF 4.2*	→ We **were leaving** the building when we heard the explosion. Wir waren gerade dabei, das Gebäude zu verlassen, ...
– dass etwas **vor etwas anderem** in der Vergangenheit stattgefunden hatte ▸ *The past perfect: GF 4.3*	→ Connor **had** already **left** when we arrived. Connor war schon gegangen, als wir ankamen.
– dass etwas **irgendwann** geschehen ist, oft mit **Auswirkungen auf die Gegenwart**	→ Jane **has left** her purse at home, so she can't pay for her bus ticket. Jane hat ihre Geldbörse zu Hause gelassen, ...
– dass ein Zustand **in der Vergangenheit begonnen** hat und **noch andauert** ▸ *The present perfect: GF 4.4*	→ We**'ve had** our dog for three years now – since 2008. Wir haben unseren Hund jetzt seit drei Jahren ...

4.1 The simple past

Last Friday Katie's family flew to Spain.
Letzten Freitag ist Katies Familie nach Spanien geflogen / flog Katies Familie nach Spanien.
Two years ago the Websters moved to Bath.
Vor zwei Jahren sind die Websters nach Bath gezogen.

Wenn man über Vergangenes berichtet, benutzt man überwiegend das ***simple past***. Man beschreibt damit Handlungen, Ereignisse und Zustände, die zu einer bestimmten Zeit in der Vergangenheit *(yesterday, last Friday, two years ago, in 2003, between 2005 and 2008, ...)* stattfanden.

! Im Deutschen wird in diesen Fällen oft das Perfekt verwendet, im Englischen jedoch nicht.

Verneinte Sätze	They didn't fly to France.	Katie didn't want to go at first.
Fragen	Did you go on holiday last year? **Where** did you go?	Did Katie like it? **When** did the Websters move to Bath?

4.2 The past progressive

What were you doing yesterday at 3.30? –
I was waiting for my sister at the school doors.
She was still talking to our Maths teacher.

Angela was just crossing the road when she saw her boyfriend.
Angela war gerade dabei, die Straße zu überqueren, ...

Das ***past progressive*** wird verwendet,

◂ um über Handlungen und Ereignisse zu sprechen, die zu einer bestimmten Zeit in der Vergangenheit noch im Gange, also noch nicht abgeschlossen waren.

◂ wenn man beschreiben will, was gerade vor sich ging *(she was just crossing the road)*, als etwas anderes passierte *(she saw her boyfriend)*.

Verneinte Sätze	You weren't listening.	It wasn't snowing when we left the house.
Fragen	Were you watching TV? **What** were they doing?	Was she crossing the road when it happened? **What** was she doing?

▸▸▸

4.3 The past perfect

When Emma arrived home, her parents had already eaten.
Als Emma zu Hause eintraf, hatten ihre Eltern bereits gegessen.

Wenn man sagen will, dass etwas noch <u>vor etwas anderem</u> in der Vergangenheit stattgefunden hatte, dann benutzt man das ***past perfect***.

Verneinte Sätze	They hadn't gone to bed.	Emma hadn't eaten anything all day.
Fragen	Had you seen that film before? **What** had they done?	Had Emma eaten when she came home? **Where** had she been all day?

4.4 The present perfect

Will Smith is great. I've seen most of his films.
Luke has **already** done his Maths homework, but he has**n't** started his French **yet**.
Have you **ever** been to Paris?
– No, I haven't. But I've **always** wanted to go.

Mel has lost her mobile. Her dad is very angry.

! Das ***present perfect*** hat mit der **Vergangenheit <u>und</u> mit der Gegenwart** zu tun. Es wird verwendet,

◂ wenn man sagen will, **dass** jemand etwas getan hat oder **dass** etwas geschehen ist. Dabei ist nicht wichtig, wann es geschehen ist – ein genauer Zeitpunkt wird nicht genannt. Das *present perfect* steht oft mit Adverbien der <u>unbestimmten</u> Zeit wie *already, just, never, ever, not ... yet*.
Oft hat die Handlung Auswirkungen auf die Gegenwart (Mels Vater ist wütend, weil sie ihr Handy verloren hat).

We've had our new car **since April**.
Wir haben unser neues Auto <u>seit April</u>.

since **+ Zeitpunkt**

We've had our new car **for three months**.
Wir haben unser neues Auto <u>seit drei Monaten</u>.

for **+ Zeitraum**

◂ für **Zustände**, die in der Vergangenheit begonnen haben und jetzt noch andauern (oft mit ***since*** bzw. ***for***).

! Im Deutschen steht in diesen Fällen meist das Präsens, im Englischen <u>muss</u> das *present perfect* stehen.

Verneinte Sätze	I haven't been to Paris yet.	Luke hasn't done his French homework.
Fragen	Have you been to Paris? **What** have you done?	Has Mel found her mobile yet? **Which** of these films have you seen already?

Additional information

4.5 The present perfect progressive

I've **been writing** e-mails all day.
Ich **schreibe** (schon) den ganzen Tag E-Mails.

We've **been learning** French for four years.
Wir **lernen** seit vier Jahren Französisch.

Auch das ***present perfect progressive*** hat mit der Vergangenheit <u>und</u> mit der Gegenwart zu tun. Es wird verwendet für **Vorgänge** und **Handlungen**, die in der Vergangenheit begonnen haben und jetzt noch andauern (oft mit ***since*** bzw. ***for***).

! Auch hier steht im Deutschen meist das Präsens – aber im Englischen das *present perfect progressive*.

GF 5 Talking about the future Über die Zukunft sprechen

Du möchtest ausdrücken,

– dass etwas für die Zukunft **geplant** ist ▸ *The going to-future: GF 5.1*	→ I'm **going to watch** the new Bond film tonight. Ich sehe mir heute Abend den neuen Bond-Film an.
– wie etwas in der Zukunft **sein wird** (**Vorhersagen, Vermutungen**) ▸ *The will-future: GF 5.2*	→ It **will be** warm and sunny in Spain. I'm sure you'**ll like** it there. Es wird warm und sonnig sein in Spanien. Ich bin sicher, dass es dir dort gefallen wird.
– dass etwas für die Zukunft **fest verabredet** ist (es steht schon im Kalender) ▸ *The present progressive: GF 5.3*	→ We'**re having** a party on Saturday. Would you like to come? Wir geben nächsten Samstag eine Party. ...

5.1 The *going to*-future

Das **Futur mit *going to*** wird verwendet,

My boyfriend says he's going to be an engineer.
Mein Freund sagt, er will Ingenieur werden.

◂ wenn man über **Vorhaben, Pläne, Absichten** für die Zukunft sprechen will.

Look at those clouds. There's going to be a storm.
... Es wird ein Gewitter geben.

◂ um auszudrücken, dass etwas **wahrscheinlich gleich geschehen wird** – es gibt bereits deutliche **Anzeichen** dafür (*hier:* die Wolken am Himmel).

5.2 The *will*-future

Das **Futur mit *will*** wird verwendet,

It will be cold and windy, and we will get some rain in the afternoon.
I'll be 15 next October.

◂ um **Vorhersagen** über die Zukunft zu äußern. Oft geht es dabei um Dinge, die man nicht beeinflussen kann, z. B. das Wetter.

I expect Ella will be late again as usual.
Ich nehme an, Ella kommt wie üblich wieder zu spät.

◂ um eine **Vermutung** auszudrücken (oft eingeleitet mit *I think, I'm sure, I expect, maybe*).

Just a moment. I'll open the door for you.
Moment. Ich mache Ihnen die Tür auf.
I won't tell anyone what's happened. I promise.
Ich sage niemandem, was passiert ist. ...

◂ wenn man sich **spontan** – also ohne es im Voraus geplant zu haben – zu etwas **entschließt**. Oft geht es dabei um **Hilfsangebote** oder **Versprechen**.

5.3 The present progressive (future meaning)

We're driving to Scotland next Friday to visit my grandparents.
I'm meeting a friend in town tonight.

Das ***present progressive*** wird verwendet, wenn etwas **für die Zukunft fest geplant** oder **fest verabredet** ist (manchmal spricht man vom *diary future*). Durch eine Zeitangabe wie *tonight* oder aus dem Zusammenhang muss klar sein, dass es um etwas Zukünftiges geht.

Additional information

5.4 The simple present (future meaning)

The next train to Bath **goes** in ten minutes.
The next drawing class **starts** on 2 September.

Das ***simple present*** wird verwendet, wenn ein **zukünftiges Geschehen** durch einen **Fahrplan**, ein **Programm** oder Ähnliches festgelegt ist (manchmal spricht man vom *timetable future*). Verben wie *arrive, leave, go, open, close, start, stop* werden häufig so verwendet.

GF 6 The simple form and the progressive form
Die einfache Form und die Verlaufsform

6.1 Simple and progressive form in contrast

Einfache Form und Verlaufsform im Vergleich

	Simple form	Progressive form
Present tense	sing(s)	am/are/is singing
Present perfect	have/has sung	have/has been singing
Past tense	sang	was/were singing
Past perfect	had sung	had been singing
***will*-future**	will sing	will be singing

Anders als im Deutschen gibt es im Englischen eine **einfache Form *(simple form)*** und eine **Verlaufsform *(progressive form)*** des Verbs.

The simple form

1a Olivia plays tennis every Saturday.
(regelmäßig, jeden Samstag)

2a Mr Bale works in an office in the city centre.
(immer, jeden Tag)

3a Ella left home at 7.15.
(die Handlung ist beendet)

◄ Die ***simple form*** wird verwendet

- für regelmäßig oder wiederholt stattfindende Handlungen (**1a**)
- für Dauerzustände (wenn etwas immer so ist) (**2a**)
- für abgeschlossene Handlungen (**3a**).

The progressive form

1b Olivia is playing tennis right now.
(sie ist gerade dabei, das Spiel ist im Gange)

2b This week Mr Bale is working at home.
(nur diese Woche, denn sein Büro wird renoviert)

3b Ella was leaving the house when she heard the explosion.
(als sie die Explosion hörte, war sie dabei zu gehen)

◄ Die ***progressive form*** wird verwendet

- für Handlungen, die gerade im Verlauf sind (**1b**)
- für vorübergehende Zustände (wenn etwas nur vorübergehend der Fall ist) (**2b**)
- für Handlungen, die zu einem bestimmten Zeitpunkt noch nicht abgeschlossen sind (**3b**).

He was washing the dishes when he heard a funny noise.
Er war gerade beim Abwaschen, ...

! Im Deutschen gibt es keine Verlaufsform.
Aber manchmal sagt und hört man Sätze wie „Ich bin gerade dabei, meine Hausaufgaben zu machen" oder „Er war (gerade) beim Abwaschen", um zum Ausdruck zu bringen, dass etwas im Gange und noch nicht abgeschlossen ist bzw. war.

! Beachte:
Nur **Tätigkeitsverben *(activity verbs)*** wie *do, drink, go, sit, write* können in der *progressive form* verwendet werden.

► *Tätigkeits- und Zustandsverben: 6.2–6.3 (p. 167)*

6.2 Activity verbs

(in a shop window) This shop repairs bikes!
(on the phone) Jack is repairing his bike. Can he call you back?

It gets dark very early here in winter.
At 6 o'clock it was already getting dark.

Tätigkeitsverben

Tätigkeitsverben bezeichnen **Tätigkeiten** *(do, go, read, repair, ...)* oder **Vorgänge** *(become, get, rain, ...)*. Sie beschreiben also, was jemand **tut** oder was **geschieht**. Tätigkeitsverben können sowohl in der *simple form* als auch in der *progressive form* verwendet werden.

6.3 State verbs

Zustandsverben

Zustandsverben *(state verbs)* bezeichnen **Zustände**. Sie werden in der Regel **nur in der *simple form*** verwendet.

Zu den **Zustandsverben** gehören

You don't look very happy. What's wrong?
Emily seems really happy at her new school.
Jake's uncle owns a nice house in the country.

– Verben, die **Eigenschaften**, **Besitz** oder **Zugehörigkeit** ausdrücken: *be, look* („aussehen"), *seem, sound, mean* („bedeuten"), *need, own* („besitzen"), *belong, ...*

Do you believe their story?
I don't know the answer to question 5.
Anna didn't understand what Julie meant.

– Verben des **Meinens** und des **Wissens**: *believe, know, mean* („meinen"), *remember, suppose, understand, ...*

Lucy doesn't like people who talk a lot.
I don't mind waiting for you here.
Chips aren't very healthy, but I love them.

– Verben des **Mögens** und **Wollens**: *like, love, hate, mind, want, ...*

GF 7 The passive Das Passiv

7.1 Active and passive

Active: **Alexander Fleming** discovered penicillin in 1928.
Alexander Fleming entdeckte 1928 das Penicillin.

Passive: **Penicillin** was discovered in 1928.
Penicillin wurde 1928 entdeckt.

Active: The manager asked **Mel** to help out.
Passive: **Mel** was asked to help out.
Mel wurde gebeten auszuhelfen.

Active: The manager paid **her** £6 an hour.
Passive: **She** was paid £6 an hour.
Ihr wurden £6 die Stunde bezahlt. / Sie erhielt £6 die Stunde.

Aktiv und Passiv

◄ Beide Sätze beschreiben denselben Sachverhalt, betrachten ihn aber aus unterschiedlichen Blickwinkeln:

- Der **Aktivsatz** handelt von Fleming und informiert uns über eine Entdeckung, die er 1928 machte.
- Der **Passivsatz** handelt von Penicillin und informiert uns über den Zeitpunkt seiner Entdeckung.

◄ Das Passiv lässt sich im Englischen von allen Verben bilden, die im Aktivsatz ein Objekt haben.

7.2 Use

1 A new sports centre has been opened in Paddington. ... ist eröffnet worden ...
2 The first goal was scored in the seventh minute. ... wurde erzielt ...
3 Breakfast is served from 7 to 10.30 am. ... wird serviert ...
4 The bank robbers have been sent to prison. ... sind ins Gefängnis gesteckt worden ...

This picture was painted by **a 12-year-old girl.**
... wurde von einem 12-jährigen Mädchen gemalt.

Part of this building was destroyed by **fire.**
... wurde durch ein Feuer zerstört.

Gebrauch

In **Passivsätzen** steht nicht, wer die Handlung ausführt. Oft ist das unwichtig oder nicht bekannt (Sätze 1 und 2), manchmal ist es auch offensichtlich und daher nicht erwähnenswert (Sätze 3 und 4).

Das Passiv findet man oft in Nachrichten, in Zeitungsartikeln (z. B. über Unfälle, Sportereignisse, Verbrechen), in offiziellen Texten, in technischen Beschreibungen und auf Schildern.

! Wenn in Passivsätzen „Täter“ oder „Verursacher“ doch genannt werden sollen, dann verwendet man die Präposition ***by ...*** („von“, „durch“).

7.3 Form

Form

Das Passiv bildet man mit einer **Form von *be*** und der 3. Form des Verbs (Partizip Perfekt, *past participle*).

Simple present	I am often invited to parties.	... werde oft eingeladen
Simple past	The bridge was built in the 1950s.	... wurde gebaut
Present perfect	All the sandwiches have been eaten.	... sind gegessen worden
***will*-future**	Our new CD will be released next week.	... wird veröffentlicht werden
Modals	Mobile phones must be turned off now. Concert tickets can be bought online.	... müssen ausgeschaltet werden ... können gekauft werden

GF 8 Modals and their substitutes
Modale Hilfsverben und ihre Ersatzverben

8.1 Substitutes

1 I'd love to be able to speak Spanish.
Ich würde liebend gern Spanisch sprechen können.
2 Being able to speak Spanish must be great.
Spanisch sprechen zu können muss toll sein.
3 We weren't allowed to use a dictionary.
Wir durften kein Wörterbuch benutzen.

Ersatzverben

Modale Hilfsverben *(can, may, must, ...)* können **nicht alle Zeitformen** bilden. Daher gibt es zu bestimmten modalen Hilfsverben **Ersatzverben**, von denen man
- den Infinitiv (1),
- die *-ing*-Form (2)
- und alle Zeitformen (3, *simple past*) bilden kann.

„können": *can – (to) be able to*

My little brother can / is able to swim.

present: *can* und *am/is/are able to*

Tim could / was able to read when he was four.
I could smell fire, but I couldn't see any smoke.

past: *could* und *was/were able to*
could steht vor allem in verneinten Sätzen und Fragen sowie mit Verben der Wahrnehmung *(smell, see, hear, ...)*.

Jacob hasn't been able to finish his essay.

present perfect: *have/has been able to*

I'm taking driving lessons, so next year I'll be able to drive.

will-future: *will/won't be able to*

„dürfen": *can, may – (to) be allowed to*

Can / May I have a sleepover on Friday, Mum?
We aren't allowed to stay up late in the week.

present: *can, may* und *am/is/are allowed to*

Under-12s couldn't / weren't allowed to see the film without an adult.

past: *could* und *was/were allowed to*

I've always been allowed to have pets.

present perfect: *have/has been allowed to*

Will you be allowed to go to the party on Friday?

will-future: *will/won't be allowed to*

Jeans must not be worn at this school.
At my school we're not allowed to wear jeans.

! Für ausdrückliche **Verbote** wird *must not (mustn't)* oder *be not allowed to* verwendet.

„müssen": *must – (to) have to*

Teacher You must work harder, Noah.
His teacher says Noah has to work harder.
I needn't get up at 6 tomorrow. / I don't have to get up at 6 tomorrow.

present: *must* und *have/has to*
(*have/has to* ist häufiger als *must*)
! **Verneinung:**
needn't oder *don't/doesn't have to*

I had to rewrite my essay.
We didn't have to wait long.

past: *had to*
! **Verneinung:** *didn't have to*

Lauren has had to go to the dentist's.

present perfect: *have/has had to*

You will have to go to the dentist's too if you eat so many sweets.

will-future: *will/won't have to*

▶▶▶

8.2 Modals – what do they express?

Modale Hilfsverben – was drücken sie aus?

Fähigkeit

I can speak French and a little German.	Ich **kann** Französisch und ein bisschen Deutsch.
My sister could read when she was only four.	Meine Schwester **konnte** lesen, als sie erst vier war.

Bitte / Aufforderung

Can I borrow this CD?	**Kann** ich diese CD ausleihen?
Can you be quiet, please?	**Kannst** du bitte leise sein?
Could you show me how to start the DVD?	**Könntest** du mir zeigen, wie man die DVD startet?
Would you help me to wash the dishes?	**Würdest** du mir helfen abzuwaschen?

Erlaubnis / Verbot

You can use my ruler.	Du **kannst** mein Lineal benutzen.
May I use your phone, please?	**Darf** ich mal dein Telefon benutzen, bitte?
You can't take photos in the museum.	Du **darfst** im Museum **nicht** fotografieren.
In 1968, children could leave school at 15.	... **konnten/durften** Kinder mit 15 die Schule verlassen.
But they couldn't vote till they were 21.	Aber sie **konnten/durften** erst mit 21 wählen.
You mustn't tell Mel about the concert. It's a surprise.	Du **darfst** Mel **nichts** von dem Konzert erzählen. ...

Vorschlag / Ratschlag

Can/Can't we go on a bike trip?	**Können** wir **(nicht)** eine Radtour machen?
You could talk to your teacher.	Du **könntest (doch)** mit deiner Lehrerin sprechen.
You should tell her the truth.	Du **solltest** ihr die Wahrheit sagen.

Angebot

Can/May I help you with your bags?	**Kann/Darf** ich Ihnen mit Ihren Taschen helfen?
Would you like to stay for dinner?	**Möchtest** du (**nicht**) zum Essen bleiben?

Notwendigkeit, Verpflichtung

You've got a cold. You must stay at home.	Du hast eine Erkältung. Du **musst** zuhause bleiben.
You needn't tell Mel about the concert. She already knows.	Du **brauchst** Mel **nicht** von dem Konzert zu erzählen. ...
Bicycles should be left outside.	Fahrräder **sollten** draußen abgestellt werden.

Möglichkeit, Wahrscheinlichkeit

That must be Luke.	Das **muss** Luke sein.
– No, it can't be Luke. Luke is in Spain.	– Nein, das **kann nicht** Luke sein. Luke ist in Spanien.
Where's Dad? – He could be at Grandma's.	... – Er **könnte** bei Oma sein.
Sarah may still be at her friend's.	Sarah ist **vielleicht** noch bei ihrer Freundin.
John might come today if he's in town.	John kommt **vielleicht** heute vorbei, ...
Kathy should be here by now.	Kathy **sollte** jetzt (eigentlich) hier sein.
There's someone at the door. It will be Janet.	Es ist jemand an der Tür. Das **wird** Janet sein.

GF 9 Conditional sentences Bedingungssätze

9.1 Type 1 and type 2

Typ 1 und Typ 2

If you run, you'll catch the bus.
Wenn du rennst, kriegst du den Bus noch.

If you miss the bus, you can take / should take / must take a taxi.
Wenn du den Bus verpasst, kannst/sollst/musst du ein Taxi nehmen.

◄ **Typ 1** („**Was ist, wenn …"-Sätze**)
Diese Bedingungssätze beziehen sich auf die **Gegenwart** oder die **Zukunft**.
Sie drücken aus, was unter bestimmten Bedingungen **geschieht** oder **geschehen kann/soll** usw.

***if*-Satz (Bedingung)**	**Hauptsatz (Folge)**
If you run,	*you'll catch the bus.*
If you miss the bus,	*you can take a taxi.*
simple present	**– *will-future* – *can/should/must* + Infinitiv**

If you ran, you would catch the bus.
Wenn du rennen würdest, würdest du den Bus noch kriegen.

If you caught the bus, you could be home in time for dinner.
Wenn du den Bus kriegen würdest, könntest du rechtzeitig zum Abendessen daheim sein.

◄ **Typ 2** („**Was wäre, wenn …"-Sätze**)
Diese Bedingungssätze beziehen sich auch auf die **Gegenwart** oder die **Zukunft**.
Sie drücken aus, was unter bestimmten Bedingungen **geschehen würde** oder **könnte**.

***if*-Satz (Bedingung)**	**Hauptsatz (Folge)**
If you ran,	*you would catch/could catch/might catch the bus.*
simple past	***would/could/might* + Infinitiv**

Additional information

9.2 Type 3

Typ 3

If you had run, you would have caught the bus.
Wenn du gerannt wärst, hättest du den Bus noch gekriegt.

If you had caught the bus, you could have had dinner with us.
Wenn du den Bus gekriegt hättest, hättest du mit uns Abendbrot essen können.

◄ **Typ 3** („**Was wäre gewesen, wenn …"-Sätze**)
Diese Bedingungssätze beziehen sich auf die **Vergangenheit**.
Sie drücken aus, was unter bestimmten Bedingungen **geschehen wäre** oder **hätte geschehen können**.
Der Sprecher stellt sich nur vor, was geschehen wäre, aber in Wirklichkeit nicht geschehen ist:
Wenn du gerannt wärst, hättest du den Bus erwischt – aber da du nicht gerannt bist …

***if*-Satz (Bedingung)**	**Hauptsatz (Folge)**
If you had run,	*you would have caught/could have caught the bus.*
past perfect	***would/could* + *have* + Partizip Perfekt**

GF 10 Relative clauses Relativsätze

10.1 Use

1 Isn't that **the boy** who/that stole your mobile?
... der Junge, der dein Handy gestohlen hat?

2 That's **the shop** that/which sells cheap CDs.
... der Laden, der billige CDs verkauft.

Gebrauch

Relativsätze beziehen sich auf ein **Nomen**.
Sie bestimmen dieses Nomen genauer: Erst durch den Relativsatz weiß man, wer oder was genau gemeint ist.

Relativsätze werden mit den Relativpronomen ***who*** oder ***that*** für **Personen (1)** und ***that*** oder ***which*** für **Dinge (2)** eingeleitet.

10.2 Contact clauses

1 There's **the boy** who I invited to my party.
or There's **the boy** I invited to my party.
... der Junge, den ich ... eingeladen habe.

2 These are **the photos** that Dad took.
or These are **the photos** Dad took.
... die Fotos, die Dad gemacht hat.

3 Jake is **the boy** who invited us to the party.
... der Junge, der uns ... eingeladen hat.

4 This is **the photo** that won first prize.
... das Foto, das den ersten Preis gewonnen hat.

Relativsätze ohne Relativpronomen

Wenn das Relativpronomen **Objekt des Relativsatzes** ist, wird es oft **weggelassen (1, 2)**.
Relativsätze ohne Relativpronomen werden *contact clauses* genannt.

! Wenn – wie in **3** und **4** – das **Relativpronomen direkt vor dem Verb** steht, dann ist es **Subjekt** und darf <u>**nicht**</u> weggelassen werden.

GF 11 Indirect speech Die indirekte Rede

11.1 Statements

Aussagesätze

Direct speech

Kate says, 'I **love** basketball. I'**m training** hard for our next match.'

◄ In der **direkten Rede** wird **wörtlich** wiedergegeben, was jemand sagt oder gesagt hat. Direkte Rede steht in Anführungszeichen (deutsch: **„...“**; englisch: **'...'**).

Indirect speech (reporting verb: simple present)

Kate says that she loves basketball. She says she's training hard for their next match.

◄ In der **indirekten Rede** (*indirect* oder *reported speech*) wird **berichtet**, was jemand sagt oder gesagt hat. Die indirekte Rede wird mit Verben wie *say, tell sb., add, answer, explain, think* eingeleitet.

Indirect speech (reporting verb: simple past)

Kate said that she loved basketball. She told me she was training hard for their next match.

◄ Steht das **einleitende Verb im *simple past*** (*she said, told me, answered* usw.), werden die Zeitformen der direkten Rede meist um eine Zeitstufe in die Vergangenheit „zurückverschoben“ *(backshift of tenses)*.

He said his name was Alex.
Er sagte, dass er Alex heißt.

! Im Englischen steht vor der indirekten Rede **kein Komma** und das Wort *that* wird oft weggelassen.

Veränderungen der Zeitformen bei einleitendem Verb im *simple past*

	Direct speech	Indirect speech
present ► past	'I don't like football.' 'I'm training hard.'	She **said** she didn't like football. She **added** that she was training hard.
past ► past perfect	'We played very well last week.'	She **said** they had played very well last week.
can* ► *could	'I can get you a ticket for our next match.'	She **told** me she could get me a ticket for their next match.
***will*-future ► *would* + infinitive**	'It'll be fun.'	She **said** it would be fun.
***going to*-future ► *was/were going to* + infinitive**	'We're going to have a party after the match.'	She **said** they were going to have a party after the match.
present perfect ► past perfect	'I've never been so excited.'	She **added** that she had never been so excited.

- Verben im *past perfect* bleiben unverändert, da man sie nicht weiter „zurückverschieben“ kann.
- In der Umgangssprache bleiben *past*-Formen der direkten Rede oft unverändert, werden also nicht ins *past perfect* „zurückverschoben“:
  Kate We played very well last week. ► Kate said they played very well last week.

►►►

11.2 Questions

Fragen

Auch bei Fragen in der indirekten Rede werden die Zeitformen in die Vergangenheit „zurückverschoben“, wenn das einleitende Verb im *simple past* steht.

Direct question (yes/no question) — ‘Do you train every day, Kate?’

Indirect question — Alex asked Kate **if/whether** she trained every day.

◄ Handelt es sich bei der direkten Frage um eine **Frage ohne Fragewort** *(yes/no question)*, dann wird die indirekte Frage mit ***if*** oder ***whether*** („ob“) eingeleitet.

Direct question (with question word) — ‘**When** did you join the team?’

Indirect question — Alex wanted to know **when** Kate had joined the team.
..., wann Kate sich der Mannschaft angeschlossen hat.

◄ Wenn die direkte **Frage mit einem Fragewort** beginnt (*why, how, what, when, where* usw.), dann wird das Fragewort in der indirekten Frage beibehalten.

11.3 Advice, requests, commands

Ratschläge, Bitten, Aufforderungen

Kate advised Alex not to miss their next match.
Kate riet Alex, ihr nächstes Spiel nicht zu verpassen.

◄ **Ratschläge** können mit ***advise sb. to do sth.*** (bzw. ***advise sb. not to do sth.***) wiedergegeben werden.

Alex asked Kate to get him some tickets.
Alex bat Kate, ihm Eintrittskarten zu besorgen.

◄ **Bitten** werden meist mit ***ask sb. to do sth.*** (bzw. ***ask sb. not to do sth.***) wiedergegeben.

◄ **Aufforderungen** und **Anordnungen** werden meist mit ***tell sb. to do sth.*** (bzw. ***tell sb. not to do sth.***) wiedergegeben.

GF 12 Adjectives: comparison Adjektive: Steigerung

12.1 Forms

Formen

	Komparativ (Comparative)	Superlativ (Superlative)
clean	cleaner	cleanest
big	bigger	biggest
happy	happier	happiest
useful	more useful	most useful
famous	more famous	most famous
expensive	more expensive	most expensive
difficult	more difficult	most difficult
good	better	best
bad	worse	worst
much/many	more	most
(a) little	less	least

Steigerungsformen werden verwendet, um Personen oder Dinge miteinander zu vergleichen.

◀ **Steigerung** mit *-er/-est*:
- **einsilbige** Adjektive
- **zweisilbige** Adjektive, die auf **-*y*** enden

◀ **Steigerung** mit *more/most*:
- die meisten **zweisilbigen** Adjektive, die nicht auf **-*y*** enden
- Adjektive mit **mehr als zwei Silben**

◀ **unregelmäßige Steigerung**:
- ***good, bad***
- ***much/many, (a) little***

Additional information

She's cleverer / more clever than her sister.
Sie ist cleverer als ihre Schwester.

That's the stupidest / most stupid thing I've ever heard.
Das ist das Dümmste, was ich je gehört habe.

Manche zweisilbigen Adjektive können mit *-er/-est* oder mit *more/most* gesteigert werden; Beispiele: *clever, simple, stupid*.
Wenn du dir nicht sicher bist, musst du die Steigerungsformen in einem Wörterbuch nachschlagen.

12.2 The adjective in comparisons

Das Adjektiv in Vergleichen

Ella is as **old** as John. — ◀ *as ... as* „so ... wie"

She's not as **old** as Lucy. — ◀ *not as ... as* „nicht so ... wie"

Lucy is **old**er than her.
(*nicht:* ... older than ~~she~~)

◀ **Komparativ + *than***:
older than „älter als"
more expensive than „teurer ... als"

Lucy is the **old**est.

◀ ***the* + Superlativ:**
the oldest „der/die älteste, am ältesten"

Grammatical terms (Grammatische Fachbegriffe)

active ['æktɪv]	Aktiv	*Beckham **scored** the final goal.*
activity verb [æk'tɪvəti vɜːb]	Tätigkeitsverb	*do, go, make, read, repair*
adjective ['ædʒɪktɪv]	Adjektiv	*good, red, new, boring*
adverb ['ædvɜːb]	Adverb	*always, badly, here, really, today*
adverb of frequency ['friːkwənsi]	Häufigkeitsadverb	*always, often, never*
adverb of indefinite time [ɪnˌdefɪnət 'taɪm]	Adverb der unbestimmten Zeit	*already, ever, just, never*
adverb of manner ['mænə]	Adverb der Art und Weise	*badly, happily, quietly, well*
advice *(no pl)* [əd'vaɪs]	Rat, Ratschlag	*You should see a doctor.*
article ['ɑːtɪkl]	Artikel	*the, a/an*
auxiliary [ɔːg'zɪliəri]	Hilfsverb	*be, have, do; will, can, must*
backshift of tenses ['bækʃɪft]	Verschiebung der Zeitformen	*'I'm sorry.'* ►
	(bei der indirekten Rede)	*Sam said he **was** sorry.*
command [kə'mɑːnd]	Befehl, Aufforderungssatz	*Open your books. Don't talk.*
comparison [kəm'pærɪsn]	Steigerung	*old – older – oldest*
conditional sentence [kənˌdɪʃənl 'sentəns]	Bedingungssatz	*I'd call him if I knew his number.*
conjunction [kən'dʒʌŋkʃn]	Konjunktion	*and, or, but; because, before*
contact clause ['kɒntækt klɔːz]	Relativsatz ohne Relativpronomen	*She's the girl **I love**.*
countable noun ['kaʊntəbl]	zählbares Nomen	*girl – girls, pound – pounds*
definite article ['defɪnət]	bestimmter Artikel	*the*
direct speech [ˌdaɪrekt 'spiːtʃ]	direkte Rede, wörtliche Rede	***'I'm sorry.'***
future ['fjuːtʃə]	Zukunft, Futur	
gerund ['dʒerənd]	Gerundium	*I like **dancing**. **Dancing** is fun.*
***going to*-future**	Futur mit *going to*	***I'm going to watch** TV tonight.*
***if*-clause** ['ɪf klɔːz]	*if*-Satz, Nebensatz mit *if*	***If I see Jack**, I'll tell him.*
imperative [ɪm'perətɪv]	Imperativ (Befehlsform)	*Open your books. Don't talk.*
indirect speech [ˌɪndərekt 'spiːtʃ]	indirekte Rede	*Sam said **(that) he was sorry**.*
infinitive [ɪn'fɪnətɪv]	Infinitiv (Grundform des Verbs)	*(to) open, (to) see, (to) read*
irregular verb [ɪˌregjələ 'vɜːb]	unregelmäßiges Verb	*(to) go – went – gone*
main clause	Hauptsatz	***I like Scruffy** because I like dogs.*
modal, modal auxiliary [ˌməʊdl‿ɔːg'zɪliəri]	modales Hilfsverb, Modalverb	*can, could, may, must*
negative statement [ˌnegətɪv 'steɪtmənt]	verneinter Aussagesatz	*I don't like bananas.*
noun [naʊn]	Nomen, Substantiv	*Sophie, girl, brother, time*
object ['ɒbdʒɪkt]	Objekt	*My sister is writing **a letter**.*
object form ['ɒbdʒɪkt fɔːm]	Objektform (der Personalpronomen)	*me, you, him, her, it, us, them*
object question ['ɒbdʒɪkt ˌkwestʃən]	Frage nach dem Objekt	*Who does Jake love?*
participle ['pɑːtɪsɪpl]	Partizip	*planning, taking; planned, taken*
participle clause [ˌpɑːtɪsɪpl 'klɔːz]	Partizipialsatz	*I saw a boy **playing in the street**.*
passive ['pæsɪv]	Passiv	*The goal **was scored** by Beckham.*
past [pɑːst]	Vergangenheit	
past participle [ˌpɑːst 'pɑːtɪsɪpl]	Partizip Perfekt	*cleaned, planned, gone, taken*
past perfect [ˌpɑːst 'pɜːfɪkt]	Plusquamperfekt, Vorvergangenheit	*He cried – he **had hurt** his knee.*
past progressive [ˌpɑːst prə'gresɪv]	Verlaufsform der Vergangenheit	*At 7.30 I **was having** dinner.*
personal pronoun [ˌpɜːsənl 'prəʊnaʊn]	Personalpronomen	*I, you, he, she, it, we, they;*
	(persönliches Fürwort)	*me, you, him, her, it, us, them*
plural ['plʊərəl]	Plural, Mehrzahl	
positive statement [ˌpɒzətɪv 'steɪtmənt]	bejahter Aussagesatz	*I like oranges.*
possessive determiner [pəˌzesɪv dɪ'tɜːmɪnə]	Possessivbegleiter (besitzanzeigender Begleiter)	*my, your, his, her, its, our, their*
possessive form [pəˌzesɪv fɔːm]	s-Genitiv	*Jo's brother; my sister's room*
possessive pronoun [pəˌzesɪv 'prəʊnaʊn]	Possessivpronomen	*mine, yours, his, hers, ours, theirs*

preposition [ˌprepəˈzɪʃn]	Präposition	*after, at, in, next to, under*
present [ˈpreznt]	Gegenwart	
present participle [ˌpreznt ˈpɑːtɪsɪpl]	Partizip Präsens	*cleaning, planning, going, taking*
present perfect [ˌpreznt ˈpɜːfɪkt]	*present perfect*	*We**'ve made** a cake for you.*
present perfect progressive [ˌpreznt ˌpɜːfɪkt prəˈgresɪv]	Verlaufsform des *present perfect*	*We**'ve been waiting** for an hour.*
present progressive [ˌpreznt prəˈgresɪv]	Verlaufsform der Gegenwart	*The Hansons **are having** lunch.*
progressive form [prəˈgresɪv fɔːm]	Verlaufsform	
pronoun [ˈprəʊnaʊn]	Pronomen, Fürwort	
quantifier [ˈkwɒntɪfaɪə]	Mengenangabe	*some, a lot of, many, much*
question tag [ˈkwestʃən tæg]	Frageanhängsel	*This place is great, **isn't it?***
question word [ˈkwestʃən wɜːd]	Fragewort	*what?, when?, where?, how?*
reflexive pronoun [rɪˌfleksɪv ˈprəʊnaʊn]	Reflexivpronomen	*myself, yourself, themselves*
regular verb [ˌregjələ ˈvɜːb]	regelmäßiges Verb	*(to) help – helped – helped*
relative clause [ˌrelətɪv ˈklɔːz]	Relativsatz	*There's the girl **who helped me**.*
relative pronoun [ˌrelətɪv ˈprəʊnaʊn]	Relativpronomen	*who, that, which, whose*
reported speech [rɪˌpɔːtɪd ˈspiːtʃ]	indirekte Rede	*Sam said **(that) he was sorry**.*
request [rɪˈkwest]	Bitte	*Can you help me with this?*
short answer [ˌʃɔːt‿ˈɑːnsə]	Kurzantwort	*Yes, I am. / No, I don't.*
simple form [ˈsɪmpl fɔːm]	einfache Form	
simple past [ˌsɪmpl ˈpɑːst]	einfache Form der Vergangenheit	*Jo **wrote** two letters yesterday.*
simple present [ˌsɪmpl ˈpreznt]	einfache Form der Gegenwart	*I always **go** to school by bike.*
singular [ˈsɪŋgjələ]	Singular, Einzahl	
state verb [ˈsteɪt vɜːb]	Zustandsverb	*be, know, like, sound, want*
statement [ˈsteɪtmənt]	Aussagesatz	
subject [ˈsʌbdʒɪkt]	Subjekt	***My sister** is writing a letter.*
subject form [ˈsʌbdʒɪkt fɔːm]	Subjektform (der Personalpronomen)	*I, you, he, she, it, we, they*
subject question [ˈsʌbdʒɪkt ˌkwestʃən]	Frage nach dem Subjekt	*Who loves Jake?*
subordinate clause [səˌbɔːdɪnət ˈklɔːz]	Nebensatz	*I like Scruffy **because I like dogs**.*
substitute [ˈsʌbstɪtjuːt]	Ersatzverb (eines modalen Hilfverbs)	*be able to, be allowed to, have to*
tense [tens]	Zeitform	
uncountable noun [ʌnˈkaʊntəbl]	nicht zählbares Nomen	*bread, milk, money, news, work*
verb [vɜːb]	Verb	*hear, open, help, go*
***will*-future**	Futur mit *will*	*I think it **will be** cold tonight.*
word order [ˈwɜːd‿ɔːdə]	Wortstellung	
yes/no question	Entscheidungsfrage	*Are you 13? Do you like comics?*

Das **Vocabulary** (S. 178–189) enthält alle neuen Wörter und Wendungen aus Band 6, die du lernen musst. Sie stehen in der Reihenfolge, in der sie in den Units vorkommen.

Das **Dictionary** (S. 190–226) enthält den Wortschatz der Bände 1 bis 6 in alphabetischer Reihenfolge. Dort kannst du nachschlagen, was ein Wort bedeutet, wie man es ausspricht oder wie es genau geschrieben wird.

So ist das Vocabulary aufgebaut:

- Hier siehst du, wo die Wörter vorkommen.
  p. 6 = Seite 6
  p. 10/P 1 = Seite 10, Übung 1
- Die Lautschrift zeigt dir, wie ein Wort ausgesprochen und betont wird.
- Eingerückte Wörter lernst du am besten zusammen mit dem vorausgehenden Wort, weil die beiden zusammengehören.
- Die blauen Kästen solltest du dir besonders gut ansehen.

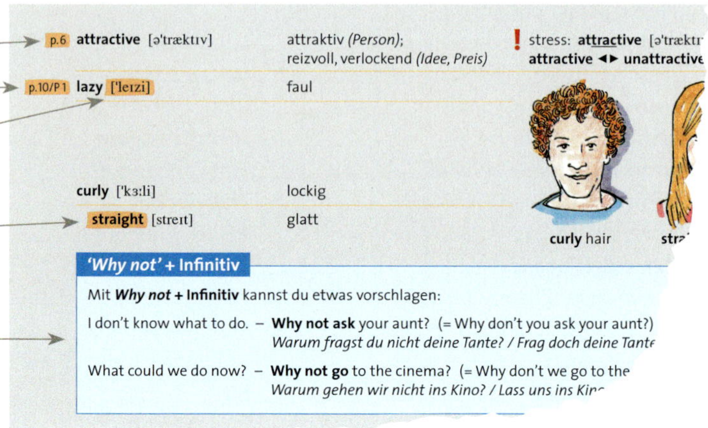

Tipps zum Wörterlernen findest du im Skills File auf Seite 133.

Abkürzungen:

n = *noun* | *v* = *verb*
adj = *adjective* | *adv* = *adverb*
prep = *preposition* | *conj* = *conjunction*

pl = *plural* | *no pl* = *no plural*
p. = page | pp. = pages
sb. = somebody | sth. = something
jn. = jemanden | jm. = jemandem

AE = *American English* | *BE* = *British English*

infml = *informal* (umgangssprachlich, informell)

Symbole:

! Hier stehen Hinweise auf Besonderheiten, bei denen man leicht Fehler machen kann.

◄► ist das „Gegenteil"-Zeichen: **attractive ◄► unattractive**

~ Die **Tilde** in den Beispielsätzen steht für das neue Wort. Beispiel:
(to) **fancy** sb. – If I ~ a boy, I just call him and ask him out.

Unit 1: Love life!

p. 6	**charming** ['tʃɑːmɪŋ]	charmant	She's quite ~. It's impossible not to like her.
	good-looking [ˌgʊd'lʊkɪŋ]	gut aussehend	
	(to) **fancy** sb. ['fænsi] *(infml)*	auf jn. stehen	If I ~ a boy, I just call him and ask him out.
	arrogant ['ærəgənt]	arrogant, überheblich	**!** stress: **arrogant** ['ærəgənt]
	loyal (to sb.**)** ['lɔɪəl]	loyal (gegenüber jm.)	a ~ friend = a good, reliable friend **!** stress: **loyal** ['lɔɪəl]
	bossy ['bɒsi]	herrisch	
	attractive [ə'træktɪv]	attraktiv *(Person)*; reizvoll, verlockend *(Idee, Preis)*	**!** stress: **attractive** [ə'træktɪv] **attractive ◄► unattractive**
	appearance [ə'pɪərəns]	Aussehen, (äußere) Erscheinung	He dresses terribly. He just doesn't care about his ~.

curly hair

straight hair

	curly ['kɜ:li]	lockig	
	straight [streɪt]	glatt	
	sense of humour [ˌsens‿əv 'hju:mə]	(Sinn für) Humor	**!** German: Sie hat **(viel) Humor**. – English: She's got **a great sense of humour**. German: Er hat **keinen Humor**. – English: He's got **no sense of humour.** **!** stress: **humour** ['hju:mə]
	peanut ['pi:nʌt]	Erdnuss	a couple of **peanuts** 
	unlike [ˌʌn'laɪk]	anders als; im Gegensatz zu	John is very arrogant, ~ his younger brother, who is really charming.
p.7	**lovable** ['lʌvəbl]	liebenswert	
	thin [θɪn]	dünn	**!** German: **dünn** ◄► **dick** English: **1. thin** ◄► **fat** *(people, animals)* **2. thin** ◄► **thick** *(books, ice, soup, ...)*
	in a friendly/strange/ different **way**	auf freundliche/seltsame/ andere Art und Weise	He looked at her **in a strange ~** and suddenly she felt very scared. When you paraphrase something you try to say it **in a different ~**.
	episode ['epɪsəʊd]	Folge *(einer Fernsehserie)*	**!** stress: **episode** ['epɪsəʊd]
	chat-up line *(infml)*	Anmachspruch	I can never think of a good **~-~ line** when I meet someone I fancy.
	(to) **chat** sb. **up (-tt-)** *(infml)*	jn. anquatschen, anbaggern	If you fancy the team captain, why don't you ~ him **up**?

PART A Real-life relationships

p.8/1	(to) **make friends (with** sb.**)**	Freunde finden; sich anfreunden (mit jm.)	The youth club is a great place to **make** new ~. At college I **made ~ with** a student from China.
	(to) **suggest** sth. **(to** sb.**)** [sə'dʒest]	(jm.) etwas vorschlagen	'Let's go for a walk,' Kelly **~ed to** Anthony. **!** My teacher **suggested** that we ask our parents. *(not:* ... ~~suggested to ask~~ ...) verb: (to) **suggest** – noun: **suggestion**
	mean [mi:n]	gemein	He took the little boys' ball away. That was really ~.
	situation [ˌsɪtʃu'eɪʃn]	Situation, Lage	**!** stress: **situation** [ˌsɪtʃu'eɪʃn]
	instead of *(prep)* [ɪn'sted‿əv]	statt, anstatt, anstelle von	This week's disco is on Friday **~ of** Saturday.
	instead *(adv)* [ɪn'sted]	stattdessen, dafür	I don't like coffee. I'll have tea ~.
p.9/2	(to) **break up (with** sb.**)** [ˌbreɪk‿'ʌp], **broke** [brəʊk], **broken** ['brəʊkən]	sich trennen (von jm.)	Why did you ~ ~ **with** your boyfriend?
	(to) **mess things up** *(infml)*	alles durcheinanderbringen, alles vermasseln	

	whether ['weðə]	ob	I don't know ~ I can come to your party or not. ! German **ob** = **1. if; 2. whether** **whether** ist etwas förmlicher als **if.**
	(to) **flirt** [flɜːt]	flirten	
	Why not tell her ...?	Warum erzählst/sagst du ihr nicht ...?	

'*Why not*' + Infinitiv

Mit ***Why not*** **+ Infinitiv** kannst du etwas vorschlagen:

I don't know what to do. – **Why not ask** your aunt? (= Why don't you ask your aunt?)
Warum fragst du nicht deine Tante? / Frag doch deine Tante.

What could we do now? – **Why not go** to the cinema? (= Why don't we go to the cinema?)
Warum gehen wir nicht ins Kino? / Lass uns ins Kino gehen.

p.9/4	**exam** [ɪg'zæm]	Prüfung, Examen	

exams

(to) **take/do an exam**	eine Prüfung ablegen
(to) **pass an exam**	eine Prüfung bestehen
(to) **fail an exam**	eine Prüfung nicht bestehen; durchfallen

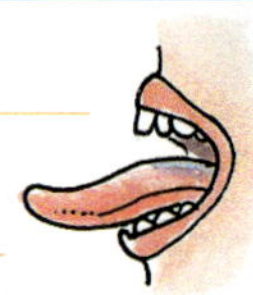

	(to) **repeat** sth. [rɪ'piːt]	etwas wiederholen	(to) say, write or do sth. again
p.10/P 1	**tongue** [tʌŋ]	Zunge	! pronunciation: **tongue** [tʌŋ]
	(to) **suppose** [sə'pəʊz]	annehmen, vermuten	She's the boss, so I ~ she's right.
	lazy ['leɪzi]	faul	**lazy ◄► hard-working**
	(to) **mention** sth. **(to** sb.**)** ['menʃn]	etwas erwähnen (jm. gegenüber)	My friends will help you if you ~ my name. I missed the meeting because no one **~ed** it **to** me. (= No one told me about it.)
p.11/P 3	(to) **keep** sth. **going**	etwas in Gang halten, etwas aufrechterhalten	(to) **keep** a conversation / a relationship / a party / a fire **going**
	I **didn't catch** your name. [kætʃ]	Ich habe deinen Namen nicht verstanden.	I **didn't** ~ your name. / I **didn't** ~ what you said. Could you repeat it, please?
	around here	hier in/aus der Gegend	Do you live **around** ~? / Are you from **around** ~?
	(to) **encourage** [ɪn'kʌrɪdʒ]	*(jn.)* ermutigen, ermuntern; *(etwas)* fördern	My parents **~d** me to apply for the job. At this school, we'd like to ~ interest in history.

PART B On-screen relationships

p.12/1	**romantic** [rəʊ'mæntɪk]	romantisch; Liebes-	
	in fact [ɪn 'fækt]	tatsächlich; in Wirklichkeit; um genau zu sein	It might look difficult, but **in** ~ it's quite easy. Yes, I know her. **In** ~, we were in the same class.
	the film/novel **is set in** ...	der Film/Roman spielt in ...	The film **is** ~ **in** 16th century London.
	(to) **direct** a film/play [də'rekt]	bei einem Film/Theaterstück Regie führen	The film **was ~ed** by Sofia Coppola. verb: (to) **direct** – noun: **director** („Regisseur/in")

	the film **stars** ... [stɑːz]	der Film hat ... in der Hauptrolle / in den Hauptrollen	The film ~ Johnny Depp and Keira Knightley.
	law [lɔː]	Jura, Rechtswissenschaften	**!** **law** = **1.** Gesetz; **2.** Jura, Rechtswissenschaften
	racism ['reɪsɪzəm]	Rassismus	
	fantasy ['fæntəsi]	Fantasy(film, -roman)	
	(to) **be based on** [beɪst]	basieren auf	The film **is ~ on** a book by Stephenie Meyer.
	pregnant ['pregnənt]	schwanger	**!** She's **six months pregnant**. = ... **im sechsten Monat schwanger**.
	control (of/over) [kən'trəʊl]	Kontrolle (über)	Keep calm and don't lose ~. (= ... verlier nicht die Beherrschung.)
	(to) **bite** [baɪt], **bit** [bɪt], **bitten** ['bɪtn]	beißen	In the last episode, he is **bitten** by a vampire and dies.
	special effects *(pl)* [ˌspeʃl‿ɪ'fekts]	Spezialeffekte	
	effect [ɪ'fekt]	(Aus-)Wirkung, Effekt	The cold weather had a bad ~ on all the plants.
p.13/2	4 **out of** 5	4 von 5	19 ~ **of** 28 students in our form are girls.
p.13/3	**religion** [rɪ'lɪdʒn]	Religion	**!** stress: **religion** [rɪ'lɪdʒn]

Religions

Person	Adjective	Building
Christian ['krɪstʃən]	**Christian**	**church, cathedral**
Catholic ['kæθlɪk]	**Catholic**	
Protestant ['prɒtɪstənt]	**Protestant**	
Hindu ['hɪnduː]	**Hindu**	**temple** ['templ] *Tempel*
Jew [dʒuː]	**Jewish**	**synagogue** ['sɪnəgɒg] *Synagoge*
Muslim ['mʊzlɪm]	**Muslim**	**mosque** [mɒsk] *Moschee*

Other 'religion words':

religious [rɪ'lɪdʒəs] *religiös; gläubig*
service ['sɜːvɪs] *Gottesdienst*
mass [mæs] *Messe*
priest [priːst] *Priester*
minister ['mɪnɪstə] *Pfarrer/in, Pastor/in*
nun [nʌn] *Nonne*

	intelligent [ɪn'telɪdʒənt]	intelligent, klug	**!** stress: **intelligent** [ɪn'telɪdʒənt]
	patient ['peɪʃnt]	geduldig	The train is late so we'll have to be ~. **patient ◄► impatient** (ungeduldig)
p.14/P 1	**reviewer** [rɪ'vjuːə]	Rezensent/in, Kritiker/in *(von Filmen, Büchern usw.)*	
	costume ['kɒstjuːm]	(Bühnen-)Kostüm	**!** stress: **costume** ['kɒstjuːm]

a costume **a suit** **!**

	sentimental [ˌsentɪ'mentl]	sentimental	Do you cry when you watch a ~ film?
p.14/P 2	**award** [ə'wɔːd]	Auszeichnung, Preis	The Oscar is the most famous film ~.

p.15/P 3	**dramatic** [drə'mætɪk]	dramatisch	noun: **drama** – adjective: **dramatic**
	bet [bet]	Wette	
	(to) **bet (-tt-)** [bet], **bet, bet**	wetten	I ~ you can't run faster than me.
	environment [ɪn'vaɪrənmənt]	Umwelt	

Unit 2: The world we live in

p.28	**appliance** [ə'plaɪəns]	Gerät *(meist elektrisch)*	Most homes have **~s** like dishwashers and washing machines.
	console ['kɒnsəʊl]	Konsole, Steuerpult	
	toothbrush ['tu:θbrʌʃ]	Zahnbürste	
	hairdryer ['heədraɪə]	Föhn, Haartrockner	
	dry [draɪ]	trocken	
	razor ['reɪzə]	Rasierapparat, Rasierer	
	microwave ['maɪkrəweɪv]	Mikrowelle	
	(to) **unplug** sth. **(-gg-)** [ˌʌn'plʌg]	den Stecker von etwas herausziehen	
	charger ['tʃɑ:dʒə]	Ladegerät	

Some more appliances

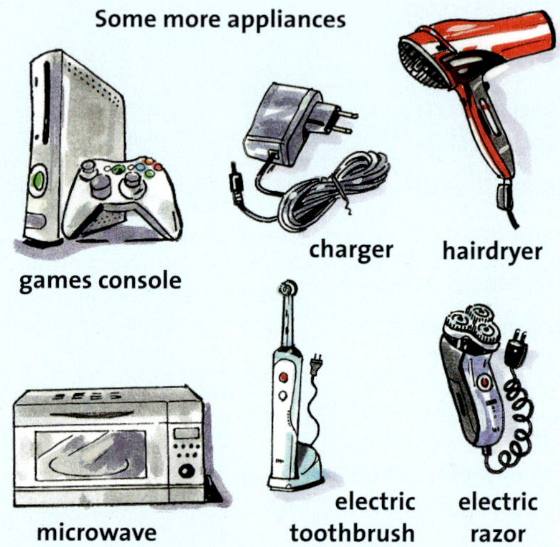

	heating ['hi:tɪŋ]	Heizung	It was really cold in our classroom today. The ~ wasn't working.
	heat [hi:t]	Hitze, Wärme	It's so hot in here. I can't sleep in this ~. **heat ◄► cold**
	(to) **heat** [hi:t]	heizen, erhitzen	We use oil to ~ our flat in winter.
p.29	**footprint** ['fʊtprɪnt]	Fußabdruck	
	fossil fuel [ˌfɒsl 'fju:əl]	fossiler Brennstoff	Oil and gas are **~ ~s**.
	carbon dioxide (CO_2) [ˌkɑ:bən daɪ'ɒksaɪd], [ˌsi:‿əʊ 'tu:]	Kohlendioxid (CO_2)	! stress: **dioxide** [daɪ'ɒksaɪd] ! Oft wird nur das Wort **carbon** („Kohlenstoff") verwendet, wenn eigentlich **carbon dioxide** gemeint ist.
	atmosphere ['ætməsfɪə]	Atmosphäre	! Betonung und Aussprache: **atmosphere** ['ætməsfɪə]
	greenhouse ['gri:nhaʊs]	Gewächshaus, Treibhaus	
	global warming [ˌgləʊbl 'wɔ:mɪŋ]	Erwärmung der Erdatmosphäre, globaler Temperaturanstieg	
	climate ['klaɪmət]	Klima	! pronunciation: **climate** ['klaɪmət]
	conditions *(pl)* [kən'dɪʃnz]	Bedingungen, Verhältnisse	**living ~** („Lebensbedingungen"), **weather ~** („Wetterverhältnisse, -bedingungen")
	amount (of) [ə'maʊnt]	Menge, Betrag	You can now add a small **~ of** salt to the soup. £ 300! I wouldn't pay that ~ for a pair of jeans.

emission [i'mɪʃn]	Emission, (Schadstoff-)Ausstoß	! stress: **e<u>mi</u>ssion** [i'mɪʃn]

tonne [tʌn]	Tonne *(Gewichtseinheit)*	1000 kilos ! pronunciation: **tonne** [tʌn]
(to) **be made up (of)**	zusammengesetzt sein (aus); bestehen (aus)	This pie chart **is ~ up of** five sections.

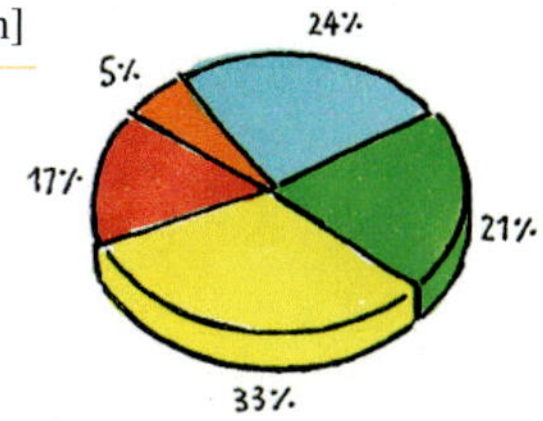

target ['tɑ:gɪt]	Ziel; Zielscheibe	What's your personal ~ for the coming year? Houses with open windows are easy **~s** for thieves.
(to) **reduce** [rɪ'dju:s]	verringern, vermindern, reduzieren	Look, they've **~d** the price from £ 25 to £ 15.
insulation [ˌɪnsju'leɪʃn]	Isolierung, Wärmedämmung	

PART A Living with technology

p.30/1 **invention** [ɪn'venʃn] Erfindung

Verbs and nouns

(to) **act**	handeln, sich verhalten	(to) **pollute** [pə'lu:t]	verschmutzen, verunreinigen
action ['ækʃn]	Tat, Handlung; Handeln	**pollution**	Verschmutzung
(to) **discuss** sth. [dɪ'skʌs]	etwas besprechen, über etwas diskutieren	(to) **react (to)**	reagieren (auf)
discussion	Diskussion	**reaction (to)** [ri'ækʃn]	Reaktion (auf)
(to) **invent** [ɪn'vent]	erfinden	(to) **suggest** [sə'dʒest]	vorschlagen
invention	Erfindung	**suggestion** [sə'dʒestʃən]	Vorschlag

scientist ['saɪəntɪst]	(Natur-)Wissenschaftler/in	
(to) **develop (from ... into)** [dɪ'veləp]	(sich) entwickeln (aus ... zu)	We are trying to ~ a new kind of computer. After a boring start, our trip **~ed into** a real adventure.
army ['ɑ:mi]	Armee, Heer	! stress: **<u>ar</u>my** ['ɑ:mi]
forever (*BE auch:* **for ever**) [fər'evə]	für immer	
(to) **carry** ['kæri]	tragen	! • He's **carrying** a suitcase. (Er trägt einen Koffer.) • He's **wearing** jeans and a red shirt. (Er trägt Jeans und ein rotes Hemd.)

	in the 1970s	in den 70er-Jahren *(des 20. Jahrhunderts)*	
	since then	seitdem	He broke his leg last week and he's been in hospital **~ then**.
	fat [fæt]	Fett	
	billion ['bɪljən]	Milliarde(n)	1,000,000,000
	(to) **create** [kri'eɪt]	schaffen, erschaffen, erzeugen	(to) make, (to) produce, (to) design, (to) invent
	(to) **allow** sb. **to do** sth. [ə'laʊ]	jm. erlauben, etwas zu tun; jm. ermöglichen, etwas zu tun	My parents don't ~ me to stay out after 10. The internet ~ you to keep in touch with family and friends.
p. 31	**choice** [tʃɔɪs]	Wahl, Auswahl	verb: (to) **choose** – noun: **choice**
p. 31/2	**power** ['paʊə]	Kraft, Energie, Strom	
	power station ['paʊə steɪʃn]	Kraftwerk, Elektrizitätswerk	
	experiment [ɪk'sperɪmənt]	Experiment	**!** stress: **exp<u>e</u>riment** [ɪk'sperɪmənt]
p. 32/P 2	**second** ['sekənd]	Sekunde	There are 60 **~s** in a minute.
p. 33/P 4	**compliment** ['kɒmplɪmənt]	Kompliment	**!** stress: **<u>com</u>pliment** ['kɒmplɪmənt]
	Congratulations. [kən,grætʃu'leɪʃnz]	Herzlichen Glückwunsch!	**!** Wenn man zum Geburtstag gratuliert, sagt man **Happy birthday**.
p. 33/P 5	**application** [,æplɪ'keɪʃn] *(kurz auch:* **app***)*	Anwendung, Anwendungsprogramm, -software; App	It's a useful little ~ that you can download from the internet.

PART B Saving the planet

p. 34/1	(to) **take** sb. **through** sth.	etwas mit jm. (genau) durchgehen	If you need help with the software, I can ~ you **through** the instructions.
	heavy ['hevi]	schwer *(von Gewicht)*; heftig, stark	**!** **heavy** = **1.** schwer – a **heavy** suitcase **2.** heftig, stark – **heavy** storms, **heavy** traffic, a **heavy** smoker 
	kettle ['ketl]	(Wasser-)Kessel, Wasserkocher	
	(to) **be a no-no** ['nəʊ nəʊ] *(infml)*	tabu sein, nicht in Frage kommen	Religious discrimination **is a** big **~-~**.
	one by one	einer nach dem anderen	She opened her presents **~ by ~**.
	all alone [,ɔːl_ə'ləʊn]	ganz allein	She was **~ alone**. Everybody else had left.
	gone [gɒn]	weg, fort	I went back to get my purse, but it was **~**.
	(to) **pretend** [prɪ'tend]	so tun, als ob	Lilly **~ed** to be asleep when her mum entered the bedroom.
	coat [kəʊt]	Mantel	

p.35/1	**responsible** [rɪ'spɒnsəbl]	verantwortlich; verantwortungsbewusst	The team captain is ~ for organizing matches. We need a reliable and ~ person to look after the house while we're away.
	(to) **break down** [ˌbreɪk 'daʊn]	zusammenbrechen; *(Gerät)* ausfallen, eine Panne haben	He **broke ~** when he heard the bad news. On our way to Italy our car **broke ~** so we had to spend two days in a hotel in Würzburg.
	the machine **kept** breaking down	das Gerät fiel immer wieder aus	Why do you **keep** asking the same question?

(to) keep

1. keep	behalten	Can I **keep** your pen or do you want it back?
2. keep	aufbewahren	Butter should be **kept** in the fridge.
3. keep sth. warm/fresh ...	etwas warm/frisch ... halten	Good insulation **keeps** your house warm.
4. keep in touch	in Verbindung bleiben; Kontakt halten	Nice meeting you. Let's **keep in touch**.
5. keep (on) doing sth.	etwas weiter tun; etwas immer wieder tun	We **kept (on) walking** till we got to a small village. My little brother **keeps asking** silly questions.
6. keep sth. going	etwas in Gang halten; etwas aufrechterhalten	**Keep** the fire **going** – it's getting really cold. I find it difficult to **keep** a conversation **going**.

	freezing ['friːzɪŋ]	eisig; eiskalt	It's ~ (cold) outside. There's even ice on the windows.
	(to) **rip** sb. **off** (-pp-) [ˌrɪp‿'ɒf] *(infml)*	jn. übers Ohr hauen, jn. abzocken	I wouldn't shop there. It's much too expensive and they'll ~ you **off** if they can.
	evil ['iːvl]	böse *(bösartig, feindselig)*, übel, schlimm	an ~ monster; an ~ smell
	24/7 (twenty-four seven)	rund um die Uhr, sieben Tage die Woche	= twenty-four hours, seven days a week
	meter ['miːtə]	*(Gas-, Strom-)*Zähler	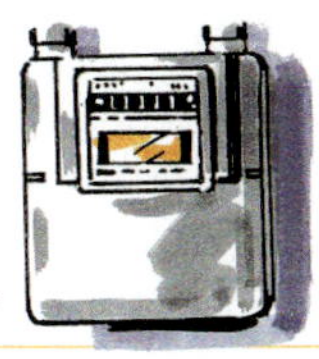 a **gas meter**
	(to) **melt** [melt]	schmelzen	The sun came out, and the snow began to ~. The sun **~ed** the ice on the windows.
	power cut ['paʊə kʌt]	Stromabschaltung, Stromausfall	
	bone [bəʊn]	Knochen	
	it **gives me the creeps** [kriːps] *(infml)*	es ist mir unheimlich; es ist mir nicht geheuer	Let's get out of this place. It **gives me the ~**. That man **gives me the ~**. He looks so scary.
p.36 /P 1	(to) **make a difference**	etwas bewirken, etwas bewegen	Help to save the planet! Get involved! You can **make a ~**!
	low [ləʊ]	niedrig	**low** ◄► **high**
p.37/P 3	**solar** ['səʊlə]	Solar-, Sonnen-	! stress: **solar** ['səʊlə]
	(to) **waste** sth. **(on)** [weɪst]	etwas verschwenden (für)	'Don't ~ your time and money on computer games,' my dad keeps telling me.

p.37/P 4	**outline** ['aʊtlaɪn]	Gliederung	
	point of view [ˌpɔɪnt‿əv 'vjuː]	Standpunkt, Sichtweise	from my **point of ~** (aus meiner Sicht; von meinem Standpunkt aus gesehen)
	on the one hand ... on the other hand	einerseits ... andererseits	**On the one ~**, technology makes life easier for us. **On the other ~**, our appliances use a lot of energy.
	however [haʊ'evə]	jedoch, allerdings	The summer is usually very hot here. This year, **~**, it has been quite cool.

Unit 3: Have your say!

p.46	**Have your say!**	*etwa:* Übe dein Mitspracherecht aus! / Rede mit!	Adults shouldn't decide everything. Young people should **have their ~** too.
	issue ['ɪʃuː]	Thema, (Streit-)Frage	Global warming is one of the big **~s** of our time.
	facilities *(pl)* [fə'sɪlətiz]	Einrichtungen, Anlagen	We need more sports **~** for kids in this area.
	(to) **vote** [vəʊt]	wählen *(zur Wahl gehen)*	

(to) care

Which issues do you **care about** most?	Welche Themen liegen dir besonders am Herzen? / Welche Themen sind dir am wichtigsten?
I **care about** health and the environment.	Mir sind Gesundheit und Umwelt wichtig.
Do you **care** enough to stand up and have your say?	Ist es dir wichtig genug, dass du aufstehst und deine Meinung sagst?
A lot of people just **don't care**.	Vielen Menschen ist es einfach egal.
Who cares about fashion? I don't!	Wen interessiert schon Mode? Mich nicht!

p.47	(to) **speak out** [ˌspiːk‿'aʊt]	seine Meinung (offen) sagen	If nobody **speaks ~**, people won't see that there's a problem.
	trade [treɪd]	Handel	the activity of buying and selling
	on charge [tʃɑːdʒ]	am Ladegerät; am Netz *(zum Aufladen)*	
	(to) **charge** [tʃɑːdʒ]	(auf)laden *(Batterie, Handy)*	
	wish [wɪʃ]	Wunsch	
	peace [piːs]	Friede(n)	**peace ◄► war**
	politician [ˌpɒlə'tɪʃn]	Politiker/in	**!** stress: **politics** ['pɒlətɪks] *(Politik)* **political** [pə'lɪtɪkl] *(politisch)* **politician** [ˌpɒlə'tɪʃn] *(Politiker/in)*

Politics (I)

Politicians usually belong to political **parties**.	**party** ['pɑːti] Partei
In a **democracy**, the citizens elect **members of parliament (MPs)**.	**democracy** [dɪ'mɒkrəsi] Demokratie **member of parliament** Parlamentsmitglied, Abgeordnete/r
After living in the UK for five years, foreign citizens can apply for British **citizenship**.	**citizenship** ['sɪtɪzənʃɪp] Staatsbürgerschaft
In the UK, the **prime minister (PM)** is the head of the government.	**prime minister** [ˌpraɪm 'mɪnɪstə] Premierminister/in, Ministerpräsident/in

Politics (II)

The head of a city government or **town council** is called 'mayor'. The mayor and the **town councillors** usually work in the **town hall**.

Germany has a written **constitution** containing its basic laws. The UK has no written constitution.

town council ['kaʊnsl] Stadtrat *(Gremium)*
town councillor ['kaʊnsələ] Stadtrat/-rätin
town hall ['hɔːl] Rathaus

constitution [ˌkɒnstɪ'tjuːʃn] Verfassung

campaign [kæm'peɪn]	Kampagne, (Werbe-)Feldzug	! spelling: **campaign**
demonstration [ˌdemən'streɪʃn]	Demonstration	
petition [pə'tɪʃn]	Unterschriftensammlung, Petition	

PART A Your right to be heard

p.48/1	(to) **get married (to** sb.**)**	(jn.) heiraten	I was born eight months after my parents **got** ~. (to) **get married** ◄► (to) **get divorced** (heiraten) (sich scheiden lassen)
	cigarette [ˌsɪgə'ret]	Zigarette	
	likely ['laɪkli]	wahrscheinlich	Everyone is angry, so it's ~ that lots of people will join the protests.
	(to) **be likely to be/do** sth.	wahrscheinlich etwas sein/tun	It**'s** ~ **to be** sunny in the afternoon. We**'re** ~ **to finish** the project in time.
p.48/2	(to) **take** sb./sth. **seriously**	jn./etwas ernst nehmen	My older sister doesn't ~ **me seriously**.
	public ['pʌblɪk]	Öffentlichkeit	! **in public** – **in der Öffentlichkeit**
	as long as *(conj)*	solange, sofern	There'll be no trouble **as** ~ **as** you don't break the rules.
	view (about/on) [vjuː]	Ansicht (über/zu)	Tell us what you think, Jake. We haven't heard your ~ yet.
	equal ['iːkwəl]	gleich *(Rechte, Bezahlung usw.)*	Do women and men always have ~ rights? Divide £1 into five ~ parts. – Easy. 20 p.
	unless [ən'les]	es sei denn; wenn ... nicht	You'll get into trouble with your parents ~ you work harder. (= ... if you don't work harder)
p.49/2	**It doesn't matter.**	Es spielt keine Rolle. / Es macht nichts (aus).	Sorry, I forgot the potatoes. – **It doesn't** ~. We can have rice instead.
	mosquito [mə'skiːtəʊ]	Moskito, Stechmücke	
	(to) **make** sth. **up**	etwas bilden, etwas ausmachen	People under 35 **make** ~ almost half the city's population. This pie chart **is made** ~ **of** five sections.
	(to) **make sense**	sinnvoll sein, einen Sinn ergeben	That doesn't **make** ~ **to** me. (= Das leuchtet mir nicht ein.)
	tax [tæks]	*(die)* Steuer	The ~ on petrol is about 70 % of the price.

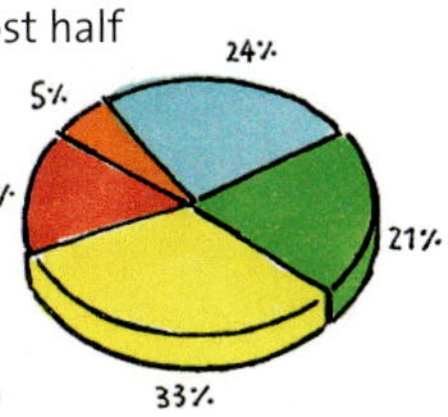

surely

Mit **surely** will man den Leser oder Hörer zur Zustimmung bewegen.	**Surely** we are old enough to make our own decisions. *Wir sind **doch wohl** alt genug, für uns selbst zu entscheiden.* (Ich bin davon überzeugt, und ich möchte, dass man mir zustimmt.) **Surely** we should ask her first. *Wir sollten sie **doch wohl** erst fragen.*
In verneinten Sätzen bringt **surely** zum Ausdruck, dass man überrascht ist oder dass man etwas kaum glauben kann. (Oft stehen solche Sätze mit Fragezeichen.)	**Surely** that's **not** snow, in the middle of June!? *Das ist **doch kein** Schnee, mitten im Juni!? /* *Das ist **doch nicht wirklich** Schnee, mitten im Juni!?* You do**n't** believe that, **surely**? *Das glaubst du **doch wohl nicht wirklich**, oder?*

p.49/3	(to) **criticize (for)** ['krɪtɪsaɪz]	kritisieren (wegen)	The report **~d** schools **for** giving too much homework. ! stress: **criticize** ['krɪtɪsaɪz]
	sensible ['sensəbl]	vernünftig	What a silly idea! Try and be more ~. ! *Nicht verwechseln:* **sensible** ['sensəbl] = vernünftig **sensitive** ['sensətɪv] = sensibel
p.50/P 1	(to) **take action** ['ækʃn]	handeln; etwas unternehmen	We can't just wait and do nothing. We'll have to **~ action**.
p.50/P 2	**device** [dɪ'vaɪs]	Vorrichtung, Gerät	My bike has a little ~ that counts the miles I've cycled.
	disgusting [dɪs'gʌstɪŋ]	widerlich, ekelhaft	The food was ~. I felt sick after eating it.
p.51/P 4	**corridor** ['kɒrɪdɔː]	Gang, Korridor	a school **corridor** 
	moderator ['mɒdəreɪtə]	Vermittler/in, Moderator/in	! **presenter** = Moderator/in *(von Fernsehshow, Nachrichten)* **moderator** = Vermittler/in *(z. B. in Konflikten, Diskussionen)*

PART B Speaking out

p.52	**novel** ['nɒvl]	Roman	
	narrator [nə'reɪtə]	Erzähler/in	
	(to) **ignore** [ɪg'nɔː]	ignorieren, nicht beachten	
	(to) **be awake** [ə'weɪk]	wach sein	(to) **be awake** ◄► (to) **be asleep**
	(to) **figure** sth. **out** ['fɪgə]	etwas ausrechnen; etwas herausfinden, herauskriegen	I can't ~ **out** how this machine works.
	whose [huːz]	deren, dessen *(Relativpronomen)*	What's the name of the boy ~ father comes from India?

	(to) **bury** ['beri]	begraben, vergraben; beerdigen	He died on holiday in Spain and was **buried** there. ! pronunciation: **bury** ['beri]
	(to) **challenge** ['tʃælɪndʒ]	herausfordern; infrage stellen	I **~d** my teacher to a game of table tennis. Journalists have **~d** what the mayor said.
p.53	**... what's on his mind** [maɪnd]	... was ihn beschäftigt / ... was ihm durch den Kopf geht	Do you want to tell me **what's on your ~**?
	(to) **recognize** ['rekəgnaɪz]	erkennen; anerkennen	I didn't ~ her. She'd been to the hairdresser's. It's important to ~ the rights of all citizens.
	(to) **stare (at** sb.**)** [steə]	(jn. an)starren	You mustn't ~ **at** people. It's rude.
p.55/P 3	**conflict** ['kɒnflɪkt]	Konflikt	! stress: **conflict** ['kɒnflɪkt]
	No worries. ['wʌriz] *(infml)*	Kein Problem! / Ist schon in Ordnung!	Sorry, I'm late. – **No ~**, we still have lots of time.
	Can I have a word with you?	Kann ich mal kurz mit dir reden?	
	I didn't mean to ...	Ich wollte nicht ...; Es war nicht meine Absicht, zu ...	I'm sorry, **I didn't ~ to** be rude. **I didn't ~ to** hurt you. Can you forgive me?

battery ['bætri, 'bætəri]	Batterie	

Das **Dictionary** enthält den Wortschatz der Bände 1 bis 6 von *English G 21*.
Wenn du wissen möchtest, was ein Wort bedeutet, wie man es ausspricht oder wie es geschrieben wird, kannst du hier nachschlagen.

Im **Dictionary** werden folgende **Abkürzungen und Symbole** verwendet:

jm. = jemandem	sb. = somebody	*pl* = *plural*	*AE* = *American English*
jn. = jemanden	sth. = something	*no pl* = *no plural*	*infml* = *informal*

- ° Mit diesem Kringel sind Wörter markiert, die nicht zum Lernwortschatz gehören.
- ► Der Pfeil verweist auf Kästchen im **Vocabulary** (S. 178–189), in denen du weitere Informationen zu diesem Wort findest.

Die **Fundstellenangaben** zeigen, wo ein Wort zum ersten Mal vorkommt.
Die Ziffern in Klammern bezeichnen Seitenzahlen:

I, II, III usw.	= Band 1, 2, 3 usw.
VI 1 (13)	= Band 6, Unit 1, Seite 13
VI 1 (13/181)	= Band 6, Unit 1, Seite 181 (im Vocabulary, zu Seite 13)

Tipps zur Arbeit mit einem Wörterbuch findest du im Skills File auf Seite 136.

Tipp

Auf der **Audio-CD im Workbook** findest du sowohl dieses englisch-deutsche Wörterverzeichnis als auch ein deutsch-englisches Wörterverzeichnis mit dem Lernwortschatz der Bände 1–6.

A

a [ə]
1. ein, eine I
2. once/twice a week einmal/zweimal pro Woche III • **a bit** ein bisschen, etwas II • **a few** ein paar, einige II • **a little** ein bisschen, wenig IV • **a lot (of)** eine Menge, viel, viele II • **He likes her a lot.** Er mag sie sehr. I

able ['eɪbl]**: be able to do sth.** etwas tun können; fähig sein / in der Lage sein, etwas zu tun III

Aboriginal [ˌæbə'rɪdʒənl] *(bezüglich der Ureinwohner Australiens)* Aborigine- V

Aborigine [ˌæbə'rɪdʒəni] Ureinwohner/in *(Australiens)* V

about [ə'baʊt]
1. über I
2. ungefähr II
3. be about to do sth. im Begriff sein, etwas zu tun; kurz davor sein, etwas zu tun V
about yourself über dich (selbst) III • **ask about sth.** nach etwas fragen I • **How about ...?** Wie wär's mit ...? III • **This is about Mr Green.** Es geht um Mr Green. I
What about ...? 1. Was ist mit ...? / Und ...? I; **2.** Wie wär's mit ...? I
What are you talking about? Wovon redest du? I • **What was the best thing about ...?** Was war das Beste an ...? II

above [ə'bʌv] oben; über, oberhalb (von) IV

°**abridged** [ə'brɪdʒd] gekürzt *(Buch)*

accent ['æksənt] Akzent II

accident ['æksɪdənt] Unfall II

ache [eɪk] wehtun IV

across [ə'krɒs]
1. (quer) über III
2. hinüber, herüber III

act [ækt]
1. handeln VI 2 (30/183)
2. sich verhalten IV
3. aufführen, spielen I
°**Act out** ... Spiele/Spielt ... vor.

action ['ækʃn] Tat, Handlung; Handeln VI 2 (30/183) • **take action** handeln; etwas unternehmen VI 3 (50)

action film ['ækʃn fɪlm] Actionfilm V

active ['æktɪv] aktiv, tätig IV

activity [æk'tɪvəti] Aktivität, Tätigkeit I

actor ['æktə] Schauspieler/in II

actually ['æktʃuəli]
1. eigentlich; in Wirklichkeit III
2. nebenbei bemerkt; übrigens IV

ad [æd] *(infml)* Anzeige, Inserat; *(im Fernsehen)* Werbespot V

°**adapted** [ə'dæptɪd] adaptiert; bearbeitet

add (to) [æd] hinzufügen, ergänzen, addieren (zu) I

addicted [ə'dɪktɪd]**: be addicted (to sth.)** abhängig (von etwas) sein, süchtig (nach etwas) sein V

address [ə'dres] Adresse, Anschrift II

adjust to sth. [ə'dʒʌst] sich an etwas anpassen; sich an etwas gewöhnen V

admission [əd'mɪʃn] Eintritt, Eintrittspreis IV

adult ['ædʌlt] Erwachsene(r) III

advantage (over sb./sth.) [əd'vɑːntɪdʒ] Vorteil (gegenüber jm./etwas) IV

adventure [əd'ventʃə] Abenteuer IV

advert ['ædvɜːt] Anzeige, Inserat; *(im Fernsehen)* Werbespot V

advertise ['ædvətaɪz] Werbung machen (für); inserieren V

advertisement [əd'vɜːtɪsmənt] Anzeige, Inserat; *(im Fernsehen)* Werbespot V

advice *(no pl)* [əd'vaɪs] Rat, Ratschläge V

advise [əd'vaɪz] beraten; raten *(einen Rat geben)* V

adviser [əd'vaɪzə] Betreuer/in, Berater/in V • **customer adviser** Kundenbetreuer/in, -berater/in V

afraid [ə'freɪd]
1. be afraid (of) Angst haben (vor) I
2. I'm afraid leider II

African American [ˌæfrɪkən_ə'merɪkən] afro-amerikanisch; Afro-Amerikaner/in IV

after ['ɑːftə] nach *(zeitlich)* I
after that danach I

after ['ɑːftə] nachdem II

afternoon [ˌɑːftə'nuːn] Nachmittag I • **in the afternoon** nachmittags, am Nachmittag I • **on Friday afternoon** freitagnachmittags, am Freitagnachmittag I

again [ə'gen] wieder; noch einmal I

against [ə'genst] gegen III

age [eɪdʒ] Alter III • **kids my age** Kinder in meinem Alter / meines Alters V
agent: travel agent ['trævl_eɪdʒənt] Reisebürokaufmann/-kauffrau V **travel agent's** Reisebüro V
ago [ə'gəʊ]: **a minute ago** vor einer Minute I
agree (on) [ə'gri:] sich einigen (auf) I • **agree with sb./sth.** jm./etwas zustimmen; mit jm./etwas übereinstimmen II
aid: first aid [,fɜ:st_'eɪd] Erste Hilfe V
air [eə] Luft III • °**air conditioning** *(no pl)* ['eə kən,dɪʃnɪŋ] Klimatisierung, Klimaanlage
airport ['eəpɔ:t] Flughafen III
alarm clock [ə'lɑ:m klɒk] Wecker V **set the alarm clock** den Wecker stellen V
album ['ælbəm] Album III
alcohol ['ælkəhɒl] Alkohol V
alive [ə'laɪv] am Leben, lebendig IV
all [ɔ:l] alle; alles I • **2 all** [,tu:_'ɔ:l] 2 beide (2:2 unentschieden) III **all alone** ganz allein VI 2 (34) • **all day** den ganzen Tag (lang) I • **all over the world** auf der ganzen Welt III • **all right** gut, in Ordnung II • **all the time** die ganze Zeit I • **all the way** den ganzen Weg IV • **from all over the UK/ the world/England** aus dem gesamten Vereinigten Königreich / aus der ganzen Welt / aus ganz England III • **not (...) at all** [ət_'ɔ:l] überhaupt nicht, ganz und gar nicht; überhaupt kein/e V • **This is all wrong.** Das ist ganz falsch. I
allow sb. to do sth. [ə'laʊ] jm. erlauben, etwas zu tun; jm. ermöglichen, etwas zu tun VI 2 (30)
°**allowance** [ə'laʊəns] Freibetrag; erlaubte Menge
allowed [ə'laʊd]: **be allowed** erlaubt sein IV • **be allowed to do sth.** etwas tun dürfen III
almost ['ɔ:lməʊst] fast, beinahe III
alone [ə'ləʊn] allein I • **all alone** ganz allein VI 2 (34) • **leave sb. alone** jn. in Ruhe lassen V
along [ə'lɒŋ]: **along the street** entlang der Straße / die Straße entlang II • °**sing along** mitsingen
alphabet ['ælfəbet] Alphabet I
°**alphabetical** [,ælfə'betɪkl] alphabetisch
already [ɔ:l'redi] schon, bereits II
also ['ɔ:lsəʊ] auch II
although [ɔ:l'ðəʊ] obwohl III
always ['ɔ:lweɪz] immer I
am [,eɪ_'em]: **7 am** 7 Uhr morgens/ vormittags I
amazing [ə'meɪzɪŋ] erstaunlich, unglaublich II
ambitious [æm'bɪʃəs] ehrgeizig V
ambulance ['æmbjələns] Krankenwagen III
American football [ə,merɪkən 'fʊtbɔ:l] Football I
amnesty ['æmnəsti] Amnestie, Begnadigung IV
amount (of) [ə'maʊnt] Menge, Betrag VI 2 (29)
an [ən] ein, eine I
ancestor ['ænsestə] Vorfahre/Vorfahrin V
and [ənd, ænd] und I • **and so on** *(short:* **etc.** [et'setərə]*)* und so weiter (usw.) IV
angel ['eɪndʒl] Engel II
angry (about sth. / with sb.) ['æŋgri] wütend, böse (über etwas / auf jn.) II
animal ['ænɪml] Tier II
anniversary [,ænɪ'vɜ:səri] Jahrestag IV • **anniversary of sb.'s death** jemandes Todestag IV
announce [ə'naʊns] ankündigen, bekanntgeben III
announcement [ə'naʊnsmənt] Durchsage, Ansage; Ankündigung, Bekanntgabe III
annoy sb. [ə'nɔɪ] jn. ärgern, belästigen III
annoyed [ə'nɔɪd] verärgert V • **get annoyed (with sb.; at/about sth.)** sich ärgern (über jn.; über etwas) V
annoying [ə'nɔɪɪŋ]: **My dad is annoying.** Mein Vater geht mir auf die Nerven. III
anorak ['ænəræk] Anorak, Windjacke III
another [ə'nʌðə] ein(e) andere(r, s); noch ein(e) I • **another 45 p** weitere 45 Pence, noch 45 Pence II
answer ['ɑ:nsə] antworten; beantworten I
answer (to) ['ɑ:nsə] Antwort (auf) I
anti- ['ænti] anti- V • **anti-social** asozial; antisozial VI 3 (49)
any ['eni] jede(r, s) (beliebige); irgendein(e) IV • **any ...?** (irgend)welche ...? I • **any time** jederzeit IV • **not (...) any** kein, keine I • **not (...) any more** nicht mehr III
anybody ['enibɒdi] (irgend)jemand II; jede(r) IV • **anybody else?** sonst noch jemand? IV • **not (...) anybody** niemand II
anyone ['eniwʌn] (irgend)jemand; jede(r) IV
anything ['eniθɪŋ] (irgend)etwas II; alles, was es auch sei / egal was IV **anything else** irgendetwas anderes IV • **anything else?** sonst noch etwas? IV • **not (...) anything** nichts II
anyway ['eniweɪ]
1. sowieso I
2. trotzdem II
3. aber egal, ...; wie auch immer, ...; wie dem auch sei, ... III
anywhere ['eniweə] irgendwo(hin) II • **not (...) anywhere** nirgendwo(hin) II
apart [ə'pɑ:t] auseinander, getrennt IV
apartment [ə'pɑ:tmənt] Wohnung IV
apologize (to sb. for sth.) [ə'pɒlədʒaɪz] sich (bei jm. für etwas) entschuldigen V
apology [ə'pɒlədʒi] Entschuldigung *(Bitte um Verzeihung)* V
appear [ə'pɪə] erscheinen IV
appearance [ə'pɪərəns] Aussehen, (äußere) Erscheinung VI 1 (6)
appetite ['æpɪtaɪt] Appetit III
apple ['æpl] Apfel I
appliance [ə'plaɪəns] Gerät *(meist elektrisch)* VI 2 (28)
► S.182 Appliances
application [,æplɪ'keɪʃn]
1. Bewerbung V • **letter of application** Bewerbungsschreiben V
2. *(kurz auch:* **app***)* Anwendung, Anwendungsprogramm, -software; App VI 2 (33)
apply for sth. [ə'plaɪ] sich um/für etwas bewerben; etwas beantragen V
appointment [ə'pɔɪntmənt] Termin, Verabredung I • °**make appointments** einen Termin machen, eine Verabredung treffen
apprentice [ə'prentɪs] Auszubildende(r), Lehrling V
apprenticeship [ə'prentɪʃɪp] Lehre, Ausbildung V
April ['eɪprəl] April I
°**archery** ['ɑ:tʃəri] Bogenschießen
archive ['ɑ:kaɪv] Archiv IV
are [ɑ:] bist; sind; seid I • **How are you?** Wie geht es dir/Ihnen/euch? II • **The pencils are 35 p.** Die Bleistifte kosten 35 Pence. I • **You're joking, aren't you?** Du machst Witze, nicht wahr? / Das ist nicht dein Ernst, oder? II
area ['eəriə] Bereich; Gebiet, Gegend III; Fläche V
argue ['ɑ:gju:] sich streiten, sich zanken I

argument ['ɑːgjumənt]
1. Argument, Begründung III
2. Streit III
arm [ɑːm] Arm I
armchair ['ɑːmtʃeə] Sessel I
army ['ɑːmi] Armee, Heer VI 2 (30)
around [ə'raʊnd] um ... (herum); in ... umher, durch III • **around here** hier in/aus der Gegend VI 1 (11) • **around six** um sechs herum, gegen sechs III • **around the lake** um den See (herum) III **around the town** in der Stadt umher, durch die Stadt • **jump/run/walk around** herumspringen/-rennen / umherspazieren III
arrival (arr) [ə'raɪvl] Ankunft III
arrive [ə'raɪv] ankommen, eintreffen II
arrogant ['ærəgənt] arrogant, überheblich VI 1 (6)
art [ɑːt] Kunst I
article ['ɑːtɪkl] (Zeitungs-)Artikel III
artificial [ˌɑːtɪ'fɪʃl] künstlich, Kunst- III
artist ['ɑːtɪst] Künstler/in III **make-up artist** Maskenbildner/in V
artistic [ɑː'tɪstɪk] künstlerisch V
as *(prep)* [əz, æz] als IV • **as a firefighter** als Feuerwehrmann, -frau IV
as *(conj)* [əz, æz] als, während II **as you can see** wie du sehen kannst II • **as if** als ob IV • **as long as** solange, sofern VI 3 (48)
as ... as [əz, æz] so ... wie II • **as big/exciting as** so groß/aufregend wie II • **just as ... as** genauso ... wie V
as usual ['juːʒuəl] wie immer, wie üblich V
ask [ɑːsk] fragen I • **ask about sth.** nach etwas fragen I • **ask questions** Fragen stellen I • **ask sb. the way** jn. nach dem Weg fragen II • **ask sb. for directions** jn. nach dem Weg fragen; jn. um eine Wegbeschreibung bitten IV • **ask sb. out** sich mit jm. verabreden; jn. einladen, mit einem auszugehen V • **ask sb. to do sth.** jn. (darum) bitten, etwas zu tun V
asleep [ə'sliːp]**: be asleep** schlafen I
°**aspect** ['æspekt] Aspekt, Seite
Assembly [ə'sembli] Versammlung *(morgendliche Schulversammlung, oft mit Andacht)* III
assess [ə'ses] einschätzen, beurteilen V
assessment [ə'sesmənt] Einschätzung, Beurteilung V
assistant [ə'sɪstənt]**: childcare assistant** Kinderpfleger/in V • **dentist's assistant** Zahnarzthelfer/in V **vet's assistant** Tierarzthelfer/in V
association [əˌsəʊsi'eɪʃn] Verband, Vereinigung V
at [ət, æt]**: at 7 Hamilton Street** in der Hamiltonstraße 7 I • **at 8.45** um 8.45 I • **at a time** gleichzeitig, auf einmal V • **at break** in der Pause *(zwischen Schulstunden)* II **at first** zuerst, am Anfang IV **at home** daheim, zu Hause I **at last** endlich, schließlich I **at least** zumindest, wenigstens I **at night** nachts, in der Nacht I **at once** sofort V • **at school** in der Schule I • **at that table** an dem Tisch (dort) / an den Tisch (dort) I • **at the bottom (of)** unten, am unteren Ende (von) II **at the butcher's** beim Metzger/Fleischer III • **at the chemist's** beim Apotheker III • **at the end (of)** am Ende (von) I • **at the Shaws' house** im Haus der Shaws/bei den Shaws zu Hause I • **at the station** am Bahnhof I • **at the top (of)** oben, am oberen Ende, an der Spitze (von) I • **at the weekend** am Wochenende I • **at work** bei der Arbeit / am Arbeitsplatz I **not (...) at all** [ət‿'ɔːl] überhaupt nicht, ganz und gar nicht; überhaupt kein/e V
ate [et, eɪt] *siehe* **eat**
athletics [æθ'letɪks] Leichtathletik III
Atlantic: the Atlantic (Ocean) [ətˌlæntɪk‿'əʊʃn] der Atlantische Ozean, der Atlantik IV
atmosphere ['ætməsfɪə] Atmosphäre VI 2 (29)
attach (to) [ə'tætʃ] anhängen, anheften *(an Brief, Mail)* V
attack [ə'tæk] angreifen III
attack [ə'tæk] Angriff III
attention [ə'tenʃn] Aufmerksamkeit V • **draw sb's attention to sth.** jn. auf etwas aufmerksam machen; jemandes Aufmerksamkeit auf etwas lenken V
attitude (to, towards) ['ætɪtjuːd] Haltung (gegenüber), Einstellung (zu, gegenüber) IV
attract [ə'trækt] anziehen, anlocken V
attraction [ə'trækʃən] Attraktion IV
attractive [ə'træktɪv] attraktiv *(Person)*; reizvoll, verlockend *(Idee, Preis)* VI 1 (6)
audience ['ɔːdɪəns] Publikum; Zuschauer/innen, Zuhörer/innen II
August ['ɔːgəst] August I
aunt [ɑːnt] Tante I • **auntie** ['ɑːnti] Tante II
auto ['ɔːtəʊ] *(AE)* Auto, PKW IV
autograph ['ɔːtəgrɑːf] Autogramm V
autumn ['ɔːtəm] Herbst I
avenue ['ævənjuː] Allee IV
average ['ævərɪdʒ] Durchschnitt, durchschnittlich, Durchschnitts- IV
avoid [ə'vɔɪd] vermeiden, aus dem Weg gehen V
awake [ə'weɪk]**: be awake** wach sein VI 3 (52)
away [ə'weɪ] weg, fort I
award [ə'wɔːd] Auszeichnung, Preis VI 1 (14)
awesome ['ɔːsəm] *(AE, infml)* klasse, großartig IV
awful ['ɔːfl] furchtbar, schrecklich II

B

baby ['beɪbi] Baby I • **have a baby** ein Baby/Kind bekommen II
back [bæk] Rücken V • **in the back** hinten, im hinteren Teil V
back (to) [bæk] zurück (nach) I **Good to have you back.** Schön, dass du wieder da bist. IV
back door [ˌbæk 'dɔː] Hintertür II
background ['bækgraʊnd] Hintergrund II • **background file** *etwa:* Hintergrundinformation(en) II
backpack ['bækpæk] *(AE)* Rucksack IV
°**backwards** ['bækwədz] nach hinten
bacon ['beɪkən] Schinkenspeck II
bad [bæd] schlecht, schlimm • **bad timing** schlechtes Timing III • **be bad at sth.** in etwas schlecht sein, etwas schlecht können III
badly ['bædli]**: do badly (in)** schlecht abschneiden (in) III
badminton ['bædmɪntən] Badminton, Federball I • **badminton racket** Badmintonschläger III
bag [bæg] Tasche, Beutel, Tüte I **sleeping bag** ['sliːpɪŋ bæg] Schlafsack V
bagel ['beɪgl] Bagel *(ringförmiges Gebäck)* IV
baggy ['bægi] weit (geschnitten) *(Hose)* V
bagpipes *(pl)* ['bægpaɪps] Dudelsack III
bakery ['beɪkəri] Bäckerei III

ball [bɔːl]
1. Ball I
2. Ball *(Tanzveranstaltung)* IV
ban (-nn-) [bæn] verbieten; ein (Aufenthalts-)Verbot erteilen V
banana [bəˈnɑːnə] Banane I
band [bænd] Band, (Musik-)Gruppe I
bank [bæŋk] Bank, Sparkasse I
bank robber [ˈbæŋk ˌrɒbə] Bankräuber/in I
bar [bɑː]
1. Bar II
2. bar chart [ˈbɑː tʃɑːt] Balkendiagramm V
barbecue [ˈbɑːbɪkjuː] Grillfest, Grillparty V
baseball [ˈbeɪsbɔːl] Baseball I
baseball cap Baseballmütze II
based [beɪst]**: be based on** basieren auf VI 1 (12)
basement [ˈbeɪsmənt] Keller(geschoss) V
basic [ˈbeɪsɪk] grundlegend; Grund-, Haupt- V
basket [ˈbɑːskɪt] Korb I • **a basket of apples** ein Korb Äpfel I
basketball [ˈbɑːskɪtbɔːl] Basketball I
°**bastard** [ˈbɑːstəd] *(infml, abwertend)* Mistkerl, Schweinehund
bath [bɑːθ] Bad, Badewanne II
have a bath baden, ein Bad nehmen II
bathroom [ˈbɑːθruːm] Badezimmer I
battery [ˈbætri, ˈbætəri] Batterie VI 3 (55)
bay [beɪ] Bucht III
be [biː]**, was/were, been** sein I
be with sb. mit jemandem zusammen sein IV • **be a no-no** *(infml)* tabu sein, nicht in Frage kommen VI 2 (34)
beach [biːtʃ] Strand II • **on the beach** am Strand II
bean [biːn] Bohne IV
bear [beə] Bär II
beard [bɪəd] Bart IV
beat [biːt]**, beat, beaten** schlagen; besiegen III
beaten [ˈbiːtn] *siehe* **beat**
beautiful [ˈbjuːtɪfl] schön I
beauty [ˈbjuːti] Schönheit III
became [bɪˈkeɪm] *siehe* **become**
because [bɪˈkɒz] weil I • **because of** [bɪˈkɒz‿əv] wegen V
become [bɪˈkʌm]**, became, become** werden II
bed [bed] Bett I • **Bed and Breakfast (B&B)** [ˌbed‿ən ˈbrekfəst] Frühstückspension I • **go to bed** ins Bett gehen I

bedroom [ˈbedruːm] Schlafzimmer I
beef [biːf] Rindfleisch III
been [biːn] *siehe* **be**
°**beer** [bɪə] Bier
before [bɪˈfɔː] vor *(zeitlich)* I
before [bɪˈfɔː] bevor II
beg (for) (-gg-) [beg] betteln (um); (eindringlich) bitten (um) IV
began [bɪˈgæn] *siehe* **begin**
begin (-nn-) [bɪˈgɪn]**, began, begun** beginnen, anfangen (mit) III
beginning [bɪˈgɪnɪŋ] Beginn, Anfang; Einleitung II
begun [bɪˈgʌn] *siehe* **begin**
behave [bɪˈheɪv] sich verhalten, sich benehmen V • **Behave yourself!** Benimm dich! V
behaviour [bɪˈheɪvjə] Verhalten, Benehmen V
behind [bɪˈhaɪnd] hinter II
belief [bɪˈliːf] Glaube, Überzeugung V
believe [bɪˈliːv] glauben III
bell [bel] Klingel, Glocke III
belong to [bɪˈlɒŋ] gehören (zu) IV
below [bɪˈləʊ] unten; unter, unterhalb (von) IV
bench [bentʃ] (Sitz-)Bank IV
°**bend** [bend]**, bent, bent** (ver)biegen
°**bent** [bent] *siehe* **bend**
best [best] am besten II • **the best ...** der/die/das beste ...; die besten I • **What was the best thing about ...?** Was war das Beste an ...? II • **Best wishes** *etwa:* Alles Gute / Mit besten Grüßen *(als Briefschluss)* IV
bestseller [ˌbestˈselə, ˈbestˌselə] Bestseller, Verkaufsschlager VI 1 (12)
bet [bet] Wette VI 1 (15)
bet (-tt-) [bet]**, bet, bet** wetten VI 1 (15/182)
better [ˈbetə] besser I • °**better lock the door** mach besser/lieber die Tür zu • **like sth. better** etwas lieber mögen II
between [bɪˈtwiːn] zwischen II
°**beverage** [ˈbevərɪdʒ] Getränk
°**beyond the story** [bɪˈjɒnd] über die Geschichte hinaus
Bible: the Bible [ˈbaɪbl] die Bibel V
big [bɪg] groß I • **big wheel** [ˌbɪg ˈwiːl] Riesenrad III
bike [baɪk] Fahrrad I • **bike ride** (Rad-)Fahrt II • **ride a bike** Rad fahren I
bill [bɪl]
1. Rechnung III
2. *(AE)* Geldschein V
billion [ˈbɪljən] Milliarde(n) VI 2 (30)
bin [bɪn] Mülltonne II

biography [baɪˈɒgrəfi] Biografie III
biology [baɪˈɒlədʒi] Biologie I
bird [bɜːd] Vogel I
birth [bɜːθ] Geburt V • **date of birth** Geburtsdatum V • **place of birth** Geburtsort V
birthday [ˈbɜːθdeɪ] Geburtstag I
Happy birthday. Herzlichen Glückwunsch zum Geburtstag. I • **My birthday is in May.** Ich habe im Mai Geburtstag. I • **My birthday is on 13th June.** Ich habe am 13. Juni Geburtstag. I • **When's your birthday?** Wann hast du Geburtstag? I
biscuit [ˈbɪskɪt] Keks, Plätzchen I
bit [bɪt]
1. a bit ein bisschen, etwas II
2. °**bit** kleines Teil, Stückchen
bit [bɪt] *siehe* **bite**
bite [baɪt]**, bit, bitten** beißen VI 1 (12)
bitten [ˈbɪtn] *siehe* **bite**
black [blæk] schwarz I
blame sb. (for) [bleɪm] jm. die Schuld geben (an); jm. Vorwürfe machen (wegen) III
blanket [ˈblæŋkɪt] Decke *(zum Zudecken)* V
bled [bled] *siehe* **bleed**
bleed [bliːd]**, bled, bled** bluten V
bleep [bliːp] piepsen II
bleep [bliːp] Piepton II
blew [bluː] *siehe* **blow**
block [blɒk] (Häuser-, Wohn-)Block IV
block sth. [blɒk] etwas sperren V
blog [blɒg] *(von web log)* Blog *(Internet-Tagebuch)* IV
blond [blɒnd] blond, hell IV
blood [blʌd] Blut IV
bloody [ˈblʌdi] blutig V
blow [bləʊ]**, blew, blown** wehen, blasen III
blown [bləʊn] *siehe* **blow**
blue [bluː] blau I
board [bɔːd]
1. (Wand-)Tafel I • **on the board** an der/die Tafel I • **bulletin board** *(AE)* schwarzes Brett, Anschlagtafel IV • **notice board** *(BE)* Anschlagtafel, schwarzes Brett I
2. on board an Bord V
boat [bəʊt] Boot, Schiff I
body [ˈbɒdi] Körper I
bodyguard [ˈbɒdigɑːd] Bodyguard, Leibwächter/in IV
bold print [ˌbəʊld ˈprɪnt] Fettdruck III
bone [bəʊn] Knochen VI 2 (35)
book [bʊk] Buch I • **book review** [rɪˈvjuː] Buchkritik, Buchbesprechung V

book [bʊk] buchen, reservieren V
booked [bʊkt]**: fully booked** ausgebucht V
boot [buːt] Stiefel I
border ['bɔːdə] Grenze IV
bored [bɔːd] gelangweilt IV
boring ['bɔːrɪŋ] langweilig I
born [bɔːn]**: be born** geboren sein/werden II
borough ['bʌrə, *AE:* 'bɜːrəʊ] (Stadt-)Bezirk IV
borrow sth. (from) ['bɒrəʊ] (sich) etwas (aus)leihen, (sich) etwas borgen (von) V
boss [bɒs] Chef/in, Boss III
bossy ['bɒsi] herrisch VI 1 (6)
both [bəʊθ] beide I
bottle ['bɒtl] Flasche I • **a bottle of milk** eine Flasche Milch I
childproof bottle kindersichere Flasche V
bottom ['bɒtəm] unteres Ende II
at the bottom (of) unten, am unteren Ende (von) II
bought [bɔːt] *siehe* **buy**
bowl [bəʊl] Schüssel I • **a bowl of cornflakes** eine Schale Cornflakes I
box [bɒks] Kasten, Kästchen, Kiste I • **phone box** Telefonzelle V
sandwich box Brotdose I
boy [bɔɪ] Junge I
boyfriend ['bɔɪfrend] (fester) Freund IV
°**bracket** ['brækɪt] Klammer *(in Texten)*
brainstorm ['breɪnstɔːm] brainstormen *(so viele Ideen wie möglich sammeln)* III
°**branch** ['brɑːntʃ] Zweig
brave [breɪv] tapfer, mutig III
bread *(no pl)* [bred] Brot I
break [breɪk] Pause I • **at break** in der Pause *(zwischen Schulstunden)* II • **take a break** eine Pause machen IV
break [breɪk]**, broke, broken** (zer-)brechen; kaputt gehen IV
break a journey eine Reise unterbrechen III • **break down** zusammenbrechen; *(Gerät)* ausfallen, eine Panne haben VI 2 (35) • **break up (with sb.)** sich trennen (von jm.) VI 1 (9)
breakable ['breɪkəbl] zerbrechlich IV
breakdance ['breɪkdɑːns] Breakdance IV
breakfast ['brekfəst] Frühstück I
have breakfast frühstücken I
breath [breθ] Atem V • **out of breath** außer Atem V • **take a deep breath** tief Luft holen V

breathe (in/out) [briːð] (ein-/aus-)atmen V
°**bride** [braɪd] Braut
bridge [brɪdʒ] Brücke I
bridle path ['braɪdl pɑːθ] Reitweg III
bright [braɪt] hell, leuchtend II
brilliant ['brɪliənt] genial, toll III
bring [brɪŋ]**, brought, brought** (mit-, her)bringen I
British ['brɪtɪʃ] britisch; Brite, Britin II
brochure ['brəʊʃə] Prospekt, Broschüre II
broke [brəʊk] *siehe* **break**
broken ['brəʊkən] *siehe* **break**
broken ['brəʊkən] gebrochen; zerbrochen, kaputt, defekt II
brother ['brʌðə] Bruder I
brought [brɔːt] *siehe* **bring**
brown [braʊn] braun I
°**bubble** ['bʌbl] Blase
budgie ['bʌdʒi] Wellensittich I
build [bɪld]**, built, built** bauen II
builder ['bɪldə] Bauarbeiter/in V
building ['bɪldɪŋ] Gebäude II
built [bɪlt] *siehe* **build**
bulletin board ['bʊlətɪn bɔːd] *(AE)* schwarzes Brett, Anschlagtafel IV
bully ['bʊli] einschüchtern, tyrannisieren II
bully ['bʊli] (Schul-)Tyrann III
bunk (bed) [bʌŋk] Etagenbett, Koje II
burger ['bɜːgə] Burger IV
burn [bɜːn] brennen; verbrennen IV
bury ['beri] begraben, vergraben; beerdigen VI 3 (52)
bus [bʌs] Bus I • **bus stop** ['bʌs stɒp] Bushaltestelle III
bush [bʊʃ] Busch, Strauch V • **the bush** der Busch *(unkultiviertes, „wildes" Land in Australien, Afrika)* V
business ['bɪznəs] Geschäft; Handel IV • **do business with** Geschäfte machen mit; Handel treiben mit V • **Mind your own business.** Das geht dich nichts an! / Kümmere dich um deine eigenen Angelegenheiten! II • **start a business** eine Firma gründen V
busy ['bɪzi]
1. belebt, verkehrsreich; hektisch III
2. beschäftigt V
3. besetzt *(Telefon, Leitung)* V
but [bət, bʌt]
1. aber I
2. sondern IV
butcher ['bʊtʃə] Fleischer/in, Metzger/in III • **at the butcher's** beim Fleischer/Metzger III

°**butt** [bʌt] *(infml)* Hintern
butter ['bʌtə] Butter III
button ['bʌtn] Knopf III
buy [baɪ]**, bought, bought** kaufen I
by [baɪ]
1. von I
2. an; (nahe) bei II
3. by car/train/bike/... mit dem Auto/Zug/Rad/... II
4. bis spätestens; nicht später als **by ten o'clock** bis (spätestens) zehn Uhr III • **by the way** übrigens II • **by two degrees / ten per cent** um zwei Grad / zehn Prozent V • **go by** vergehen, vorübergehen *(Zeit)* V • **one by one** einer nach dem anderen VI 2 (34)
Bye. [baɪ] Tschüs! I

C

cab [kæb] Taxi IV • **get a cab** ein Taxi nehmen IV
cabin ['kæbɪn] Hütte III
cable ['keɪbl] Kabel *(auch kurz für Kabelfernsehen)* IV
café ['kæfeɪ] *(kleines)* Restaurant, Imbissstube, Café II
cafeteria [ˌkæfə'tɪəriə] Cafeteria; *(USA)* Schulmensa IV
cage [keɪdʒ] Käfig I
cake [keɪk] Kuchen, Torte I
°**calculate** ['kælkjuleɪt] berechnen, ermitteln
°**calculator** ['kælkjuleɪtə] Taschenrechner
calendar ['kælɪndə] Kalender I
call [kɔːl]
1. rufen; anrufen I
2. nennen I
call sb. names jn. mit Schimpfwörtern hänseln, jm. Schimpfwörter nachrufen III
call [kɔːl] Anruf, Telefongespräch I
wake-up call Weckanruf V
called [kɔːld]**: be called** heißen, genannt werden III
caller ['kɔːlə] Anrufer/Anruferin V
calm [kɑːm] ruhig, still V
calm down [ˌkɑːm 'daʊn] sich beruhigen II
calorie ['kæləri] Kalorie IV
came [keɪm] *siehe* **come**
camel ['kæml] Kamel II
camera ['kæmərə] Kamera, Fotoapparat I
camp [kæmp] zelten III
camp [kæmp] Camp, (Ferien-)Lager IV
campaign [kæm'peɪn] Kampagne, (Werbe-)Feldzug VI 3 (47)

can [kən, kæn]
1. können I
2. dürfen I
Can I help you? Kann ich Ihnen helfen? / Was kann ich für Sie tun? *(im Geschäft)* I
can [kæn] Dose, Büchse V
canal [kə'næl] Kanal III
cancer ['kænsə] Krebs *(Krankheit)* V
candidate ['kændɪdət] Kandidat/in, Bewerber/in V
canned [kænd] Dosen-; ... in Dosen V
canoe [kə'nu:] Kanu III
canoe [kə'nu:] paddeln, Kanu fahren III
canteen [kæn'ti:n] Kantine, Schulmensa II
canyon ['kænjən] Schlucht IV
cap [kæp] Mütze, Kappe II
capital ['kæpɪtl] Hauptstadt III
capital letter [,kæpɪtl 'letə] Großbuchstabe III
°**captain** ['kæptɪn] Kapitän/in
caption ['kæpʃn] Bildunterschrift III
car [kɑ:] Auto I • **car park** Parkplatz III • **racing car** ['reɪsɪŋ kɑ:] Rennwagen V
caravan ['kærəvæn] Wohnwagen II
carbon ['kɑ:bən] Kohlenstoff; *(oft auch kurz für:)* Kohlendioxid VI 2 (29/182)
carbon dioxide (CO_2) [,kɑ:bən daɪ'ɒksaɪd], [,si:_əʊ 'tu:] Kohlendioxid (CO_2) VI 2 (29)
°**carbon footprint** [,kɑ:bən 'fʊtprɪnt] „CO_2-Fußabdruck", CO_2-Bilanz
card [kɑ:d] (Spiel-, Post-)Karte I
credit card ['kredɪt kɑ:d] Kreditkarte V
care about sth. [keə] etwas wichtig nehmen V • **They don't care.** Es ist ihnen egal. VI 3 (46/186) • **Who cares?** Wen interessiert das (schon)? VI 3 (46/186)
► S.186 (to) care
career [kə'rɪə] Karriere III
careful ['keəfl]
1. vorsichtig II
2. sorgfältig, gründlich II
3. aufmerksam V
careless ['keələs] nachlässig; unvorsichtig, leichtsinnig V
caretaker ['keəteɪkə] Hausmeister/in II
carrot ['kærət] Möhre, Karotte I
carry ['kæri] tragen VI 2 (30)
cartoon [kɑ:'tu:n] Cartoon (Zeichentrickfilm; Bilderwitz) II
case [keɪs] Fall II
cash [kæʃ] Bargeld V • **pay cash** bar bezahlen V
castle ['kɑ:sl] Burg, Schloss II
cat [kæt] Katze I
catch [kætʃ], **caught, caught** fangen; erwischen II • **I didn't catch your name.** Ich habe deinen Namen nicht verstanden. VI 1 (11)
cathedral [kə'θi:drəl] Kathedrale, Dom III
► S.181 Religions
Catholic ['kæθlɪk] Katholik/in; katholisch VI 1 (13/181)
► S.181 Religions
cattle *(pl)* ['kætl] Rinder V
caught [kɔ:t] *siehe* **catch**
cause [kɔ:z] verursachen IV
cause (of sth.) [kɔ:z] Grund, Ursache (für etwas) IV
cave [keɪv] Höhle V
CD [,si:'di:] CD I • **CD player** CD-Spieler I
ceilidh ['keɪli] *Musik- und Tanzveranstaltung, vor allem in Schottland und Irland* III
cellphone ['selfəʊn] *(AE)* Handy, Mobiltelefon IV
Celsius (C) ['selsiəs] Celsius IV
cent (c) [sent] Cent I • **per cent (%)** [pə 'sent] Prozent III
centimetre (cm) ['sentɪmi:tə] Zentimeter III
central ['sentrəl] Zentral-, Mittel- III
centre ['sentə] Zentrum, Mitte I
city centre Stadtzentrum, Innenstadt I • **sports centre** Sportzentrum I
century ['sentʃəri] Jahrhundert II
certainly ['sɜ:tnli] bestimmt, sicher(lich); gerne, selbstverständlich, klar V
certificate [sə'tɪfɪkət] Zertifikat, Bescheinigung V
chair [tʃeə] Stuhl I
challenge ['tʃælɪndʒ] herausfordern; infrage stellen VI 3 (52)
champion ['tʃæmpiən] Meister/in, Champion I
championship ['tʃæmpiənʃɪp] Meisterschaft III
chance [tʃɑ:ns] Chance, Möglichkeit IV
change [tʃeɪndʒ]
1. (sich) ändern; (sich) verändern IV
2. wechseln IV
3. umsteigen III
4. sich umziehen IV
change channels umschalten *(Fernsehen)* VI 2 (32)
change [tʃeɪndʒ]
1. (Ver-)Änderung, Wechsel IV
2. Wechselgeld I; Kleingeld IV
channel ['tʃænl] Kanal, Sender IV
change channels umschalten *(Fernsehen)* VI 2 (32) • **hop channels** zappen IV
character ['kærəktə]
1. Charakter, Wesen IV
2. Person, Figur *(in Roman, Film, Theaterstück)* IV
charge [tʃɑ:dʒ] (auf)laden *(Batterie, Handy)* VI 3 (47/186)
charge [tʃɑ:dʒ]**: on charge** am Ladegerät; am Netz *(zum Aufladen)* VI 3 (47)
charger ['tʃɑ:dʒə] Ladegerät VI 2 (28)
charming ['tʃɑ:mɪŋ] charmant VI 1 (6)
chart [tʃɑ:t] Diagramm V
charts [tʃɑ:ts] Charts, Hitliste III
chat (-tt-) [tʃæt] plaudern; chatten II • **chat sb. up** *(infml)* jn. anquatschen, anbaggern VI 1 (7/179)
chat room ['tʃæt ru:m] Chatroom III
chat-up line ['tʃæt_ʌp laɪn] *(infml)* Anmachspruch VI 1 (7)
cheap [tʃi:p] billig I
check [tʃek]
1. (über)prüfen, kontrollieren I
2. check in einchecken *(Hotel, Flughafen)* V
3. check out auschecken *(Hotel)* V
°**checklist** ['tʃeklɪst] Checkliste
checkpoint ['tʃekpɔɪnt] Kontrollpunkt *(hier auch: zur Selbstüberprüfung)* I
cheek [tʃi:k] Wange IV
cheeky ['tʃi:ki] frech, dreist V
cheer [tʃɪə] jubeln, Beifall klatschen II
cheerleader ['tʃɪəli:də] Cheerleader *(Stimmungsanheizer/in bei Sportereignissen* IV
cheese [tʃi:z] Käse I • **cream cheese** Frischkäse IV
chef [ʃef] Koch, Köchin *(Berufsbezeichnung)* V
chemist ['kemɪst] Drogerie, Apotheke II • **at the chemist's** beim Apotheker III
cheque (for) [tʃek] Scheck (über) V
cherry ['tʃeri] Kirsche II
chicken ['tʃɪkɪn] Huhn; (Brat-)Hähnchen I
child [tʃaɪld], *pl* **children** ['tʃɪldrən] Kind I • **only child** Einzelkind V
childcare ['tʃaɪldkeə] Kinderbetreuung V • **childcare assistant** Kinderpfleger/in V
childproof ['tʃaɪldpru:f] kindersicher *(Flasche, Verschluss)* V
chips *(pl)* [tʃɪps]
1. *(BE)* Pommes frites I

2. (potato) chips *(AE)* Kartoffelchips IV
chocolate ['tʃɒklət] Schokolade I
choice [tʃɔɪs] Wahl, Auswahl VI 2 (31)
choir ['kwaɪə] Chor I
choose [tʃu:z]**, chose, chosen** (sich) aussuchen, (aus)wählen I
chorus ['kɔ:rəs] Refrain III
chose [tʃəʊz] *siehe* **choose**
chosen ['tʃəʊzn] *siehe* **choose**
Christian ['krɪstʃən] Christ/in; christlich V
► S.181 Religions
Christmas ['krɪsməs] Weihnachten I
church [tʃɜ:tʃ] Kirche I
► S.181 Religions
cigarette [ˌsɪgə'ret] Zigarette VI 3 (48)
cinema ['sɪnəmə] Kino I • **go to the cinema** ins Kino gehen II
circle ['sɜ:kl] Kreis IV
circus ['sɜ:kəs] (runder) Platz III
citizen ['sɪtɪzn] (Staats-)Bürger/in, Staatsangehörige(r) IV
citizenship ['sɪtɪzənʃɪp] Staatsbürgerschaft VI 3 (47/186)
► S.186 Politics
city ['sɪti] (Groß-)Stadt I • **city centre** Stadtzentrum, Innenstadt I
civil ['sɪvl]**: civil rights** *(pl)* Bürgerrechte IV • **civil war** Bürgerkrieg IV
clap (-pp-) [klæp] (Beifall) klatschen IV
°**clarification** [ˌklærəfɪ'keɪʃn] Klärung
class [klɑ:s]
1. (Schul-)Klasse I
2. Unterricht; Kurs IV
°**class rep** *(kurz für:* **class representative***)* Kurs-, Klassensprecher/in
class teacher Klassenlehrer/in I
classical ['klæsɪkl] klassisch III
classmate ['klɑ:smeɪt] Klassenkamerad/in, Mitschüler/in I
classroom ['klɑ:sru:m] Klassenzimmer I
clean [kli:n] sauber II
clean [kli:n] sauber machen, putzen I • **I clean my teeth.** Ich putze mir die Zähne. I • **clean up** säubern; aufräumen VI 2 (37)
cleaner ['kli:nə] Putzfrau, -mann II
clear [klɪə] klar, deutlich I
clever ['klevə] schlau, klug I
cleverness ['klevənəs] Klugheit, Schlauheit IV
click on sth. [klɪk] etwas anklicken II
cliff [klɪf] Klippe, Felsen III
climate ['klaɪmət] Klima VI 2 (29)
climate change ['klaɪmət tʃeɪndʒ] (der) Klimawandel VI 2 (29)
climb [klaɪm] klettern; hinaufklettern (auf) I • **Climb a tree.** Klettere auf einen Baum. I
clinic ['klɪnɪk] Klinik II
clock [klɒk] (Wand-, Stand-, Turm-) Uhr I • **alarm clock** [ə'lɑ:m klɒk] Wecker V
clone [kləʊn] Klon III
close (to) [kləʊs] nahe (bei, an) III
That was close. Das war knapp. II
close [kləʊz] schließen, zumachen I
closed [kləʊzd] geschlossen II
°**closing phrase** ['kləʊzɪŋ freɪz] Grußformel *(am Briefende)*
clothes *(pl)* [kləʊðz, kləʊz] Kleider, Kleidung(sstücke) II
cloud [klaʊd] Wolke II
cloudless ['klaʊdləs] wolkenlos IV
cloudy ['klaʊdi] bewölkt II
clown [klaʊn] Clown/in II
club [klʌb] Klub; Verein I
°**clue** [klu:] Hinweis
coach [kəʊtʃ] Trainer/in, Coach III
coast [kəʊst] Küste III
coat [kəʊt] Mantel VI 2 (34)
code: dress code ['dres kəʊd] Kleiderordnung IV
coffee ['kɒfi] Kaffee IV • **coffee to go** Kaffee zum Mitnehmen IV
coin [kɔɪn] Münze V
cola ['kəʊlə] Cola I
cold [kəʊld] kalt I • **be cold** frieren I
cold [kəʊld]
1. Kälte IV
2. Erkältung II
have a cold erkältet sein, eine Erkältung haben II
collect [kə'lekt] sammeln I
collection [kə'lekʃn] Sammlung IV
collector [kə'lektə] Sammler/in II
college ['kɒlɪdʒ] berufliche Fach(hoch)schule V
colony ['kɒləni] Kolonie V
colour ['kʌlə] kolorieren, färben, bunt an-, ausmalen III
colour ['kʌlə] Farbe I • **What colour is ...?** Welche Farbe hat ...? I
colourful ['kʌləfl] farbenfroh, farbenprächtig, farbig V
column ['kɒləm] Säule III
°**combine** [kəm'baɪn] kombinieren, verbinden
come [kʌm]**, came, come** kommen I • **come home** nach Hause kommen I • **come in** hereinkommen I • **Come on. 1.** Na los, komm. II; **2.** Ach komm! / Na hör mal! II
°**We've come a long way.** Wir sind weit gekommen. *(Wir haben viel erreicht.)*
comedy ['kɒmədi] Komödie IV
comfortable ['kʌmftəbl] bequem, behaglich IV • **Make yourself comfortable.** Machs dir bequem. IV
comic ['kɒmɪk] Comic-Heft I
°**command** [kə'mɑ:nd] Befehl, Aufforderung
comment ['kɒment] Kommentar, Bemerkung IV
Commonwealth ['kɒmənwelθ]**: the Commonwealth** *Gemeinschaft der Länder des ehemaligen Britischen Weltreichs* III
communicate [kə'mju:nɪkeɪt] sich verständigen, kommunizieren V
communication [kəˌmju:nɪ'keɪʃn] Kommunikation V
community [kə'mju:nəti] *(politische)* Gemeinde V • **community hall** Gemeindehalle, Gemeindesaal; Gemeinschaftshalle, Gemeinschaftssaal III
company ['kʌmpəni] Firma, Gesellschaft III
compare [kəm'peə] vergleichen IV
compared to [kəm'peəd] verglichen mit VI 3 (49)
comparison [kəm'pærɪsn] Steigerung; Vergleich II
competition [ˌkɒmpə'tɪʃn] Wettbewerb, Wettkampf IV
complain (about sth.) [kəm'pleɪn] sich (über etwas) beschweren, sich (über etwas) beklagen III
complete [kəm'pli:t] vollständig, völlig V
°**complete** [kəm'pli:t] vervollständigen, ergänzen
complicated ['kɒmplɪkeɪtɪd] kompliziert V
compliment ['kɒmplɪmənt] Kompliment VI 2 (33)
computer [kəm'pju:tə] Computer I
concert ['kɒnsət] Konzert III • **rock concert** Rockkonzert V
conclusion [kən'klu:ʒn] Schluss(folgerung) IV • **draw conclusions** Schlüsse ziehen, schlussfolgern IV
°**conditioning: air conditioning** *(no pl)* ['eə kənˌdɪʃnɪŋ] Klimatisierung, Klimaanlage
conditions *(pl)* [kən'dɪʃnz] Bedingungen, Verhältnisse VI 2 (29)
confidence ['kɒnfɪdəns] Selbstvertrauen; Vertrauen V
confident ['kɒnfɪdənt] selbstbewusst, (selbst)sicher; zuversichtlich V

conflict ['kɒnflɪkt] Konflikt VI 3 (55)
Congratulations. [kən,grætʃu'leɪʃnz] Herzlichen Glückwunsch! VI 2 (33)
connect (to/with) [kə'nekt] verbinden (mit) V
connection [kə'nekʃn] Verbindung V
conscious ['kɒnʃəs] bewusst; bei Bewusstsein V
console ['kɒnsəʊl] Konsole, Steuerpult VI 2 (28)
constitution [,kɒnstɪ'tju:ʃn] Verfassung VI 3 (47/187)
► S.187 Politics
contact ['kɒntækt] Kontakt, Verbindung V • **contacts** *(pl) Liste von Bekannten/Kontakten (im Handy, im Mailprogramm)* V
contact sb. ['kɒntækt] sich mit jm. in Verbindung setzen V
contain [kən'teɪn] enthalten IV
context ['kɒntekst] Zusammenhang, Kontext IV • °**from the context** aus dem Zusammenhang, aus dem Kontext
continent ['kɒntɪnənt] Kontinent V
continue [kən'tɪnju] fortsetzen; weitermachen (mit) V
contrast ['kɒntrɑ:st] Kontrast, Gegensatz V
control (of/over) [kən'trəʊl] Kontrolle (über) VI 1 (12) • **remote control** [rɪ,məʊt kən'trəʊl] Fernbedienung IV
control sth. (-ll-) [kən'trəʊl] etwas kontrollieren, die Kontrolle über etwas haben VI 3 (49)
conversation [,kɒnvə'seɪʃn] Gespräch, Unterhaltung IV
cook [kʊk] kochen, zubereiten II
cook [kʊk] Koch/Köchin III
cooker ['kʊkə] Herd I
cookie ['kʊkɪ] *(AE)* Keks IV
cool [ku:l]
1. kühl II
2. cool I
copy ['kɒpi] kopieren; abschreiben II
copy ['kɒpi]
1. Kopie, Abschrift II
2. Exemplar III
corner ['kɔ:nə] Ecke I • **on the corner of Green Street and London Road** Green Street, Ecke London Road II
cornflakes ['kɔ:nfleɪks] Cornflakes I
correct [kə'rekt] berichtigen, korrigieren II
correct [kə'rekt] richtig III
corridor ['kɒrɪdɔ:] Gang, Korridor VI 3 (51)
°**cos** [kɒz] *BE infml für* **because**

cost [kɒst], **cost, cost** kosten IV
cost [kɒst] Kosten VI 2 (36)
costume ['kɒstju:m] (Bühnen-)Kostüm VI 1 (14)
cotton ['kɒtn] Baumwolle IV
couch [kaʊtʃ] Couch, Sofa V
couch potato *(infml)* Stubenhocker/in *(jd., der viel vor dem Fernseher sitzt)* V
could [kəd, kʊd]
1. **he could ...** er konnte ... II
2. **he could ...** er könnte ... III
count [kaʊnt] zählen II
countable ['kaʊntəbl] zählbar IV
countdown ['kaʊntdaʊn] Countdown III
counter ['kaʊntə] Theke, Ladentisch IV
country ['kʌntri] Land *(auch als Gegensatz zur Stadt)* II • **in the country** auf dem Land II
countryside ['kʌntrisaɪd] Land(schaft), Natur IV
couple ['kʌpl]: **a couple of weeks** ein paar Wochen IV
course [kɔ:s] Kurs, Lehrgang III
course: of course [əv 'kɔ:s] natürlich, selbstverständlich I
court [kɔ:t]
1. Platz, Court *(für Squash, Badminton, Tennis)* III
2. Gericht(shof) IV
cousin ['kʌzn] Cousin, Cousine I
cover ['kʌvə] (CD-)Hülle I
cow [kaʊ] Kuh II
crash (into) [kræʃ] zusammenstoßen (mit); hineinfahren (in) IV
crazy ['kreɪzi] verrückt III
cream [kri:m] Sahne; Creme IV; Salbe V • **cream cheese** Frischkäse IV
create [kri'eɪt] schaffen, erschaffen, erzeugen VI 2 (30)
credit card ['kredɪt kɑ:d] Kreditkarte V • **pay by credit card** mit Kreditkarte bezahlen V
creeps [kri:ps]: **it gives me the creeps** *(infml)* es ist mir unheimlich; es ist mir nicht geheuer VI 2 (35)
cricket ['krɪkɪt] Kricket *(Schlagballspiel)* V
crime [kraɪm] Kriminalität; Verbrechen IV • **crime film** Krimi IV **crime series** Krimiserie IV • **crime story** Krimi IV
crisps *(pl)* [krɪsps] Kartoffelchips I
criticize (for) ['krɪtɪsaɪz] kritisieren (wegen) VI 3 (49)
crocodile ['krɒkədaɪl] Krokodil II
cross [krɒs] Kreuz V

cross [krɒs] überqueren II • **cross a time zone** eine Zeitzone passieren/durchqueren IV
cross [krɒs]: **be cross (with)** böse, sauer sein (auf) I
crowd [kraʊd] (Menschen-)Menge, Masse; *(infml auch:)* Clique, Gruppe IV
crowded ['kraʊdɪd] überfüllt, voll IV
cruel ['kru:əl] grausam IV
crush [krʌʃ]: **have a crush on sb.** in jn. verknallt sein III
cry [kraɪ] weinen IV
culture ['kʌltʃə] Kultur IV • **culture shock** Kulturschock V
cup [kʌp]
1. Tasse III
2. Pokal III
a cup of tea eine Tasse Tee III
cupboard ['kʌbəd] Schrank I
curly ['kɜ:li] lockig VI 1 (6)
curriculum vitae [kə,rɪkjələm 'vi:taɪ] **(CV)** Lebenslauf V
curry ['kʌri] Curry(gericht) III
curtain ['kɜ:tn] Vorhang IV
customer ['kʌstəmə] Kunde, Kundin II • **customer adviser** Kundenbetreuer/in, -berater/in V
cut (-tt-) [kʌt], **cut, cut** schneiden III • **cut sth. down** etwas zurückschneiden; *(Baum)* fällen VI 2 (36) **cut sth. off** etwas abtrennen, abschneiden III • **cut the grass** Rasen mähen IV
CV [si: 'vi:] **(curriculum vitae)** Lebenslauf V
cycle ['saɪkl] (mit dem) Rad fahren II • **cycle path** Radweg II
°**cyclist** ['saɪklɪst] Radfahrer/in

D

dad [dæd] Papa, Vati; Vater I
daily ['deɪli] täglich IV
dance [dɑ:ns] tanzen I
dance [dɑ:ns] Tanz I • **dance floor** Dancefloor, Tanzfläche IV
dancer ['dɑ:nsə] Tänzer/in II
dancing ['dɑ:nsɪŋ] Tanzen I **dancing lessons** Tanzstunden, Tanzunterricht I
danger ['deɪndʒə] Gefahr III • **in danger** in Gefahr V
dangerous ['deɪndʒərəs] gefährlich II
dark [dɑ:k] dunkel I
dark Dunkelheit VI 2 (34)
date [deɪt] Datum I • **date of birth** Geburtsdatum V • **to date** bis heute V

daughter ['dɔ:tə] Tochter I
day [deɪ] Tag I • **one day** eines Tages I • **days of the week** Wochentage I • **day out** Tagesausflug III
dead [ded] tot I
deal [di:l]**: It's a deal.** Abgemacht! III • **make a deal** ein Abkommen / eine Abmachung treffen III
dear [dɪə] Schatz, Liebling I • **Oh dear!** Oje! II
dear [dɪə]**: Dear Jay ...** Lieber Jay, ... I • **Dear Sir or Madam** Sehr geehrte Damen und Herren *(Anrede in Briefen)* IV
death [deθ] Tod IV
debate [dɪ'beɪt] debattieren IV
debate [dɪ'beɪt] Debatte IV
December [dɪ'sembə] Dezember I
decide (on sth.) [dɪ'saɪd] (etwas) beschließen; sich (für etwas) entscheiden IV
decision [dɪ'sɪʒn] Entscheidung V
make a decision eine Entscheidung treffen/fällen V
deep [di:p] tief IV
deer, *pl* **deer** [dɪə] Reh, Hirsch II
definite ['defɪnət] fest, bestimmt; endgültig, eindeutig V
°**definition** [ˌdefɪ'nɪʃn] Definition
degree [dɪ'gri:] Grad II
deli ['deli] Deli *(Lebensmittelgeschäft und Fastfoodrestaurant)* IV
delicious [dɪ'lɪʃəs] köstlich, lecker II
democracy [dɪ'mɒkrəsi] Demokratie VI 3 (47/186)
► S.186 Politics
demonstration [ˌdemən'streɪʃn] Demonstration VI 3 (47)
dentist ['dentɪst] Zahnarzt, -ärztin IV • **dentist's assistant** Zahnarzthelfer/in V
department store [dɪ'pɑ:tmənt stɔ:] Kaufhaus II
departure (dep) [dɪ'pɑ:tʃə] Abfahrt, Abflug; Abreise III
depressed [dɪ'prest] deprimiert, niedergeschlagen IV
depressing [dɪ'presɪŋ] deprimierend, trostlos IV
describe sth. (to sb.) [dɪ'skraɪb] (jm.) etwas beschreiben II
description [dɪ'skrɪpʃn] Beschreibung II
desert ['dezət] Wüste V
deserve [dɪ'zɜ:v] verdienen *(zu Recht bekommen)* V
design [dɪ'zaɪn] entwerfen, gestalten II
design [dɪ'zaɪn] Design; Gestaltung; Entwurf V
designer [dɪ'zaɪnə] Designer/in V
fashion designer Modedesigner/in V
desk [desk] Schreibtisch I
destroy [dɪ'strɔɪ] zerstören III
detail ['di:teɪl] Detail, Einzelheit II
°**detailed** ['di:teɪld] detailliert, ausführlich
detective [dɪ'tektɪv] Detektiv/in I
private detective [ˌpraɪvət dɪ'tektɪv] Privatdetektiv/in V
determined [dɪ'tɜ:mɪnd]**: be determined (to do sth.)** (fest) entschlossen sein (etwas zu tun) V
develop (from ... into) [dɪ'veləp] (sich) entwickeln (aus ... zu) VI 2 (30)
device [dɪ'vaɪs] Vorrichtung, Gerät VI 3 (50)
dial (*BE:* **-ll-**) ['daɪəl] *(Telefonnummer)* wählen V
°**dialogue** ['daɪəlɒg] Dialog
diary ['daɪəri] Tagebuch; Terminkalender I
dice, *pl* **dice** [daɪs] Würfel II
°**dictate** [dɪk'teɪt] diktieren
dictionary ['dɪkʃənri] Wörterbuch, *(alphabetisches)* Wörterverzeichnis I
did [dɪd] *siehe* **do** • **Did you go ...?** Bist du ... gegangen? / Seid ihr ... gegangen? I • **we didn't sing** wir sangen nicht / wir haben nicht gesungen I
die (of) *(-ing form:* **dying***)* [daɪ] sterben (an) II
difference ['dɪfrəns] Unterschied IV
make a difference etwas bewirken, etwas bewegen VI 2 (36)
different (from) ['dɪfrənt] verschieden, unterschiedlich; anders (als) I
difficult ['dɪfɪkəlt] schwierig, schwer I
dining room ['daɪnɪŋ ru:m] Esszimmer I
dinner ['dɪnə] Abendessen, Abendbrot I • **have dinner** Abendbrot essen I
dinosaur ['daɪnəsɔ:] Dinosaurier IV
direct a film/play [də'rekt] bei einem Film/Theaterstück Regie führen VI 1 (12)
directions *(pl)* [də'rekʃnz] Wegbeschreibung(en) IV
director: film director ['fɪlm dəˌrektə] Regisseur/in IV
dirty ['dɜ:ti] schmutzig II
disabled [dɪs'eɪbld] (körper)behindert III
disadvantage [ˌdɪsəd'vɑ:ntɪdʒ] Nachteil IV
disagree (with) [ˌdɪsə'gri:] nicht übereinstimmen (mit); anderer Meinung sein (als) III
disappear [ˌdɪsə'pɪə] verschwinden II
disappoint [ˌdɪsə'pɔɪnt] enttäuschen IV
disappointed (about/in) [ˌdɪsə'pɔɪntɪd] enttäuscht (von/über) IV
discipline ['dɪsəplɪn] Disziplin V
disc jockey (DJ) ['dɪsk dʒɒki, 'di: dʒeɪ] Diskjockey (DJ)
disco ['dɪskəʊ] Disko I
discover [dɪ'skʌvə] entdecken; herausfinden IV
discriminate against sb. [dɪ'skrɪmɪneɪt] jn. diskriminieren, jn. benachteiligen IV
discrimination (against) [dɪˌskrɪmɪ'neɪʃn] Diskriminierung (von), Benachteiligung (von) IV
discuss sth. [dɪ'skʌs] etwas besprechen, über etwas diskutieren VI 2 (30/183)
discussion [dɪ'skʌʃn] Diskussion II
written discussion Erörterung VI 2 (37)
disease [dɪ'zi:z] Krankheit V
disgusting [dɪs'gʌstɪŋ] widerlich, ekelhaft VI 3 (50)
dish [dɪʃ] Gericht *(Speise)* III
dishwasher ['dɪʃwɒʃə] Geschirrspülmaschine I
display [dɪ'spleɪ]**: be on display** ausgestellt sein/werden IV
divide sth. into sth. [dɪ'vaɪd] etwas (auf)teilen (in) V
divorced [dɪ'vɔ:st] geschieden I
get divorced sich scheiden lassen VI 3 (48/187)
DJ ['di: dʒeɪ] Diskjockey III
DJ ['di: dʒeɪ] *(Musik/CDs/Platten)* auflegen *(in der Disko)* III
do [du:]**, did, done** tun, machen I
Do you like ...? Magst du ...? I
do a gig einen Auftritt haben, ein Konzert geben III • **do a good job** gute Arbeit leisten II • **do a project** ein Projekt machen, durchführen II • **do an exam** eine Prüfung ablegen VI 1 (9/180) • **do an exercise** eine Übung machen II
do badly/well (in) schlecht/gut abschneiden (in) III • **do research** recherchieren IV • **do sport** Sport treiben I • **do work experience** ein Praktikum machen V • **How are you doing?** Wie geht's? V
doable ['du:əbl] machbar IV
doctor ['dɒktə] Doktor; Arzt/Ärztin II • **to the doctor's** zum Arzt III
°**document** ['dɒkjumənt] dokumentieren

documentary [ˌdɒkju'mentri] Dokumentarfilm, -beitrag IV
dog [dɒg] Hund I
dollar ($) ['dɒlə] Dollar IV
dolphin ['dɒlfɪn] Delfin V
done [dʌn] *siehe* **do**
don't [dəʊnt]**: Don't listen to Dan.** Hör/Hört nicht auf Dan. I • **I don't know.** Ich weiß es nicht. I • **I don't like ...** Ich mag ... nicht. / Ich mag kein(e) ... I
door [dɔ:] Tür I • **fireproof door** ['faɪəpru:f] feuerfeste Tür V
doorbell ['dɔ:bel] Türklingel I
dorm [dɔ:m] *(infml)* Schlafsaal V
dormitory ['dɔ:mətri] Schlafsaal V
dossier ['dɒsieɪ] Mappe, Dossier *(des Sprachenportfolios)* I
double ['dʌbl] zweimal, doppelt, Doppel- I • °**double circle** Doppelkreis, „Kugellager" *(als Gesprächskreis)* • **double room** [ˌdʌbl 'ru:m] Doppelzimmer V
down [daʊn] hinunter, herunter, nach unten I • **down there** dort unten II • **fall down** hinfallen II **turn sth. down** etwas leiser stellen IV
download [ˌdaʊn'ləʊd] runterladen, downloaden III
downloadable [ˌdaʊn'ləʊdəbl] herunterladbar, zum Herunterladen IV
downstairs [ˌdaʊn'steəz] unten; nach unten I
downtown [ˌdaʊn'taʊn] (im/in das) Stadtzentrum IV • **the downtown bus** der Bus Richtung Stadtzentrum IV
drama ['drɑ:mə]
1. Schauspiel, darstellende Kunst I
2. Fernsehspiel; Drama IV
dramatic [drə'mætɪk] dramatisch VI 1 (15)
drank [dræŋk] *siehe* **drink**
draw [drɔ:]**, drew, drawn**
1. zeichnen III
2. draw conclusions Schlüsse ziehen, schlussfolgern IV
3. draw sb's attention to sth. jn. auf etwas aufmerksam machen; jemandes Aufmerksamkeit auf etwas lenken V
draw [drɔ:] Unentschieden III **Our last match was a draw, 2–2.** *(you say: two all)* Unser letztes Spiel war ein Unentschieden, 2:2. III
drawing ['drɔ:ɪŋ] Zeichnung III
drawn [drɔ:n] *siehe* **draw**
dream [dri:m] Traum I • **dream house** Traumhaus I
dream (of, about) [dri:m] träumen (von) III
dreamer ['dri:mə] Träumer/in V
dress [dres] Kleid I
dress [dres] sich kleiden; sich anziehen V
dress code ['dres kəʊd] Kleiderordnung IV
dressed [drest]**: get dressed** sich anziehen I
drew [dru:] *siehe* **draw**
drink [drɪŋk] Getränk I
drink [drɪŋk]**, drank, drunk** trinken I
drinkable ['drɪŋkəbl] trinkbar, Trink- IV
drive [draɪv]**, drove, driven** *(ein Auto / mit dem Auto)* fahren II
drive [draɪv] (Auto-)Fahrt III
driven ['drɪvn] *siehe* **drive**
driver ['draɪvə] Fahrer/in II
driving instructor ['draɪvɪŋ‿ɪnˌstrʌktə] Fahrlehrer/in V
driving licence ['draɪvɪŋ ˌlaɪsns] Führerschein V
drop (-pp-) [drɒp]
1. fallen lassen I
2. drop sb. off jn. absetzen *(aussteigen lassen)* IV
drove [drəʊv] *siehe* **drive**
drug [drʌg] Droge, Rauschgift; Medikament IV • **be on drugs** *(gewohnheitsmäßig)* Drogen nehmen IV
drum [drʌm] Trommel III • **drums** *(pl)* [drʌmz] Schlagzeug III • **play the drums** Schlagzeug spielen III
drunk [drʌŋk] *siehe* **drink**
drunk [drʌŋk] betrunken IV
dry [draɪ] trocken VI 2 (28/182)
dump sb. [dʌmp] mit jm. Schluss machen V
during *(prep)* ['djuərɪŋ] während IV
dustbin ['dʌstbɪn] Mülltonne II
DVD [ˌdi: vi:' di:] DVD I

E

each [i:tʃ] jeder, jede, jedes (einzelne) I • **each other** [i:tʃ‿'ʌðə] einander, sich (gegenseitig) III
°**eagle** ['i:gl] Adler
ear [ɪə] Ohr I
earache ['ɪəreɪk] Ohrenschmerzen II
early ['ɜ:li] früh I
earn [ɜ:n] verdienen IV
earring ['ɪərɪŋ] Ohrring I
earth [ɜ:θ] Erde IV • **on earth** auf der Erde IV
earthquake ['ɜ:θkweɪk] Erdbeben IV
east [i:st] Osten; nach Osten; östlich III
eastbound ['i:stbaʊnd] Richtung Osten III
Easter ['i:stə] Ostern; Oster- IV
easy ['i:zi] leicht, einfach I
easy-going [ˌi:zi'gəʊɪŋ] gelassen, locker III
eat [i:t]**, ate, eaten** essen I
eaten ['i:tn] *siehe* **eat**
editor ['edɪtə] Redakteur/in III
education [ˌedʒʊ'keɪʃn] Bildung IV
effect [ɪ'fekt] (Aus-)Wirkung, Effekt VI 1 (12)
°**e.g.** [ˌi:'dʒi:] *(from Latin: exempli gratia)* z.B.
egg [eg] Ei II
either ['aɪðə, 'i:ðə]**: not (...) either** auch nicht; auch kein V
elect sb. sth. [ɪ'lekt] jn. zu etwas wählen IV
election [ɪ'lekʃn] Wahl *(von Kandidaten bei einer Abstimmung)* IV
electric [ɪ'lektrɪk] elektrisch, Elektro- III
electricity [ɪˌlek'trɪsəti] Strom, Elektrizität III
electronic [ɪˌlek'trɒnɪk] elektronisch III
elementary school [ˌelɪ'mentri sku:l] *(USA) Grundschule für 6- bis 11-Jährige* IV
elephant ['elɪfənt] Elefant I
elevator ['elɪveɪtə] *(AE)* Fahrstuhl, Aufzug II
else [els]**: anything else** irgendetwas anderes IV • **anything else?** sonst noch etwas? IV • **anybody else?** ... sonst noch jemand? IV **somebody else** jemand anders IV **somewhere else** woanders IV **what else?** was (sonst) noch? IV **who else?** wen (sonst) noch? IV
e-mail, email ['i:meɪl] E-Mail I
e-mail, email ['i:meɪl] mailen VI 3 (47)
embarrassed [ɪm'bærəst]**: I'm embarrassed.** Es ist mir peinlich. IV
emission [i'mɪʃn] Emission, (Schadstoff-)Ausstoß VI 2 (29)
empty ['empti] leer I
enclose sth. [ɪn'kləʊz] etwas *(einem Brief)* beilegen V
encourage [ɪn'kʌrɪdʒ] *(jn.)* ermutigen, ermuntern; *(etwas)* fördern VI 1 (11)
end [end] enden; beenden III
end [end] Ende, Schluss I • **at the end (of)** am Ende (von) I • **in the end** schließlich, zum Schluss III

ending ['endɪŋ] Ende, (Ab-)Schluss *(einer Geschichte, eines Films usw.)* III
endless ['endləs] endlos IV
enemy ['enəmi] Feind/in II
energetic [ˌenə'dʒetɪk] aktiv, tatkräftig; dynamisch, schwungvoll V
energy ['enədʒi] Energie V
engine ['endʒɪn] Motor IV • **search engine** Suchmaschine *(im Internet)* IV
engineer [ˌendʒɪ'nɪə] Ingenieur/in II
°**engineering** [ˌendʒɪ'nɪərɪŋ] Maschinenbau
English ['ɪŋglɪʃ] Englisch; englisch I
enjoy [ɪn'dʒɔɪ] genießen II • **Enjoy yourself.** Viel Spaß / Amüsier dich gut! III
enough [ɪ'nʌf] genug I
enter ['entə]
1. betreten; eintreten (in) III
2. eingeben *(Geheimzahl)* V
entry ['entri] Eintrag, Eintragung *(im Wörterbuch/Tagebuch)* III
environment [ɪn'vaɪrənmənt] Umwelt VI 1 (15)
episode ['epɪsəʊd] Folge *(einer Fernsehserie)* VI 1 (7)
equal ['i:kwəl] gleich *(Rechte, Bezahlung usw.)* VI 3 (48)
equipment [ɪ'kwɪpmənt] Ausrüstung III
eraser [ɪ'reɪsər] *(AE)* Radiergummi IV
escape (from sb./sth.) [ɪ'skeɪp] fliehen (vor jm./aus etwas); entkommen III
especially [ɪ'speʃəli] besonders IV
essay (about, on) ['eseɪ] Aufsatz (über) I
etc. [et'setərə] und so weiter (usw.) IV
ethnic ['eθnɪk] ethnisch, Volks- IV
euro (€) ['jʊərəʊ] Euro I
even ['i:vn]
1. sogar II • **even if** sogar wenn IV
2. not even (noch) nicht einmal III
He didn't even open the letter. Er hat den Brief nicht einmal geöffnet. III
evening ['i:vnɪŋ] Abend I • **in the evening** abends, am Abend I
on Friday evening freitagabends, am Freitagabend I
event [ɪ'vent] Ereignis; Veranstaltung IV
ever? ['evə] je? / jemals? / schon mal? II
every ['evri] jeder, jede, jedes I
everybody ['evribɒdi] jeder, alle II
everyday *(adj)* ['evrideɪ] Alltags-; alltägliche(r, s) III
everyone ['evriwʌn] jeder, alle IV
everything ['evriθɪŋ] alles I
everywhere ['evriweə] überall III
evil ['i:vl] böse *(bösartig, feindselig)*, übel, schlimm VI 2 (35)
exact [ɪg'zækt] exakt, genau IV
exactly [ɪg'zæktli] genau III
exam [ɪg'zæm] Prüfung, Examen VI 1 (9) • **do/take an exam** eine Prüfung ablegen VI 1 (9/180) • **fail an exam** eine Prüfung nicht bestehen; durchfallen VI 1 (9/180)
pass an exam eine Prüfung bestehen VI 1 (9/180)
► S.180 exams
example [ɪg'zɑ:mpl] Beispiel III
for example zum Beispiel III
excellent ['eksələnt] ausgezeichnet, hervorragend IV
except [ɪk'sept] außer IV
exchange [ɪks'tʃeɪndʒ]**: exchange rate** Wechselkurs V • **exchange student** Austauschschüler/in III
excited [ɪk'saɪtɪd] begeistert, aufgeregt III
exciting [ɪk'saɪtɪŋ] aufregend, spannend I
Excuse me, ... [ɪk'skju:z mi:] Entschuldigung, ... / Entschuldigen Sie, ... I
exercise ['eksəsaɪz]
1. Übung, Aufgabe I
2. *(no pl)* (körperliche) Bewegung, Training IV
exercise book ['eksəsaɪz bʊk] Schulheft, Übungsheft I
expect [ɪk'spekt] erwarten III
expect sb. to do sth. von jm. erwarten, dass er/sie etwas tut V
expensive [ɪk'spensɪv] teuer I
experience [ɪk'spɪəriəns] Erfahrung(en), Erlebnis IV • **in my experience** meiner Erfahrung nach; nach meiner Erfahrung IV
work experience *(no pl)* ['wɜ:k‿ɪkˌspɪəriəns] Praktikum; Arbeits-, Praxiserfahrung(en) V • **do work experience** ein Praktikum machen V
experience [ɪk'spɪəriəns] erfahren, erleben IV
experiment [ɪk'sperɪmənt] Experiment VI 2 (31)
explain sth. to sb. [ɪk'spleɪn] jm. etwas erklären, erläutern II
explanation [ˌeksplə'neɪʃn] Erklärung II
explore [ɪk'splɔ:] erkunden, erforschen I
explorer [ɪk'splɔ:rə] Entdecker/in, Forscher/in II
explosion [ɪk'spləʊʒn] Explosion IV
extra ['ekstrə] zusätzlich I
extracurricular activities (*kurz:* **extracurriculars)** [ˌekstrəkə'rɪkjələz] *schulische Angebote außerhalb des regulären Unterrichts, oft als Arbeitsgemeinschaften* IV
eye [aɪ] Auge I

F

face [feɪs] Gesicht I • **face to face** von Angesicht zu Angesicht, persönlich V
facilities *(pl)* [fə'sɪlətiz] Einrichtungen, Anlagen VI 3 (46)
fact [fækt] Tatsache, Fakt III • **in fact** tatsächlich; in Wirklichkeit; um genau zu sein VI 1 (12)
factory ['fæktri] Fabrik II
fail an exam [feɪl] eine Prüfung nicht bestehen; durchfallen VI 1 (9/180)
► S.180 exams
failure *(n)* ['feɪljə] ungenügend *(USA, Schulnote)* IV
fair [feə] fair, gerecht II
faithfully ['feɪθfəli]**: Yours faithfully** Mit freundlichen Grüßen *(Briefschluss bei namentlich unbekanntem Empfänger)* IV
fall [fɔ:l]**, fell, fallen** fallen, stürzen; hinfallen II • **fall down** hinfallen II • **fall in love (with sb.)** sich verlieben (in jn.) IV • **fall off** herunterfallen (von) II
fallen ['fɔ:lən] *siehe* **fall**
false [fɔ:ls] falsch IV
familiar [fə'mɪliə]**: be familiar with sth.** vertraut sein mit; sich auskennen mit V
family ['fæməli] Familie I • **family name** Nachname, Familienname V • **family tree** (Familien-) Stammbaum I
famous (for) ['feɪməs] berühmt (für, wegen) II
fan [fæn] Fan I
fancy ['fænsi]**: fancy sb.** *(infml)* auf jn. stehen VI 1 (6) • **fancy sth.** Lust auf/zu etwas haben V
fantastic [fæn'tæstɪk] fantastisch, toll I
fantasy ['fæntəsi] Fantasy(film, -roman) VI 1 (12)
far [fɑ:] weit (entfernt) II • **so far** bisher, bis jetzt IV
farm [fɑ:m] Bauernhof, Farm II

farmer ['fɑ:mə] Bauer/Bäuerin, Landwirt/in; (Fisch-)Züchter/in III
farmhouse ['fɑ:mhaʊs] Farmhaus, Bauernhaus IV
farming ['fɑ:mɪŋ] Landwirtschaft IV
fascinating ['fæsɪneɪtɪŋ] faszinierend V
fascination [ˌfæsɪ'neɪʃn] Faszination V
fashion ['fæʃn] Mode II • **fashion designer** ['fæʃn dɪˌzaɪnə] Modedesigner/in V
fashionable ['fæʃnəbl] modisch, schick V
fast [fɑ:st] schnell II • **fast food** [ˌfɑ:st 'fu:d] Fastfood III
fat [fæt] dick; fett IV
fat [fæt] Fett VI 2 (30)
father ['fɑ:ðə] Vater I
fault [fɔ:lt]: **It's not my fault.** Es ist nicht meine Schuld. III
favour ['feɪvə]: **Would you do me a favour?** Würdest du mir einen Gefallen tun? IV
favourite ['feɪvərɪt] Lieblings- I
my favourite colour meine Lieblingsfarbe I
favourite Liebling V
fear (of) [fɪə] Angst (vor) V
February ['februəri] Februar I
fed [fed] *siehe* **feed** • **be fed up (with sth.)** [ˌfed_'ʌp] die Nase voll haben (von etwas) II
feed [fi:d], **fed, fed** füttern I
feel [fi:l], **felt, felt** sich fühlen; fühlen; sich anfühlen II • **Feel free to ask questions.** Ihr könnt jetzt gern Fragen stellen. V • **I feel sick.** Mir ist schlecht. IV • **I'm not feeling great.** Ich fühle mich nicht besonders wohl. V
feeling ['fi:lɪŋ] Gefühl III
feet [fi:t] *Plural von „foot"*
fell [fel] *siehe* **fall**
felt [felt] *siehe* **feel**
felt tip ['felt tɪp] Filzstift I
female ['fi:meɪl] weiblich III
fence [fens] Zaun IV
ferry ['feri] Fähre III
festival ['festɪvl] Fest, Festival, Festspiele III
few [fju:]: **a few** ein paar, einige II
fiction: science fiction [ˌsaɪəns 'fɪkʃn] Sciencefiction V
fiddle ['fɪdl] *(infml)* Fiedel, Geige III
play the fiddle Geige spielen III
field [fi:ld] Feld, Acker, Weide II
in the field auf dem Feld II
fight (for) [faɪt], **fought, fought** kämpfen (für, um) III
fight [faɪt] Kampf; Schlägerei IV
figure ['fɪgə] Zahl, Ziffer V
figure sth. out ['fɪgə] etwas ausrechnen; etwas herausfinden, herauskriegen VI 3 (52)
file [faɪl] **background file** *etwa:* Hintergrundinformation(en) II
grammar file *Grammatikanhang* I
skills file *Anhang mit Lern- und Arbeitstechniken* I • **sound file** Tondatei, Soundfile III
fill [fɪl] füllen; sich füllen VI 2 (34)
fill in ausfüllen; einsetzen V
film [fɪlm] Film I • **film director** Regisseur/in IV • **film review** Filmkritik, Filmbesprechung V
film star Filmstar I • **film studio** Filmstudio III • **action film** Actionfilm V
film [fɪlm] filmen III
film-maker ['fɪlmmeɪkə] Filmemacher/in III
final ['faɪnl] letzte(r, s); End- III
final score Endstand III
final ['faɪnl] Finale, Endspiel III
finally ['faɪnəli] zuletzt, als letztes V; schließlich, endlich VI 2 (34)
financial [faɪ'nænʃl] finanziell, Finanz- V
find [faɪnd], **found, found** finden I
find out (about) herausfinden (über) I
finder ['faɪndə] Finder I
fine [faɪn]
1. gut, schön; in Ordnung II
2. *(gesundheitlich)* gut II
I'm/He's fine. Es geht mir/ihm gut. II
finger ['fɪŋgə] Finger I
finish ['fɪnɪʃ] beenden, zu Ende machen; enden I
fire ['faɪə] Feuer, Brand II • **fire safety** Verhalten im Brandfall IV
fire station Feuerwache IV • **put out a fire** ein Feuer löschen IV
firefighter ['faɪəfaɪtə] Feuerwehrfrau, -mann IV
fireman/-woman ['faɪəmən, 'faɪəˌwʊmən] Feuerwehrmann/-frau II
fireproof ['faɪəpru:f] feuerfest *(Tür)* V
first [fɜ:st]
1. erste(r, s) I
2. zuerst, als Erstes I
at first zuerst, am Anfang IV • **be first** der/die Erste sein I • **first aid** [ˌfɜ:st_'eɪd] Erste Hilfe V • **first-aid kit** Erste-Hilfe-Kasten, Verbandskasten V • **first floor** erster Stock *(BE)* / Erdgeschoss *(AE)* IV
first half erste Halbzeit III • **first name** Vorname V
fish [fɪʃ] fischen, angeln III
fish, *pl* **fish** [fɪʃ] Fisch I
°**fishbowl** ['fɪʃbəʊl] Fishbowl *(gesteuerte Diskussionsform)*
fist [fɪst] Faust IV
fit (-tt-) [fɪt] passen I • **fit in** hineinpassen; sich einfügen, sich anpassen IV
fit [fɪt] fit V
fitness ['fɪtnəs] Fitness IV • **fitness instructor** [ɪn'strʌktə] Fitnesstrainer/in V
flag [flæg] Flagge, Fahne V
flash [flæʃ] Lichtblitz III
flat [flæt] Wohnung I
flat [flæt] flach V • **flat screen** ['flæt skri:n] Flachbildschirm IV
flew [flu:] *siehe* **fly**
flight [flaɪt] Flug II • **a 14-hour flight** ein 14-stündiger Flug, ein 14-Stunden-Flug III
flirt [flɜ:t] flirten VI 1 (9)
floor [flɔ:]
1. Fußboden I
2. Stock(werk) IV • **first floor** erster Stock *(BE)* / Erdgeschoss *(AE)* IV • **ground floor** *(BE)* Erdgeschoss IV • **on the second floor** im zweiten Stock *(BE)* / im ersten Stock *(AE)* IV
floppy hat ['flɒpi] Schlapphut V
°**flow chart** ['fləʊ tʃɑ:t] Flussdiagramm
°**flower** ['flaʊə] Blume; Blüte
flown [fləʊn] *siehe* **fly**
flu [flu:] Grippe V
flute [flu:t] Querflöte III
fly [flaɪ], **flew, flown** fliegen II
°**fly** [flaɪ] Fliege
fog [fɒg] Nebel II
foggy ['fɒgi] neblig II
folk (music) ['fəʊk ˌmju:zɪk] Folk *(englische, schottische, irische oder nordamerikanische Volksmusik des 20. Jahrhunderts)* III
follow ['fɒləʊ] folgen; verfolgen I
follow the rules Regeln befolgen V
°**following** ['fɒləʊɪŋ]: **the following ...** die folgenden ...
food [fu:d]
1. Essen; Lebensmittel I
2. Futter I
foot [fʊt], *pl* **feet** [fi:t] Fuß I; Fuß *(Längenmaß: 30,48 cm)* IV
football ['fʊtbɔ:l] Fußball I • **football boots** Fußballschuhe, -stiefel I
footprint ['fʊtprɪnt] Fußabdruck VI 2 (29)
footstep ['fʊtstep] Schritt V

for [fə, fɔː] für I • **for a while** für eine Weile, eine Zeit lang V • **for breakfast/lunch/dinner** zum Frühstück/Mittagessen/Abendbrot I **for example** zum Beispiel III • **for lots of reasons** aus vielen Gründen I • **for miles** meilenweit II **for sale** *(auf Schild)* zu verkaufen IV • **for the first time** zum ersten Mal IV • **for 20 minutes** seit 20 Minuten; 20 Minuten lang IV **for three days** drei Tage (lang) I **just for fun** nur zum Spaß I **What for?** Wofür? II • **What's for homework?** Was haben wir als Hausaufgabe auf? I
force [fɔːs] zwingen, erzwingen V
foreground ['fɔːgraʊnd] Vordergrund II
foreign ['fɒrən] ausländisch, fremd IV • **foreign language** Fremdsprache IV
forest ['fɒrɪst] Wald II
forever *(BE auch:* **for ever***)* [fər'evə] für immer VI 2 (30)
forgave [fə'geɪv] *siehe* **forgive**
forget (-tt-) [fə'get]**, forgot, forgotten** vergessen I
forgive [fə'gɪv]**, forgave, forgiven** vergeben, verzeihen IV
forgiven [fə'gɪvn] *siehe* **forgive**
forgot [fə'gɒt] *siehe* **forget**
forgotten [fə'gɒtn] *siehe* **forget**
fork [fɔːk] Gabel III
form [fɔːm]
1. (Schul-)Klasse I • **form teacher** Klassenlehrer/in I
2. Formular V
°**form** [fɔːm] bilden
°**formal letter** ['fɔːml] formeller/förmlicher Brief
fortunately ['fɔːtʃənətli] zum Glück IV
forum ['fɔːrəm] Forum V
forward ['fɔːwəd]
°**1.** vorwärts
2. look forward to sth. sich auf etwas freuen IV
fossil fuel [ˌfɒsl 'fjuːəl] fossiler Brennstoff VI 2 (29)
fought [fɔːt] *siehe* **fight**
found [faʊnd] *siehe* **find**
found [faʊnd] gründen IV
°**four-part** ['fɔːpɑːt] vierteilige(r, s)
fox [fɒks] Fuchs II
frame [freɪm] Rahmen; Gestell V
free [friː]
1. frei I • **free time** Freizeit, freie Zeit I
2. kostenlos I
Feel free to ask questions. Ihr könnt jetzt gern Fragen stellen. V
freedom ['friːdəm] Freiheit V
freezing ['friːzɪŋ] eisig; eiskalt VI 2 (35)
French [frentʃ] Französisch I
French fries *(AE)* [fraɪz] Pommes Frites IV
fresh [freʃ] frisch IV
Friday ['fraɪdeɪ, 'fraɪdi] Freitag I
fridge [frɪdʒ] Kühlschrank I
friend [frend] Freund/in I • **make friends (with sb.)** Freunde finden; sich anfreunden (mit jm.) VI 1 (8)
online friend Internetfreund/in V
friendliness ['frendlinəs] Freundlichkeit IV
friendly ['frendli] freundlich III
fries [fraɪz]**: French fries** *(AE)* Pommes Frites IV
frog [frɒg] Frosch II
from [frəm, frɒm]
1. aus I
2. von I
from all over the UK/the world/England aus dem gesamten Vereinigten Königreich / aus der ganzen Welt / aus ganz England III
from Monday to Friday von Montag bis Freitag III • **I'm from ...** Ich komme aus ... / Ich bin aus ... I
Where are you from? Wo kommst du her?
front [frʌnt]**: in front of** vor *(räumlich)* I • **front door** [ˌfrʌnt 'dɔː] Wohnungstür, Haustür I
fruit [fruːt] Obst, Früchte; Frucht I
fruit salad ['fruːt ˌsæləd] Obstsalat I
fruity ['fruːti] fruchtig V
fuel ['fjuːəl] Brenn-, Treib-, Kraftstoff VI 2 (29/182)
full [fʊl] voll I
fully ['fʊli]**: fully booked** ausgebucht V
fun [fʌn] Spaß I • **have fun** Spaß haben, sich amüsieren I • **Have fun!** Viel Spaß! I • **just for fun** nur zum Spaß I • **Riding is fun.** Reiten macht Spaß. I
funeral ['fjuːnərəl] Trauerfeier, Beerdigung V
funny ['fʌni] witzig, komisch I
future ['fjuːtʃə] Zukunft; Zukunfts-, zukünftig V

G

°**gallery** ['gæləri] (Bilder-)Galerie
game [geɪm] Spiel I
gang [gæŋ] Gang, (Jugend-)Bande V
gangster ['gæŋstə] Gangster/in V
garage ['gærɑːʒ]
1. Garage II
2. Autowerkstatt V
garbage ['gɑːrbɪdʒ] *(AE)* Müll, Abfall IV
garden ['gɑːdn] Garten I
gardener ['gɑːdnə] Gärtner/in IV
gas [gæs]
1. Gas IV
2. *(AE)* Benzin IV • **gas station** *(AE)* Tankstelle IV
°**gasifier** ['gæsɪfaɪə] Vergaser
gate [geɪt]
1. Tor III
2. Flugsteig III
gave [geɪv] *siehe* **give**
gear [gɪə] Ausrüstung IV
°**geek** [giːk] Freak
general ['dʒenrəl] allgemeine(r, s) III
generally ['dʒenrəli] allgemein, im Allgemeinen, generell V
generation [ˌdʒenə'reɪʃn] Generation V
geography [dʒi'ɒgrəfi] Geografie, Erdkunde I
German ['dʒɜːmən] Deutsch; deutsch; Deutsche(r) I
Germany ['dʒɜːməni] Deutschland I
get (-tt-) [get]**, got, got**
1. bekommen, kriegen II
2. holen, besorgen II
3. gelangen, (hin)kommen I
4. get angry/hot/... wütend/heiß/... werden II
5. get dressed [drest] sich anziehen I
6. get off (the train/bus) (aus dem Zug/Bus) aussteigen I • **get on (the train/bus)** (in den Zug/Bus) einsteigen I
7. get up aufstehen I
get a cab ein Taxi nehmen IV
get divorced sich scheiden lassen VI 3 (48/187) • **get involved** sich engagieren (für, bei); sich beteiligen (an) IV • **get married (to sb.)** (jn.) heiraten VI 3 (48) • **get on well/badly (with sb.)** sich gut/schlecht verstehen (mit jm.) IV • **get ready (for)** sich fertig machen (für), sich vorbereiten (auf) I • °**Get real!** *(infml)* Komm auf den Boden! / Werd vernünftig! • **get sth. off the ground** etwas auf den Weg bringen; etwas auf die Beine stellen III
get things ready Dinge fertig machen, vorbereiten I • **get to know sb.** jn. kennenlernen IV
getting by in English [ˌgetɪŋ 'baɪ] *etwa:* auf Englisch zurechtkommen I
ghost [gəʊst] Geist, Gespenst II

gig [gɪg] *(infml)* Gig, Auftritt III
do a gig einen Auftritt haben, ein Konzert geben III
giraffe [dʒəˈrɑːf] Giraffe II
girl [gɜːl] Mädchen I
girlfriend [ˈgɜːlfrend] (feste) Freundin IV
give [gɪv], **gave, given** geben I
give a talk (on sth.) einen Vortrag/eine Rede halten (über etwas) V
give sth. up auf etwas verzichten V • **give up** aufgeben, resignieren IV • **it gives me the creeps** *(infml)* es ist mir unheimlich; es ist mir nicht geheuer VI 2 (35)
given [ˈgɪvn] *siehe* **give**
glad [glæd] froh, dankbar III
glamorous [ˈglæmərəs] glamourös V
glass [glɑːs] Glas I • **a glass of water** ein Glas Wasser I
glasses *(pl)* [ˈglɑːsɪz] (eine) Brille I
global [ˈgləʊbl] global, weltweit VI 2 (29/182) • **global warming** Erwärmung der Erdatmosphäre, globaler Temperaturanstieg VI 2 (29)
glue [gluː] (auf-, ein)kleben II
glue [gluː] Klebstoff I • **glue stick** Klebestift I
go [gəʊ], **went, gone** gehen I; fahren II • **go by** vergehen, vorübergehen *(Zeit)* V • **go by car/train/bike** mit dem Auto/Zug/Rad fahren II • **go for a walk** spazieren gehen, einen Spaziergang machen II • **go home** nach Hause gehen I
go on **1.** weitermachen I; **2.** weiterreden III • **Go on.** Mach/Erzähl weiter. I • **go on a trip** einen Ausflug machen II • **go on holiday** in Urlaub fahren II • **go red** rot werden, erröten V • **go riding** reiten gehen I • **go shopping** einkaufen gehen I • **go sightseeing** auf Sightseeingtour gehen, sich Sehenswürdigkeiten ansehen V
go swimming schwimmen gehen I • **go to bed** ins Bett gehen I
go to the cinema ins Kino gehen II
go together zusammenpassen, -gehören II • **go well** gut (ver-)laufen, gutgehen III • **go with** gehören zu, passen zu III • **go out with sb.** mit jm. gehen *(als Freund/in)* V • **coffee to go** Kaffee zum Mitnehmen IV • **Let's go.** Auf geht's! I
goal [gəʊl] Tor *(im Sport)* III • **score a goal** ein Tor schießen, einen Treffer erzielen III
goalkeeper [ˈgəʊlkiːpə] Torwart, Torfrau III
gold [gəʊld] Gold IV
golden [ˈgəʊldən] goldene(r, s) IV
golf [gɒlf] Golf III
gone [gɒn]
1. weg, fort VI 2 (34)
2. *siehe* **go**
good [gʊd]
1. gut I
2. brav II
Good afternoon. Guten Tag. *(nachmittags)* I • **Good luck (with ...)!** Viel Glück (bei/mit ...)! I
Good morning. Guten Morgen. I
Good to have you back. Schön, dass du wieder da bist. IV • **be good at sth.** gut in etwas sein; etwas gut können III
Goodbye. [ˌgʊdˈbaɪ] Auf Wiedersehen. I • **say goodbye** sich verabschieden I
good-looking [ˌgʊdˈlʊkɪŋ] gut aussehend VI 1 (6)
got [gɒt] *siehe* **get**
got [gɒt]: **I've got ...** Ich habe ... I
I haven't got a chair. Ich habe keinen Stuhl. I
government [ˈgʌvənmənt] Regierung IV
governor [ˈgʌvənə] Gouverneur/in *(Oberhaupt eines US-Bundesstaates)* IV
°**GPS** [ˌdʒiː piː‿ˈes] **(Global Positioning System** [pəˈzɪʃnɪŋ]**)** Globales Positionsbestimmungssystem; Satellitennavigationssystem
grab sth. (-bb-) [græb] sich etwas schnappen IV
grade [greɪd]
1. Klasse, Jahrgangsstufe IV
2. (Schul-)Note, Zensur IV
graffiti [grəˈfiːti] Graffiti V
grammar [ˈgræmə] Grammatik I
grammar file *Grammatikanhang* I
grand [grænd] eindrucksvoll, beeindruckend IV
grandad [ˈgrændæd] Opa III
grandchild [ˈgræntʃaɪld], *pl* **grandchildren** Enkel/in I
grandfather [ˈgrænfɑːðə] Großvater I
grandma [ˈgrænmɑː] Oma I
grandmother [ˈgrænmʌðə] Großmutter I
grandpa [ˈgrænpɑː] Opa I
grandparents [ˈgrænpeərənts] Großeltern I
granny [ˈgræni] Oma II
grape [greɪp] Weintraube IV
°**graph**: **suspense graph** [səˈspens grɑːf] Spannungskurve
grass [grɑːs] Gras, Rasen IV • **cut the grass** Rasen mähen IV
great [greɪt] großartig, toll I
great-grandfather [ˌgreɪt ˈgrænfɑːðə] Urgroßvater III
great-grandmother [ˌgreɪt ˈgrænmʌðə] Urgroßmutter III
greedy [ˈgriːdi] gierig, habgierig V
green [griːn] grün I • **green energy** grüne Energie; Ökoenergie VI 2 (29)
greenhouse [ˈgriːnhaʊs] Gewächshaus, Treibhaus VI 2 (29)
grew [gruː] *siehe* **grow**
grey [greɪ] grau II
ground [graʊnd] (Erd-)Boden III
ground floor *(BE)* Erdgeschoss IV
get sth. off the ground etwas auf den Weg bringen; etwas auf die Beine stellen III
grounded [ˈgraʊndɪd]: **be grounded** Ausgehverbot/Hausarrest haben III
group [gruːp] Gruppe I • **group word** Oberbegriff II
grow [grəʊ], **grew, grown**
°**1.** wachsen
2. *(Getreide usw.)* anbauen, anpflanzen II
3. grow up [ˌgrəʊ‿ˈʌp] erwachsen werden; aufwachsen III
grown [grəʊn] *siehe* **grow**
grumble [ˈgrʌmbl] murren, nörgeln I
guess [ges] raten, erraten, schätzen III • **Guess what!** [ˌges ˈwɒt] Stell dir vor! / Stellt euch vor! IV
guest [gest] Gast I
guide [gaɪd]: **(tour) guide** (Fremden-)Führer/in, Reiseleiter/in IV
guilty [ˈgɪlti] schuldbewusst; schuldig IV
guinea pig [ˈgɪni pɪg] Meerschweinchen I
guitar [gɪˈtɑː] Gitarre I • **play the guitar** Gitarre spielen I
gun [gʌn] Gewehr IV
guy [gaɪ] *(infml)* Typ, Kerl IV
guys *(pl)* [gaɪz] *(AE, infml)* Leute III
gym [dʒɪm] Sporthalle, Turnhalle; Fitnessstudio IV

H

had [hæd] *siehe* **have** *und* **have got**
hair *(no pl)* [heə] Haar, Haare I
hairdresser [ˈheədresə] Friseur/in III
hairdryer [ˈheədraɪə] Föhn, Haartrockner VI 2 (28)
hairy [ˈheəri] haarig, behaart V
half [hɑːf], *pl* **halves** [hɑːvz] Hälfte III • **first half** erste Halbzeit III
half of ... die Hälfte der/des ... IV

half [hɑːf]**: half an hour** eine halbe Stunde III • **half past 11** halb zwölf (11.30/23.30) I • **three and a half days** dreieinhalb Tage IV
half-pipe ['hɑːfpaɪp] Halfpipe III
half-time [ˌhɑːf 'taɪm] Halbzeit(pause) III
hall [hɔːl] Flur, Diele I • **study hall** ['stʌdɪ hɔːl] *Zeit zum selbstständigen Arbeiten/Lernen in der Schule* IV • **town hall** [taʊn 'hɔːl] Rathaus VI 3 (47/187)
halves [hɑːvz] *Plural von „half"*
hamburger ['hæmbɜːgə] Hamburger I
hamster ['hæmstə] Hamster I
hand [hænd] Hand I • **on the one hand ... on the other hand** einerseits ... andererseits VI 2 (37)
handball ['hændbɔːl] Handball III
hang [hæŋ]**, hung, hung:**
Hang on. Einen Augenblick. / Sofort. / *(am Telefon)* Bleiben Sie dran. V • **hang out (with friends)** *(infml)* rumhängen, abhängen (mit Freunden/Freundinnen) III
hang up *(den Telefonhörer)* auflegen V
happen (to) ['hæpən] geschehen, passieren (mit) I
happiness ['hæpinəs] Glück IV
happy ['hæpi] glücklich, froh I
Happy birthday. Herzlichen Glückwunsch zum Geburtstag. I
happy ending Happyend II • **be happy to do sth.** gern bereit sein, etwas zu tun V
harbour ['hɑːbə] Hafen II
hard [hɑːd] hart; schwer, schwierig II • **work hard** hart arbeiten II
hard-working [ˌhɑːd 'wɜːkɪŋ] fleißig, tüchtig III
hat [hæt] Hut II
hate [heɪt] hassen, gar nicht mögen I
have [həv, hæv]**, had, had** haben, besitzen II • **have a baby** ein Baby/Kind bekommen II • **have a bath** baden, ein Bad nehmen II
have a cold erkältet sein, eine Erkältung haben II • **have a crush on sb.** in jn. verknallt sein III
Have a good holiday. Schöne Ferien! V • **Have a good time.** Viel Spaß! V • **have a look at sth.** sich etwas ansehen, einen Blick werfen auf etwas IV • **have a picnic** ein Picknick machen I • **have a sauna** in die Sauna gehen II
have a shower (sich) duschen I
have a sore throat Halsschmerzen haben II • **have a temperature** Fieber haben II • **Can I have a word with you?** Kann ich mal kurz mit dir reden? VI 3 (55) • **have breakfast/dinner** frühstücken / Abendbrot essen I • **have ... for breakfast** zum Frühstück essen/trinken I • **have fun** Spaß haben, sich amüsieren I • **have sleep-overs** Schlafpartys veranstalten III
have to do tun müssen I • **Have your say!** *etwa:* Übe dein Mitspracherecht aus! / Rede mit! VI 3 (46)
Good to have you back. Schön, dass du wieder da bist. IV
have got: I've got ... [aɪv 'gɒt] Ich habe ... I • **I haven't got a chair.** Ich habe keinen Stuhl. I
he [hiː] er I
head [hed] Kopf I • **head teacher** Schulleiter/in III
headache ['hedeɪk] Kopfschmerzen II
heading ['hedɪŋ] Überschrift, Titel IV
headless ['hedləs] kopflos IV
headline ['hedlaɪn] Schlagzeile IV
headphones *(pl)* ['hedfəʊnz] Kopfhörer III
health [helθ] Gesundheit IV
healthy ['helθi] gesund II
hear [hɪə]**, heard, heard** hören I
heard [hɜːd] *siehe* **hear**
heart [hɑːt] Herz II
heat [hiːt] heizen, erhitzen VI 2 (28/182)
heat [hiːt] Hitze, Wärme VI 2 (28/182)
heating ['hiːtɪŋ] Heizung VI 2 (28)
heaven ['hevn] Himmel *(im religiösen Sinn)* IV
heavy ['hevi]
1. schwer *(von Gewicht)* VI 2 (34)
2. heftig, stark VI 2 (34)
hedgehog ['hedʒhɒg] Igel II
held [held] *siehe* **hold**
helicopter ['helɪkɒptə] Hubschrauber, Helikopter II
Hello. [hə'ləʊ] Hallo. / Guten Tag. I
helmet ['helmɪt] Helm III
help [help] helfen I • **Can I help you?** Kann ich Ihnen helfen? / Was kann ich für Sie tun? *(im Laden)* I
help [help] Hilfe I
helpful ['helpfl]
1. nützlich, hilfreich IV
2. hilfsbereit V
helpless ['helpləs] hilflos IV
her [hə, hɜː]
1. ihr, ihre I
2. sie; ihr I
here [hɪə]
1. hier I
2. hierher I
Here you are. Bitte sehr. / Hier bitte. I
hero ['hɪərəʊ] Held/in; Idol, Vorbild V
hers [hɜːz] ihrer, ihre, ihrs II
herself [hə'self, hɜː'self] sich (selbst) III
Hi! [haɪ] Hallo! I • **Say hi to Dilip for me.** Grüß Dilip von mir. I
hid [hɪd] *siehe* **hide**
hidden ['hɪdn] *siehe* **hide**
hide [haɪd]**, hid, hidden** verstecken; sich verstecken I
high [haɪ] hoch III
highlight ['haɪlaɪt] Highlight V
high school ['haɪ skuːl] *(USA)* Schule für 14- bis 18-Jährige IV
highway ['haɪweɪ] *(USA) Fernstraße (oft mit vier oder mehr Spuren)* IV
hijacker ['haɪdʒækə] (Flugzeug-) Entführer/in IV
hike [haɪk] wandern IV
hike [haɪk] Wanderung, Marsch IV • **go on a hike** wandern gehen IV
hill [hɪl] Hügel II
hilly ['hɪli] hügelig III
him [hɪm] ihn; ihm I
himself [hɪm'self] sich (selbst) III
Hindu ['hɪnduː] Hindu; Hindu- V; hinduistisch VI 1 (13/181)
► S.181 Religions
hip hop ['hɪp hɒp] Hip Hop III
hippo ['hɪpəʊ] Flusspferd II
his [hɪz]
1. sein, seine I
2. seiner, seine, seins II
historical [hɪ'stɒrɪkl] geschichtlich, historisch V
history ['hɪstri] Geschichte I
hit (-tt-) [hɪt] **hit, hit** schlagen II
hit [hɪt] Hit III
hobby ['hɒbi] Hobby I
hockey ['hɒki] Hockey I • **hockey shoes** Hockeyschuhe I
hold [həʊld]**, held, held**
1. halten II
2. veranstalten, abhalten *(Veranstaltung, Wettbewerb)* V
hold on (to sth.) sich festhalten (an etwas) V • **hold sb. up** jn. aufhalten VI 2 (34)
hole [həʊl] Loch IV
holiday ['hɒlədeɪ]
1. Feiertag IV
2. holiday(s) Ferien I
holiday flat Ferienwohnung II
be on holiday in Urlaub sein; Ferien haben/machen II • **go on holiday** in Urlaub fahren II
a two-week holiday ein zwei-

wöchiger Urlaub III • **Have a good holiday.** Schöne Ferien! V
home [həʊm] Heim, Zuhause I
at home daheim, zu Hause I
come home nach Hause kommen I • **get home** nach Hause kommen I • **go home** nach Hause gehen I • **leave home** von zu Hause ausziehen VI 3 (48) • **old people's home** Alten-, Seniorenheim V
homeless ['həʊmləs] obdachlos IV
homelessness ['həʊmləsnəs] Obdachlosigkeit V
hometown ['həʊmtaʊn] Heimatstadt, -ort IV
homework *(no pl)* ['həʊmwɜ:k] Hausaufgabe(n) I • **do homework** die Hausaufgabe(n) machen I
What's for homework? Was haben wir als Hausaufgabe auf? I
honest ['ɒnɪst] ehrlich V
°**honey bee** ['hʌnibi:] Honigbiene
Hooray! [hu'reɪ] Hurra! II
hop channels [ˌhɒp 'tʃænəlz] zappen IV
hope [həʊp] hoffen II
hope [həʊp] Hoffnung III
horrible ['hɒrəbl] scheußlich, grauenhaft II
horror film ['hɒrə fɪlm] Horrorfilm VI 1 (14)
horse [hɔ:s] Pferd I
hospital ['hɒspɪtl] Krankenhaus II
hostel ['hɒstl] Herberge, Wohnheim III
hot [hɒt] heiß I • **hot chocolate** heiße Schokolade I
hotel [həʊ'tel] Hotel II
hotline ['hɒtlaɪn] Hotline II
hour ['aʊə] Stunde II • **half an hour** eine halbe Stunde III • **a 14-hour flight** ein 14-stündiger Flug, ein 14-Stunden-Flug III • **a 24-hour supermarket** ein Supermarkt, der 24 Stunden geöffnet ist III
hours *(pl)* ['aʊəz]
1. Öffnungszeiten IV
2. work long hours lange arbeiten V
house [haʊs] Haus I • **at the Shaws' house** im Haus der Shaws / bei den Shaws zu Hause I
how [haʊ] wie I • **How about ...?** Wie wär's mit ...? III • **How am I doing?** Wie komme ich voran? *(Wie sind meine Fortschritte?)* III
How are you? Wie geht es dir/Ihnen/euch? II • **How are you doing?** Wie geht's? V • **How do you know ...?** Woher weißt/kennst du ...? I • **how long?** seit wann?/wie lange? IV • **how many?** wie viele? I • **how much?** wie viel? I
How much is/are ...? Was kostet/kosten ...? / Wie viel kostet/kosten ...? I • **How old are you?** Wie alt bist du? I • **how to do sth.** wie man etwas tut / tun kann / tun soll IV • **How was ...?** Wie war ...? I
however [haʊ'evə] jedoch, allerdings VI 2 (37)
huge [hju:dʒ] riesig, sehr groß III
human ['hju:mən] Menschen-, menschlich IV
humour ['hju:mə] Humor VI 1 (6/179)
sense of humour (Sinn für) Humor VI 1 (6)
hundred ['hʌndrəd] hundert I
hung [hʌŋ] *siehe* **hang**
hungry ['hʌŋgri] hungrig III • **I'm hungry.** Ich habe Hunger III
hunt [hʌnt] jagen III
hunt [hʌnt] Jagd III
hurry ['hʌri] eilen; sich beeilen II
hurry up sich beeilen I
hurry ['hʌri]**: be in a hurry** in Eile sein, es eilig haben I
hurt [hɜ:t]**, hurt, hurt** wehtun; verletzen I
hurt [hɜ:t] verletzt II
husband ['hʌzbənd] Ehemann II
hutch [hʌtʃ] (Kaninchen-)Stall I

I

I [aɪ] ich I • **I'm** [aɪm] ich bin I
I'm from ... Ich komme aus ... / Ich bin aus ... I • **I'm sorry.** Tut mir leid. / Entschuldigung. I
ice [aɪs]**: ice cream** (Speise-)Eis I
ice hockey Eishockey III • **ice rink** Schlittschuhbahn II
icy ['aɪsi] eisig V
idea [aɪ'dɪə] Idee, Einfall I
ideal [aɪ'di:əl] ideal V
if [ɪf]
1. falls, wenn II
2. ob II
as if als ob IV • **even if** sogar wenn IV
ignore [ɪg'nɔ:] ignorieren, nicht beachten VI 3 (52)
ill [ɪl] krank II
illegal [ɪ'li:gl] illegal, ungesetzlich IV
illness ['ɪlnəs] Krankheit IV
°**imaginary journey** [ɪ'mædʒɪnəri] Phantasiereise
imagination [ɪˌmædʒɪ'neɪʃn] Fantasie, Vorstellung IV
imagine sth. [ɪ'mædʒɪn] sich etwas vorstellen III
immediately [ɪ'mi:diətli] sofort IV
immigrant ['ɪmɪgrənt] Einwanderer/Einwanderin IV
impatient [ɪm'peɪʃnt] ungeduldig VI 1 (13/181)
important (to) [ɪm'pɔ:tnt] wichtig (für) II
impossible [ɪm'pɒsəbl] unmöglich II
impress [ɪm'pres] beeindrucken V
impressed [ɪm'prest] beeindruckt IV
impressive [ɪm'presɪv] beeindruckend, eindrucksvoll V
improve [ɪm'pru:v] verbessern IV
in [ɪn] in I • **in ... Street** in der ...straße I • **in a friendly/strange/different way** auf freundliche/seltsame/andere Art und Weise VI 1 (7) • **in danger** in Gefahr V
in English auf Englisch I • **in fact** tatsächlich; in Wirklichkeit; um genau zu sein VI 1 (12) • **in front of** vor *(räumlich)* I • **in here** hier drinnen I • **in the afternoon** nachmittags, am Nachmittag I
in the country auf dem Land II
in the end schließlich, zum Schluss III • **in the evening** abends, am Abend I • **in the field** auf dem Feld II • **in the morning** am Morgen, morgens I • **in the photo** auf dem Foto I • **in the picture** auf dem Bild I • **in the world** (auf) der Welt IV • **in the yard** auf dem Hof II • **in time** rechtzeitig II • **in 1919** 1919, im Jahre 1919 IV • **in the 1970s** in den 70er-Jahren *(des 20. Jahrhunderts)* VI 2 (30)
°**include** [ɪn'klu:d] beinhalten, enthalten
independent [ˌɪndɪ'pendənt] unabhängig V
°**individual** [ˌɪndɪ'vɪdʒuəl] einzelne(r, s), individuelle(r, s)
indoor ['ɪndɔ:] *(nur vor Nomen)* Hallen-; im Gebäude V • **indoor market** Markthalle V • **indoor swimming pool** Hallenbad V • **indoor toilet** Innentoilette V
indoors [ˌɪn'dɔ:z] drinnen, nach drinnen V
industrial [ɪn'dʌstriəl] industriell, Industrie- IV
industry ['ɪndəstri] Industrie IV
infinitive [ɪn'fɪnətɪv] Infinitiv *(Grundform des Verbs)* I
information (about/on) *(no pl)* [ˌɪnfə'meɪʃn] Information(en) (über) II

ink [ɪŋk] Tinte V
inside [ˌɪn'saɪd]
1. innen (drin), drinnen I
2. nach drinnen II
3. innerhalb IV
4. inside the car ins Auto (hinein), ins Innere des Autos II
install [ɪn'stɔːl] installieren, einrichten II
instant messages *(pl)* [ˌɪnstənt 'mesɪdʒɪz] *Nachrichten, die man im Internet austauscht (in Echtzeit)* III
instead *(adv)* [ɪn'sted] stattdessen, dafür VI 1 (8/179)
instead of *(prep)* [ɪn'sted‿əv] statt, anstatt, anstelle von VI 1 (8)
instructions *(pl)* [ɪn'strʌkʃnz]
1. (Gebrauchs-)Anweisung(en), Anleitung(en) II
°**2.** Hinweise zur Einnahme *(bei Medikamenten)*
instructor [ɪn'strʌktə] Lehrer/in, Trainer/in V • **driving instructor** Fahrlehrer/in V • **fitness instructor** Fitnesstrainer/in V • **ski instructor** Skilehrer/in V
instrument ['ɪnstrəmənt] Instrument III
insulation [ˌɪnsju'leɪʃn] Isolierung, Wärmedämmung VI 2 (29)
intelligent [ɪn'telɪdʒənt] intelligent, klug VI 1 (13)
interest (in) ['ɪntrəst] Interesse (an) V
interested ['ɪntrəstɪd]**: be interested (in)** interessiert sein (an), sich interessieren (für) III
interesting ['ɪntrəstɪŋ] interessant I
international [ˌɪntə'næʃnəl] international III
internet ['ɪntənet] Internet III • **on the internet** im Internet IV • **surf the internet** im Internet surfen III
interview ['ɪntəvjuː]
1. Interview I
2. (job) interview Vorstellungsgespräch, Bewerbungsgespräch V
interview ['ɪntəvjuː] interviewen, befragen II
interviewer ['ɪntəvjuːə] Interviewer/in, Befrager/in V
into ['ɪntə, 'ɪntʊ] in ... (hinein) I
introduce [ˌɪntrə'djuːs]
1. introduce sb. to sb. jn. jm. vorstellen; jn. mit jm. bekanntmachen V
2. introduce sth. etwas einführen *(Thema, Mode, Methode)* V
introduction (to) [ˌɪntrə'dʌkʃn] Einführung (in) III
invent [ɪn'vent] erfinden VI 2 (30/183)
invention [ɪn'venʃn] Erfindung VI 2 (30)
invitation (to) [ˌɪnvɪ'teɪʃn] Einladung (zu) I
invite (to) [ɪn'vaɪt] einladen (zu) I
involved [ɪn'vɒlvd]**: get involved** sich engagieren (für, bei); sich beteiligen (an) IV
is [ɪz] ist I
island ['aɪlənd] Insel II
issue ['ɪʃuː] Thema, (Streit-)Frage VI 3 (46)
it [ɪt] er/sie/es I • **It's £1.** Er/Sie/Es kostet 1 Pfund. I • **It doesn't matter.** Es spielt keine Rolle. / Es macht nichts (aus). VI 3 (49) • **It gives me the creeps.** *(infml)* Es ist mir unheimlich. / Es ist mir nicht geheuer. VI 2 (35) • **It says here: ...** Hier steht: ... / Es heißt hier: ... II
its [ɪts] sein/seine; ihr/ihre I
itself [ɪt'self] sich (selbst) III

J

jacket ['dʒækɪt] Jacke, Jackett II
rainproof jacket ['reɪnpruːf] regendichte Jacke V • **weatherproof jacket** ['weðəpruːf] wetterfeste Jacke V • **windproof jacket** ['wɪndpruːf] winddichte Jacke V
jail [dʒeɪl] Gefängnis IV
jam: traffic jam ['træfɪk dʒæm] (Verkehrs-)Stau IV
January ['dʒænjuəri] Januar I
jazz [dʒæz] Jazz III
jealous (of) ['dʒeləs] neidisch (auf); eifersüchtig (auf) III
jealousy ['dʒeləsi] Eifersucht IV
jeans *(pl)* [dʒiːnz] Jeans I
Jew [dʒuː] Jude/Jüdin VI 1 (13/181)
► S.181 Religions
Jewish ['dʒuːɪʃ] jüdisch IV
► S.181 Religions
job [dʒɒb] Aufgabe, Job I • **job interview** Vorstellungsgespräch, Bewerbungsgespräch V
jobless ['dʒɒbləs] arbeitslos IV
join sb. [dʒɔɪn] sich jm. anschließen; bei jm. mitmachen II
joke [dʒəʊk] Witz I
joke [dʒəʊk] scherzen, Witze machen II
journalist ['dʒɜːnəlɪst] Journalist/in IV
journey ['dʒɜːni] Fahrt, Reise III
Have a good journey. Gute Reise! V
judge (by) [dʒʌdʒ] beurteilen, einschätzen (nach) IV
judo ['dʒuːdəʊ] Judo I • **do judo** Judo machen I
jug [dʒʌg] Krug I • **a jug of milk** ein Krug Milch I
juice [dʒuːs] Saft I
juicy ['dʒuːsi] saftig V
July [dʒu'laɪ] Juli I
jumble sale ['dʒʌmbl seɪl] Wohltätigkeitsbasar I
jump [dʒʌmp] springen II • **jump around** herumspringen III
June [dʒuːn] Juni I
junior ['dʒuːniə] Junioren-, Jugend- I
just [dʒʌst]
1. (einfach) nur, bloß I • **It's just a game.** Es ist nur/bloß ein Spiel. III
2. einfach III • **I just can't find my keys.** Ich kann einfach meine Schlüssel nicht finden. III • **Just don't listen to them.** Hör einfach nicht hin. III
3. gerade (eben), soeben II • **just then** genau in dem Moment / gerade dann III
4. just as ... as genauso ... wie V
5. just like your mother genau wie deine Mutter III

K

kangaroo [ˌkæŋgə'ruː] Känguru II
keep [kiːp]**, kept, kept** (be)halten; aufbewahren III • **keep in touch** in Verbindung bleiben, Kontakt halten III • **keep (on) doing sth.** etwas weiter tun; etwas immer wieder tun VI 2 (35/185) • **the machine kept breaking down** das Gerät fiel immer wieder aus VI 2 (35) • **keep sb. away (from)** jn. fernhalten (von) VI 3 (49) • **keep sth. going** etwas in Gang halten, etwas aufrechterhalten VI 1 (11)
keep sth. warm/cool/open etwas warm/kühl/offen halten II
► S.185 (to) keep
kept [kept] *siehe* **keep**
ketchup ['ketʃəp] Ketschup V
kettle ['ketl] (Wasser-)Kessel, Wasserkocher VI 2 (34)
key [kiː] Schlüssel II • **key ring** Schlüsselring II • **key word** Stichwort, Schlüsselwort I
keyboard ['kiːbɔːd] Keyboard *(elektronisches Tasteninstrument)* III
kick [kɪk] treten IV
kid [kɪd] Kind, Jugendliche(r) I
kill [kɪl] töten I
kilogram (kg) ['kɪləgræm]**, kilo** ['kiːləʊ] Kilogramm, Kilo (kg) III

a 150-kilogram bear ein 150 Kilogramm schwerer Bär III
kilometre (km) ['kɪləmiːtə] Kilometer III • **a ten-kilometre walk** eine Zehn-Kilometer-Wanderung III
kind [kaɪnd] freundlich, nett V
kind (of) [kaɪnd] Art III • **What kind of car ...?** Was für ein Auto ...? III
kindergarten ['kɪndəgɑːtn] Kindergarten; *(USA)* Vorschule *(für 5- bis 6-Jährige)* IV
king [kɪŋ] König I
kingdom: the United Kingdom (UK) [juˌnaɪtɪd 'kɪŋdəm, juː'keɪ] das Vereinigte Königreich III
kiss [kɪs] Kuss IV
kiss [kɪs] küssen IV
kit [kɪt] Ausrüstung V • **first-aid kit** Erste-Hilfe-Kasten, Verbandskasten V • **repair kit** Flickzeug V **survival kit** Überlebenspäckchen V
kitchen ['kɪtʃɪn] Küche I
kite [kaɪt] Drachen I
kiwi ['kiːwiː] Kiwi II
knee [niː] Knie I
knew [njuː] *siehe* **know**
knife [naɪf], *pl* **knives** [naɪvz] Messer III
knock [nɒk] Klopfen V
knock (at/on sth.) [nɒk] (an etwas) klopfen V
know [nəʊ], **knew, known**
1. wissen I
2. kennen I
know about sth. von etwas wissen; über etwas Bescheid wissen II
get to know kennenlernen IV
How do you know ...? Woher weißt du ...? / Woher kennst du ...? I • **I don't know.** Ich weiß es nicht. I • **I'll let you know.** Ich gebe dir/Ihnen Bescheid V • **..., you know.** ..., wissen Sie. / ..., weißt du. I
You know what, Sophie? Weißt du was, Sophie? I
known [nəʊn]
1. *siehe* **know**
2. bekannt IV
koala [kəʊ'ɑːlə] Koala V

L

°label ['leɪbl] beschriften, etikettieren
label ['leɪbl] Marke, Label VI 3 (47)
laid [leɪd] *siehe* **lay the table**
lain [leɪn] *siehe* **lie**
lake [leɪk] (Binnen-)See II
lamb [læm] Lamm(fleisch) III
lamp [læmp] Lampe I
land [lænd] landen II
land [lænd] Land, Grund und Boden II
landscape ['lændskeɪp] Landschaft V
lane [leɪn] Gasse, Weg III
language ['læŋgwɪdʒ] Sprache I **foreign language** Fremdsprache IV
laptop ['læptɒp] Laptop V
large [lɑːdʒ] groß II
lasagne [lə'zænjə] Lasagne I
last [lɑːst] letzte(r, s) I • **the last day** der letzte Tag I • **at last** endlich, schließlich I
last (for) [lɑːst] dauern IV
late [leɪt] spät; zu spät I • **be late** zu spät sein/kommen I • **Sorry, I'm late.** Entschuldigung, dass ich zu spät bin/komme. I
later ['leɪtə] später I
latest ['leɪtɪst] neueste(r, s) III
laugh [lɑːf] lachen I • **laugh at sb.** jn. auslachen IV
laughable ['lɑːfəbl] lächerlich IV
laughter ['lɑːftə] Gelächter II
law [lɔː]
1. Gesetz IV
2. Jura, Rechtswissenschaften VI 1 (12)
lay [leɪ] *siehe* **lie**
lay the table [leɪ], **laid, laid** den Tisch decken I
°layout ['leɪaʊt] Layout, Anordnung, Aufbau
lazy ['leɪzi] faul VI 1 (10)
leader ['liːdə] Leiter/in, (An-)Führer/in III
leaf [liːf], *pl* **leaves** [liːvz] Blatt *(an Pflanzen)* V
lean out [ˌliːn‿'aʊt] sich hinauslehnen V
learn [lɜːn] lernen I • **learn sth. about sth.** etwas über etwas erfahren, etwas über etwas herausfinden II
least [liːst] am wenigsten III • **at least** zumindest, wenigstens I
leather ['leðə] Leder III
leave [liːv], **left, left**
1. (weg)gehen; abfahren II
2. verlassen II
3. zurücklassen II
leave a message eine Nachricht hinterlassen V • **leave home** von zu Hause ausziehen VI 3 (48)
leave sb. alone jn. in Ruhe lassen V
leave sth. out etwas weglassen/auslassen IV
leaves [liːvz] *Plural von „leaf"*
left [left] *siehe* **leave**
left [left] linke(r, s) II • **look left** nach links schauen II • **on the left** links, auf der linken Seite II • **turn left** (nach) links abbiegen II
leg [leg] Bein I
legal ['liːgl] legal, gesetzlich IV
leisure ['leʒə] Freizeit • **leisure centre** Freizeitzentrum, -park II
lemon ['lemən] Zitrone III
lemonade [ˌlemə'neɪd] Limonade I
lend sb. sth. [lend], **lent, lent** jm. etwas leihen, etwas an jn. verleihen V
lent [lent] siehe **lend**
less [les] weniger IV
lesson ['lesn] (Unterrichts-)Stunde I • **lessons** *(pl)* Unterricht I
let [let], **let, let** lassen II • **Let's ...** Lass uns ... / Lasst uns ... I • **Let's go.** Auf geht's! I • **Let's look at the list.** Sehen wir uns die Liste an. / Lasst uns die Liste ansehen. I
let sb. do sth. jm. erlauben, etwas zu tun; zulassen, dass jd. etwas tut III • **I'll let you know.** Ich gebe dir/Ihnen Bescheid V
letter ['letə]
1. Buchstabe I • **capital letter** [ˌkæpɪtl 'letə] Großbuchstabe III
2. **letter (to)** Brief (an) II • **°letter to the editor** Leserbrief • **letter of application** Bewerbungsschreiben V
lettuce ['letɪs] (Kopf-)Salat II
level ['levl] (Lern-)Stand, Niveau, Grad V
library ['laɪbrəri] Bibliothek, Bücherei I
licence ['laɪsns]**: driving licence** Führerschein V • **moped licence** Mopedführerschein V
license plate ['laɪsns pleɪt] *(AE)* Nummernschild IV
lie *(-ing form:* **lying***)* [laɪ] lügen V
lie *(-ing form:* **lying***)* [laɪ], **lay, lain** liegen IV
life [laɪf], *pl* **lives** [laɪvz] Leben I
lifeguard ['laɪfgɑːd] Rettungsschwimmer/in V • **lifeguard station** Station der Rettungsschwimmer/innen V
lift [lɪft] Fahrstuhl, Aufzug II
light [laɪt] Licht III • **traffic light** (Verkehrs-)Ampel IV
like [laɪk] wie I • **What was the weather like?** Wie war das Wetter? II • **like that / like this** so IV
like [laɪk] mögen, gernhaben I **like sth. better** etwas lieber mögen II • **I like swimming/dancing.**

Ich schwimme/tanze gern. I • **I'd like ... (= I would like ...)** Ich hätte gern ... / Ich möchte gern ... I • **I'd like to talk about ... (= I would like to talk about ...)** Ich möchte/würde gern über ... reden I • **Would you like ...?** Möchtest du ...? / Möchten Sie ...? I • **Would you like some?** Möchtest du etwas/ein paar? / Möchten Sie etwas/ein paar? I

likeable ['laɪkəbl] liebenswert, nett, sympathisch IV

likely ['laɪkli] wahrscheinlich VI 3 (48) • **be likely to be/do sth.** wahrscheinlich etwas sein/tun VI 3 (48/187)

line [laɪn]
1. Zeile II
°2. Linie
3. (U-Bahn-)Linie III
4. *(AE)* Schlange, Reihe *(wartender Menschen)* IV

link [lɪŋk] verbinden, verknüpfen I

link [lɪŋk] Verbindung, Verknüpfung III

linking word ['lɪŋkɪŋ wɜ:d] Bindewort II

lion ['laɪən] Löwe II

list [lɪst] Liste I

list [lɪst] auflisten, aufzählen II

listen (to) ['lɪsn] zuhören; sich etwas anhören I • **listen for sth.** auf etwas horchen, achten III

listener ['lɪsənə] Zuhörer/in II

listing ['lɪstɪŋ]: **TV listings** *(pl)* das Fernsehprogramm IV

little ['lɪtl]
1. klein I
2. wenig IV

live [lɪv] leben, wohnen I • **live on sth.** von etwas leben; sich von etwas ernähren V

live music [laɪv] Livemusik II

lives [laɪvz] *Plural von „life"*

living room ['lɪvɪŋ ru:m] Wohnzimmer I

local ['ləʊkl] Orts-, örtlich II; Lokal-, IV • **local paper** Lokalzeitung IV

location [ləʊ'keɪʃn]
1. (Wohn-)Ort III
2. (Veranstaltungs-)Ort III
3. Drehort

lock [lɒk] abschließen; sperren III

lock [lɒk] Schleuse III

logical ['lɒdʒɪkl] logisch V

logo ['ləʊgəʊ] Logo III

lonely ['ləʊnli] einsam III

long [lɒŋ] lang I • **work long hours** lange arbeiten V • **as long as** *(conj)* solange, sofern VI 3 (48)

look [lʊk]
1. schauen, gucken I
2. **look different/great/old** anders/toll/alt aussehen I
look after sth./sb. auf etwas/jn. aufpassen; sich um etwas/jn. kümmern II • **look at** ansehen, anschauen I • **look for** suchen II
look forward to sich auf etwas freuen IV • **look left/right** nach links/rechts schauen II • **look round** sich umsehen I • **look sth. up** etwas nachschlagen III • **look up (from)** hochsehen, aufschauen (von) II

look [lʊk]
1. **look (at)** Blick (auf) • **have a look at sth.** sich etwas ansehen, einen Blick werfen auf etwas IV
2. (Gesichts-)Ausdruck V

lorry ['lɒri] Lastkraftwagen III

lose [lu:z], **lost, lost** verlieren II

lost [lɒst] *siehe* **lose**

lot [lɒt]: **a lot (of) / lots (of)** eine Menge, viel, viele II • **Thanks a lot!** Vielen Dank! I • **He likes her a lot.** Er mag sie sehr. I • **lots more** viel mehr I

loud [laʊd] laut I

lovable ['lʌvəbl] liebenswert VI 1 (7)

love [lʌv] lieben, sehr mögen II
would love to do sth. etwas gern tun wollen V

love [lʌv] Liebe II • **Love ...** Liebe Grüße, ... *(Briefschluss)* I • **fall in love (with sb.)** sich verlieben (in jn.) IV

low [ləʊ] niedrig VI 2 (36)

loyal (to sb.) ['lɔɪəl] loyal (gegenüber jm.) VI 1 (6)

luck [lʌk]: **Good luck (with ...)!** Viel Glück (bei/mit ...)! I

luckily ['lʌkɪli] zum Glück, glücklicherweise II

lucky ['lʌki]: **be lucky (with)** Glück haben (mit) III

lunch [lʌntʃ] Mittagessen I
lunch break Mittagspause I

°**lunchtime** ['lʌntʃtaɪm] Mittagszeit

lyrics *(pl)* ['lɪrɪks] Liedtext(e), Songtext(e) III

M

machine [mə'ʃi:n] Maschine, Gerät; *hier:* Automat III • **ticket machine** Fahrkartenautomat III

mad [mæd] verrückt I • **be mad about sth.** verrückt nach/auf etwas sein III

madam: Dear Sir or Madam [sɜ:, sə; 'mædəm] Sehr geehrte Damen und Herren *(Anrede in Briefen)* IV

made [meɪd] *siehe* **make**

magazine [,mægə'zi:n] Zeitschrift, Magazin I

mail [meɪl] schicken, senden *(per Post oder E-mail)*; mailen III • **mail sb.** jn. anmailen II

mailbox ['meɪlbɒks] Mailbox V

main [meɪn] Haupt- III

mainly ['meɪnli] hauptsächlich V

majority [mə'dʒɒrəti] Mehrheit IV

make [meɪk], **made, made** machen; bauen I • **make a deal** ein Abkommen / eine Abmachung treffen III • **make a decision** eine Entscheidung treffen/fällen V
make a difference etwas bewirken, etwas bewegen VI 2 (36)
make a mess alles durcheinanderbringen, alles in Unordnung bringen I • **make a point** ein Argument vorbringen III • **make a speech** eine Rede halten IV
make friends (with sb.) Freunde finden; sich anfreunden (mit jm.) VI 1 (8) • °**make notes** sich Notizen machen • **make sb. do sth.** jn. dazu bringen etwas zu tun V
make sense sinnvoll sein, einen Sinn ergeben VI 3 (49) • **be made up (of)** zusammengesetzt sein (aus); bestehen (aus) VI 2 (29)
make sth. up 1. etwas bilden, etwas ausmachen VI 3 (49); °**2.** sich etwas ausdenken • **make sure that** sich vergewissern, dass ...; dafür sorgen, dass ... IV • **Make yourself comfortable.** Machs dir bequem. IV

make-up ['meɪkʌp] Make-up II
make-up artist ['ɑ:tɪst] Maskenbildner/in V

male [meɪl] männlich III

man [mæn], *pl* **men** [men] Mann I

°**manage sth.** ['mænɪdʒ] etwas regeln

manager ['mænədʒə]
1. Manager/in III
°2. Geschäftsführer/in, Leiter/in

many ['meni] viele I • **how many?** wie viele? I

map [mæp] Landkarte, Stadtplan II

March [mɑ:tʃ] März I

march [mɑ:tʃ] Marsch, Demonstration IV

mark [mɑ:k] *(BE)* (Schul-)Note, Zensur IV

mark sth. up [,mɑ:k‿'ʌp] etwas markieren, kennzeichnen II

market ['mɑ:kɪt] Markt II

marmalade ['mɑːməleɪd] (Orangen-)Marmelade I
married (to) ['mærɪd] verheiratet (mit) I • **get married (to sb.)** (jn.) heiraten VI 3 (48)
mass [mæs] Messe *(Gottesdienst)* VI 1 (13/181)
► S.181 Religions
match [mætʃ] Spiel, Wettkampf I
°**match** [mætʃ]
1. passen zu
2. zuordnen
°Match the letters and numbers. Ordne die Buchstaben den Zahlen zu.
match day ['mætʃ deɪ] Spieltag V
mate [meɪt] *(infml)* Freund/in, Kumpel III
material [mə'tɪəriəl] Material V
maths [mæθs] Mathematik I
matter ['mætə]: **It doesn't matter.** Es spielt keine Rolle. / Es macht nichts (aus). VI 3 (49)
matter ['mætə]: **What's the matter?** Was ist los? / Was ist denn? II
°no matter what/who/... ganz gleich, was/wer/...
May [meɪ] Mai I
may [meɪ] dürfen III
maybe ['meɪbi] vielleicht I
mayor ['meə] Bürgermeister/in IV
me [miː] mir; mich I • **Me too.** Ich auch. I • **more than me** mehr als ich II • **That's me.** Das bin ich. I **Why me?** Warum ich? I
meal [miːl] Mahlzeit, Essen III
mean [miːn] gemein VI 1 (8)
mean [miːn], **meant, meant**
1. bedeuten III
2. meinen *(sagen wollen)* II
I didn't mean to ... Ich wollte nicht ...; Es war nicht meine Absicht, zu ... VI 3 (55)
meaning ['miːnɪŋ] Bedeutung III
meant [ment] *siehe* **mean**
meat [miːt] Fleisch I
mechanic [mə'kænɪk] Mechaniker/in V
medal ['medl] Medaille III
media *(pl)* ['miːdiə] Medien III
mediation [ˌmiːdi'eɪʃn] Vermittlung, Sprachmittlung, Mediation II
medicine ['medsn, 'medɪsn] Medizin V
medium ['miːdiəm] mittel(groß) II
meet [miːt], **met, met**
1. treffen; kennenlernen I
2. sich treffen I
Nice to meet you. Nett, dich kennenzulernen. III
meeting ['miːtɪŋ] Versammlung, Besprechung IV
melt [melt] schmelzen VI 2 (35)
member (of) ['membə] Mitglied (von, in) IV • **member of parliament** Parlamentsmitglied, Abgeordnete(r) VI 3 (47/186)
► S.186 Politics
men [men] *Plural von „man"*
mention sth. (to sb.) ['menʃn] etwas erwähnen (jm. gegenüber) VI 1 (10)
menu ['menjuː] Speisekarte II
mess [mes]: **be a mess** sehr unordentlich sein; fürchterlich aussehen II • **make a mess** alles durcheinanderbringen, alles in Unordnung bringen I
message ['mesɪdʒ] Nachricht III; Botschaft VI 1 (12) • **instant messages** *Nachrichten, die man im Internet austauscht (in Echtzeit)* III **leave a message** eine Nachricht hinterlassen V • **take a message** eine Nachricht entgegennehmen V • **Can I take a message for her/him?** Kann ich ihr/ihm etwas ausrichten? V • **text message** SMS III
mess things up [ˌmes_'ʌp] *(infml)* alles durcheinanderbringen, alles vermasseln VI 1 (9)
met [met] *siehe* **meet**
metal ['metl] Metall V
meter ['miːtə] *(Gas-, Strom-)*Zähler VI 2 (35)
°**methane** ['miːθeɪn] Methan(gas)
°**method** ['meθəd] Methode
metre ['miːtə] Meter II
mice [maɪs] *Plural von „mouse"*
microphone ['maɪkrəfəʊn] Mikrofon III
microwave ['maɪkrəweɪv] Mikrowelle VI 2 (28)
middle (of) ['mɪdl] Mitte I; Mittelteil II • **middle school** *(USA) Schule für 11- bis 14-Jährige* IV • **in the middle of nowhere** *(infml) etwa:* am Ende der Welt V
midnight ['mɪdnaɪt] Mitternacht III
might [maɪt]: **you might need help** du könntest (vielleicht) Hilfe brauchen III
mild [maɪld] mild III
mile [maɪl] Meile *(= ca. 1,6 km)* II
for miles meilenweit II
milk [mɪlk] Milch I
million ['mɪljən] Million III
millionaire [ˌmɪljə'neə] Millionär/in IV
mime [maɪm] pantomimisch darstellen, vorspielen II
mind [maɪnd]: **I don't mind helping/working/...** Es macht mir nichts aus zu helfen/zu arbeiten/... V
Do you mind? Stört es Sie? V • **if you don't mind** wenn Sie nichts dagegen haben V • **Would you mind waiting outside?** Würden Sie bitte draußen warten? V • **Mind your own business.** Das geht dich nichts an! / Kümmere dich um deine eigenen Angelegenheiten! II **Never mind.** *etwa:* Nicht so wichtig. / Ist (doch) egal. / Das willst du gar nicht wissen. IV
mind [maɪnd]: **say what's on your mind** sag, was dich beschäftigt / was dir durch den Kopf geht VI 3 (53)
mind map ['maɪnd mæp] Mindmap („Gedankenkarte", „Wissensnetz") I
mine [maɪn] meiner, meine, meins II
°**minimum** ['mɪnɪməm] Minimum
minister ['mɪnɪstə]
1. Pastor/in, Pfarrer/in IV
► S.181 Religions
2. **prime minister** [ˌpraɪm 'mɪnɪstə] Premierminister/in, Ministerpräsident/in VI 3 (47/186)
► S.186 Politics
minority [maɪ'nɒrəti] Minderheit IV
mints *(pl)* [mɪnts] Pfefferminzbonbons I
minus ['maɪnəs] minus IV
minute ['mɪnɪt] Minute I • **Wait a minute.** Warte mal! / Moment mal! II
mirror ['mɪrə] Spiegel II
miss [mɪs]
1. vermissen II
2. verpassen V
3. **Miss a turn.** Einmal aussetzen. II
Miss White [mɪs] Frau White *(unverheiratet)* I
missing ['mɪsɪŋ]: **be missing** fehlen II
mistake [mɪ'steɪk] Fehler I
mix [mɪks] mischen, mixen III
mix [mɪks] Mix, Mischung III
mixture ['mɪkstʃə] Mischung III
mobile (phone) ['məʊbaɪl] Mobiltelefon, Handy I
model ['mɒdl] Modell*(-flugzeug, -schiff usw.)* I; (Foto-)Modell II
role model Vorbild V
moderator ['mɒdəreɪtə] Vermittler/in, Moderator/in VI 3 (51)
modern ['mɒdən] modern III
mole [məʊl] Maulwurf II
mom [mɒm, *AE:* mɑːm] *(AE)* Mama, Mutti; Mutter III
moment ['məʊmənt] Moment III

Monday ['mʌndeɪ, 'mʌndi] Montag I • **Monday morning** Montagmorgen I
money ['mʌni] Geld I • **raise money (for)** [reɪz] Geld sammeln (für) IV
monitor ['mɒnɪtə] Bildschirm, Monitor III
monkey ['mʌŋki] Affe II
monster ['mɒnstə] Ungeheuer, Monster II
month [mʌnθ] Monat I
monument ['mɒnjumənt] Denkmal, Monument IV
moon [mu:n] Mond II
moped ['məʊped] Moped V
moped licence Mopedführerschein V
more [mɔ:] mehr I • **more and more** immer mehr V • **lots more** viel mehr I • **more than** mehr als II • **more than me** mehr als ich II **more boring (than)** langweiliger (als) II • **no more music** keine Musik mehr I • **not (...) any more** nicht mehr III
morning ['mɔ:nɪŋ] Morgen, Vormittag I • **in the morning** morgens, am Morgen I • **Monday morning** Montagmorgen I • **on Friday morning** freitagmorgens, am Freitagmorgen I
mosque [mɒsk] Moschee III
► S.181 Religions
mosquito [mə'ski:təʊ] Moskito, Stechmücke VI 3 (49)
most [məʊst] (der/die/das) meiste ...; am meisten II • **most people** die meisten Leute I • **(the) most boring** der/die/das langweiligste ...; am langweiligsten II
mostly ['məʊstli] hauptsächlich, überwiegend V
motel [məʊ'tel] Motel IV
mother ['mʌðə] Mutter I
motorbike ['məʊtəbaɪk] Motorrad V
mountain ['maʊntən] Berg II
mouse [maʊs], *pl* **mice** [maɪs] Maus I
mouth [maʊθ] Mund I
move [mu:v]
1. bewegen; sich bewegen II **Move back one space.** Geh ein Feld zurück. II • **Move on one space.** Geh ein Feld vor. II
2. **move (to)** umziehen (nach, in) II • **move in** einziehen II • **move out** ausziehen II
movement ['mu:vmənt] Bewegung II
movie ['mu:vi] Film III

MP3 player [ˌempi:'θri: ˌpleɪə] MP3-Spieler I
Mr ... ['mɪstə] Herr ... I
Mrs ... ['mɪsɪz] Frau ... I
Ms ... [mɪz, məz] Frau ... II
much [mʌtʃ] viel I • **how much?** wie viel? I • **How much is/are ...?** Was kostet/kosten ...? / Wie viel kostet/kosten ...? I • **like/love sth. very much** etwas sehr mögen / sehr lieben II
mud [mʌd] Schlamm, Matsch V
muddy ['mʌdi] schlammig, matschig, schmutzig V
muesli ['mju:zli] Müsli IV
multi- ['mʌlti] viel-, mehr-; multi-, Multi- IV • **multi-coloured** mehrfarbig IV • **multi-millionaire** Multimillionär/in IV
multiple choice [ˌmʌltɪpl 'tʃɔɪs] Multiple-Choice II
mum [mʌm] Mama, Mutti; Mutter I
murder ['mɜ:də] Mord IV
museum [mju'zi:əm] Museum I
mushroom ['mʌʃrʊm, -ru:m] Pilz III
music ['mju:zɪk] Musik I
musical ['mju:zɪkl] Musical I
musician [mju:'zɪʃn] Musiker/in III
Muslim ['mʊzlɪm] Muslim/Muslima, Muslimin; muslimisch V
► S.181 Religions
must [mʌst]
1. müssen I
2. **mustn't do** nicht tun dürfen II
must [mʌst] Muss IV
my [maɪ] mein/e I
myself [maɪ'self] mir/mich (selbst) III
mystery ['mɪstri] Geheimnis, Rätsel IV

N

name [neɪm] Name I • **call sb. names** jn. mit Schimpfwörtern hänseln, jm. Schimpfwörter nachrufen III • **family name** Nachname, Familienname V • **first name** Vorname V • **My name is ...** Ich heiße ... / Mein Name ist ... I **What's your name?** Wie heißt du? I
name [neɪm] nennen; benennen II **name after** benennen nach IV
narrator [nə'reɪtə] Erzähler/in VI 3 (52)
nation ['neɪʃn] Nation IV
national ['næʃnəl] national III **national park** Nationalpark IV

nationality [ˌnæʃə'nælɪti] Staatsangehörigkeit, Nationalität V
Native American [ˌneɪtɪv‿ə'merɪkən] Amerikanische(r) Ureinwohner/in, Indianer/in IV
natural ['nætʃrəl] Natur-, natürlich IV
nature ['neɪtʃə] Natur V
near [nɪə] in der Nähe von, nahe (bei) I
nearly ['nɪəli] fast, beinahe V
neat [ni:t] gepflegt II • **neat and tidy** schön ordentlich II
necessary ['nesəsəri] nötig, notwendig V
neck [nek] Hals, Genick V
need [ni:d] brauchen, benötigen I **need to do sth.** etwas tun müssen; etwas zu tun brauchen V
needn't do ['ni:dnt] nicht tun müssen, nicht zu tun brauchen II
negative ['negətɪv] negativ V
neighbour ['neɪbə] Nachbar/in I
nephew ['nefju:, 'nevju:] Neffe IV
nervous ['nɜ:vəs] nervös, aufgeregt I
network ['netwɜ:k]
1. (Fernseh-/Radio-) Sendernetz IV
°2. (Wörter-)Netz
never ['nevə] nie, niemals I
Never mind. [ˌnevə 'maɪnd] *etwa:* Nicht so wichtig. / Ist (doch) egal. / Das willst du gar nicht wissen. IV
new [nju:] neu I
news *(no pl)* [nju:z] Nachrichten, Neuigkeiten III • **That's good news.** Das sind gute Nachrichten. III
newspaper ['nju:speɪpə] Zeitung I
newsreader ['nju:zˌri:də] Nachrichtensprecher/in IV
next [nekst]: **be next** der/die Nächste sein I • **the next morning/day** am nächsten Morgen/Tag I **What have we got next?** Was haben wir als Nächstes? I
next to [nekst] neben II
nice [naɪs] schön, nett I • **Nice to meet you.** Nett, dich/euch/Sie kennenzulernen. III • **Nice try.** Netter Versuch. V
niece [ni:s] Nichte IV
night [naɪt] Nacht, später Abend I **at night** nachts, in der Nacht I **on Friday night** freitagnachts, Freitagnacht I
nightclub ['naɪtklʌb] Nachtklub III
°**nightmare** ['naɪtmeə] Albtraum
nil [nɪl] null III
no [nəʊ] nein I
no [nəʊ] kein, keine I • **no more music** keine Musik mehr I • **no**

one niemand IV • °**no matter what/who/...** ganz gleich, was/wer/... • **No smoking!** Rauchen verboten! III • **No way!** Auf keinen Fall! / Kommt nicht in Frage! II **No worries.** *(infml)* Kein Problem!/ Ist schon in Ordnung! VI 3 (55)
nobody ['nəʊbədi] niemand II
nod (-dd-) [nɒd] nicken (mit) II
noise [nɔɪz] Geräusch; Lärm I
noisy ['nɔɪzi] laut, lärmend II
no-no ['nəʊ nəʊ]: **be a no-no** *(infml)* tabu sein, nicht in Frage kommen VI 2 (34)
non-violent [ˌnɒn'vaɪələnt] gewaltlos, gewaltfrei IV
normal ['nɔːml] normal, üblich V
north [nɔːθ] Norden; nach Norden; nördlich III
northbound ['nɔːθbaʊnd] Richtung Norden III
north-east [ˌnɔːθ'iːst] Nordosten; nach Nordosten; nordöstlich III
north-west [ˌnɔːθ'west] Nordwesten; nach Nordwesten; nordwestlich III
nose [nəʊz] Nase I
not [nɒt] nicht I • **not (...) any** kein, keine I • **not (...) any more** nicht mehr III • **not (...) anybody** niemand II • **not (...) anything** nichts II • **not (...) anywhere** nirgendwo(hin) II • **not (...) at all** überhaupt nicht, ganz und gar nicht; überhaupt kein/e V • **not (...) either** auch nicht; auch kein V **not even** (noch) nicht einmal III **not (...) yet** noch nicht II
note [nəʊt]
1. Mitteilung, Notiz I • °**make notes** sich Notizen machen **take notes** sich Notizen machen I
2. (Geld-)Schein, Banknote V
nothing ['nʌθɪŋ] nichts II
notice ['nəʊtɪs] bemerken IV
notice board ['nəʊtɪs bɔːd] Anschlagtafel, schwarzes Brett I
novel ['nɒvl] Roman VI 3 (52)
November [nəʊ'vembə] November I
now [naʊ] nun, jetzt I • **now and then** gelegentlich, ab und zu V
nowhere ['nəʊweə] nirgendwo(hin) V • **in the middle of nowhere** *(infml) etwa:* am Ende der Welt V
number ['nʌmbə] Zahl, Ziffer, Nummer I • **number plate** Nummernschild IV
nun [nʌn] Nonne VI 1 (13/181)
▶ S.181 Religions
nurse [nɜːs] Krankenpfleger/in, Krankenschwester V
nut [nʌt] Nuss IV

O

o [əʊ] null I
ocean ['əʊʃn] Ozean IV
o'clock [ə'klɒk]: **eleven o'clock** elf Uhr I
October [ɒk'təʊbə] Oktober I
°**odd** [ɒd]: **What word is the odd one out?** Welches Wort passt nicht dazu / gehört nicht dazu?
of [əv, ɒv] von I • **two kilos of oranges** zwei Kilo Orangen III
of course [əv 'kɔːs] natürlich, selbstverständlich I
off [ɒf]: **a week/day/month ... off** eine Woche / einen Tag / einen Monat ... frei IV • **cut sth. off** etwas abtrennen, abschneiden III **fall off** herunterfallen (von) II **get off (the train/bus)** (aus dem Zug/Bus) aussteigen I • **get sth. off the ground** etwas auf den Weg bringen; etwas auf die Beine stellen III • **take sth. off** etwas ausziehen *(Kleidung)* II • **take 10 c off** 10 Cent abziehen I • **tear sth. off** etwas abreißen IV • **turn sth. off** etwas ausschalten III
offer ['ɒfə] anbieten IV
offer ['ɒfə] Angebot IV
office ['ɒfɪs]
1. Büro V • **office worker** Büroangestellte(r) V
2. **ticket office** Kasse *(für den Verkauf von Eintrittskarten)* IV; Fahrkartenschalter III
officer ['ɒfɪsə]: **police officer** Polizist/in, Polizeibeamter, -beamtin V
official [ə'fɪʃl] offiziell, amtlich, Amts- V
often ['ɒfn] oft, häufig I
Oh dear! [əʊ 'dɪə] Oje! II
Oh well ... [əʊ 'wel] Na ja ... / Na gut ... I
oil [ɔɪl] Öl III
oily ['ɔɪli] ölig V
OK [əʊ'keɪ] okay, gut, in Ordnung I **I'll/You'll/She'll/ ... be OK.** Mir/ Dir/Ihr/ ... wird nichts passieren. IV
old [əʊld] alt I • **old people's home** Alten-, Seniorenheim V • **a sixteen-year-old** ein/e Sechzehnjährige/r III • **a sixteen-year-old girl** ein sechzehnjähriges Mädchen III
old-fashioned [ˌəʊld'fæʃnd] altmodisch III
Olympic Games [əˌlɪmpɪk 'geɪmz] *(kurz:* **the Olympics** [ə'lɪmpɪks]*)* Olympische Spiele; die Olympiade IV
on [ɒn]
1. auf I
2. weiter III
3. an, eingeschaltet *(Radio, Licht usw.)* II
and so on *(short:* **etc.** [et'setərə]*)* und so weiter (usw.) IV • **be on** gezeigt werden, laufen *(im Fernsehen/Kino)* IV • **be on holiday** in Urlaub sein; Ferien haben/machen II • **go on holiday** in Urlaub fahren II • **on a shift** in einer Schicht IV • **on 13th June** am 13. Juni I **on board** an Bord V • **on charge** am Ladegerät; am Netz *(zum Aufladen)* VI 3 (47) • **on Friday** am Freitag I • **on Friday afternoon** freitagnachmittags, am Freitagnachmittag I • **on Friday evening** freitagabends, am Freitagabend I **on Friday morning** freitagmorgens, am Freitagmorgen I • **on Friday night** freitagnachts, Freitagnacht I • **on the beach** am Strand II • **on the board** an die Tafel I • **on the corner of Green Street and London Road** Green Street, Ecke London Road II • **on the internet** im Internet IV • **on the left** links, auf der linken Seite II • **on the one hand ... on the other hand** einerseits ... andererseits VI 2 (37) • **on the phone** am Telefon I • **on the plane** im Flugzeug II • **on the radio** im Radio I **on the right** rechts, auf der rechten Seite II • **on the train** im Zug I • **on TV** im Fernsehen I **straight on** geradeaus weiter II **What page are we on?** Auf welcher Seite sind wir? I
once [wʌns]
1. einmal III • **once a week** einmal pro Woche III
2. einst, früher einmal III
3. **at once** sofort V
one [wʌn] eins, ein, eine I • **one by one** einer nach dem anderen VI 2 (34) • **one day** eines Tages I **a new one** ein neuer / eine neue / ein neues II • **my old ones** meine alten II • **no one** niemand IV
one-day ticket [ˌwʌn deɪ 'tɪkɪt] Tages(fahr)karte III
onion ['ʌnjən] Zwiebel III
online [ˌɒn'laɪn] online, Online- III **online friend** Internetfreund/in V

only ['əʊnli]
1. nur, bloß I
2. erst III
3. **the only guest** der einzige Gast I • **only child** Einzelkind V
on-screen [,ɒn'skri:n] Leinwand- VI 1 (12)
onto ['ɒntə, 'ɒntʊ] auf (... hinauf) III
open ['əʊpən] öffnen, aufmachen I
open ['əʊpən] offen, geöffnet II
open-air [,əʊpən_'eə] im Freien; Freilicht- III
opening ['əʊpənɪŋ]**: opening hours** Öffnungszeiten IV • **°opening sentence** Einleitungssatz
opera ['ɒprə] Oper III
operation (on) [,ɒpə'reɪʃn] Operation (an) III
opinion [ə'pɪnjən] Meinung III • **in my opinion** meiner Meinung nach III
opposite ['ɒpəzɪt] Gegenteil I
°**opposite** ['ɒpəzɪt] gegenteilige(r, s), entgegengesetzte(r, s)
or [ɔ:] oder I
orange ['ɒrɪndʒ] orange(farben) I
orange ['ɒrɪndʒ] Orange, Apfelsine I • **orange juice** ['ɒrɪndʒ dʒu:s] Orangensaft I
order ['ɔ:də] bestellen IV
order ['ɔ:də]
1. Befehl, Anweisung, Anordnung V
°2. Reihenfolge • **°in the right order** in der richtigen Reihenfolge • **°word order** Wortstellung
organization [,ɔ:gənaɪ'zeɪʃn] Organisation V
organize ['ɔ:gənaɪz] ordnen, organisieren III
organized ['ɔ:gənaɪzd] (gut) organisiert V
original *(n; adj)* [ə'rɪdʒənl] Original; Original- IV
orphan ['ɔ:fn] Waise, Waisenkind V
other ['ʌðə] andere(r, s) I • **the others** die anderen I • **the other way round** anders herum II • **on the one hand ... on the other hand** einerseits ... andererseits VI 2 (37)
Ouch! [aʊtʃ] Autsch! I
our ['aʊə] unser, unsere I
ours ['aʊəz] unserer, unsere, unseres II
ourselves [aʊə'selvz] uns (selbst) III
out heraus, hinaus; draußen II
out of ... aus ... (heraus/hinaus) I
4 out of 5 4 von 5 VI 1 (13) • **out of breath** [breθ] außer Atem V • **day out** Tagesausflug III

outback ['aʊtbæk]**: the outback** *(Australien)* das Hinterland V
outdoor ['aʊtdɔ:] *(nur vor Nomen)* Außen-; im Freien, Freiluft- V
outdoor activities Aktivitäten im Freien V • **outdoor swimming pool** Freibad V • **outdoor temperature** Außentemperatur V
outdoors [,aʊt'dɔ:z] im Freien, (nach) draußen V
outfit ['aʊtfɪt] Outfit *(Kleidung; Ausrüstung)* II
outline ['aʊtlaɪn] Gliederung VI 2 (37)
outside [,aʊt'saɪd]
1. draußen I
2. nach draußen II
3. **outside his room** vor seinem Zimmer; außerhalb seines Zimmers I
over ['əʊvə]
1. über, oberhalb von I
2. **be over** vorbei/zu Ende sein I
over there da drüben, dort drüben I • **over to ...** hinüber zu/nach ... II
all over the world auf der ganzen Welt III • **from all over the UK/ the world/England** aus dem gesamten Vereinigten Königreich / aus der ganzen Welt / aus ganz England III
overnight [,əʊvə'naɪt] über Nacht V
own [əʊn]
1. **our own pool** unser eigenes Schwimmbad II
2. **on my/our/... own** [əʊn] allein, selbstständig *(ohne Hilfe)* V
owner ['əʊnə] Besitzer/in V

P

Pacific [pə'sɪfɪk]**: the Pacific (Ocean)** der Pazifische Ozean, der Pazifik IV
pack [pæk] packen, einpacken II
packet ['pækɪt] Päckchen, Packung, Schachtel I • **a packet of mints** ein Päckchen/eine Packung Pfefferminzbonbons I
paddle ['pædl] paddeln III
paddle ['pædl] Paddel III
pads *(pl)* [pædz] (Knie- usw.) Schützer III
page [peɪdʒ] (Buch-, Heft-)Seite I
What page are we on? Auf welcher Seite sind wir? I
paid [peɪd] *siehe* **pay**
pain [peɪn] Schmerz V
painful ['peɪnfl] schmerzhaft IV
paint [peɪnt] (an)malen I
painter ['peɪntə] Maler/in II
pair [peə]**: a pair (of)** ein Paar II

palace ['pæləs] Palast, Schloss III
panic ['pænɪk]**: Don't panic!** Keine Panik. / Bleib ruhig. IV
pants *(pl)* [pænts] *(AE)* Hose IV
paper ['peɪpə]
1. Papier I
2. Zeitung II • **local paper** Lokalzeitung IV
paragraph ['pærəgrɑ:f] Absatz *(in einem Text)* II
Paralympics [,pærə'lɪmpɪks] Paralympische Spiele *(Olympische Spiele für Sportler/innen mit körperlicher Behinderung)* III
paramedic [,pærə'medɪk] Sanitäter/in II
paraphrase ['pærəfreɪz] umschreiben, anders ausdrücken III
parcel ['pɑ:sl] Paket I
parents ['peərənts] Eltern I
park [pɑ:k] Park I • **park ranger** *Ranger sind eine Art Aufseher/in in Nationalparks, die auch Führungen machen und als Wald- und Wildhüter/innen arbeiten* IV
parliament ['pɑ:ləmənt] Parlament III • **member of parliament** Parlamentsmitglied, Abgeordnete(r) VI 3 (47/186)
► S.186 Politics
parrot ['pærət] Papagei I
part [pɑ:t] Teil I • **take part (in)** teilnehmen (an) III
partner ['pɑ:tnə] Partner/in I
party ['pɑ:ti]
1. *(politische)* Partei VI 3 (47/186)
► S.186 Politics
2. Party I
pass [pɑ:s]
1. (herüber)reichen, weitergeben I
pass round herumgeben I • **°pass sth. on** etwas weitergeben
2. **pass an exam** eine Prüfung bestehen VI 1 (9/180)
► S.180 exams
passenger ['pæsɪndʒə] Passagier/in, Fahrgast, Reisende(r) V
passport ['pɑ:spɔ:t] (Reise-)Pass V
past [pɑ:st] Vergangenheit I
past [pɑ:st] vorbei (an), vorüber (an) II • **half past 11** halb zwölf (11.30/ 23.30) I • **quarter past 11** Viertel nach elf (11.15/23.15) I
pasta *(no pl)* ['pæstə] Pasta, Nudeln, Teigwaren IV
path [pɑ:θ] Pfad, Weg II • **bridle path** Reitweg III
patient ['peɪʃnt] Patient/in V
patient ['peɪʃnt] geduldig VI 1 (13)
pavement ['peɪvmənt] Gehweg, Bürgersteig IV

pay (for) [peɪ], **paid, paid** bezahlen II • **pay by credit card** mit Kreditkarte bezahlen V • **pay cash** bar bezahlen V
pay [peɪ] Bezahlung, Lohn V
PE [ˌpiː_ˈiː], **Physical Education** [ˌfɪzɪkəl_edʒuˈkeɪʃn] Turnen, Sportunterricht I
pea [piː] Erbse III
peace [piːs] Friede(n) VI 3 (47)
peanut [ˈpiːnʌt] Erdnuss VI 1 (6)
pen [pen] Kugelschreiber, Füller I
pence (p) *(pl)* [pens] Pence *(Plural von „penny")*
pencil [ˈpensl] Bleistift I • **pencil case** [ˈpensl keɪs] Federmäppchen I • **pencil sharpener** [ˈpensl ʃɑːpnə] Bleistiftanspitzer I
penny [ˈpeni] *kleinste britische Münze* I
people [ˈpiːpl] Menschen, Leute I
old people's home Alten-, Seniorenheim V
pepper [ˈpepə] Pfeffer III
per [pɜː, pə] pro III • **per cent (%)** [pə ˈsent] Prozent III
percentage [pəˈsentɪdʒ] Prozentsatz, prozentualer Anteil V
perfect [ˈpɜːfɪkt] perfekt; ideal; vollkommen IV
°**perfume** [ˈpɜːfjuːm] Parfüm
perhaps [pəˈhæps] vielleicht V
period [ˈpɪərɪəd] (Unterrichts-/Schul-)Stunde IV
person [ˈpɜːsn] Person II
personal [ˈpɜːsənl] persönliche(r, s) III
°**personal stereo** [ˌpɜːsənl ˈsteriəʊ] *Überbegriff für tragbare Musikabspielgeräte wie etwa MP3-Spieler*
pet [pet] Haustier I • **pet shop** Tierhandlung I
petition [pəˈtɪʃn] Unterschriftensammlung, Petition VI 3 (47)
petrol [ˈpetrəl] Benzin IV • **petrol station** Tankstelle IV
phone [fəʊn] Telefon I • **on the phone** am Telefon I • **phone box** Telefonzelle V • **phone call** Anruf, Telefongespräch I • **phone number** Telefonnummer I
phone [fəʊn] telefonieren, anrufen I
photo [ˈfəʊtəʊ] Foto I • **in the photo** auf dem Foto I • **take photos** Fotos machen, fotografieren I
°**photocopy** [ˈfəʊtəʊkɒpi] Fotokopie
°**phrase** [freɪz] Ausdruck, (Rede-)Wendung
piano [piˈænəʊ] Klavier, Piano I
play the piano Klavier spielen I
pick [pɪk]
°**1. pick out** aussuchen, auswählen
2. pick sb. up jn. abholen III
3. pick sth. up etwas hochheben, aufheben II
picnic [ˈpɪknɪk] Picknick I • **have a picnic** ein Picknick machen I
picture [ˈpɪktʃə] Bild I • **in the picture** auf dem Bild I • **picture story** Bildergeschichte IV
pie [paɪ] Obstkuchen; Pastete II
pie chart Tortendiagramm, Kreisdiagramm V
piece [piːs]: **a piece of** ein Stück I
a piece of paper ein Stück Papier I
piercing [ˈpɪəsɪŋ] Piercing VI 1 (10)
pig [pɪg] III
pill [pɪl] Pille, Tablette V
°**pine tree** [ˈpaɪn triː] Kiefer *(Nadelbaum)*
pink [pɪŋk] pink(farben), rosa I
pipe [paɪp] Pfeife III
pirate [ˈpaɪrət] Pirat, Piratin I
pitch [pɪtʃ] Spielfeld III
pizza [ˈpiːtsə] Pizza I
place [pleɪs] Ort, Platz I • **at someone's place** bei jemandem zu Hause V • **place of birth** Geburtsort V • **take place** stattfinden IV
°**placemat** [ˈpleɪsmæt] Set, Platzdeckchen
plan [plæn] Plan I
plan (-nn-) [plæn] planen I
plane [pleɪn] Flugzeug II • **on the plane** im Flugzeug II
planet [ˈplænɪt] Planet II
plant [plɑːnt] Pflanze V
plant [plɑːnt] pflanzen, einpflanzen V
plantation [plɑːnˈteɪʃn] Plantage IV
plastic [ˈplæstɪk] Plastik V
plate [pleɪt] Teller I • **a plate of chips** ein Teller Pommes frites I
license plate *(AE)* Nummernschild IV • **number plate** *(BE)* Nummernschild IV
platform [ˈplætfɔːm] Bahnsteig, Gleis III
play [pleɪ] spielen I • **play football** Fußball spielen I • **play the drums** Schlagzeug spielen III • **play the fiddle** Geige spielen III • **play the guitar** Gitarre spielen I • **play the piano** Klavier spielen I
play [pleɪ] Theaterstück I
player [ˈpleɪə] Spieler/in I
pleasant [ˈpleznt] angenehm V
please [pliːz] bitte *(in Fragen und Aufforderungen)* I
plot [plɒt] Handlung *(eines Romans, Films, Theaterstücks)* IV
plug [plʌg] Stecker III
plus [plʌs] plus IV
pm [ˌpiː_ˈem]: **7 pm** 7 Uhr abends / 19 Uhr I
pocket [ˈpɒkɪt] Tasche *(an Kleidungsstück)* II • **pocket money** Taschengeld II
poem [ˈpəʊɪm] Gedicht I
point [pɔɪnt] Punkt II • **make a point** ein Argument vorbringen III • **point of view** Standpunkt, Sichtweise VI 2 (37) • **10.4 (ten point four)** 10,4 (zehn Komma vier) III
point (at/to sth.) [pɔɪnt] zeigen, deuten (auf etwas) II
poison [ˈpɔɪzn] Gift V
poisonous [ˈpɔɪzənəs] giftig V
police *(pl)* [pəˈliːs] Polizei I • **police officer** Polizist/in, Polizeibeamter, -beamtin V • **police station** Polizeiwache, Polizeirevier II
policeman [pəˈliːsmən] Polizist II
policewoman [pəˈliːswʊmən] Polizistin II
°**policy** [ˈpɒləsi] Politik, Vorgehensweise
polite [pəˈlaɪt] höflich IV
political [pəˈlɪtɪkl] politisch V
politician [ˌpɒləˈtɪʃn] Politiker/in VI 3 (47)
politics [ˈpɒlɪtɪks] (die) Politik V
► S.186 Politics
pollute [pəˈluːt] verschmutzen, verunreinigen VI 2 (30/183)
polluted [pəˈluːtɪd] verseucht, verunreinigt V
pollution [pəˈluːʃn] (Umwelt-)Verschmutzung V
poltergeist [ˈpəʊltəgaɪst] Poltergeist I
ponytail [ˈpəʊniteɪl] Pferdeschwanz *(Frisur)* III
pool [puːl] (Schwimm-)Becken III
poor [pɔː, pʊə]
1. arm I • **poor Sophie** (die) arme Sophie I
°**2.** schlecht, armselig
pop (music) [pɒp] Pop(musik) III
popcorn [ˈpɒpkɔːn] Popcorn II
popular (with) [ˈpɒpjulə] populär, beliebt (bei) III
population [ˌpɒpjuˈleɪʃn] Bevölkerung, Einwohner(zahl) IV
pork [pɔːk] Schweinefleisch III
positive [ˈpɒzətɪv] positiv V
possibility [ˌpɒsəˈbɪləti] Möglichkeit, Chance IV
possible [ˈpɒsəbl] möglich II
post [pəʊst] Post *(Briefe, Päckchen, ...)* III • **post office** [ˈpəʊst_ɒfɪs] Postamt II

post [pəʊst] posten *(ins Netz stellen)* V
postcard ['pəʊstkɑːd] Postkarte II
postcode ['pəʊstkəʊd] Postleitzahl V
poster ['pəʊstə] Poster I
potato [pə'teɪtəʊ], *pl* **potatoes** Kartoffel I • **potato chips** *(AE)* Kartoffelchips IV • **couch potato** *(infml)* Stubenhocker/in *(jd., der viel vor dem Fernseher sitzt)* V
poultry ['pəʊltri] Geflügel IV
pound (£) [paʊnd] Pfund *(britische Währung)* I
°**pour** [pɔː] strömen; schütten, gießen
poverty ['pɒvəti] Armut V
power ['paʊə] Kraft, Energie, Strom VI 2 (31)
power cut ['paʊə kʌt] Stromabschaltung, Stromausfall VI 2 (35)
power station ['paʊə steɪʃn] Kraftwerk, Elektrizitätswerk VI 2 (31)
practice ['præktɪs] *hier:* Übungsteil I
practise ['præktɪs] üben; trainieren I
pray [preɪ] beten V
prayer ['preə] Gebet V
pregnant ['pregnənt] schwanger VI 1 (12)
prejudice ['predʒudɪs] Vorurteil IV
prejudiced ['predʒədɪst]**: be prejudiced (against)** voreingenommen sein (gegen), Vorurteile haben (gegenüber) IV
prepare (for) [prɪ'peə] vorbereiten; sich vorbereiten (auf) II
prescription [prɪ'skrɪpʃn] Rezept *(für Medikamente)* V
present ['preznt]
1. Gegenwart I
2. Geschenk I
present [prɪ'zent] präsentieren V
presentation [ˌprezn'teɪʃn] Präsentation, Vorstellung I
presenter [prɪ'zentə] Moderator/in II
president ['prezɪdənt] Präsident/in IV
press [pres] drücken III
°**pressure** ['preʃə] Druck
pretend [prɪ'tend] so tun, als ob VI 2 (34)
pretty ['prɪti] hübsch I
pretty healthy/good/... ['prɪti] ziemlich gesund/gut/... II
price [praɪs] (Kauf-)Preis I
priest [priːst] Priester VI 1 (13/181)
► S.181 Religions
primary school ['praɪməri skuːl] Grundschule V
prime minister [ˌpraɪm 'mɪnɪstə] Premierminister/in, Ministerpräsident/in VI 3 (47/186)
► S.186 Politics
prime time ['praɪm taɪm] Hauptsendezeit IV
°**principal** ['prɪnsəpl] Schulleiter/in
print [prɪnt] drucken V
print: bold print [ˌbəʊld 'prɪnt] Fettdruck III
printer ['prɪntə] Drucker V
prison ['prɪzn] Gefängnis V
prisoner ['prɪznə] Gefangene(r) V
private detective [ˌpraɪvət dɪ'tektɪv] Privatdetektiv/in V
prize [praɪz] Preis, Gewinn I
probably ['prɒbəbli] wahrscheinlich II
problem ['prɒbləm] Problem II
produce [prə'djuːs] produzieren, herstellen III
product ['prɒdʌkt] Produkt IV
production [prə'dʌkʃn] Produktion, Herstellung IV
profile ['prəʊfaɪl] Porträt, Steckbrief III; Profil V
programme ['prəʊgræm]
1. Programm I
2. (Fernseh-)Sendung IV
project (about, on) ['prɒdʒekt] Projekt (über, zu) I • **do a project** ein Projekt machen, durchführen II
promise ['prɒmɪs] versprechen II
pronunciation [prəˌnʌnsi'eɪʃn] Aussprache I
proof *(no pl)* [pruːf] Beweis(e) II
protect sb. (from sth.) [prə'tekt] jn. (be)schützen (vor etwas) III
protest [prə'test] protestieren IV
protest ['prəʊtest] Protest IV
Protestant ['prɒtɪstənt] Protestant/in; protestantisch VI 1 (13/181)
► S.181 Religions
proud (of sb./sth.) [praʊd] stolz (auf jn./etwas) II
province ['prɒvɪns] Provinz III
PS [ˌpiː_'es] **(postscript** ['pəʊstskrɪpt]**)** PS *(Nachschrift unter Briefen)* III
pub [pʌb] Kneipe, Lokal II
public ['pʌblɪk] Öffentlichkeit VI 3 (48)
public ['pʌblɪk] öffentlich V
public transport *(no pl)* öffentliche Verkehrsmittel, öffentlicher Personennahverkehr V
publish ['pʌblɪʃ] veröffentlichen III
pull [pʊl] ziehen I
pullover ['pʊləʊvə] Pullover II
punctual ['pʌŋktʃuəl] pünktlich V
punish ['pʌnɪʃ] bestrafen V
punishment ['pʌnɪʃmənt] Bestrafung, Strafe V
purple ['pɜːpl] violett; lila I
purse [pɜːs] Geldbörse II
push [pʊʃ] drücken, schieben, stoßen I
put (-tt-) [pʊt]**, put, put** legen, stellen, *(etwas wohin)* tun I • **put out a fire** ein Feuer löschen IV • **put sth. on** etwas anziehen *(Kleidung)* II • °**put sth. on the wall** etwas an die Wand hängen • °**put sth. together** etwas zusammenstellen, zusammenfügen • °**Put up your hand.** Heb deine Hand. / Hebt eure Hand.
puzzled ['pʌzld] verwirrt II
pyjamas *(pl)* [pə'dʒɑːməz] Schlafanzug II
pyramid ['pɪrəmɪd] Pyramide IV

Q

qualification [ˌkwɒlɪfɪ'keɪʃn] Abschluss, Qualifikation V
quality ['kwɒləti] Qualität; Eigenschaft V
quarter ['kwɔːtə]**: quarter past 11** Viertel nach 11 (11.15/23.15) I
quarter to 12 Viertel vor 12 (11.45/23.45) I
queen [kwiːn] Königin III
question ['kwestʃn] Frage I • **ask questions** Fragen stellen I
°**question word** Fragewort
°**questionnaire** [ˌkwestʃə'neə] Fragebogen
queue [kjuː] *(BE)* Schlange, Reihe *(wartender Menschen)* IV
queue [kjuː] sich anstellen, anstehen V
quick [kwɪk] schnell I
quiet ['kwaɪət] leise, still, ruhig I
quite bad/quick/good ... [kwaɪt] ziemlich schlimm/schnell/gut/... II
quiz [kwɪz], *pl* **quizzes** ['kwɪzɪz] Quiz, Ratespiel I
°**quotation mark** [kwəʊ'teɪʃn mɑːk] Anführungszeichen
°**quote** [kwəʊt] Zitat

R

rabbit ['ræbɪt] Kaninchen I
rabbit-proof kaninchen-sicher, kaninchen-fest V
race [reɪs] Rasse V
racing car ['reɪsɪŋ kɑː] Rennwagen V
racism ['reɪsɪzəm] Rassismus VI 1 (12)

racist ['reɪsɪst] rassistisch; Rassist/in V
racket ['rækɪt]: **badminton racket** Badmintonschläger III • **tennis racket** Tennisschläger VI 3 (48)
radio ['reɪdiəʊ] Radio I • **on the radio** im Radio I
raft [rɑːft] Schlauchboot *(wildwassertauglich)* IV
rafting ['rɑːftɪŋ] Rafting *(Wildwasserfahren mit dem Schlauchboot)* IV
railway ['reɪlweɪ] Eisenbahn II
rain [reɪn] Regen II
rain [reɪn] regnen II
rainforest ['reɪnfɒrɪst] Regenwald V
rainproof ['reɪnpruːf] regendicht *(Kleidung)* V
rainy ['reɪni] regnerisch II
raise money (for) [reɪz] Geld sammeln (für) IV
ran [ræn] *siehe* **run**
rang [ræŋ] *siehe* **ring**
ranger ['reɪndʒə]: **(park) ranger** *eine Art Aufseher/in in Nationalparks, die auch Führungen machen und als Wald- und Wildhüter/innen arbeiten* IV
rap [ræp] Rap *(rhythmischer Sprechgesang)* I
rapids *(pl)* ['ræpɪdz] Stromschnellen III
rate: **exchange rate** [ɪks'tʃeɪndʒ reɪt] Wechselkurs V
°**ration** ['ræʃn] Ration
°**rationing** ['ræʃənɪŋ] Rationierung
razor ['reɪzə] Rasierapparat, Rasierer VI 2 (28)
RE [ˌɑːr_'iː], **Religious Education** [rɪˌlɪdʒəs_edʒu'keɪʃn] Religion, Religionsunterricht I
react (to) [ri'ækt] reagieren (auf) V
reaction (to) [ri'ækʃn] Reaktion (auf) VI 2 (30/183)
read [riːd], **read, read** lesen I
read on weiterlesen III • °**read out** vorlesen • °**Read out loud.** Lies laut vor. • °**Read the poem to a partner.** Lies das Gedicht einem Partner / einer Partnerin vor.
read [red] *siehe* **read**
reader ['riːdə] Leser/in II
ready ['redi] bereit, fertig I • **get ready (for)** sich fertig machen (für), sich vorbereiten (auf) I • **get things ready** Dinge fertig machen, vorbereiten I
real [rɪəl] echt, wirklich I • **real-life** im wirklichen Leben, aus dem wirklichen Leben VI 1 (8)
realistic [ˌriːə'lɪstɪk] realistisch, wirklichkeitsnah III
reality [ri'æləti] Wirklichkeit, Realität IV
°**realize** ['riːəlaɪz] verwirklichen, realisieren
really ['rɪəli] wirklich I
reason ['riːzn] Grund, Begründung I • **for lots of reasons** aus vielen Gründen I
receipt [rɪ'siːt] Quittung; Kassenbon V
receive [rɪ'siːv] empfangen IV
recent ['riːsnt] jüngste(r, s), aktuelle(r, s); vor kurzem *(geschehen, entstanden usw.)* V
recently ['riːsntli] in letzter Zeit; neulich, vor kurzem V
reception [rɪ'sepʃn] Rezeption, Empfang *(in einem Hotel)* V
°**receptionist** [rɪ'sepʃənɪst] Rezeptionist/in; Empfangsdame
recognize ['rekəgnaɪz] (wieder)erkennen V; anerkennen VI 3 (53)
recommend sth. to sb. [ˌrekə'mend] jm. etwas empfehlen V
record [rɪ'kɔːd] *(Musik / einen Film)* aufnehmen III
record ['rekɔːd] Schallplatte III
recorder [rɪ'kɔːdə] Blockflöte III
recording [rɪ'kɔːdɪŋ] Aufnahme, Aufzeichnung III
recycle [ˌriː'saɪkl] wiederverwerten, wiederverwenden VI 2 (36)
recycled [ˌriː'saɪkld] wiederverwertet, wiederverwendet, recycelt II
recycling [ˌriː'saɪklɪŋ] Wiederverwertung, Recycling II
red [red] rot I • **go red** rot werden, erröten V
reduce [rɪ'djuːs] verringern, vermindern, reduzieren VI 2 (29)
reef [riːf] Riff V
refer to **(-rr-)** [rɪ'fɜː] sich beziehen auf III
reference ['refrəns] Referenz, Empfehlung V
reggae ['regeɪ] Reggae III
regular ['regjələ] normal *(Größenangabe bei Getränken, Fastfood)* IV
rehearsal [rɪ'hɜːsl] Probe *(am Theater)* I
rehearse [rɪ'hɜːs] proben *(am Theater)* I
relations *(pl)* [rɪ'leɪʃnz] Beziehungen *(zwischen Ländern, Firmen, Organisationen)* V
relationship [rɪ'leɪʃnʃɪp] Beziehung V
relax [rɪ'læks] (sich) entspannen, sich ausruhen II
relaxed [rɪ'lækst] locker, entspannt III
release [rɪ'liːs] *(CD, Film)* herausbringen, auf den Markt bringen III
reliable [rɪ'laɪəbl] zuverlässig, verlässlich V
religion [rɪ'lɪdʒn] Religion VI 1 (13)
▸ S.181 Religions
religious [rɪ'lɪdʒəs] religiös; gläubig VI 1 (13/181)
▸ S.181 Religions
remember sth./sb. [rɪ'membə]
1. sich an etwas/jn. erinnern I
2. sich etwas/jn. merken I
3. einer Person/Sache gedenken V
remote control [rɪˌməʊt kən'trəʊl] Fernbedienung IV
rent [rent] Miete V
rent sth. [rent] etwas mieten, etwas leihen V
repair sth. [rɪ'peə] etwas reparieren V • **repair kit** Flickzeug V
repeat [rɪ'piːt] Wiederholung *(einer Fernsehsendung)* IV
repeat sth. [rɪ'piːt] etwas wiederholen VI 1 (9)
reply [rɪ'plaɪ]: **in reply to your letter/article/...** in Beantwortung Ihres Briefes/Artikels/... V
report (on) [rɪ'pɔːt] Bericht, Reportage (über) I
report (to sb.) [rɪ'pɔːt] (jm.) berichten II
represent [ˌreprɪ'zent] repräsentieren, vertreten III
°**request** [rɪ'kwest] Bitte
rerun ['riːrʌn] *(AE)* Wiederholung *(einer Fernsehsendung)* IV
rescue helicopter ['reskjuː ˌhelɪkɒptə] Rettungshubschrauber II
research (on) *(no pl)* [rɪ'sɜːtʃ, 'riːsɜːtʃ] Recherche, Nachforschung(en) IV **do research** recherchieren IV
respect [rɪ'spekt] achten, respektieren V
respect [rɪ'spekt] Achtung, Respekt V • **out of respect** aus Achtung, aus Respekt V
responsible [rɪ'spɒnsəbl] verantwortlich; verantwortungsbewusst VI 2 (35)
rest [rest] Rest II
restaurant ['restrɒnt] Restaurant II
result [rɪ'zʌlt] Ergebnis, Resultat I
return (to) [rɪ'tɜːn] zurückkehren (nach, zu) V
return ticket [rɪ'tɜːn ˌtɪkɪt] Rückfahrkarte II
°**reverse** [rɪ'vɜːs] umgekehrte(r, s), entgegengesetzte(r, s)
review [rɪ'vjuː]: **film/book review** Film-/Buchkritik, Film-/Buchbesprechung V

reviewer [rɪ'vjuːə] Rezensent/in, Kritiker/in *(von Filmen, Büchern usw.)* VI 1 (14)
revise [rɪ'vaɪz]
1. überarbeiten III
2. wiederholen III
revision [rɪ'vɪʒn] Wiederholung *(des Lernstoffs)* I
rhino ['raɪnəʊ] Nashorn II
rice [raɪs] Reis III
rich [rɪtʃ] reich II
ridden ['rɪdn] *siehe* **ride**
riddle ['rɪdl] Rätsel III
ride [raɪd], **rode, ridden** reiten I • **go riding** reiten gehen I • **ride a bike** Rad fahren I
ride [raɪd]: **(bike) ride** (Rad-)Fahrt II • **take a ride** eine Fahrt machen III
ridiculous [rɪ'dɪkjələs] lächerlich, albern V
right [raɪt] richtig I • **all right** [ɔːl 'raɪt] gut, in Ordnung II • **be right** Recht haben I • **That's right.** Das ist richtig. / Das stimmt. I • **You need a school bag, right?** Du brauchst eine Schultasche, stimmt's? / nicht wahr? I
right [raɪt] rechte(r, s) II • **look right** nach rechts schauen II • **on the right** rechts, auf der rechten Seite II • **turn right** (nach) rechts abbiegen II
right [raɪt]: **right now** jetzt sofort; jetzt gerade I
right [raɪt] Recht IV
rim [rɪm] Kante IV
ring [rɪŋ] Ring II
ring [rɪŋ], **rang, rung** klingeln, läuten II
ringtone ['rɪŋtəʊn] Klingelton III
rip sb. off (-pp-) [ˌrɪp_'ɒf] *(infml)* jn. übers Ohr hauen, jn. abzocken VI 2 (35)
rise [raɪz], **rose, risen** (auf)steigen IV
risen ['rɪzn] *siehe* **rise**
river ['rɪvə] Fluss II
RnB [ˌɑːr_ən'biː] RnB *(Rhythm and Blues; Form des Blues, in der Rhythmus eine große Rolle spielt; moderner RnB enthält Rap- und Hip Hop-Elemente)* III
road [rəʊd] Straße I • **Park Road** [ˌpɑːk 'rəʊd] Parkstraße I
rock [rɒk]
1. Fels, Felsen III
2. **rock concert** Rockkonzert V
rock star Rockstar V
rock and roll [ˌrɒk_ən 'rəʊl] Rock and Roll IV
rode [rəʊd] *siehe* **ride**

role [rəʊl] Rolle III • **role play** Rollenspiel II • **role model** Vorbild V
roll [rəʊl] Brötchen I
Roman ['rəʊmən] römisch; Römer, Römerin II
romance [rəʊ'mæns, 'rəʊmæns] Romanze; Romantik IV
romantic [rəʊ'mæntɪk] romantisch; Liebes- VI 1 (12)
room [ruːm] Raum, Zimmer I
double room Doppelzimmer V
single room Einzelzimmer V
rose [rəʊz] *siehe* **rise**
round [raʊnd] rund II
round [raʊnd] um ... (herum); in ... umher II • **the other way round** anders herum II
route [ruːt] Strecke, Route IV
royal ['rɔɪəl] königlich III
rubber ['rʌbə] Radiergummi I
rubbish ['rʌbɪʃ] (Haus-)Müll, Abfall II
rucksack ['rʌksæk] Rucksack III
rude [ruːd] unhöflich, unverschämt II
rule [ruːl] Regel, Vorschrift IV
follow the rules Regeln befolgen V
ruler ['ruːlə] Lineal I
run [rʌn] (Wett-)Lauf II
run (-nn-) [rʌn], **ran, run**
1. laufen, rennen I • **run around** herumrennen III
2. **run sth.** etwas leiten, führen *(Hotel, Firma usw.)* V
rung [rʌŋ] *siehe* **ring**
runner ['rʌnə] Läufer/in II
running ['rʌnɪŋ]: **running shoes** Laufschuhe III • **running track** Laufbahn *(Sport)* III • **running water** fließendes Wasser V
rush hour ['rʌʃ_aʊə] Hauptverkehrszeit III

S

sad [sæd] traurig II
saddle ['sædl] Sattel III
sadness ['sædnəs] Traurigkeit IV
safe (from) [seɪf] sicher, in Sicherheit (vor) II
safety ['seɪfti] Sicherheit IV • **fire safety** Verhalten im Brandfall IV
said [sed] *siehe* **say**
sailor ['seɪlə] Seemann, Matrose II
salad ['sæləd] Salat *(als Gericht oder Beilage)* I
sale [seɪl] (Aus-, Schluss-)Verkauf IV • **for sale** *(auf Schild)* zu verkaufen IV

salmon ['sæmən], *pl* **salmon** Lachs III
salt [sɔːlt] Salz III • **salt water** Salzwasser V
same [seɪm]: **the same ...** der-/die-/dasselbe ...; dieselben ... I • **be/look the same** gleich sein/aussehen I
sandwich ['sænwɪtʃ] Sandwich, *(zusammengeklapptes)* belegtes Brot I • **sandwich box** Brotdose I
sang [sæŋ] *siehe* **sing**
sat [sæt] *siehe* **sit**
satellite ['sætəlaɪt] Satellit IV
Saturday ['sætədeɪ, 'sætədi] Samstag, Sonnabend I
sauna ['sɔːnə] Sauna II • **have a sauna** in die Sauna gehen II
sausage ['sɒsɪdʒ] (Brat-, Bock-) Würstchen, Wurst I
save [seɪv]
1. retten II
2. sparen II
3. etwas (ab)speichern *(Daten, Telefonnummern)* V
saw [sɔː] *siehe* **see**
saxophone ['sæksəfəʊn] Saxophon III
say [seɪ], **said, said** sagen I • **It says here: ...** Hier steht: ... / Es heißt hier: ... II • **say goodbye** sich verabschieden I • **Say hi to Dilip for me.** Grüß Dilip von mir. I • **say sorry** sich entschuldigen II
say [seɪ]: **Have your say!** *etwa:* Übe dein Mitspracherecht aus! / Rede mit! VI 3 (46)
scan a text (-nn-) [skæn] einen Text schnell nach bestimmten Wörtern/Informationen absuchen II
scared [skeəd] verängstigt II • **be scared (of)** Angst haben (vor) I
scarf [skɑːf], *pl* **scarves** [skɑːvs] Schal III
scary ['skeəri] unheimlich; gruselig I
scene [siːn] Szene I
schedule [*AE:* 'skedʒuːl, *BE:* 'ʃedjuːl] *(AE)*
1. Stundenplan IV
2. Fahrplan IV
school [skuːl] Schule I • **at school** in der Schule I • **school bag** Schultasche I • **school subject** Schulfach I • **primary school** Grundschule V • **secondary school** weiterführende Schule V
science ['saɪəns] Naturwissenschaft I • **science fiction** Sciencefiction V
scientist ['saɪəntɪst] (Natur-)Wissenschaftler/in VI 2 (30)

score [skɔː] Spielstand; Punktestand III • **final score** Endstand III • **What's the score now? – 2–0.** (*you say:* **two nil**) Wie steht es jetzt? (*beim Sport*) – 2:0 III
score (a goal) [skɔː] ein Tor schießen, einen Treffer erzielen III
scream [skriːm] schreien III
screen [skriːn] Leinwand; Bildschirm VI 1 (12) • **flat screen** Flachbildschirm IV
sea [siː] Meer, (*die*) See I • **sea snake** Seeschlange V
search (for) [sɜːtʃ] suchen (nach), durchsuchen IV
search engine ['sɜːtʃ‿ˌendʒɪn] Suchmaschine (*im Internet*) IV
seat [siːt] (Sitz-)Platz V
second ['sekənd] Sekunde VI 2 (32)
second ['sekənd] zweite(r, s) I; zweitens VI 2 (37) • **second floor** zweiter Stock (*BE*) / erster Stock (*AE*) IV • **second-hand** [ˌsekənd 'hænd] gebraucht; aus zweiter Hand III
secondary school ['sekəndri skuːl] weiterführende Schule V
secret ['siːkrət] geheim V
secret ['siːkrət] Geheimnis V
secretly ['siːkrətli] heimlich V
section ['sekʃn] Abschnitt, Teil, (Themen-)Bereich III
see [siː], **saw, seen**
1. sehen I
2. see sb. jn. besuchen, jn. aufsuchen II
I see. Ich verstehe. / Aha. / Ach so. V • **See?** Siehst du? I • **See you.** Tschüs. / Bis bald. I • **Wait and see!** Wart's ab! III
seem (to be / to do) [siːm] (zu sein / zu tun) scheinen IV
seen [siːn] *siehe* **see**
segregate ['segrɪgeɪt] trennen (*nach Rasse, Religion, Geschlecht*) IV
segregation [ˌsegrɪ'geɪʃn] (Rassen-)Trennung IV
sell [sel], **sold, sold** verkaufen II
be sold out ausverkauft sein; vergriffen sein III
semester [sɪ'mestə] Semester (*Schulhalbjahr in den USA*) IV
semi-final [ˌsemi'faɪnl] Halbfinale III
send (to) [send], **sent, sent** schicken, senden (an) II
sense [sens] Sinn VI 1 (6/179) • **make sense** sinnvoll sein, einen Sinn ergeben VI 3 (49) • **sense of humour** (Sinn für) Humor VI 1 (6)
sensible ['sensəbl] vernünftig VI 3 (49)
sensitive ['sensətɪv] sensibel VI 3 (49/188)
sent [sent] *siehe* **send**
sentence ['sentəns] Satz I
sentimental [ˌsentɪ'mentl] sentimental VI 1 (14)
separate ['seprət] getrennt, separat V
September [sep'tembə] September I
series, *pl* **series** ['sɪəriːz] (Sende-)Reihe, Serie II
serious ['sɪəriəs] ernst, ernsthaft IV
seriously? ['sɪəriəsli] im Ernst? IV
take sb./sth. seriously jn./etwas ernst nehmen VI 3 (48)
serve [sɜːv] bedienen (*Kunden*) V
service ['sɜːvɪs]
°**1.** Dienst
2. Gottesdienst VI 1 (13/181)
► S.181 Religions
set (-tt-) [set], **set, set**
1. set the alarm clock den Wecker stellen V
2. the film/novel is set in ... der Film/Roman spielt in ... VI 1 (12)
settle ['setl] sich niederlassen, siedeln; besiedeln V
settler ['setlə] Siedler/in V
setup ['setʌp] Setup II
sex [seks] Geschlecht III
shack [ʃæk] Hütte, Baracke V
°**shade** [ʃeɪd] Schatten
shadow ['ʃædəʊ] Schatten IV
shake [ʃeɪk], **shook, shaken** schütteln; zittern V
shaken ['ʃeɪkən] *siehe* **shake**
shame [ʃeɪm]: **It's a shame.** Es ist ein Jammer / eine Schande. V
shampoo [ʃæm'puː] Shampoo, Haarwaschmittel III
shape [ʃeɪp] Form V
share sth. (with sb.) [ʃeə] sich etwas teilen (mit jm.) I
she [ʃiː] sie I
sheep, *pl* **sheep** [ʃiːp] Schaf II
sheet [ʃiːt] Blatt, Bogen (*Papier*) V
shelf [ʃelf], *pl* **shelves** [ʃelvz] Regal(brett) I
shift [ʃɪft] Schicht (*bei der Arbeit*) IV
shine [ʃaɪn], **shone, shone** scheinen (*Sonne*) II
ship [ʃɪp] Schiff I
shirt [ʃɜːt] Hemd I
shock [ʃɒk] Schock V
shocked [ʃɒkt] schockiert IV
shocking ['ʃɒkɪŋ] schockierend V
shoe [ʃuː] Schuh I
shone [ʃɒn] *siehe* **shine**
shook [ʃʊk] *siehe* **shake**
shoot [ʃuːt], **shot, shot**
1. schießen, erschießen III
°**2.** fotografieren
shop [ʃɒp] Laden, Geschäft I
shop assistant ['ʃɒp‿əˌsɪstənt] Verkäufer/in I • **shop window** Schaufenster II
shop (-pp-) [ʃɒp] einkaufen (gehen) I
shoplift ['ʃɒplɪft] Ladendiebstahl begehen V
shoplifting ['ʃɒplɪftɪŋ] Ladendiebstahl V
shopping ['ʃɒpɪŋ] (das) Einkaufen I
go shopping einkaufen gehen I
shopping list Einkaufsliste I
short [ʃɔːt] kurz I; klein (*Person*) IV
shorts (*pl*) [ʃɔːts] Shorts, kurze Hose I
shot [ʃɒt] *siehe* **shoot**
should [ʃəd, ʃʊd]: **You should have told me.** Du hättest es mir sagen sollen. V • **Why should I ... ?** Warum sollte ich ... ? III
shoulder ['ʃəʊldə] Schulter I
shout [ʃaʊt] schreien, rufen I
show [ʃəʊ] Show, Vorstellung I
show [ʃəʊ], **showed, shown**
1. zeigen I
2. show (sth.) off (mit etwas) angeben V
shower ['ʃaʊə] Dusche I • **have a shower** (sich) duschen I • **take a shower** (sich) duschen VI 2 (36)
shown [ʃəʊn] *siehe* **show**
shut up [ˌʃʌt‿'ʌp], **shut, shut** den Mund halten II
shy [ʃaɪ] schüchtern, scheu II
sick [sɪk]
1. I feel sick. Mir ist schlecht. IV
2. (*besonders AE*) krank V
side [saɪd] Seite II
sidewalk ['saɪdwɔːk] (*AE*) Gehweg, Bürgersteig IV
sights (*pl*) [saɪts] Sehenswürdigkeiten II
sightseeing ['saɪtsiːɪŋ] Sightseeing (*Besichtigung der lokalen Sehenswürdigkeiten*) V
sign [saɪn] Schild, Zeichen III
sign [saɪn] unterschreiben IV
silence ['saɪləns] Stille; Schweigen III
silent letter [ˌsaɪlənt 'letə] „stummer" Buchstabe (*nicht gesprochener Buchstabe*) II
silly ['sɪli] albern, dumm I
similar (to) ['sɪmələ] ähnlich wie V
simple ['sɪmpl] einfach, nicht kompliziert V
since [sɪns]
1. da, weil IV

2. since April 4th seit dem 4. April IV • **since then** seitdem VI 2 (30)
sincerely [sɪn'sɪəli]**: Yours sincerely** Mit freundlichen Grüßen/Herzliche Grüße *(Briefschluss bei namentlich bekanntem Empfänger)* IV
sing [sɪŋ]**, sang, sung** singen I
°sing along mitsingen
singer ['sɪŋə] Sänger/in II
single ['sɪŋgl] ledig, alleinstehend I
single (ticket) einfache Fahrkarte *(nur Hinfahrt)* III • **single room** Einzelzimmer V
single ['sɪŋgl] Single III
sink [sɪŋk] Spüle, Spülbecken I
sir [sɜː, sə]**: Dear Sir or Madam** Sehr geehrte Damen und Herren *(Anrede in Briefen)* IV
sister ['sɪstə] Schwester I • **sister city** *(AE)* Partnerstadt IV
sit (-tt-) [sɪt]**, sat, sat** sitzen; sich setzen I • **sit down** sich hinsetzen II • **Sit with me.** Setz dich zu mir. / Setzt euch zu mir. I
site [saɪt] (Internet-)Seite VI 2 (30)
situation [ˌsɪtʃu'eɪʃn] Situation, Lage VI 1 (8)
size [saɪz] Größe I
skate [skeɪt] Inliner/Skateboard fahren I
skateboard ['skeɪtbɔːd] Skateboard I
skater ['skeɪtə] Skateboardfahrer/in III
skates *(pl)* [skeɪts] Inliner I
sketch [sketʃ] Sketch I
ski [skiː] Ski fahren/laufen III
ski [skiː] Ski III • **ski instructor** ['skiː‿ɪnˌstrʌktə] Skilehrer/in V
ski slope ['skiː sləʊp] Skipiste III
skill [skɪl] Fähigkeit, Fertigkeit V
skills file ['skɪlz faɪl] *Anhang mit Lern- und Arbeitstechniken* I
skim a text (-mm-) [skɪm] einen Text überfliegen *(um den Inhalt grob zu erfassen)* III
skin [skɪn] Haut IV
skinny ['skɪni] mager IV
skirt [skɜːt] Rock II
sky [skaɪ] Himmel II
skyline ['skaɪlaɪn] Skyline *(Horizont; Silhouette)* IV
skyscraper ['skaɪskreɪpə] Wolkenkratzer IV
slave [sleɪv] Sklave, Sklavin II
sledge [sledʒ] Schlitten III
sleep [sliːp]**, slept, slept** schlafen I
sleep [sliːp] Schlaf III
sleeping bag ['sliːpɪŋ bæg] Schlafsack V
sleepless ['sliːpləs] schlaflos IV
sleepover ['sliːpəʊvə] Schlafparty III
slept [slept] *siehe* **sleep**
°slide [slaɪd] rutschen, gleiten
slide [slaɪd] Folie *(bei einer Computerpräsentation);* Dia V
slogan ['sləʊgən] Slogan V
slow [sləʊ] langsam II
slum [slʌm] Slum, Elendsviertel V
small [smɔːl] klein I
smart [smɑːt] clever, schlau II
smell [smel] riechen II
smell [smel] Geruch II
smile [smaɪl] lächeln I • **smile at sb.** jn. anlächeln II
smile [smaɪl] Lächeln II
smoke [sməʊk] rauchen III • **No smoking!** Rauchen verboten. III
smoke [sməʊk] Rauch III
snack [snæk] Snack, Imbiss II
snake [sneɪk] Schlange I • **sea snake** ['siː sneɪk] Seeschlange V
snow [snəʊ] Schnee II
snowball ['snəʊbɔːl] Schneeball IV
snowshoe ['snəʊʃuː] Schneeschuh III
snowshoeing ['snəʊʃuːɪŋ] Schneeschuhwandern III
snowstorm ['snəʊstɔːm] Schneesturm VI 2 (35)
so [səʊ]
1. also; deshalb, daher I • **So?** Und? / Na und? II
°2. sodass
3. so sweet so süß I • **so far** bisher, bis jetzt IV
3. so that sodass, damit III
4. Do you really think so? Meinst du wirklich? / Glaubst du das wirklich? II
soap [səʊp] Seife I • **soap opera** ['səʊp‿ɒprə] *(kurz:* **soap***)* Seifenoper IV
soccer ['sɒkə] Fußball IV
social ['səʊʃl] sozial, Sozial- IV
°social networking site [ˌsəʊʃl 'netwɜːkɪŋ saɪt] *Website zur Bildung und Unterhaltung sozialer Netzwerke*
sock [sɒk] Socke, Strumpf I
soda ['səʊdə] *(AE)* Limonade IV
sofa ['səʊfə] Sofa I
soft [sɒft] weich IV • **soft drink** alkoholfreies Getränk IV
software ['sɒftweə] Software II
solar ['səʊlə] Solar-, Sonnen- VI 2 (37)
sold [səʊld] *siehe* **sell** • **be sold out** ausverkauft sein; vergriffen sein III
soldier ['səʊldʒə] Soldat/in IV
solve [sɒlv] lösen V
some [səm, sʌm] einige, ein paar I
some cheese/juice etwas Käse/Saft I
somebody ['sʌmbədi] jemand I
Find/Ask somebody who ... Finde/Frage jemanden, der ... II • **somebody else** jemand anders IV
°somehow ['sʌmhaʊ] irgendwie
someone ['sʌmwʌn] jemand IV
something ['sʌmθɪŋ] etwas II
sometimes ['sʌmtaɪmz] manchmal I
somewhere ['sʌmweə] irgendwo(hin) II • **somewhere else** woanders IV • **somewhere to stay** ein Platz zum Übernachten V
son [sʌn] Sohn I
song [sɒŋ] Lied, Song I
soon [suːn] bald I
sore [sɔː]**: have a sore throat** Halsschmerzen haben II
sorry ['sɒri]**: (I'm) sorry.** Entschuldigung. / Tut mir leid. I • **Sorry, I'm late.** Entschuldigung, dass ich zu spät bin/komme. I • **Sorry?** Wie bitte? I • **say sorry** sich entschuldigen II
sort [sɔːt] Art, Sorte II
SOS [ˌes‿əʊ‿'es] SOS *(internationales Funknotsignal)* V
sound [saʊnd] klingen, sich *(gut usw.)* anhören I
sound [saʊnd] Laut; Klang I
sound file ['saʊnd faɪl] Tondatei, Soundfile III
soundtrack ['saʊndtræk] Soundtrack, Filmmusik V
soup [suːp] Suppe II
source [sɔːs] Quelle *(von Information, Energie usw.)* IV
south [saʊθ] Süden; nach Süden; südlich III
southbound ['saʊθbaʊnd] Richtung Süden III
south-east [ˌsaʊθ'iːst] Südosten; nach Südosten; südöstlich III
south-west [ˌsaʊθ'west] Südwesten; nach Südwesten; südwestlich III
souvenir [ˌsuːvə'nɪə] Souvenir, Mitbringsel IV
space [speɪs] Platz *(Raum)* IV
Move back one space. Geh ein Feld zurück. II • **Move on one space.** Geh ein Feld vor. II
spaghetti [spə'geti] Spaghetti II
sparkling water ['spɑːklɪŋ] Mineralwasser mit Kohlensäure, Sprudel IV
speak (to) [spiːk]**, spoke, spoken** sprechen (mit), reden (mit) II
speak out seine Meinung (offen) sagen VI 3 (47)

special ['speʃl]**: a special day** ein besonderer Tag I • **What's special about ...?** Was ist das Besondere an ...? V • **special effects** *(pl)* Spezialeffekte VI 1 (12)
specific [spə'sɪfɪk] bestimmte(r, s), spezifische(r, s) IV
speech [spi:tʃ] Rede IV • **make a speech** eine Rede halten IV
spell [spel] buchstabieren I
spelling ['spelɪŋ] (Recht-)Schreibung, Schreibweise III
spend [spend]**, spent, spent: spend money (on)** Geld ausgeben (für) II • **spend time (on)** Zeit verbringen (mit) II
spent [spent] *siehe* **spend**
spicy ['spaɪsi] würzig, scharf gewürzt III
splash [splæʃ] spritzen IV
spoke [spəʊk] *siehe* **speak**
spoken ['spəʊkən] *siehe* **speak**
spoon [spu:n] Löffel III
sport [spɔ:t] Sport; Sportart I
do sport *(BE)* Sport treiben I
sports centre Sportzentrum I
sports hall Sporthalle III
sportsman ['spɔ:tsmən] Sportler IV
sportswoman ['spɔ:tswʊmən] Sportlerin IV
sporty ['spɔ:ti] sportlich III
spot (-tt-) [spɒt] entdecken III
spotlight ['spɒtlaɪt] Spotlight IV
spray [spreɪ] sprühen V
spring [sprɪŋ]
1. Frühling I
2. Quelle V
spy [spaɪ] Spion/in I
square [skweə] Platz III • **square km (sq km)** Quadratkilometer IV
squeeze [skwi:z] drücken; (aus-)pressen III
squirrel ['skwɪrəl] Eichhörnchen II
stadium ['steɪdiəm] Stadion III
stage [steɪdʒ] Bühne III
stairs *(pl)* [steəz] Treppe; Treppenstufen I
stamp [stæmp] Briefmarke I
stand [stænd]**, stood, stood** stehen; sich (hin)stellen II
star [stɑ:]
1. Stern II
2. (Film-, Pop-)Star I • **rock star** ['rɒk stɑ:] Rockstar V
star [stɑ:]**: the film stars ...** der Film hat ... in der Hauptrolle / in den Hauptrollen VI 1 (12)
stare (at sb.) [steə] (jn. an)starren VI 3 (53)
start [stɑ:t] starten, anfangen, beginnen (mit) I • **start a business** eine Firma gründen V
start [stɑ:t] Start IV
state [steɪt] Staat III
statement ['steɪtmənt] Aussage, Feststellung III
station ['steɪʃn] Bahnhof I • **at the station** am Bahnhof I • **fire station** Feuerwache IV • **gas station** *(AE)* Tankstelle IV • **lifeguard station** ['laɪfgɑ:d] Station der Rettungsschwimmer/innen V
petrol station *(BE)* Tankstelle IV
statue ['stætʃu:] Statue II
stay [steɪ]
1. bleiben I • **stay out** draußen bleiben, wegbleiben III
2. wohnen, übernachten II • **stay with** wohnen bei III • **somewhere to stay** ein Platz zum Übernachten V
stay [steɪ] Aufenthalt V • **Have a pleasant stay.** Einen angenehmen Aufenthalt! V
steak [steɪk] Steak III
steal [sti:l]**, stole, stolen** stehlen II
steel [sti:l] Stahl III • **steel drum** Steeldrum III
step [step]
1. Schritt I
2. Treppenstufe IV
stereo ['steriəʊ] Stereoanlage I
stew [stju:] Eintopf(gericht) III
°**stick** [stɪk] Stock
stick [stɪk]**, stuck, stuck**
1. (auf)kleben V
2. **stick sth. up** etwas aufhängen *(und dabei mit Klebstoff befestigen)* V
3. **stick out of sth.** aus etwas herausragen, herausstehen III
sticker ['stɪkə] Sticker IV
still [stɪl] (immer) noch I
°**still** [stɪl] Standfoto
stole [stəʊl] *siehe* **steal**
stolen ['stəʊlən]
1. *siehe* **steal**
2. gestohlene(r) V
stomach ['stʌmək] Magen II
stomach ache Magenschmerzen, Bauchweh II
stone [stəʊn] Stein II
stood [stʊd] *siehe* **stand**
stop (-pp-) [stɒp]
1. aufhören I
2. anhalten I
Stop that! Hör auf damit! / Lass das! I
stop [stɒp] Halt IV
store [stɔ:] (ein)lagern, aufbewahren V
storm [stɔ:m] Sturm; Gewitter II
stormy ['stɔ:mi] stürmisch II
story ['stɔ:ri] Geschichte, Erzählung I
straight *(adj)* [streɪt] glatt VI 1 (6)
straight on *(adv)* [streɪt_'ɒn] geradeaus weiter II
strange [streɪndʒ] seltsam, sonderbar; fremd III
strawberry ['strɔ:bəri] Erdbeere II
street [stri:t] Straße I • **at 7 Hamilton Street** in der Hamiltonstraße 7 I
strength [streŋθ] Stärke, Kraft V
stress [stres] Betonung III
stressful ['stresfl] anstrengend, stressig V
strict [strɪkt] streng III
strike [straɪk] Streik III • **be on strike** streiken, sich im Streik befinden III • **go on strike** streiken, in den Streik treten III
strong [strɒŋ] stark II
structure ['strʌktʃə] strukturieren, aufbauen II
stuck [stʌk]
1. *siehe* **stick**
°2. **be stuck** festsitzen
student ['stju:dənt] Schüler/in; Student/in I • **exchange student** Austauschschüler/in III
studio ['stju:diəʊ] Studio III
study ['stʌdi] studieren; sorgfältig durchlesen; lernen IV • **study hall** *Zeit zum selbstständigen Arbeiten/ Lernen in der Schule* IV • **study skills** *(pl)* Lern- und Arbeitstechniken I
stuff [stʌf] Zeug, Kram II
stupid ['stju:pɪd] blöd, dämlich II
style [staɪl] Stil V
subject ['sʌbdʒɪkt] Schulfach I
suburb ['sʌbɜ:b] Vorort V
subway ['sʌbweɪ]**: the subway** *(AE)* die U-Bahn II
succeed (in sth.) [sək'si:d] Erfolg haben, erfolgreich sein (mit etwas, bei etwas) IV
success [sək'ses] Erfolg III
successful [sək'sesfl] erfolgreich III
such (a) [sʌtʃ] so (ein/e), solch (ein/e); solche V
suddenly ['sʌdnli] plötzlich, auf einmal I
suffer (from sth.) ['sʌfə] (an/unter etwas) leiden IV
sugar ['ʃʊgə] Zucker II
suggest sth. (to sb.) [sə'dʒest] (jm.) etwas vorschlagen VI 1 (8)
suggestion [sə'dʒestʃən] Vorschlag IV
suit [su:t] Anzug V; (Damen-)Kostüm VI 1 (14/181)
suitable ['su:təbl] geeignet, passend V

suitcase ['su:tkeɪs] Koffer II
sum sth. up (-mm-) [ˌsʌm_'ʌp] etwas zusammenfassen V
summarize sth. ['sʌməraɪz] etwas zusammenfassen IV
summary ['sʌməri] Zusammenfassung IV
summer ['sʌmə] Sommer I
sun [sʌn] Sonne II
Sunday ['sʌndeɪ, 'sʌndi] Sonntag I
sung [sʌŋ] *siehe* **sing**
sunglasses *(pl)* ['sʌnglɑ:sɪz] (eine) Sonnenbrille I
sunny ['sʌni] sonnig II
sunscreen ['sʌnskri:n] Sonnenschutzmittel V
super ['su:pə] super IV
supermarket ['su:pəmɑ:kɪt] Supermarkt II
superstar ['su:pəstɑ:] Superstar V
support [sə'pɔ:t] unterstützen IV **support a team** eine Mannschaft unterstützen; Fan einer Mannschaft sein III
supporter [sə'pɔ:tə] Anhänger/in, Fan III
suppose [sə'pəʊz] annehmen, vermuten VI 1 (10)
sure [ʃʊə, ʃɔ:] klar, sicher IV • **be sure** sicher sein II • **make sure that ...** sich vergewissern, dass ...; dafür sorgen, dass ... IV
surely ['ʃʊəli, 'ʃɔ:li] doch wohl; doch sicher VI 3 (49/188)
► S.188 surely
surf [sɜ:f]**: surf the internet** im Internet surfen III
surfboard ['sɜ:fbɔ:d] Surfbrett II
surfing ['sɜ:fɪŋ]**: go surfing** wellenreiten gehen, surfen gehen II
surname ['sɜ:neɪm] Nachname V
surprise [sə'praɪz] Überraschung III
surprise sb. [sə'praɪz] jn. überraschen III
surprised (at sth.) [sə'praɪzd] überrascht (über/von etwas) III
surprising [sə'praɪzɪŋ] überraschend, erstaunlich V
survey (on) ['sɜ:veɪ] Umfrage, Untersuchung (über) II
survival [sə'vaɪvl] Überleben V **survival kit** Überlebenspäckchen V
survive [sə'vaɪv] überleben II
°**suspense** [sə'spens] Spannung
swam [swæm] *siehe* **swim**
swap sth. (for sth.) (-pp-) [swɒp] etwas (ein)tauschen (für etwas/gegen etwas) IV
°**sway** [sweɪ] *hier:* hin- und herwiegen
sweat [swet] schwitzen IV
sweat [swet] Schweiß IV
sweatshirt ['swetʃɜ:t] Sweatshirt I
sweet [swi:t] süß I
sweetheart ['swi:thɑ:t] Liebling, Schatz II
sweets *(pl)* [swi:ts] Süßigkeiten I
swim (-mm-) [swɪm]**, swam, swum** schwimmen I • **go swimming** schwimmen gehen I
swimmer ['swɪmə] Schwimmer/in II
swimming ['swɪmɪŋ]**: swimming pool** [pu:l] Schwimmbad, Schwimmbecken I • **swimming trunks** *(pl)* [trʌŋks] Badehose III **indoor swimming pool** Hallenbad V • **outdoor swimming pool** Freibad V
swimsuit ['swɪmsu:t] Badeanzug III
°**swipe a card** [swaɪp] eine Karte durchziehen
swum [swʌm] *siehe* **swim**
syllable ['sɪləbl] Silbe I
°**sympathetic** [ˌsɪmpə'θetɪk] verständnisvoll, mitfühlend
synagogue ['sɪnəgɒg] Synagoge VI 1 (13/181)
► S.181 Religions
synonym ['sɪnənɪm] Synonym *(Wort mit gleicher oder sehr ähnlicher Bedeutung)* IV
system ['sɪstəm] System IV

T

table ['teɪbl] Tisch I
table tennis ['teɪbl tenɪs] Tischtennis I • **table tennis bat** Tischtennisschläger III
take [teɪk]**, took, taken**
1. nehmen I
2. (weg-, hin)bringen I
3. dauern, *(Zeit)* brauchen III
take action handeln; etwas unternehmen VI 3 (50) • **take a break** eine Pause machen IV • **take a deep breath** tief Luft holen V **take a message** eine Nachricht entgegennehmen V • **Can I take a message for her/him?** Soll ich ihr/ihm etwas ausrichten? V • **take an exam** eine Prüfung ablegen VI 1 (9/180) • **take a ride** eine Fahrt machen III • **take a shower** duschen VI 2 (36) • **take notes** sich Notizen machen I • **take out** herausnehmen I • **take part (in)** teilnehmen (an) III • **take photos** Fotos machen, fotografieren I **take place** stattfinden IV • **take sb./sth. seriously** jn./etwas ernst nehmen VI 3 (48) • **take sb. through sth.** etwas mit jm. (genau) durchgehen VI 2 (34) • **take sth. off** etwas ausziehen *(Kleidung)* II • **take 10 c off** 10 Cent abziehen I • **take sth. over** etwas übernehmen; etwas in seine Gewalt bringen IV • °**Take turns.** Wechselt euch ab. • **We'll take them.** *(beim Einkaufen)* Wir nehmen sie. I
taken ['teɪkən] *siehe* **take**
talent ['tælənt] Talent, Begabung III
talk (to sb. about sth.) [tɔ:k] (mit jm. über etwas) reden, sich (mit jm. über etwas) unterhalten I
talk [tɔ:k] Vortrag, Rede V • **give a talk (on sth.)** einen Vortrag/eine Rede halten (über etwas) V
tall [tɔ:l] hoch *(Bäume, Türme usw.)*; groß *(Person)* IV
target ['tɑ:gɪt] Ziel; Zielscheibe VI 2 (29)
tattoo [tə'tu:] Tattoo IV
taught [tɔ:t] *siehe* **teach**
tax [tæks] *(die)* Steuer VI 3 (49)
taxi ['tæksi] Taxi III
tea [ti:] Tee; *(auch:) leichte Nachmittags- oder Abendmahlzeit* I
teach [ti:tʃ]**, taught, taught** unterrichten, lehren I
teacher ['ti:tʃə] Lehrer/in I • **head teacher** Schulleiter/in III
team [ti:m] Team, Mannschaft I
tear [tɪə] Träne IV
tear sth. off [teə]**, tore, torn** etwas abreißen IV
teaspoon ['ti:spu:n] Teelöffel III
technical ['teknɪkl] technisch V
technician [tek'nɪʃn] Techniker/in V
°**technique** [tek'ni:k] Technik, Methode
technology [tek'nɒlədʒi] Technologie V
teddy ['tedi] Teddybär III
teen [ti:n] Teenager-, Jugend- III
teenager ['ti:neɪdʒə] Teenager, Jugendliche(r) II
teeth [ti:θ] *Plural von „tooth"*
telephone ['telɪfəʊn] Telefon I **telephone number** Telefonnummer I • **What's your telephone number?** Was ist deine Telefonnummer? I
television (TV) ['telɪvɪʒn] Fernsehen I
tell (about) [tel]**, told, told** erzählen (von), berichten (über) I • **Tell me your names.** Sagt mir eure Namen. I • **tell sb. the way** jm. den Weg beschreiben II • **tell sb. to do sth.**

jm. sagen, dass er/sie etwas tun soll V
temperature ['temprətʃə] Temperatur II • **have a temperature** Fieber haben II
temple ['templ] Tempel VI 1 (13/181)
► S.181 Religions
tennis ['tenɪs] Tennis I
tennis racket ['tenɪs rækɪt] Tennisschläger VI 3 (48)
tense [tens] (grammatische) Zeit, Tempus III
tent [tent] Zelt IV
term [tɜːm] Trimester II
terrible ['terəbl] schrecklich, furchtbar I
terrified ['terɪfaɪd]: **be terrified (of)** schreckliche Angst haben (vor) IV
terrorist ['terərɪst] Terrorist/in; Terror-, terroristisch IV
test [test] Test, Prüfung II
text [tekst] Text I • **text message** SMS III • **skim a text** einen Text überfliegen *(um den Inhalt grob zu erfassen)* III
text sb. [tekst] jm. eine SMS schicken III
than [ðæn, ðən] als II • **more than** mehr als II • **more than me** mehr als ich II
thank [θæŋk]: **Thank you.** Danke (schön). I • **Thanks.** Danke. I
Thanks a lot! Vielen Dank! I
Thanks very much! Danke sehr! / Vielen Dank! II
that [ðət, ðæt]
1. das (dort) I
2. jene(r, s) I
That's me. Das bin ich. I • **That's right.** Das ist richtig. / Das stimmt. I • **That's up to you.** Das liegt bei dir. / Das kannst/musst du (selbst) entscheiden. III • **that's why** deshalb, darum V
that [ðət, ðæt] der, die, das; die *(Relativpronomen)* III
that [ðət, ðæt] dass I • **so that** sodass, damit III
that far/good/bad/... [ðæt] so weit/gut/schlecht/... III
the [ðə, ði] der, die, das; die I
theatre ['θɪətə] Theater II
°**theft** [θeft] Diebstahl
their [ðeə] ihr, ihre *(Plural)* I
theirs [ðeəz] ihrer, ihre, ihrs II
them [ðəm, ðem] sie; ihnen I
themselves [ðəm'selvz] sich (selbst) III
then [ðen] dann, danach I • **now and then** gelegentlich, ab und zu V • **since then** seitdem VI 2 (30)
there [ðeə]
1. da, dort I
2. dahin, dorthin I
down there dort unten II • **over there** da drüben, dort drüben I
there are es sind (vorhanden); es gibt I • **there's** es ist (vorhanden); es gibt I • **there isn't a ...** es ist kein/e ...; es gibt kein/e ... I
thermometer [θə'mɒmɪtə] Thermometer II
these [ðiːz] diese, die (hier) I
they [ðeɪ] sie *(Plural)* I
thick [θɪk] dick VI 1 (7/179)
thief [θiːf], *pl* **thieves** [θiːvz] Dieb/in II
thin [θɪn] dünn VI 1 (7)
thing [θɪŋ] Ding, Sache I • **What was the best thing about ...?** Was war das Beste an ...? II
think [θɪŋk], **thought, thought** glauben, meinen, denken I
think about 1. nachdenken über II; 2. denken über, halten von II
think of 1. denken über, halten von II; 2. denken an; sich ausdenken II
third [θɜːd] dritte(r, s) I
third [θɜːd]: **a third** ein Drittel V
this [ðɪs]
1. dies (hier) I
2. diese(r, s) I
This is Isabel. Hier spricht Isabel. / Hier ist Isabel. *(am Telefon)* II
this morning/afternoon/evening heute Morgen/Nachmittag/Abend I • **this way** 1. hier entlang, in diese Richtung II; 2. so, auf diese Weise VI 3 (47)
those [ðəʊz] die (da), jene (dort) I
thought [θɔːt] *siehe* **think**
thought [θɔːt] Gedanke IV
thoughtful ['θɔːtfl] nachdenklich; aufmerksam, rücksichtsvoll V
thousand ['θaʊznd] tausend I
threaten ['θretn] (be)drohen V
°**three-part** dreiteilige(r, s)
threw [θruː] *siehe* **throw**
thriller ['θrɪlə] Thriller VI 1 (12)
thrilling ['θrɪlɪŋ] aufregend, spannend V
throat [θrəʊt] Hals, Kehle II
through [θruː] durch II
throw [θrəʊ], **threw, thrown** werfen I • **throw up** sich übergeben IV
thrown [θrəʊn] *siehe* **throw**
Thursday ['θɜːzdeɪ, 'θɜːzdi] Donnerstag I
°**tick** [tɪk] Häkchen
°**tick** [tɪk] ankreuzen, ein Häkchen machen
ticket ['tɪkɪt]
1. Eintrittskarte I
2. Fahrkarte II
ticket machine Fahrkartenautomat III • **ticket office** Kasse *(für den Verkauf von Eintrittskarten)* IV; Fahrkartenschalter III
one-day ticket Tages(fahr)karte III • **return ticket** Rückfahrkarte II
single (ticket) einfache Fahrkarte *(nur Hinfahrt)* III
tidy ['taɪdi] aufräumen I
tidy ['taɪdi] ordentlich, aufgeräumt II
tie [taɪ] Krawatte V
tie *(-ing form:* **tying***)* [taɪ] binden V
tiger ['taɪgə] Tiger II
tight [taɪt]
1. fest IV
2. dicht, eng V
till [tɪl] bis *(zeitlich)* I
time [taɪm]
1. Zeit; Uhrzeit I
2. **time(s)** Mal(e); -mal II
at a time gleichzeitig, auf einmal V • **any time** jederzeit IV • **cross a time zone** [zəʊn] eine Zeitzone passieren IV • **for the first time** zum ersten Mal IV • **Have a good time.** Viel Spaß! V • **in time** rechtzeitig II • **three times** dreimal III • **What's the time?** Wie spät ist es? I
°**timeline** ['taɪmlaɪn] Zeitachse, Zeitleiste
timetable ['taɪmteɪbl]
1. Stundenplan I
2. Fahrplan II
timing ['taɪmɪŋ]: **bad timing** schlechtes Timing III
tiny ['taɪni] winzig V
tip [tɪp]
1. Tipp II
2. Spitze IV
tired ['taɪəd] müde I • **be tired of sth.** genug von etwas haben, etwas satt haben IV
title ['taɪtl] Titel, Überschrift I
to [tə, tu]
1. zu, nach I • **to Jenny's** zu Jenny I • °**to the front** nach vorn
2. **an e-mail to** eine E-Mail an I
write to schreiben an I
3. **quarter to 12** Viertel vor 12 (11.45/23.45) I
4. **try to help/to play/...** versuchen, zu helfen/zu spielen/... I
5. um zu II
6. **from Monday to Friday** von Montag bis Freitag III
toast [təʊst] Toast(brot) I
toaster ['təʊstə] Toaster VI 2 (34)
tobacco [tə'bækəʊ] Tabak II

today [tə'deɪ] heute I
toe [təʊ] Zeh I
together [tə'geðə] zusammen I
toilet ['tɔɪlət] Toilette I
told [təʊld] *siehe* **tell**
tomato [tə'mɑːtəʊ], *pl* **tomatoes** Tomate II
tomorrow [tə'mɒrəʊ] morgen I
tomorrow's weather das Wetter von morgen II
tongue [tʌŋ] Zunge VI 1 (10)
tonight [tə'naɪt] heute Nacht, heute Abend I • **tonight's programme** das Programm von heute Abend; das heutige Abendprogramm II
tonne [tʌn] Tonne *(Gewichtseinheit)* VI 2 (29)
too [tuː]: **from Bristol too** auch aus Bristol I • **Me too.** Ich auch. I
too much/big/... [tuː] zu viel/groß/ ... I
took [tʊk] *siehe* **take**
tool [tuːl] Werkzeug IV
tooth [tuːθ], *pl* **teeth** [tiːθ] Zahn I
toothache ['tuːθeɪk] Zahnschmerzen II
toothbrush ['tuːθbrʌʃ] Zahnbürste VI 2 (28)
toothless ['tuːθləs] zahnlos IV
top [tɒp]
1. Spitze, oberes Ende I • **at the top (of)** oben, am oberen Ende, an der Spitze (von) I • **on top (of sth.)** [ɒn 'tɒp] oben, oben drauf (auf etwas) V
2. Top, Oberteil I
topic ['tɒpɪk] Thema, Themenbereich I • **topic sentence** *Satz, der in das Thema eines Absatzes einführt* II
tore [tɔː] *siehe* **tear**
torn [tɔːn] *siehe* **tear**
tornado [tɔː'neɪdəʊ] Tornado, Wirbelsturm II
tortoise ['tɔːtəs] Schildkröte I
touch [tʌtʃ] berühren, anfassen II
touch [tʌtʃ]: **keep in touch** in Verbindung bleiben, Kontakt halten III
°**tough** [tʌf] zäh
tour [tʊə]: **tour (of the house)** Rundgang, Tour (durch das Haus) I • **tour guide** (Fremden-)Führer/in, Reiseleiter/in IV
tourist ['tʊərɪst] Tourist/in II
tourist information Fremdenverkehrsamt II
towards sb./sth. [tə'wɔːdz] auf jn./etwas zu II
towel ['taʊəl] Handtuch IV
tower ['taʊə] Turm I
town [taʊn] (Klein-)Stadt I
town council ['kaʊnsl] Stadtrat *(Gremium)* VI 3 (47/187)
► S.187 Politics
town councillor ['kaʊnsələ] Stadtrat/-rätin VI 3 (47/187)
► S.187 Politics
town hall [taʊn 'hɔːl] Rathaus VI 3 (47/187)
► S.187 Politics
track [træk]
1. Stück, Titel, Track *(auf einer CD)* III
°**2.** Pfad
trade [treɪd] Handel VI 3 (47)
tradition [trə'dɪʃn] Tradition IV
traditional [trə'dɪʃənl] traditionell III
traffic ['træfɪk] Verkehr II • **traffic jam** (Verkehrs-)Stau IV • **traffic light** (Verkehrs-)Ampel IV
train [treɪn] Zug I • **on the train** im Zug I
train [treɪn]
1. trainieren III
2. train (as sth.) eine Ausbildung (zu/als etwas) machen V
trainers *(pl)* ['treɪnəz] Turnschuhe II
training ['treɪnɪŋ]
1. (berufliche) Ausbildung V
2. training session ['seʃn] Trainingsstunde, -einheit III
tram [træm] Straßenbahn III
translate (from ... into) [træns'leɪt] übersetzen (aus ... ins) III
translation [træns'leɪʃn] Übersetzung III
°**transparency** [træns'pærənsi] Folie *(für Overheadprojektoren)*
transport ['trænspɔːt] Beförderung, Transport III • **public transport** *(no pl)* [,pʌblɪk 'trænspɔːt] öffentliche Verkehrsmittel, öffentlicher Personennahverkehr V
trash [træʃ] *(AE)* Abfall, Müll V
travel (-ll-) ['trævl] reisen II
travel ['trævl] *(das)* Reisen VI 2 (34)
travel agent ['trævl_,eɪdʒənt] Reisebürokaufmann/-kauffrau V
travel agent's Reisebüro V
Travelcard ['trævlkɑːd] Tages-/Wochen-/Monatsfahrkarte *(der Londoner Verkehrsbetriebe)* III
tree [triː] Baum I
trendy ['trendi] modisch, schick III
trick [trɪk]
1. (Zauber-)Kunststück, Trick I
do tricks (Zauber-)Kunststücke machen I
2. Streich II
trip [trɪp] Reise; Ausflug I • **go on a trip** einen Ausflug machen II
trouble ['trʌbl] Schwierigkeiten, Ärger II • **be in trouble** in Schwierigkeiten sein; Ärger kriegen II
troublemaker ['trʌblmeɪkə] Randalierer/in, Unruhestifter/in V
trousers *(pl)* ['traʊzəz] Hose II
truck [trʌk] Lastwagen V
true [truː] wahr II
trumpet ['trʌmpɪt] Trompete III
try [traɪ]
1. versuchen I
2. probieren, kosten I
try and do sth. / try to do sth. versuchen, etwas zu tun I • **try on** anprobieren *(Kleidung)* I
try [traɪ] Versuch V • **Nice try.** Netter Versuch. V
T-shirt ['tiːʃɜːt] T-Shirt I
tsunami [tsuː'nɑːmi] Tsunami IV
tube [tjuːb]: **the Tube** *(no pl)* die Londoner U-Bahn III
Tuesday ['tjuːzdeɪ, 'tjuːzdi] Dienstag I
tune [tjuːn] Melodie III
tunnel ['tʌnl] Tunnel II
turkey ['tɜːki] Truthahn, Pute/Puter III
turn [tɜːn]
1. sich umdrehen II • **turn left/right** (nach) links/rechts abbiegen II • **turn to sb.** sich jm. zuwenden; sich an jn. wenden I
2. turn sth. on/off etwas ein-, ausschalten III
3. turn sth. down/up etwas leiser/lauter stellen IV; etwas höher/niedriger stellen VI 2 (28)
turn [tɜːn]: **It's your turn.** Du bist dran / an der Reihe. I • **Miss a turn.** Einmal aussetzen. II • °**Take turns.** Wechselt euch ab. • **Whose turn is it?** Wer ist dran / an der Reihe? II
turtle ['tɜːtl] Wasserschildkröte V
TV [tiː'viː] Fernsehen I • **on TV** im Fernsehen I • **watch TV** fernsehen I • **TV listings** *(pl)* das Fernsehprogramm IV • °**TV dinner** *(infml)* Fertiggericht
twenty-four seven (24/7) rund um die Uhr, sieben Tage die Woche VI 2 (35)
twice [twaɪs] zweimal • **twice a week** zweimal pro Woche III
°**twilight** ['twaɪlaɪt] Dämmerung, Zwielicht
twin [twɪn]: **twin brother** Zwillingsbruder I • **twins** *(pl)* Zwillinge I
twin town Partnerstadt IV
two all [,tuː‿'ɔːl] 2 beide (2:2 unentschieden) III
type [taɪp] Typ III
typical (of) ['tɪpɪkl] typisch (für) V

U

ugly ['ʌgli] hässlich V
unattractive [ˌʌnə'træktɪv] unattraktiv; wenig verlockend VI 1 (6/178)
unbelievable [ˌʌnbɪ'li:vəbl] unglaublich IV
uncle ['ʌŋkl] Onkel I
unclear [ˌʌn'klɪə] unklar III
uncomfortable [ʌn'kʌmftəbl] unbequem, unbehaglich IV
unconscious [ʌn'kɒnʃəs] bewusstlos V
uncool [ˌʌn'ku:l] *(infml)* uncool III
uncountable [ʌn'kaʊntəbl] unzählbar IV
under ['ʌndə] unter I
underground ['ʌndəgraʊnd]**: the underground** die U-Bahn II
°**underline** [ˌʌndə'laɪn] unterstreichen
°**underlined** [ˌʌndə'laɪnd] unterstrichen
understand [ˌʌndə'stænd]**, understood, understood** verstehen, begreifen I
understandable [ˌʌndə'stændəbl] verständlich IV
understood [ˌʌndə'stʊd] *siehe* **understand**
unemployment [ˌʌnɪm'plɔɪmənt] Arbeitslosigkeit V
unfair [ˌʌn'feə] unfair, ungerecht III
unforgettable [ˌʌnfə'getəbl] unvergesslich V
unforgivable [ˌʌnfə'gɪvəbl] unverzeihlich V
unfortunately [ʌn'fɔ:tʃənətli] leider IV
unfriendly [ʌn'frendli] unfreundlich III
unhappy [ʌn'hæpi] unglücklich III
unhealthy [ʌn'helθi] ungesund III
uniform ['ju:nɪfɔ:m] Uniform I
unit ['ju:nɪt] Lektion, Kapitel I
united: the United Kingdom (UK) [juˌnaɪtɪd 'kɪŋdəm] ([ˌju: 'keɪ]) das Vereinigte Königreich *(Großbritannien und Nordirland)* III • **the United States (US)** [juˌnaɪtɪd 'steɪts] ([ˌju:‿'es]) die Vereinigten Staaten *(von Amerika)* III
university [ˌju:nɪ'vɜ:səti] Universität IV
unkind [ˌʌn'kaɪnd] unfreundlich V
unless [ən'les] es sei denn; wenn ... nicht VI 3 (48)
unlike [ˌʌn'laɪk] anders als; im Gegensatz zu VI 1 (6)
unlock [ˌʌn'lɒk] aufschließen; entsperren III
unplug sth. (-gg-) [ˌʌn'plʌg] den Stecker von etwas herausziehen VI 2 (28)
unpopular [ʌn'pɒpjələ] unbeliebt, unpopulär VI 1 (15)
unreadable [ʌn'ri:dəbl] unleserlich IV
unsafe [ʌn'seɪf] nicht sicher, gefährlich III
untidy [ʌn'taɪdi] unordentlich III
until [ən'tɪl] bis III
unwanted [ˌʌn'wɒntɪd] unerwünscht, ungewollt V
up [ʌp] hinauf, herauf, nach oben I
up the hill den Hügel hinauf II
That's up to you. Das liegt bei dir. / Das kannst/musst du (selbst) entscheiden. III
upset (about) [ˌʌp'set] aufgebracht, gekränkt, mitgenommen (wegen) III
upset sb. (-tt-) [ʌp'set]**, upset, upset** jn. ärgern, kränken, aus der Fassung bringen III
upstairs [ˌʌp'steəz] oben; nach oben I
us [əs, ʌs] uns I
use [ju:z] benutzen, verwenden I; verbrauchen *(Energie)* VI 2 (28)
used to ['ju:st tə]**: I used to be excited.** Früher war ich (immer) aufgeregt. V
useful ['ju:sfl] nützlich III
usual ['ju:ʒuəl]**: as usual** wie immer, wie üblich V
usually ['ju:ʒuəli] meistens, gewöhnlich, normalerweise I

V

vacation [və'keɪʃn, *AE:* veɪ'keɪʃn] *(AE)* Urlaub, Ferien III
valley ['væli] Tal II
valuable ['væljuəbl] wertvoll IV
°**vampire** ['væmpaɪə] Vampir/in
vandalism ['vændəlɪzəm] Vandalismus, Zerstörungswut V
vandalize ['vændəlaɪz] mutwillig beschädigen, mutwillig zerstören V
vegetable ['vedʒtəbl] *(ein)* Gemüse III
vegetarian [ˌvedʒə'teəriən] vegetarisch; Vegetarier/in IV
°**verse** [vɜ:s] Strophe, Vers
version ['vɜ:ʃn] Version, Fassung IV
very ['veri] sehr I • **like/love sth. very much** etwas sehr mögen/sehr lieben II • **Thanks very much!** Danke sehr! / Vielen Dank! II
vet [vet] Tierarzt/-ärztin V • **vet's assistant** [ˌvets‿ə'sɪstənt] Tierarzthelfer/in V
victim ['vɪktɪm] Opfer III
video ['vɪdiəʊ] Video III
view [vju:]
1. Aussicht, Blick II
2. view (about/on) Ansicht (über/zu) VI 3 (48)
point of view Standpunkt, Sichtweise VI 2 (37)
°**view** [vju:] betrachten; *(im Fernsehen/Kino)* anschauen
viewer ['vju:ə] Zuschauer/in IV
village ['vɪlɪdʒ] Dorf I
violence ['vaɪələns] Gewalt; Gewalttätigkeit IV
violent ['vaɪələnt] gewalttätig; gewaltsam IV
violin [ˌvaɪə'lɪn] Violine, Geige III
virus ['vaɪrəs], *pl* **viruses** ['vaɪrəsəz] Virus V
visit ['vɪzɪt] besuchen II
visit ['vɪzɪt] Besuch II
visitor ['vɪzɪtə] Besucher/in, Gast I
visual ['vɪʒuəl] visuell; optisch V
vitae: curriculum vitae [kəˌrɪkjələm 'vi:taɪ] **(CV)** Lebenslauf V
vocabulary [və'kæbjələri] Vokabelverzeichnis, Wörterverzeichnis I
voice [vɔɪs] Stimme IV
volleyball ['vɒlibɔ:l] Volleyball I
volume ['vɒlju:m] Lautstärke IV
volunteer [ˌvɒlən'tɪə] sich freiwillig melden, sich bereit erklären IV
volunteer [ˌvɒlən'tɪə] Freiwillige(r) IV
vote [vəʊt] wählen *(zur Wahl gehen)* VI 3 (46) • **vote for sb.** für jn. stimmen IV

W

wait (for) [weɪt] warten (auf) I
Wait a minute. Warte mal! / Moment mal! II • **I can't wait to see ...** ich kann es kaum erwarten, ... zu sehen I • **Wait and see!** Wart's ab! III
waiter ['weɪtə] Kellner II
waiting room ['weɪtɪŋ ru:m] Wartezimmer IV
waitress ['weɪtrəs] Kellnerin II
wake up [ˌweɪk‿'ʌp]**, woke, woken** aufwachen III • **wake sb. (up)** jn. (auf)wecken III
wake-up call ['weɪk‿ʌp ˌkɔ:l] Weckanruf V
walk [wɔ:k] (zu Fuß) gehen I
walk around herumlaufen, umherspazieren III • **walk around**

the town in der Stadt umhergehen, durch die Stadt gehen III
walk off weggehen IV
walk [wɔ:k] Spaziergang II • **a ten-kilometre walk** eine Zehn-Kilometer-Wanderung III • **go for a walk** spazieren gehen, einen Spaziergang machen II
wall [wɔ:l] Wand; Mauer II
want [wɒnt] (haben) wollen I
want to do sth. etwas tun wollen I • **want sb. to do sth.** wollen, dass jm. etwas tut IV • **want to be sth.** etwas werden wollen *(beruflich)* V
war [wɔ:] Krieg IV
wardrobe ['wɔ:drəʊb] Kleiderschrank I
warm [wɔ:m] warm II
warn sb. (about sth.) [wɔ:n] jn. (vor etwas) warnen III
was [wəz, wɒz]**: (I/he/she/it) was** *siehe* **be**
wash [wɒʃ] waschen I • **I wash my face.** Ich wasche mir das Gesicht. I
washing machine ['wɒʃɪŋ məˌʃi:n] Waschmaschine I
waste [weɪst] Verschwendung VI 3 (47)
waste sth. (on) [weɪst] etwas verschwenden (für) VI 2 (37)
watch [wɒtʃ] beobachten, sich etwas ansehen; zusehen I
watch TV fernsehen I
watch [wɒtʃ] Armbanduhr I
water ['wɔ:tə] Wasser I • **running water** fließendes Wasser *(Leitungswasser)* V • **salt water** Salzwasser V
waterproof ['wɔ:təpru:f] wasserdicht *(Kleidung, Uhr)* V
wave [weɪv] winken II
way [weɪ]
1. Weg II • **all the way** den ganzen Weg IV • **ask sb. the way** jn. nach dem Weg fragen II • **on the way (to)** auf dem Weg (zu/nach) II • **tell sb. the way** jm. den Weg beschreiben II • **°We've come a long way.** Wir sind weit gekommen. *(Wir haben viel erreicht.)*
2. Richtung II • **the other way round** anders herum II • **the wrong way** in die falsche Richtung II • **this way** hier entlang, in diese Richtung II • **which way?** in welche Richtung? / wohin? II
3. Art und Weise III • **in a friendly/strange/different way** auf freundliche/seltsame/andere Art und Weise VI 1 (7) • **the way you ...** so wie du ..., auf dieselbe Weise wie du ... IV • **this way** so, auf diese Weise VI 3 (47)
by the way übrigens II • **No way!** Auf keinen Fall! / Kommt nicht in Frage! II
we [wi:] wir I
weak [wi:k] schwach II
weakness ['wi:knəs] Schwäche, Schwachpunkt V
wear [weə]**, wore, worn** tragen, anhaben *(Kleidung)* I
weather ['weðə] Wetter II
weatherproof ['weðəpru:f] wetterfest *(Kleidung)* V
webcam ['webkæm] Webcam III
website ['websaɪt] Website II
wedding ['wedɪŋ] Hochzeit, Trauung V
Wednesday ['wenzdeɪ, 'wenzdi] Mittwoch I
week [wi:k] Woche I • **days of the week** Wochentage I • **a two-week holiday** ein zweiwöchiger Urlaub III
weekend [ˌwi:k'end] Wochenende I
at the weekend am Wochenende I
welcome ['welkəm]
1. Welcome (to Bristol). Willkommen (in Bristol). I
2. You're welcome. Gern geschehen. / Nichts zu danken. I
welcome sb. (to) ['welkəm] jn. begrüßen, willkommen heißen (in) I
They welcome you to ... Sie heißen dich in ... willkommen I
well [wel]
1. gut II
2. *(gesundheitlich)* gut; gesund, wohlauf II
do well (in) gut abschneiden (in) III • **go well** gut (ver)laufen, gutgehen III • **You did well.** Das hast du gut gemacht. II • **Oh well ...** Na ja ... / Na gut ... I • **Well, ...** Nun, ... / Also, ... I • **°Well done!** [ˌwel 'dʌn] Gut gemacht!
Welsh [welʃ] walisisch; Walisisch II
went [went] *siehe* **go**
were [wə, wɜ:]**: (we/you/they) were** *siehe* **be**
west [west] Westen; nach Westen; westlich III
westbound ['westbaʊnd] Richtung Westen III
western ['westən] westlich, West- III
western ['westən] Western VI 1 (14)
wet [wet] nass III
whale [weɪl] Wal(fisch) V
what [wɒt]
1. was I
2. welche(r, s) I
What about ...? 1. Was ist mit ...? / Und ...? I; **2.** Wie wär's mit ...? I
What are you talking about? Wovon redest du? I • **What colour is ...?** Welche Farbe hat ...? I
What for? Wofür? II • **What have we got next?** Was haben wir als Nächstes? I • **What kind of car ...?** Was für ein Auto ...? III • **What page are we on?** Auf welcher Seite sind wir? I • **What's for homework?** Was haben wir als Hausaufgabe auf? I • **... what's on his mind** ... was ihn beschäftigt / ... was ihm durch den Kopf geht VI 3 (53) • **What's the matter?** Was ist los? / Was ist denn? II • **What's the time?** Wie spät ist es? I
What's your name? Wie heißt du? I • **What's your telephone number?** Was ist deine Telefonnummer? I • **What was the weather like?** Wie war das Wetter? II • **I don't know what to do.** Ich weiß nicht, was ich machen soll. IV
whatever [wɒt'evə] was (auch) immer IV
wheel [wi:l] Rad III • **big wheel** Riesenrad III
wheelchair ['wi:ltʃeə] Rollstuhl I
when [wen] wann I • **When's your birthday?** Wann hast du Geburtstag? I
when [wen]
1. wenn I
2. als I
whenever [wen'evə] wann immer IV
where [weə]
1. wo I
2. wohin I
Where are you from? Wo kommst du her? I
wherever [weər'evə] wo auch immer IV
whether ['weðə] ob VI 1 (9)
which [wɪtʃ]**: Which picture ...?** Welches Bild ...? I • **which way?** in welche Richtung? / wohin? II
which [wɪtʃ] der, die, das; die *(Relativpronomen)* III
while [waɪl] während III
while [waɪl]**: for a while** für eine Weile, eine Zeit lang V
whisky ['wɪski] Whisky II
whisper ['wɪspə] flüstern I
whistle ['wɪsl] pfeifen II
whistle ['wɪsl] (Triller-)Pfeife III

white [waɪt] weiß I
who [huː]
1. wer I
2. wen/wem II
who [huː] der, die, das; die *(Relativpronomen)* III • **Find/Ask somebody who ...** Finde/Frage jemanden, der ... II
whoever [huː'evə] wer auch immer IV
whole [həʊl] ganze(r, s), gesamte(r, s) III
whole-grain ['həʊlgreɪn] Vollkorn- IV
whose [huːz] deren, dessen *(Relativpronomen)* VI 3 (52)
whose? [huːz] wessen? II • **Whose are these?** Wem gehören diese? II **Whose turn is it?** Wer ist dran / an der Reihe? II
why [waɪ] warum I • **that's why** deshalb, darum V • **Why me?** Warum ich? I • **Why not tell her ...?** Warum erzählst/sagst du ihr nicht ...? VI 1 (9) • **Why should I ... ?** Warum sollte ich ... ? III
► S.180 'Why not' + Infinitiv
wide [waɪd] weit, breit IV
wife [waɪf], *pl* **wives** [waɪvz] Ehefrau II
wild [waɪld] wild II
will [wɪl]: **you'll be cold (= you will be cold)** du wirst frieren; ihr werdet frieren II • **you won't be cold** [wəʊnt] **(= you will not be cold)** du wirst nicht frieren; ihr werdet nicht frieren II
win (-nn-) [wɪn], **won, won** gewinnen I
win [wɪn] Sieg III
wind [wɪnd] Wind I
window ['wɪndəʊ] Fenster I
windproof ['wɪndpruːf] winddicht V
windy ['wɪndi] windig I
wine [waɪn] Wein IV
wing [wɪŋ] Flügel IV
winner ['wɪnə] Gewinner/in, Sieger/in II
winter ['wɪntə] Winter I
°**wish** [wɪʃ] wünschen
wish [wɪʃ] Wunsch VI 3 (47) • **Best wishes** *etwa:* Alles Gute / Mit besten Grüßen *(als Briefschluss)* IV
with [wɪð]
1. mit I
2. bei I
be with sb. mit jemandem zusammen sein IV • **go with** gehören zu, passen zu III • **Sit with me.** Setz dich zu mir. / Setzt euch zu mir. I
without [wɪ'ðaʊt] ohne I

witness ['wɪtnəs] Zeuge/Zeugin V
wives [waɪvz] *Plural von „wife"*
woke [wəʊk] *siehe* **wake**
woken ['wəʊkən] *siehe* **wake**
wolf [wʊlf], *pl* **wolves** [wʊlvz] Wolf II
woman ['wʊmən], *pl* **women** ['wɪmɪn] Frau I
won [wʌn] *siehe* **win**
wonder ['wʌndə] sich fragen, gern wissen wollen II
won't [wəʊnt]: **you won't be cold (= you will not be cold)** du wirst nicht frieren; ihr werdet nicht frieren II
wood [wʊd] Holz III
woodpecker ['wʊdpekə] Specht II
woods *(pl)* [wʊdz] Wald, Wälder III
word [wɜːd] Wort I • **Can I have a word with you?** Kann ich mal kurz mit dir reden? VI 3 (55)
word building ['wɜːd bɪldɪŋ] Wortbildung II
°**word order** ['wɜːd‿ɔːdə] Wortstellung
wore [wɔː] *siehe* **wear**
work [wɜːk]
1. arbeiten I
2. funktionieren III
work hard hart arbeiten II • **work long hours** lange arbeiten V
work on sth. an etwas arbeiten I
work out gut ausgehen IV
work sth. out etwas herausarbeiten, herausfinden IV • °**work sth. through** etwas durcharbeiten
work [wɜːk] Arbeit I • **at work** bei der Arbeit / am Arbeitsplatz I
work experience *(no pl)* Praktikum; Arbeits-, Praxiserfahrung(en) V • **do work experience** ein Praktikum machen V
worker ['wɜːkə] Arbeiter/in II
office worker ['ɒfɪs wɜːkə] Büroangestellte(r) V
workplace ['wɜːkpleɪs] Arbeitsplatz IV
worksheet ['wɜːkʃiːt] Arbeitsblatt I
workshop ['wɜːkʃɒp] Workshop, Lehrgang III
world [wɜːld] Welt I • **all over the world** auf der ganzen Welt III
from all over the world aus der ganzen Welt III • **in the world** (auf) der Welt IV
worn [wɔːn] *siehe* **wear**
worried (about) ['wʌrid] beunruhigt (wegen), besorgt (wegen/um) IV
worry ['wʌri] Sorge, Kummer II
No worries. *(infml)* Kein Problem! / Ist schon in Ordnung! VI 3 (55)

worry (about) ['wʌri] sich Sorgen machen (wegen, um) I • **Don't worry.** Mach dir keine Sorgen. I
worrying ['wʌriɪŋ] beunruhigend, sorgenvoll V
worse [wɜːs] schlechter, schlimmer II
worst [wɜːst]: **(the) worst** am schlechtesten, schlimmsten; der/die/das schlechteste, schlimmste II
would [wəd, wʊd]: **I/you/... would ...** ich würde / du würdest / ... III • **I'd like ... (= I would like ...)** Ich hätte gern ... / Ich möchte gern ... I
Would you like ...? Möchtest du ...? / Möchten Sie ...? I • **Would you like some?** Möchtest du etwas/ein paar? / Möchten Sie etwas/ein paar? I • **I'd like to talk about ... (= I would like to talk about ...)** Ich möchte über ... reden / Ich würde gern über ... reden I
write [raɪt], **wrote, written** schreiben I • **write down** aufschreiben I • **write to** schreiben an I
writer ['raɪtə] Schreiber/in; Schriftsteller/in II
written ['rɪtn] *siehe* **write**
written discussion [ˌrɪtn dɪ'skʌʃn] Erörterung VI 2 (37)
wrong [rɒŋ] falsch, verkehrt I
be wrong 1. falsch sein I; 2. sich irren, Unrecht haben II • **the wrong way** in die falsche Richtung II
wrote [rəʊt] *siehe* **write**

X

°**xenophobic** [ˌzenə'fəʊbɪk] fremdenfeindlich

Y

yard [jɑːd] Hof II • **in the yard** auf dem Hof II
yawn [jɔːn] gähnen II
year [jɪə]
1. Jahr I
2. Jahrgangsstufe I
a sixteen-year-old ein/e Sechzehnjährige/r III • **a sixteen-year-old girl** ein sechzehnjähriges Mädchen III
yellow ['jeləʊ] gelb I
yes [jes] ja I
yesterday ['jestədeɪ, 'jestədi] gestern I • **yesterday morning/afternoon/evening** gestern Morgen/

Nachmittag/Abend I • **yesterday's homework** die Hausaufgaben von gestern II
yet [jet]**: not (...) yet** noch nicht II
yet? schon? II
yoga ['jəʊgə] Yoga I
you [juː]
1. du; Sie I
2. ihr I • **you two** ihr zwei I
3. dir; dich; euch I
4. man III
young [jʌŋ] jung I
your [jɔː]
1. dein/e I
2. Ihr I
3. euer/eure I
yours [jɔːz]
1. deiner, deine, deins II
2. Ihrer, Ihre, Ihrs II
3. eurer, eure, eures II
yourself [jɔː'self] dir/dich (selbst) III
yourselves [jɔː'selvz] euch (selbst) III
youth [juːθ] Jugend, Jugend- III
youth group Jugendgruppe IV
youth hostel Jugendherberge III
yuck [jʌk] igitt III

Z

zebra ['zebrə] Zebra II
zero ['zɪərəʊ] null I
zone [zəʊn] Zone, Gebiet IV
zoo [zuː] Zoo IV

First names
(Vornamen)

Abraham ['eɪbrəhæm]
Adisa [ə'di:sə]
Adrian ['eɪdriən]
Afra ['æfrə]
Alex ['ælɪks]
Alexis [ə'leksɪs]
Ally ['æli]
Amy ['eɪmi]
Andrew ['ændru:]
Arnie ['ɑ:ni]
Arnold ['ɑ:nəld]
Barry ['bæri]
Baz, Bazza [bæz], ['bæzə]
Becky ['beki]
Belinda ['bə'lɪndə]
Bella ['belə]
Bex [beks]
Brad [bræd]
Cate [keɪt]
Celia ['si:liə]
Charlie ['tʃɑ:li]
Chaz [tʃæz]
Chris [krɪs]
Dani ['dæni]
Daniel ['dænjəl]
David ['deɪvɪd]
Davina [də'vi:nə]
Dayamayee [ˌdaɪəmaɪ'i:]
Denny ['deni]
Diana [daɪ'ænə]
Dizzy ['dɪzi]
Dustin ['dʌstɪn]
Earl [3:l]
Edward ['edwəd]
Elizabeth [i'lɪzəbəθ]
Ella ['elə]
Fay [feɪ]
Felice [fə'li:s]
Gary ['gæri]
George [dʒɔ:dʒ]
Hailey ['heɪli]
Hanif ['hænɪf]
Harita [hə'ri:tə]
Helen ['helən]
Holly ['hɒli]
Jake [dʒeɪk]
James [dʒeɪmz]
Jane [dʒeɪn]
Jay [dʒeɪ]
Jérôme [dʒə'rəʊm]
Jess [dʒes]
Jill [dʒɪl]
Joseph ['dʒəʊzɪf]
Josh [dʒɒʃ]
Julia ['dʒu:liə]
Julian ['dʒu:liən]
Julie ['dʒu:li]
Juno ['dʒu:nəʊ]
Kate [keɪt]
Katy ['keɪti]
Kristen ['krɪstən]
Laura ['lɔ:rə]
Laurie ['lɒri]
Layla ['leɪlə]
Leo ['li:əʊ]
Lucy ['lu:si]
Maggie ['mægi]
Marc [mɑ:k]
Maria [mə'ri:ə]
Martin ['mɑ:tɪn]
Matty ['mæti]
Mel [mel]
Melinda [mə'lɪndə]
Michael ['maɪkəl]
Mike [maɪk]
Minty ['mɪnti]
Morpheus ['mɔ:fiəs]
Morris ['mɒrɪs]
Murat [mu:'rɑ:t]
Nadia ['nɑ:diə]
Nat [næt]
Neil [ni:l]
Neo ['ni:əʊ]
Nikki ['nɪki]
Oliver ['ɒlɪvə]
Paris ['pærɪs]
Parminder [pɑ:'mɪndə]
Patricia [pə'trɪʃə]
Paulie ['pɔ:li]
Penelope [pə'neləpi]
Petra ['petrə]
Phil [fɪl]
Philip ['fɪlɪp]
Rebecca [ri'bekə]
Reg [redʒ]
Robert ['rɒbət]
Roger ['rɒdʒə]
Rose [rəʊz]
Ruby ['ru:bi]
Saci ['sæʃi]
Sarah ['seərə]
Sean [ʃɔ:n]
Seb [seb]
Sharon ['ʃærən]
Sherman ['ʃ3:mən]
Stephenie ['stefəni]
Sue [su:]
Tasha ['tæʃə]
Tina ['ti:nə]
Toby ['təʊbi]
Tony ['təʊni]
Tyler ['taɪlə]
Wendy ['wendi]
Zooey ['zəʊi]

Family names
(Familiennamen)

Alexie [ə'leksi]
Beckham ['bekəm]
Blair [bleə]
Blanchett ['blɑ:ntʃɪt]
Bleaker ['bli:kə]
Boateng ['bwɑ:teŋ]
Broun [braʊn]
Clooney ['klu:ni]
Dee [di:]
Deschanel [ˌdeɪʃə'nel]
Ford [fɔ:d]
Gordon-Levitt [ˌgɔ:dn 'levɪt]
Halse Anderson [ˌhæls_'ændəsən]
Kennedy ['kenədi]
Lincoln ['lɪŋkən]
Livingstone ['lɪvɪŋstən]
Lloyd [lɔɪd]
Martin ['mɑ:tɪn]
McBeath [mək'bi:θ]
McCormick [mə'kɔ:mɪk]
Meyer ['maɪə]
Minton ['mɪntən]
Mitchell ['mɪtʃəl]
Munslow ['mʌnsləʊ]
Nagra ['nɑ:grə]
Neck [nek]
Nutt [nʌt]
Parker ['pɑ:kə]
Patel [pə'tel]
Pattinson ['pætɪnsən]
Petrakis [pə'trɑ:kɪs]
Pitt [pɪt]
Presley ['presli], ['prezli]
Pym [pɪm]
Roberts ['rɒbəts]
Sandburg ['sændb3:g]
Shrimpton ['ʃrɪmptən]
Smith [smɪθ]
Stewart ['stju:ət]
Thompson ['tɒmpsən]
Webber ['webə]
Wilde [waɪld]

Place names
(Ortsnamen)

Banff [bænf]
Bavaria [bə'veəriə] *Bayern*
Birmingham ['b3:mɪŋəm]
Brighton ['braɪtn]
Bristol ['brɪstl]
Broughton ['brɔ:tn]
Cambridge ['keɪmbrɪdʒ]
Cape Breton [ˌkeɪp 'bretɒn]
Cardiff ['kɑ:dɪf]
Cashel ['kæʃl]
Chicago [ʃɪ'kɑ:gəʊ]
Colorado [ˌkɒlə'rɑ:dəʊ]
Delhi ['deli]
Edinburgh ['edɪnbərə]
Fort William [ˌfɔ:t 'wɪljəm]
Glasgow ['glɑ:zgəʊ]
Hallow Road [ˌhæləʊ 'rəʊd]
Hamilton ['hæmltən]
Helsinki [hel'sɪŋki]
Hexham ['heksəm]
Hobart ['həʊbɑ:t]
Holborn ['həʊbən]
Hove [həʊv]
Iveragh Peninsula [ˌaɪvrə pə'nɪnsjʊlə]
Launceston ['lɒnsəstən]
Liverpool ['lɪvəpu:l]
London ['lʌndən]
Malaga ['mæləgə]
Manchester ['mæntʃɪstə]
Marineland [mə'ri:nlənd]
Marseille [mɑ:'seɪ]
Melbourne ['melbən]
Michigan ['mɪʃɪgən]
Mt. Cameron [ˌmaʊnt 'kæmrən]
Niagara Falls [naɪˌægərə 'fɔ:lz]
Norfolk Broads [ˌnɔ:fək 'brɔ:dz]
Norwich ['nɒrɪdʒ]
Nova Scotia [ˌnəʊvə 'skəʊʃə]
Ontario [ɒn'teəriəʊ]
Ottawa ['ɒtəwə]
Oxford ['ɒksfəd]
Peterborough ['pi:təbərə]
Piccadilly [ˌpɪkə'dɪli]
Rearden ['rɪədn]
Spokane [spəʊ'kæn]
St Pauls [sənt 'pɔ:lz]
Stranraer [stræn'rɑ:]
Sydney ['sɪdni]
Tianjin [tiˌæn'dʒɪn]
Toronto [tə'rɒntəʊ]
Toulouse [tu:'lu:z]
Venice ['venɪs] *Venedig*
Victoria [vɪk'tɔ:riə]
Washington ['wɒʃɪŋtən]
Wellington ['welɪŋtən]
Wellpinit ['welpɪnɪt]

Other names
(Andere Namen)

Arsenal ['ɑ:snəl]
Aviator ['eɪvieɪtə]
Beluga [bə'lu:gə]
Boeing ['bəʊɪŋ]
Celtic Tiger [ˌkeltɪk 'taɪgə]
Galadriel [gə'lɑ:driəl]
Matrix ['meɪtrɪks]
Meatrix ['mi:trɪks]
Moopheus ['mu:fiəs]
Titanic [taɪ'tænɪk]
Vatican ['vætɪkən]
Volpi Cup ['vɒlpi kʌp]

Country/Continent	Adjective	Person	People
Africa ['æfrɪkə] *Afrika*	African ['æfrɪkən]	an African	the Africans
America [ə'merɪkə] *Amerika*	American [ə'merɪkən]	an American	the Americans
Asia ['eɪʃə, 'eɪʒə] *Asien*	Asian ['eɪʃn, 'eɪʒn]	an Asian	the Asians
Australia [ɒ'streɪliə] *Australien*	Australian [ɒ'streɪliən]	an Australian	the Australians
Austria ['ɒstriə] *Österreich*	Austrian ['ɒstriən]	an Austrian	the Austrians
Belgium ['beldʒəm] *Belgien*	Belgian ['beldʒən]	a Belgian	the Belgians
Canada ['kænədə] *Kanada*	Canadian [kə'neɪdiən]	a Canadian	the Canadians
China ['tʃaɪnə] *China*	Chinese [ˌtʃaɪ'ni:z]	a Chinese	the Chinese
Croatia [krəʊ'eɪʃə] *Kroatien*	Croatian [krəʊ'eɪʃn]	a Croatian	the Croatians
the Czech Republic [ˌtʃek rɪ'pʌblɪk] *Tschechien, die Tschechische Republik*	Czech [tʃek]	a Czech	the Czechs
Denmark ['denmɑ:k] *Dänemark*	Danish ['deɪnɪʃ]	a Dane [deɪn]	the Danes
Egypt ['i:dʒɪpt] *Ägypten*	Egyptian [i'dʒɪpʃn]	an Egyptian	the Egyptians
England ['ɪŋglənd] *England*	English ['ɪŋglɪʃ]	an Englishman/-woman	the English
Europe ['jʊərəp] *Europa*	European [ˌjʊərə'pi:ən]	a European	the Europeans
Finland ['fɪnlənd] *Finnland*	Finnish ['fɪnɪʃ]	a Finn [fɪn]	the Finns
France [frɑ:ns] *Frankreich*	French [frentʃ]	a Frenchman/-woman	the French
Germany ['dʒɜ:məni] *Deutschland*	German ['dʒɜ:mən]	a German	the Germans
(Great) Britain ['brɪtn] *Großbritannien*	British ['brɪtɪʃ]	a Briton ['brɪtn]	the British
Greece [gri:s] *Griechenland*	Greek [gri:k]	a Greek	the Greeks
Holland ['hɒlənd] *Holland, die Niederlande*	Dutch [dʌtʃ]	a Dutchman/-woman	the Dutch
Hungary ['hʌŋgəri] *Ungarn*	Hungarian [hʌŋ'geəriən]	a Hungarian	the Hungarians
India ['ɪndiə] *Indien*	Indian ['ɪndiən]	an Indian	the Indians
Ireland ['aɪələnd] *Irland*	Irish ['aɪrɪʃ]	an Irishman/-woman	the Irish
Italy ['ɪtəli] *Italien*	Italian [ɪ'tæliən]	an Italian	the Italians
Japan [dʒə'pæn] *Japan*	Japanese [ˌdʒæpə'ni:z]	a Japanese	the Japanese
Malaysia [mə'leɪʒə, mə'leɪziə] *Malaysia*	Malaysian [mə'leɪʒn, mə'leɪziən]	a Malaysian	the Malaysians
the Netherlands ['neðələndz] *die Niederlande, Holland*	Dutch [dʌtʃ]	a Dutchman/-woman	the Dutch
New Zealand [ˌnju: 'zi:lənd] *Neuseeland*	New Zealand [ˌnju: 'zi:lənd]	a New Zealander	the New Zealanders
Nigeria [naɪ'dʒɪəriə] *Nigeria*	Nigerian [naɪ'dʒɪəriən]	a Nigerian	the Nigerians
Norway ['nɔ:weɪ] *Norwegen*	Norwegian [nɔ:'wi:dʒən]	a Norwegian	the Norwegians
Pakistan [ˌpækɪ'stæn, ˌpɑ:kɪ'stɑ:n] *Pakistan*	Pakistani [ˌpækɪ'stæni, ˌpɑ:kɪ'stɑ:ni]	a Pakistani	the Pakistanis
the Philippines ['fɪlɪpi:nz] *die Philippinen*	Philippine ['fɪlɪpi:n]	a Filipino [ˌfɪlɪ'pi:nəʊ]/ Filipina [ˌfɪlɪ'pi:nə]	the Filipinos/ Filipinas
Poland ['pəʊlənd] *Polen*	Polish ['pəʊlɪʃ]	a Pole [pəʊl]	the Poles
Portugal ['pɔ:tʃʊgl] *Portugal*	Portuguese [ˌpɔ:tʃu'gi:z]	a Portuguese	the Portuguese
Russia ['rʌʃə] *Russland*	Russian ['rʌʃn]	a Russian	the Russians
Scotland ['skɒtlənd] *Schottland*	Scottish ['skɒtɪʃ]	a Scotsman/-woman, a Scot [skɒt]	the Scots, the Scottish
Slovakia [sləʊ'vɑ:kiə, sləʊ'vækiə] *die Slowakei*	Slovak ['sləʊvæk]	a Slovak	the Slovaks
Slovenia [sləʊ'vi:niə] *Slowenien*	Slovenian [sləʊ'vi:niən], Slovene ['sləʊvi:n]	a Slovene, a Slovenian	the Slovenes, the Slovenians
Spain [speɪn] *Spanien*	Spanish ['spænɪʃ]	a Spaniard ['spænɪəd]	the Spaniards
Sweden ['swi:dn] *Schweden*	Swedish ['swi:dɪʃ]	a Swede [swi:d]	the Swedes
Switzerland ['swɪtsələnd] *die Schweiz*	Swiss [swɪs]	a Swiss	the Swiss
Tanzania [ˌtænzə'ni:ə] *Tansania*	Tanzanian [ˌtænzə'ni:ən]	a Tanzanian	the Tanzanians
Turkey ['tɜ:ki] *die Türkei*	Turkish ['tɜ:kɪʃ]	a Turk [tɜ:k]	the Turks
the United Kingdom (the UK) [juˌnaɪtɪd 'kɪŋdəm, ju:'keɪ] *das Vereinigte Königreich (Großbritannien und Nordirland)*	British ['brɪtɪʃ]	a Briton ['brɪtn]	the British
the United States of America (the USA) [juˌnaɪtɪd ˌsteɪts_əv_ə'merɪkə, ˌju:_es_'eɪ] *die Vereinigten Staaten von Amerika*	American [ə'merɪkən]	an American	the Americans
Wales [weɪlz] *Wales*	Welsh [welʃ]	a Welshman/-woman	the Welsh

Getting ready for a test 1 Revision ▸ pp. 20–23

1 A holiday by the sea is more exciting ▸ p. 20

1. I think that ... is more/less exciting than ...
2. In my opinion ... is/isn't as comfortable as ...
3. ... is/isn't as cool as ...
4. ... are more/less crowded than ...
5. ... is more/less expensive than ...
6. ... is more/less interesting than ...
7. ... is/isn't as exciting as ...

2 SPEAKING Making holiday plans ▸ p. 20

1	B	4	G	7	E
2	D	5	F	8	I
3	C	6	A	9	H

3 SPEAKING Likes and dislikes ▸ p. 20

(individual answers)

4 WORDS A teenage magazine ▸ p. 21

a) cinema & TV: channel, cable, presenter, plot, cartoon, prime time, repeat (n.), scene, ... • sport: active, athletics, competition, exercise, pitch, train, ... • health: fruit, healthy food, vegetables, menu, whole-grain, ... • music: concert, sound file, label, recommend, release, lyrics, playlist, ... • books: comic, novel, plot, release, writer, recommend, ... • computer: menu, link, cable, install, save, surf the internet, ...

b) 1 exercise
2 active
3 released
4 install
5 repeat
6 concert

5 WORDS Talking about religions ▸ p. 21

a) 1 English
2 cathedral
3 palace
4 technician
5 bell
6 believe

b) 1 Muslim
2 Protestant
3 synagogue
4 priest
5 bell
6 believe

6 WORDS The world of soap opera ▸ p. 22

a) 1 father
2 uncle
3 granddaughter
4 wife
5 lover
6 ex-husband

b) 1 divorced
2 love
3 relationship
4 baby
5 father
6 single

7 Are you fit and healthy? ▸ p. 22

a) 1 Do you live a healthy life?
2 Do you play any sport in your free time?
3 How often do you train every week?
4 Do you go to school by bike?
5 Is the food that you eat healthy?
6 How many meals do you have every day?
7 What do you usually have for breakfast?
8 How often do you eat fresh fruit and vegetables?
9 Do you get enough sleep every night?
10 What else do you do to stay fit and healthy?

b) (individual answers)

c) (individual answers)

d) (individual answers)

8 Being a teenage mum is not easy ▸ p. 23

a) -------------

b) 1 Rebecca got pregnant because she sometimes forgot to take the pill.
2 When she told her parents that she was pregnant they were really upset.
3 Rebecca lives alone with her son because her boyfriend left them to live his own life.
4 Rebecca thinks you shouldn't be a mum at 16 because you have to grow up quickly and a baby isn't always sweet.
5 In the future, Rebecca wants to go back and finish school.
6 Rebecca wants help from her parents because it will be hard to study and be a mum at the same time.
7 Maria thinks Rebecca should talk to her parents about her plans for the future.
8 Maria thinks that Rebecca's parents will try and help her when they see how much Rebecca has grown up.

9 SPEAKING Giving your opinion ▸ p. 23

a) (individual dialogues)

b) (individual answers)

Getting ready for a test 1 Practice test ▸ pp. 24–26

1 LISTENING What can we do this weekend? ▸ p. 24

a) B

b)

Helen's ideas	Tina's reaction
– go to the theatre	– boring; wants sth. more modern
– play new computer game	– not interested in computers
– each stay at home and listen to music	– wants to do sth. with Helen
– listen to music and watch TV together	– only repeats on TV on Saturday evening
– watch 'Strictly Come Dancing'	– no more dancing films please
– watch 'The Breakfast Club'	– seen it hundreds of times

2 SPEAKING Holidays plans ▸ p. 24

(individual answers)

3 LISTENING Living together ▸ p. 25

1 D 3 D 5 D
2 C 4 A 6 C

4 LISTENING Radio adverts ▸ p. 25

a) 1: true, 2: false

b) 3: false, 4: true

c) 5: true, 6: false

5 SPEAKING Too young to be a mum? ▸ p. 26

(model answer)

1 I can see two teenage girls. The girl in the first picture is pregnant and she is on her own. She is looking quite serious. In the second picture there is a young girl with a baby on her knees. She is looking down at her child but she isn't smiling.
2 I don't think the girls in the photos are very happy. They aren't smiling and might be thinking about the problems they have as a teenage mum. Maybe they had to leave school or their boyfriends broke up with them. They probably can't get a job or go out in the evenings like their friends can because they have to look after their babies.
3 It must have been a shock when their friends and families heard the news. Nobody expects teenagers to become pregnant; especially when they haven't finished school yet.
4 Teenagers usually don't have to worry about anyone except themselves, but teenage parents have to look after a baby too. They cannot go out and meet friends. Teenage mothers especially may not be able to go to school and get an education just as easily as their friends can because they first have to find someone who looks after their baby when they're at school.
5 The baby's father should do just as much as the mother, for example look after the child and try to help with money for the baby's food, clothes, etc.
6 I think there is no "best" age to have a baby, but maybe one should have finished school first and at least one of the parents should have a job.

6 PRESENTATION My lifestyle ▸ p. 26

(individual answers)

Getting ready for a test 2 Revision ▸ pp. 38–41

1 WORDS Travel ▸ p. 38

a) air: airport, flight, plane, gate, (to) land, … • railway: platform, train, the Tube, underground, … • road: cab, (to) cycle, (to) drive, motorway, petrol station, rush hour, traffic jam, truck, … • sea: ferry, boat, harbour, ship, …

b)
1 went
2 picked
3 travel
4 broke down
5 drive
6 ask

2 London's underground ▸ p. 38

1 opened
2 was
3 have been added
4 were pulled
5 came
6 travelled
7 has risen
8 appeared

3 Transport in London ▸ p. 38

1 I always try to sit at the top so I can enjoy the view.
2 I was in a terrible traffic jam yesterday. It took one hour to drive from Piccadilly to Tower Bridge! I don't think that I'll go into London by car again.
3 I want to reduce my carbon footprint, so I sold my car a long time ago.
4 When I got to the stop, the last bus had left early.
5 My husband and I always use the Tube on Saturdays when we go shopping.

4 WORDS After the accident ▸ p. 39

1 unconscious
2 operations
3 alcohol
4 drunk
5 healthy
6 hurts
7 headache
8 threw up
9 sweat
10 ambulance

5 Reporting what people said ▸ p. 39

1 He told me (that) I had had an accident.
2 He said (that) Julie was still unconscious.
3 He added (that) we had to have an operation.
4 He asked if we had drunk any alcohol before the accident.
5 He asked if I and Julie had had a cold recently.
6 He wanted to know if we felt any pain.
7 He told me (that) I had thrown up after the accident.

6 STUDY SKILLS Writing ▸ p. 39

1 *F* 23-year-old truck driver (who)
2 *D* one of the worst accidents (what)
3 *A* driving at over 80 miles per hour (why/how)
4 *B* when broken glass flew into it (how/why)
5 *C* in the late afternoon rush hour (when)
6 *E* St Pauls and Eastville Park (where)

7 WORDS For a greener world ▸ p. 40

a)
1 sun
2 oil
3 waste
4 pollute
5 solar power
6 trees

b)
1 c
2 a
3 g
4 f
5 h
6 d

8 Our green holiday ▸ p. 40

1 So did you enjoy your holiday?
2 Where did you stay?
3 How did you find out about it?
4 So what was special about it?
5 And was it organic food?
6 Anyway, what else did you do?
7 How far was it? And did you have good weather?

9 Ben's blog ▸ p. 41

1 I did not/didn't take the bus.
2 Unfortunately, they did not/didn't have any.
3 I did not/didn't choose the big, red apples from Italy.
4 I was not/wasn't allowed to buy organic eggs.
5 Could not/couldn't find a second-hand clothes shop that was open!
6 I just was not/wasn't able to find one made in this country.

10 WRITING A written discussion ▸ p. 41

a) B, D, A, C

b) Introduction: You often hear people say ... / So the question is ... / ...

Arguments: On the one hand ... / On the other hand ... / First ... / Second ... / ...
Conclusion: After looking at both sides / ...

c) (individual answers)

Getting ready for a test 2 Practice test ▸ pp. 42–44

1 LANGUAGE Congestion charge ▸ p. 42

1	B	5	B	9	A
2	A	6	C	10	A
3	A	7	C	11	C
4	C	8	B	12	A

2 WRITING A visit to the doctor's ▸ p. 43

a) (model answer)

(1) I was cycling home yesterday and suddenly a dog ran out in front of me and I fell off my bike.
(2) Yes, I do. In my left arm. It hurts really badly. It's so bad that I wasn't able to sleep last night.
(3) Yes, I've got a terrible headache, and I've also got stomach ache.
(4) Well, I'm a bit embarrassed about this, but I ... well, I threw up in the middle of the road.
(5) Yes, I did. And cold too. I was so cold that I was shivering.
(6) So what about my arm. Is it broken or not?
(7) School tomorrow – are you sure? OK. Bye. And thank you.

b) (individual answers)

3 WRITING A report ▸ p. 43

(individual answers)

4 WRITING A shopping survey ▸ p. 44

(model answers)

1 I usually help to write our family shopping list because it helps my mum to remember what to buy. Another advantage is that I can decide or at least suggest what I'd like to eat.

2 I think it is a good thing to buy organic food as one can be sure that it is healthier.
A disadvantage of organic food, however, is that it can be quite expensive.

3 I think eating more vegetables is healthy because they contain many vitamins. Also, the production of vegetables causes less CO_2 than the production of meat.

4 Buying recycled paper sounds like a good idea because it takes lots of trees to produce new paper and that destroys the forests.

5 Yes, I use plastic bags more than once because I don't want to waste them. They are fine even when you use them a second or third time.

6 I sometimes buy clothes at second hand shops or flea markets if they're of good quality. Also, it's fun because you can find interesting things if you're lucky.

5 WRITING A letter to a newspaper ▸ p. 44

(model answer)

I would like to comment on the article 'Child slaves work for western fashion companies'. I have to say that I was shocked when I read it. It makes me sad when I think about children who have to work under these conditions – instead of going to school or having free time! Here in the western world all that children have to do is go to school. I think working is really bad for children and that children in developing countries often are not given the chance to get a good education. Children should not have to work anywhere in the world. To help them, we, the customers in western countries should boycott products from companies that use children for the production of their clothes.

6 WRITING Opinions ▸ p. 44

(individual answers)

Getting ready for a test 3 Revision ► pp. 56–58

1 WORDS Getting involved ► p. 56

1 protest
2 speech
3 have
4 part
5 start
6 raise
7 volunteered
8 march
9 vote

2 READING Which event? ► p. 56

(model answers)

a) I'd choose RSPCA Volunteer Information Day for Lily because she doesn't have much money, and if she becomes a volunteer she can help animals in trouble by looking after them instead of spending money on them.

b) Ella should go to 'Queen's Park project week' because there she can practise her garden skills. When the work is done she can even go hiking in the beautiful park that she helped to create.
If I was Adam I would choose Event 1 'Film and discussion', because he is interested in global warming and the documentary is about climate change.

3 Are you going to work in the holidays? ► p. 57

a)
1 Are you going to work in the holidays?
2 ... I am / I'm going to look for a job.
3 ... Sam and I are going to work in Mum's shop.
4 Yeah, but we're / we are not going to do it for the whole holidays.
5 And after that we are / we're going to spend a week with Dad in London.
6 And is he going to show you all the sights?
7 But he is / he's not going to spend too much time with us – I hope!
8 What kind of job are you going to look for?
9 I am / I'm not going to work in a shop or anywhere inside.

b) (individual dialogues)

4 WORDS Paraphrasing ► p. 57

1 e Partei *(party)*
2 f Untertitel *(subtitle)*
3 b Abgeordnete/r *(MP)*
4 d TV-Gastgeber/in *(chat-show host)*
5 c Ziel *(goal)*
6 a Wirtschaft *(economy)*

5 EVERYDAY ENGLISH Making suggestions ► p. 57

a)
1 B
2 A
3 A
4 B
5 B
6 B

b) (model answer)
After lunch you could watch a film at the cinema right next to the Italian restaurant. Why don't you phone the cinema for the film times? After the film we could meet in the café on the other side of the street. I suggest that I pick you up on my way home. If I were you, I'd order a café crema while you wait there.

6 WORDS Politics ► p. 58

1 elect
2 citizen
3 responsibility
4 discriminates against
5 the majority
6 illegal
7 criticize

7 READING What does it mean? ► p. 58

a) (model answer)
1 opposition, maximum, region, conference
2 popularity, collection
3 permitted, sit

c) (individual answers)

Getting ready for a test 3 Practice test ▸ pp. 59–62

1 READING Events ▸ p. 59

Jill E; Megan A; Sally D; Ben B; Ethan C

2 MEDIATION An advertisement ▸ p. 60

1. Arbeit in einem internationalen Jugendcamp, Wohnen im Dorf mit Jugendlichen aus aller Welt
2. Hauptsächlich Organisation des Tages- und Abendprogramms für die Jugendlichen
3. Man sollten zwischen 17 und 20 Jahre alt sein und gut mit Jugendlichen umgehen können; man sollte organisiert sein und gut im Team arbeiten.
4. 25 Pfund Taschengeld pro Woche
5. Übernahme der Reisekosten, kostenlose Unterkunft und Verpflegung (Frühstück und zwei warme Mahlzeiten)

3 MEDIATION Helping a visitor to Germany ▸ p. 60

(model answer)
You could go to the youth club in *Böllstraße*, where they're going to show a DVD about German politics. They are going to explain the goals of the most important political parties or give information about different areas of politics. The film is illustrated by cartoons and funny drawings and it has English subtitles. It starts at 7.30 pm and takes about 45 minutes. There's going to be a discussion and some live music afterwards.
You could also go to a live talk show where MPs from different European countries are going to discuss Europe's future. The talk starts at 6.30 pm and will be over at about 8 pm and it's at the *Fernsehzentrum Köln*. The whole discussion is going to be translated into English.

4 READING Notices, short ads and signs ▸ p. 61

1	false	5	true	9	false
2	false	6	false	10	false
3	true	7	true	11	true
4	false	8	true	12	false

5 READING A news report ▸ p. 62

1. A false B false C true D not in the text
2. A
3. B
4. A For Will Black, free recycling at all schools is very important, so that schools would have a reason to recycle as much as possible.
   B Barbara McKenzie cares about cheaper tickets for public transport for young people and wants young people to pay only half of what adults pay.
   C Jack Smith would like more places for young people, for example for music concerts.
5. (model answer)
   This statement is false because the text says that this year's main sitting of Youth Parliament will be held at the University of Ulster in Northern Ireland. However, there will probably be a sitting in the House of Commons sometime during the year.

Unit 2 Part A

1 Inventions that changed the world ► Unit 2, Part A (p. 30)

One of these inventions is actually a joke! Can you guess which one it is? Here is the answer:

The last invention (number 10) is a joke. (Did you notice that the date on the article was 1st April?) The Language Mediator hasn't been invented yet – so your language teacher's job is safe for now! But scientists in America are trying to develop one which can be used by the army.

Unit 3 Lead-in

1 What's the right age? ► Unit 3, Part A (p. 48)

Ages for Germany:	
get married:	18
drive a car (on your own):	18 (in Begleitung eines Erwachsenen:17)
vote in an election:	18 (bei Kommunalwahlen in vielen 16) Bundesländern:
buy cigarettes	18
buy alcohol	16 (Bier,Wein) bzw. 18 (Schnaps, Liköre, Alkopops)
leave home	18

Unit 3 Lead-in

5 How much do you care? ▸ Unit 3, Lead-in (p. 47)

QUIZ

a) Calculate your score.

1:	A = 2	B = 3	C = 1
2:	A = 1	B = 3	C = 2
3:	A = 2	B = 1	C = 3
4:	A = 1	B = 2	C = 3
5:	A = 2	B = 3	C = 1
6:	A = 2	B = 1	C = 3
7:	A = 3	B = 2	C = 1

b) Read your result.

17–21 points

Wow! No one cares more than you, right? A fair world, human rights, peace – all these things are really important to you. If you think something is unfair, you speak out and you work hard to change things.
That's impressive! You have your own opinions and you want everyone to agree with you. Hmm, just a minute! We're not saying you're bossy, but ... Our advice to you: It's great that you care so much, but remember that it's important to listen to other people too. If you want to change someone's opinion, you can't just shout: 'How stupid. You can't possibly believe that!' You might be more successful if you say in a calm way: 'That's an interesting argument. I see what you mean, but ...' Try it!

12–16 points

You care a lot and you try to do as much as you can to make the world a better place. Like most people, you know that you probably could do more. But sometimes you think: 'The problems in the world are just too big and I am too small. I can't change the world.' Our advice to you: Remember that it's always just one person or one small group that changes the world. If you don't like something, it's important to speak out. You don't have to be a politician or the boss of a big company. The things you say and the actions that you take can make a difference!

7–11 points

You probably think you already know what your result says. You've heard it a million times: Young people are lazy ... they only think about themselves ... they're not interested ... they just don't care. Is it true? We don't think so. Actually, you're just a normal teenager! You care about lots of things: sport, fashion, friends, family, music, going out, having fun. Of course you want the world to be a better place, but you think no one listens to your generation. Our advice to you: Remember it's your world too. Have your say when things happen that you don't like! Next time you think something is important, speak out and get involved. If you do, you will probably find life is more interesting than you thought.

Illustrationen

Silke Bachmann, Hamburg (S. 52; 111 TF 5 (u. 125)); **Roland Beier**, Berlin (S. 32; 36 2. v. oben re.; 54; 81; 83; 107; 132; 133; 135; 137; 138; 140; 141 oben; 142; 144 unten; 147–189); **Carlos Borrell**, Berlin (Umschlaginnenseite 2); **Gareth Evans**, Berlin (S. 73 oben, unten li. (u. 139 unten)); **Dylan Gibson**, Pitlochry (S. 55; 111 TF1 (u. 116)); **Karin Mall**, Berlin (S. 29 Mitte; 72 (u. 139 oben u. Mitte); 73 Mitte re., unten re.); **Alfred Schüssler**, Frankfurt/Main (S. 48; 49; 51 unten; 75)

Bildquellen

action press, Hamburg (S. 122 unten re.: REX FEATURES LTD.); **Alamy**, Abingdon (Inhaltsverz. (u. 28 (M) mobile charger): Chas Spradbery (RF), Inhaltsverz. Juno film still re. (u. 13): PHOTOS 12, Inhaltsverz. (u. 46 Bild D): David Levenson; S. 7 oben lesbian couple: Image Source Pink (RF); S. 15 oben Mitte Tyler & Chaz (M): GlowImages (RF); S. 25 oben 2. v. li.: Wedding Day; S. 26 oben re.: Catchlight Visual Services, unten: Image Source; S. 30 Bild 2: shinypix, Bild 5: Finnbar Webster; S. 41 unten: British Retail Photography; S. 46 Bild F (u. 134 oben): Beyond Fotomedia GmbH; S. 51 oben: Blend Images, Mitte: DBURKE; S. 90 Bild G: Somos Images (RF); S. 99 oben re.: Boel Ferm; S. 107 oben: ClassicStock; S. 114 oben: David Lyons; S. 131 re.: vario images GmbH & Co.KG; S. 133 unten: Horizon International Images Limited); **The Associated Press**, New York (S. 62: PA Wire); **The Bridgeman Art Library** (S. 130 unten re.: George Washington (oil on canvas), Stuart, Gilbert (1755–1828)/ Sterling & Francine Clark Art Institute, Williamstown, USA); **www.carbonfootprint.com** (S. 28/29 Hintergrund, 29 unten); **CBC** (S. 50: stills from news report "The mosquito". Copyright © CBC Vancouver); **Cinetext**, Frankfurt/Main (Inhaltsverz. Juno poster: 20th Century Fox; S. 98: Delphi); **Corbis**, Düsseldorf (Inhaltsverz. (u. 6 Ed): moodboard (RF); S. 10 unten (u. 104): cultura (RF); S. 20 oben: Biscuit Eight LLC (RF); S. 80 oben: Monalyn Gracia (RF); S. 86: Matilda Hartman; S. 88 unten: Asia Images/Alex Mares-Manton; S. 89 oben: Image Source (RF); S. 92: Blend Images/Jose Luis Pelaez, Inc. (RF); S. 130 unten li., oben re.); **Corel Library** (S. 146 oben); **Cornelsen Verlag**, Berlin (Inhaltsverz. (u. 13) film still from DVD Juno review; S. 14; S. 122 li.); **Philip Devlin**, Berlin (S. 89 unten); **Financial Times**, London (S. 134 unten); **Ellen Forney** (S. 16–18: From THE ABSOLUTELY TRUE DIARY OF A PART-TIME INDIAN by Sherman Alexie. Copyright © 2007 by Sherman Alexie. Illustrations copyright 2007 by Ellen Forney. By permission of LITTLE, BROWN & COMPANY.); **Fotex**, Hamburg (S. 8 unten: Susa); **Fotolia**, Berlin (S. 9 oben: martins (RF); S. 36 oben li.: Dustin Lyson; S. 99 oben li.: Phototom); **Getty Images**, München (Inhaltsverz. (u. 6 Toby): A J James (RF), Inhaltsverz. (u. 6 Minty): Thinkstock (RF); S. 21: Lisa Zador; S. 76: Fuse (RF); S. 87 oben: Winston Davidian (RF); S. 95 unten: Pieter Folkens; S. 111 TF 6 li. (u. 131 li.): AFP; S. 113; S. 146 unten woman (M): Terry Vine); **GRACE**, New York (S. 111 TF 3 (u. 121 unten): Produced by Free Range Studios, www.freerangestudios.com, in conjunction with GRACE/Sustainable Table, www.sustainabletable.org. Copyright © 2003 GRACE. Reproduced and distributed with the permission of GRACE); **Hachette**, London (S. 34: from "The Carbon Diaries" by Saci Lloyd, first published in the UK by Hodder Children's, an imprint of Hachette Children's Books, 338 Euston Road, London NW1 3BH); **iStockphoto**, Calgary (Inhaltsverz. (u. 7 Peanut): Don Bayley, Inhaltsverz. (u. 29 oben li.): Ian Bracegirdle, Inhaltsverz. (u. 28) toothbrush (M): alejandro Soto, mobile (M) (u. 30 Bild 7): Amanda Rhode, airplane (M): Björn Kindler, fridge (M): pixel107, washing machine (M): Oman Mirzaie, controller (M): Michal Rozanski, MP3 (M): yuriyza, laptop (M): Rafal Zdeb, DVD player (M): Uyen Le, flats (M): Chris Schmidt, houses (M): Matthew Dixon, hair dryer (M): Don Nichols); S. 6 oben gay couple: Libby Chapman, oben Hintergrund blond girl: mammamaart, oben Hintergrund group of friends: mandygodbehear, oben girl with headphones: Skip ODonnell; S. 7 oben Hintergrund group: Don Bayley, oben Hintergrund re. friends: Chris Schmidt; S. 9 Mitte: asiseeit; S. 10 oben: Lukasz Kulicki; S. 15 oben re. Alexis (M): Zlata Zubenko, oben li. Hailey (M): MoniqueRodriguez; S. 20 unten:Linda Bucklin; S. 24 unten: mbbirdy; S. 25 oben li.: Adam James; S. 26 oben li.: Lone Elisa Plougmann; S. 28 unten: johanna goodyear; S. 29 oben 2. v. li.: Josef Friedhuber, oben 2. v. re.: Andy Green, oben re.: Anton Prado PHOTOGRAPHY; S. 30 Bild 3: Niels Laan, Bild 4: Paula Connelly, Bild 8: Marie Fields, Bild 10: subjug; S. 36 oben re.: ranplett; S. 40 oben: Robert Byron; S. 41 oben: Borut Trdina; S. 44: Sally Llanes; S. 61: kelvin wakefield; S. 84: Morgan Lane Studios; S. 99 Mitte re.: Dan Moore; S. 111 TF2 (u. 114 unten): Mikhail Bistrov; 115 oben re.: mocker_bat; S. 123: Shelly Perry; S. 124 unten 2. v. li.: poco_bw, unten 2. v. re.: 4FR; S. 144 oben: james steidl); **ITN Source** (S. 31: still from "Bang goes the theory – The Human Power Station". Courtesy of ITN Source); **Brent Martin**, Cambridge, NZ (S. 33 oben); **www.offthemark.com** (S. 80 Mitte: Cartoon copyrighted by Mark Parisi); **Photofusion**, London (Inhaltsverz. (u. 46 Bild B): Janine Wiedel; S. 46 Bild A: Joanne OBrien); **Photolibrary**, London (Inhaltsverz. (u. 46 Bild C): INC SUPERSTOCK, Inhaltsverz. (u. 6 Bex): Design Pics Inc (RF); S. 88 oben: age fotostock/Saxpixcom Saxpixcom); **Picture Alliance**, Frankfurt/Main (S. 11: chromorange; S. 33 unten map (M): dieKLEINERT.de; S. 91: dpa; S. 111 TF 6 re. (u. 130 oben li.): dpa; S. 115 unten li.: abaca; S. 122 oben:

dpa); **Picture Desk**, London (S. 12 oben li.: THE KOBAL COLLECTION / WATERMARK, unten: THE KOBAL COLLECTION / FILM COUNCIL / BEND IT FILMS, oben re.: THE KOBAL COLLECTION / MAVERICK FILMS; S. 121 oben: THE KOBAL COLLECTION / WARNER BROS); **Marion Schönenberger**, Berlin (S. 64–74 li.); **Shutterstock**, New York (Inhaltsverz. Jake (M) (u. 8 oben): Yuri Arcurs, Inhaltsverz. oben Hintergrund (u. 8 oben Hintergrund): Binkski, Inhaltsverz. oben li. Monster (u. 8/9 oben u. Hintergrund): Elise Gravel, Inhaltsverz. (u. 28) underground (M): Michal Rosak, car (M): efiplus, jumping woman (M): Sergey Rusakov, dancing boy (M): AYAKOVLEV.COM, bus (M): James Steidl, dishwasher (M): akva, razor (M): Carla Donofrio; S. 6 oben Asian boy: Apollofoto; S. 7 oben re. boy and girl: Tracy Whiteside; S. 9 mobile (M): Jaroslaw Grudzinski; S. 13 unten: Fejas; S. 22 oben: Deklofenak, unten: Denis Vrublevski; S. 23 oben: Tomasz Trojanowski, unten: Elena Elisseeva; S. 24 oben: blueking, Mitte: PSD photography; S. 25 oben re.: Elzbieta Sekowska, oben 2. v. re.: AZPworldwide, unten: Planner; S. 30 Bild 1: jeff Metzger; S. 33 unten smartphones (M): Danylchenko Iaroslav, icons (M): Maisei Raman (1), Hudyma Natallia (4), jamaican (1), magicinfoto (6); S. 36 unten li.: Gualberto Becerra, re. 2. v. unten: Sergey Peterman; S. 38 oben: Lance Bellers, unten: Chris Jenner; S. 40 unten: Inc; S. 42: Stephen Finn; S. 43: Monkey Business Images; S. 46 Bild E: Lisa F. Young; S. 46/47 Hintergrund: Chen Ping Hung; S. 56 oben (M): stephenkirsh, unten: Galina Barskaya; S. 64 (u. 71 unten Hintergrund): Nick Lamb; S. 74 oben re.: Maceofoto; S. 80 unten re.: Galyna Andrushko, unten li.: AVAVA; S. 87 unten: Marijus Seskauskas; S. 90 oben: Klaus-Peter Adler, Bild A: Alexander Raths, Bild B: Monkey Business Images, Bild C: Andresr, Bild D: Titov Andriy, Bild E: Andrey Arkusha, Bild F: empipe, Bild H: Yuri Arcurs, Bild I: Dmitriy Shironosov, Bild J: Vibrant Image Studio, Bild K: Patrizia Tilly, Bild L: Piotr Marcinski; S. 94: Algecireño; S. 95 oben re.: VanHart, Mitte 2. v. li.: Carlos E. Santa Maria, Mitte 2. v. re.: Anton Novik, Mitte re. (M): Anton Novik; S. 97: Alexey Stiop; S. 99 unten li. printer (M): Natalia Siverina, unten li. sign (M): aispl, unten re.: Andre Blais; S. 102 li.: Kuzma, re.: Fedorov Oleksiy; S. 111 TF 4 (u. 124 li.): RS; S. 112/113 Hintergrund: Mitar Vidakovic; S. 115 oben li.: mikeledray, unten re.: kolosigor; S. 124 unten Mitte: vgstudio, unten re.: Alen; S. 141 unten: Holger Mette; S. 144 Mitte: Tatiana Popova; S. 146 unten leaves (M): debra hughes, unten face (M): Doreen Salcher, unten tree (M): Alexei Novikov); **Andy Singer**, Saint Paul, MN (Inhaltsverz. Cartoon (u. 36)); **Thomas Thesen**, Seoul (S. 146 Mitte); **ullstein bild**, Berlin (S. 15 unten: united archives; S. 122 Mitte re.: Rauhe; S. 131 2. v. re.: BPA, 2. v. li.: BPA)

Titelbild

Corbis, Düsseldorf (cyclist (M): Patrik Giardino); **Getty Images**, München (high-rise building (M): Bryan Mullennix)

Liedquellen

S. 13: *All I Want is You* Musik & Text: Barry Polisar © Rainbow Morning Music Alle Rechte für Deutschland, Österreich, Schweiz bei Sony/ATV Music Publishing (Germany) GmbH; **S. 112:** *LOVE IS ALL AROUND* Musik & Text: Reg Presley © Dick James Music Ltd./Universal Music Publishing GmbH, *BYE BYE LOVE*. Text: Bordleaux Bryant, Felice Bryant © Acuff Rose Music. Alle Rechte für Deutschland, Österreich, Schweiz bei Sony/ATV Music Publishing (Germany) GmbH

Textquellen

S. 16–18: *The Absolutely True Diary of a Part-time Indian*. Extracts from THE ABSOLUTELY TRUE DIARY OF A PART-TIME INDIAN by Sherman Alexie. Copyright © 2007 by Sherman Alexie. Illustrations copyright by Ellen Forney. By permission of LITTLE, BROWN & COMPANY; **S. 34–35:** *The Carbon Diaries 2015*. Abridged and adapted from "The Carbon Diaries" by Saci Lloyd, first published in the UK by Hodder Children's, an imprint of Hachette Children's Books, 338 Euston Road, London NW1 3BH; **S. 52–53:** *A class debate*. Adapted from SPEAK by Laurie Halse Anderson. Copyright © 1999 by Laurie Halse Anderson. Reprinted by permission of Farrar, Straus and Giroux, LLC.; **S. 112:** *Goodbye* from "For Beauty Douglas" (Allison & Busby), © Adrian Mitchell 1982, reprinted with permission of United Agents Ltd. Adrian Mitchell's poetry should not be used for examination purposes, *Celia Celia* from "For Beauty Douglas" (Allison & Busby), © Adrian Mitchell 1982, reprinted with permission of United Agents Ltd. Adrian Mitchell's poetry should not be used for examination purposes, *One parting*. From "HONEY AND SALT", copyright © 1963 by Carl Sandburg and renewed 1991 by Margaret Sandburg, Helga Sandburg Crile and Janet Sandburg, reprinted by permission of Houghton Mifflin Harcourt Publishing House; **S. 116–119:** *Cate Blanchett wants to be my friend on Facebook*. Alex Broun, Greenwich, Australia / www.alexbroun.com; **S. 125–128:** *If only Papa hadn't danced*. Copyright © 2009 by Patricia McCormick. Veröffentlichung mit Genehmigung Nr. 68535 der Paul & Peter Fritz AG in Zürich; **S. 136:** Auszug v. S. 516 aus „English G 2000 Wörterbuch – Das Wörterbuch zum Lehrwerk". Herausgegeben von der Langenscheidt-Redaktion Wörterbücher und der Cornelsen-Redaktion Englisch. © 2007 Cornelsen Verlag GmbH & Co. OHG, Berlin und Langenscheidt KG, Berlin und München.

Infinitive	Simple past form	Past participle	
(to) **be**	**was/were**	**been**	sein
(to) **beat**	**beat**	**beaten**	schlagen; besiegen
(to) **become**	**became**	**become**	werden
(to) **begin**	**began**	**begun**	beginnen, anfangen (mit)
(to) **bet**	**bet**	**bet**	wetten
(to) **bite** [aɪ]	**bit** [ɪ]	**bitten** [ɪ]	beißen
(to) **bleed** [iː]	**bled** [e]	**bled** [e]	bluten
(to) **blow**	**blew**	**blown**	wehen, blasen
(to) **break**	**broke**	**broken**	(zer)brechen; kaputt gehen
(to) **bring**	**brought**	**brought**	(mit-, her)bringen
(to) **build**	**built**	**built**	bauen
(to) **buy**	**bought**	**bought**	kaufen
(to) **catch**	**caught**	**caught**	fangen; erwischen
(to) **choose** [uː]	**chose** [əʊ]	**chosen** [əʊ]	(aus)wählen; (sich) aussuchen
(to) **come**	**came**	**come**	kommen
(to) **cost**	**cost**	**cost**	kosten
(to) **cut**	**cut**	**cut**	schneiden
(to) **do**	**did**	**done** [ʌ]	tun, machen
(to) **draw**	**drew**	**drawn**	zeichnen
(to) **drink**	**drank**	**drunk**	trinken
(to) **drive** [aɪ]	**drove**	**driven** [ɪ]	*(ein Auto)* fahren
(to) **eat**	**ate** [et, eɪt]	**eaten**	essen
(to) **fall**	**fell**	**fallen**	(hin)fallen, stürzen
(to) **feed**	**fed**	**fed**	füttern
(to) **feel**	**felt**	**felt**	(sich) fühlen; sich anfühlen
(to) **fight**	**fought**	**fought**	kämpfen
(to) **find**	**found**	**found**	finden
(to) **fly**	**flew**	**flown**	fliegen
(to) **forget**	**forgot**	**forgotten**	vergessen
(to) **forgive**	**forgave**	**forgiven**	vergeben, verzeihen
(to) **get**	**got**	**got**	bekommen; holen; werden; (hin)kommen
(to) **give**	**gave**	**given**	geben
(to) **go**	**went**	**gone** [ɒ]	gehen, fahren
(to) **grow**	**grew**	**grown**	wachsen; anbauen, anpflanzen
(to) **hang**	**hung**	**hung**	hängen
(to) **have (have got)**	**had**	**had**	haben, besitzen
(to) **hear** [ɪə]	**heard** [ɜː]	**heard** [ɜː]	hören
(to) **hide** [aɪ]	**hid** [ɪ]	**hidden** [ɪ]	(sich) verstecken
(to) **hit**	**hit**	**hit**	schlagen
(to) **hold**	**held**	**held**	halten
(to) **hurt**	**hurt**	**hurt**	wehtun; verletzen
(to) **keep**	**kept**	**kept**	(be)halten
(to) **know** [nəʊ]	**knew** [njuː]	**known** [nəʊn]	wissen; kennen
(to) **lay** the table	**laid**	**laid**	den Tisch decken
(to) **leave**	**left**	**left**	(weg)gehen; abfahren; verlassen; zurücklassen

Infinitive	Simple past form	Past participle	
(to) **lend**	**lent**	**lent**	verleihen
(to) **let**	**let**	**let**	lassen
(to) **lie** [aɪ]	**lay** [eɪ]	**lain** [eɪ]	liegen
(to) **lose** [uː]	**lost** [ɒ]	**lost** [ɒ]	verlieren
(to) **make**	**made**	**made**	machen; bauen; bilden
(to) **mean** [iː]	**meant** [e]	**meant** [e]	bedeuten; meinen
(to) **meet**	**met**	**met**	(sich) treffen
(to) **pay**	**paid**	**paid**	bezahlen
(to) **put**	**put**	**put**	legen, stellen, *(wohin)* tun
(to) **read** [iː]	**read** [e]	**read** [e]	lesen
(to) **ride** [aɪ]	**rode**	**ridden** [ɪ]	reiten; *(Rad)* fahren
(to) **ring**	**rang**	**rung**	klingeln, läuten
(to) **rise** [aɪ]	**rose**	**risen** [ɪ]	(auf)steigen
(to) **run**	**ran**	**run**	rennen, laufen
(to) **say** [eɪ]	**said** [e]	**said** [e]	sagen
(to) **see**	**saw**	**seen**	sehen; besuchen, aufsuchen
(to) **sell**	**sold**	**sold**	verkaufen
(to) **send**	**sent**	**sent**	schicken, senden
(to) **set** the alarm clock	**set**	**set**	den Wecker stellen
(to) **shake**	**shook**	**shaken**	schütteln; zittern
(to) **shine**	**shone** [ɒ]	**shone** [ɒ]	scheinen *(Sonne)*
(to) **shoot** [uː]	**shot**	**shot**	schießen, erschießen
(to) **show**	**showed**	**shown**	zeigen
(to) **shut up**	**shut**	**shut**	den Mund halten
(to) **sing**	**sang**	**sung**	singen
(to) **sit**	**sat**	**sat**	sitzen; sich setzen
(to) **sleep**	**slept**	**slept**	schlafen
(to) **speak**	**spoke**	**spoken**	sprechen
(to) **spend**	**spent**	**spent**	*(Zeit)* verbringen; *(Geld)* ausgeben
(to) **stand**	**stood**	**stood**	stehen; sich (hin)stellen
(to) **steal**	**stole**	**stolen**	stehlen
(to) **stick**	**stuck**	**stuck**	(auf)kleben
(to) **swim**	**swam**	**swum**	schwimmen
(to) **take**	**took**	**taken**	nehmen; (weg-, hin)bringen; dauern, *(Zeit)* brauchen
(to) **teach**	**taught**	**taught**	unterrichten, lehren
(to) **tear sth. off** [eə]	**tore**	**torn**	etwas abreißen
(to) **tell**	**told**	**told**	erzählen, berichten
(to) **think**	**thought**	**thought**	denken, glauben, meinen
(to) **throw**	**threw**	**thrown**	werfen
(to) **understand**	**understood**	**understood**	verstehen
(to) **upset**	**upset**	**upset**	ärgern, kränken, aus der Fassung bringen
(to) **wake** up	**woke**	**woken**	aufwachen; wecken
(to) **wear** [eə]	**wore** [ɔː]	**worn** [ɔː]	tragen *(Kleidung)*
(to) **win**	**won** [ʌ]	**won** [ʌ]	gewinnen
(to) **write**	**wrote**	**written**	schreiben